Algorithms for PID Controller 2024

Algorithms for PID Controller 2024

Guest Editors

Ramiro Barbosa
Paulo Moura Oliveira

MDPI Basel • Beijing • Wuhan • Barcelona • Belgrade • Novi Sad • Cluj • Manchester

Guest Editors
Ramiro Barbosa
Electrical Engineering
Polytechnic of Porto
Porto
Portugal

Paulo Moura Oliveira
Engineering Department
University of Trás-os-Montes e Alto Douro
Vila Real
Portugal

Editorial Office
MDPI AG
Grosspeteranlage 5
4052 Basel, Switzerland

This is a reprint of the Special Issue, published open access by the journal *Algorithms* (ISSN 1999-4893), freely accessible at: https://www.mdpi.com/journal/algorithms/special_issues/7IE4QZ941W.

For citation purposes, cite each article independently as indicated on the article page online and as indicated below:

Lastname, A.A.; Lastname, B.B. Article Title. *Journal Name* **Year**, *Volume Number*, Page Range.

ISBN 978-3-7258-7266-4 (Hbk)
ISBN 978-3-7258-7267-1 (PDF)
https://doi.org/10.3390/books978-3-7258-7267-1

Contents

About the Editors

Ramiro Barbosa

Ramiro Barbosa is a Coordinator Professor at the Department of Electrical Engineering at the Institute of Engineering of Porto (ISEP), Polytechnic of Porto, Portugal. He earned his PhD in Electrical and Computer Engineering from the Faculty of Engineering of the University of Porto (FEUP) in 2005. His main research interests include control systems, modelling and simulation, fractional calculus and fractional-order control, evolutionary algorithms, artificial intelligence, and robotics.

Paulo Moura Oliveira

Paulo Moura Oliveira received the Electrical Engineering degree in 1991, from UTAD University, Portugal, and MSc in Industrial Control Systems in 1994 and PhD in Control Engineering in 1998, both from Salford University, Manchester, UK. He is an Associate Professor with Habilitation at the Engineering Department of UTAD University and a senior researcher at CRIISs (Centre for Robotics in Industry and Intelligent Systems) of the INESC TEC institute in Porto. His current research interests are focused on the fields of control engineering, control engineering education, robotics, evolutionary and nature-inspired algorithms for single and multiple objective optimization problem solving, swarm optimization, intelligent control and PID control. He is the author of more than 200 peer-reviewed scientific publications.

Preface

This reprint is devoted to algorithms for the design, analysis, and implementation of PID (Proportional–Integral–Derivative) controllers, one of the most enduring and widely applied control strategies in engineering practice. Despite the rapid development of advanced control methodologies, PID control remains at the heart of industrial automation, embedded systems, and process engineering. Its apparent simplicity conceals a rich algorithmic structure that continues to evolve alongside modern computational tools. The subject of this work is the systematic development of algorithms that underpin PID controller tuning, adaptation, optimization, and digital realization. Particular attention is given to soft-computing-based methods.

The primary aim of this reprint is to bridge the gap between theoretical formulations and deployable algorithms. Rather than treating PID control merely as a set of heuristic rules, this work seeks to present it as a coherent algorithmic framework grounded in control theory, numerical methods, and systems engineering. It aspires to provide readers with both conceptual understanding and practical tools for designing reliable and efficient controllers. The motivation for writing this reprint arose from observing a persistent need for a comprehensive yet accessible treatment of PID algorithms that reflects current computational capabilities. It is addressed to researchers and practicing engineers in control engineering, automation, robotics, and related disciplines. It may also serve as a reference for professionals engaged in industrial process control and embedded system design. A foundational knowledge of linear systems and basic control theory is assumed, but the material is presented with clarity and rigour to support both study and practical application.

We hope that this work will contribute to a deeper appreciation of PID control not merely as a classical technique, but as a continuing field of algorithmic innovation.

Ramiro Barbosa and Paulo Moura Oliveira
Guest Editors

algorithms

MDPI

Article

Analytical MPC Algorithm Using Steady-State Process Model

Piotr M. Marusak

Institute of Control and Computation Engineering, Warsaw University of Technology, Nowowiejska 15/19, 00-665 Warszawa, Poland; piotr.marusak@pw.edu.pl

Abstract: For some classes of control plants (e.g., large time delay or inverse response), the PID controllers may offer unsatisfactory results; on the other hand, a Model Predictive Control (MPC) algorithm based on a linear model may offer insufficient control quality when applied to nonlinear control plants. To improve the MPC algorithm operation, one can use a steady-state process model; this paper describes how to do this skillfully. The obtained algorithm, based on the popular Dynamic Matrix Control (DMC) algorithm, is detailed. The proposed approach consists in modifying the analytical version of the DMC algorithm in such a way that it can still be expressed as the control law. Thus, the algorithm can still be applied to fast control plants, requiring short sampling times. Though the proposed approach does not modify the DMC algorithm much, it offers improvement in the control quality when the algorithm is employed in a nonlinear control plant. Experiments illustrating the efficiency of the proposed approach were conducted in the control system of a nonlinear chemical reactor. The results show improvement in the control quality compared to a case when the classical MPC algorithm is used.

Keywords: prediction; process control; model predictive control (MPC); dynamic matrix control (DMC); nonlinear control; quadratic optimization; steady-state characteristic

1. Introduction

PID control is practically standard in the case of control systems with short sampling times. Moreover, PID is still being researched and developed using modern techniques; see, e.g., [1–4]. However, in the case of control plants with difficult dynamics (e.g., long time delays, inverse response), other control techniques, like the Smith predictor (see, e.g., [5,6]) or the Model Predictive Control (MPC) algorithms, are used. The advantages of the MPC algorithms originate in using the model of the process to predict its behavior [7–12]. It is good to note that if an accurate analytical model is not available or is hard to obtain, an approach based on artificial neural networks can be applied; see, e.g., [13–15]. The MPC algorithms can be divided into two main groups. In the numerical MPC algorithms, the control signal is generated after solving an optimization task online. In the second group of analytical MPC algorithms, the control law is obtained after offline optimization. Numerous studies have been concerned with numerical algorithms; the NMPC (nonlinear model-based MPC) algorithms are based on non-convex, hard to solve, and computationally time-consuming, nonlinear optimization problems solved at each iteration; see, e.g., [16–18]. To limit drawbacks of this approach, the so-called fast NMPC algorithms, generating suboptimal solutions faster than in the standard approach, were developed; see, e.g., [19–21]. In this next group of numerical algorithms, the process model is skillfully used to formulate a prediction that is linear with respect to the control action to simplify the algorithm by formulating the optimization task as the quadratic optimization problem; see, e.g., [12,13,22–28].

The explicit algorithms can be considered as being between numerical and analytical. In the explicit approach, most of the calculations are done offline. The algorithms using a nonlinear process model are suboptimal—see, e.g., [29–31]—but the ones based on the linear model generate optimal solutions [32–34]. The main drawback of the explicit approach is that the complexity of the controller grows rapidly with the number of constraints included in the problem.

The analytical group of MPC algorithms has been researched more and more recently as the computation power of modern microcontrollers has increased, allowing the implementation of analytical MPC algorithms. However, mainly basic versions of them based on linear models have been used [35,36] or researched [37–39], including robust MPC algorithms using Linear Matrix Inequalities (LMIs) to calculate the control signal [40–42]. They offer good control performance for processes that are not highly nonlinear but may work poorly for other ones. Therefore, it is desirable to propose analytical MPC algorithms designed for nonlinear plants; an algorithm based on the fuzzy process model is proposed in [43]. The current paper contains a proposal for such an algorithm, which is a generalization of the classical analytical DMC algorithm, utilizing only a process step response and a steady-state process model.

The algorithm proposed in this article is intended to cope mainly with the nonlinearity of the control plant, but at the same time, it is also capable of dealing with delay and other non-minimum phase behaviors of control plants (for which predictive control algorithms are usually applied). Moreover, the algorithm is designed in such a way that it offers good performance with low computational demand and less computing power required by the algorithm, which means cheaper chips can be used in the embedded systems, resulting in fewer problems in the future when chips start to be rationed and access to them becomes part of the economic rivalry between countries.

Moreover, the proposed algorithm uses a relatively small modification of the DMC algorithm, so it can be easily adopted by someone who knows the popular Dynamic Matrix Control algorithm. However, introducing such a small modification requires an appropriate formulation of the control law; in this case, assuming the parameter λ varies in time and depends on the gain of the control plant at the current operating point was crucial and necessary.

2. Materials and Methods

2.1. MPC Algorithms

The MPC algorithms generate the future control signal trajectories in such a way that, predicting many sampling instants ahead, the future behavior of the control plant and the shape of control signals fulfill assumed criteria, which, for SISO (Single-Input Single-Output) control plants, are expressed in the form of the following optimization task [7,8,10,12]:

$$\arg\min_{\Delta u}\left\{J_{\mathrm{MPC}} = (\overline{\boldsymbol{y}} - \boldsymbol{y})^T \cdot (\overline{\boldsymbol{y}} - \boldsymbol{y}) + \lambda \cdot \Delta \boldsymbol{u}^T \cdot \Delta \boldsymbol{u}\right\} \tag{1}$$

where $\boldsymbol{y} = \left[y_{k+1|k}, \ldots, y_{k+p|k}\right]$, $\Delta \boldsymbol{u} = \left[\Delta u_{k|k}, \ldots, \Delta u_{k+s-1|k}\right]$, $y_{k+j|k}$ is the output value for the $(k+i)^{\mathrm{th}}$ sampling instant predicted at the kth sampling instant using a control plant model, $\Delta u_{k+i|k}$ are future changes in the manipulated variable, and $\lambda \geq 0$ is the weighting coefficient for the changes of the manipulated variable; p and s denote prediction and control horizons, respectively. The following vector defines the reference trajectory:

$$\overline{\boldsymbol{y}} = \left[\overline{y}_{k+1|k}, \ldots, \overline{y}_{k+p|k}\right]. \tag{2}$$

As a solution to the optimization problem given in (1), the optimal vector of control action is obtained in such a way that future predicted control errors are minimized (the first component of the performance index) and the control signal does not change too much (the second component). The $\Delta u_{k|k}$ element of the vector of decision variables $\Delta \boldsymbol{u}$ is applied to the control system and the algorithm passes to the next iteration. The predicted values of the output signal $y_{k+j|k}$ are derived using the control plant model the MPC algorithm is based on. In order to take into account modeling uncertainty and unmodeled disturbances, the prediction is calculated, including correction, which is the difference between the measured process output and the output of the model used by the algorithm. If a linear model is used, then (1) becomes quadratic with respect to the changes in the control signal. Moreover, a control law can be obtained if the optimization problem is solved without constraints. The DMC algorithm will now be detailed.

2.2. Analytical DMC Algorithm

The simplest MPC algorithms are based on linear process models; see e.g., [7]. One of them is the DMC algorithm, based on the process model in the form of the step response:

$$\widehat{y}_k = \sum_{n=1}^{p_d-1} a_n \cdot \Delta u_{k-n} + a_{p_d} \cdot u_{k-p_d}, \tag{3}$$

where a_n are the coefficients of the control plant step response, and p_d is the horizon of dynamics equal to the number of time instants, after which the step response coefficients can be considered fixed.

The predicted output values, calculated from Model (3), are thus given by the following formula:

$$y_{k+i|k} = \widehat{y}_{k+i} + d_k, \tag{4}$$

where $d_k = y_k - \widehat{y}_k$ is a model of unmeasured disturbances (it also includes the effect of modeling errors) acting on the process; it is calculated as the difference between the current process output measurement y_k and the output of the model described by (3). If no better information is available, it is assumed that it is constant over the entire prediction horizon. This model of unmeasurable disturbances is called a DMC-type disturbance model. After transformation of the prediction (4), one obtains the following:

$$y_{k+i|k} = \sum_{n=1}^{i} a_n \cdot \Delta u_{k-n+i} + \sum_{n=i+1}^{p_d-1} a_n \cdot \Delta u_{k-n+i} + a_{p_d} \cdot u_{k-p_d} + d_k\,, \tag{5}$$

The prediction (5) can be transformed to the following form:

$$\begin{aligned} y_{k+i|k} = y_k &+ \sum_{n=i+1}^{p_d-1} a_n \cdot \Delta u_{k-n+i} + a_{p_d} \cdot \sum_{n=p_d}^{p_d+i-1} \Delta u_{k-n+i} - \sum_{n=1}^{p_d-1} a_n \cdot \Delta u_{k-n} \\ &+ \sum_{n=1}^{i} a_n \cdot \Delta u_{k-n+i|k}. \end{aligned} \tag{6}$$

Note that in Formula (6), only the last component depends on future control changes; the others depend on the past. Thus, the other components are elements of the free response:

$$\widetilde{y}_{k+i|k} = y_k + \sum_{n=i+1}^{p_d-1} a_n \cdot \Delta u_{k-n+i} + a_{p_d} \cdot \sum_{n=p_d}^{p_d+i-1} \Delta u_{k-n+i} - \sum_{n=1}^{p_d-1} a_n \cdot \Delta u_{k-n}. \tag{7}$$

In such a case, the prediction of the process output values $\boldsymbol{y}$ expressed in the matrix–vector form can be decomposed into two parts:

$$y = \widetilde{y} + A \cdot \Delta u \ , \tag{8}$$

where $\widetilde{y} = \left[\widetilde{y}_{k+1|k}, \ldots, \widetilde{y}_{k+p|k}\right]$ is the free response of the plant, which describes the influence of the past values of control signals on the process output; the form of the free response depends on the model used for prediction—see, e.g., [7,8,10,12]. The second component in Formula (8), the forced response, depends on future changes in the control signal. The dynamic matrix A is given by the following formula:

$$A = \begin{bmatrix} a_1 & 0 & \ldots & 0 & 0 \\ a_2 & a_1 & \ldots & 0 & 0 \\ \vdots & \vdots & \ddots & \vdots & \vdots \\ a_p & a_{p-1} & \ldots & a_{p-s+2} & a_{p-s+1} \end{bmatrix} . \tag{9}$$

The free response (7) written in vector–matrix form is as follows:

$$\widetilde{y} = \overleftarrow{y} + \overleftarrow{A} \cdot \Delta \overleftarrow{u} , \tag{10}$$

where

$$\overleftarrow{A} = \begin{bmatrix} a_2 - a_1 & a_3 - a_2 & \ldots & a_{p_d} - a_{p_d-1} \\ a_3 - a_1 & a_4 - a_2 & \ldots & a_{p_d} - a_{p_d-1} \\ \vdots & \vdots & \ddots & \vdots \\ a_{p+1} - a_1 & a_{p+2} - a_2 & \ldots & a_{p_d} - a_{p_d-1} \end{bmatrix} , \tag{11}$$

$$\Delta \overleftarrow{u} = \left[\Delta u_{k-1}, \ldots, \Delta u_{k-p_d+1}\right], \tag{12}$$

$$\overleftarrow{y} = [y_k, \ldots, y_k], \tag{13}$$

where $\overleftarrow{y}$ vector has p elements.

After applying the prediction (8), the performance function (1) is transformed into a function that depends quadratically on the decision variables Δu:

$$J_{LMPC} = (\overline{y} - \widetilde{y} - A \cdot \Delta u)^T \cdot (\overline{y} - \widetilde{y} - A \cdot \Delta u) + \lambda \cdot \Delta u^T \cdot \Delta u \ . \tag{14}$$

If, in each iteration, the optimization problem with performance function (14) is solved without constraints, then it has the following solution given by the analytical formula:

$$\Delta u = \left(A^T \cdot A + \lambda \cdot I\right)^{-1} \cdot A^T \cdot (\overline{y} - \widetilde{y}) \ . \tag{15}$$

After substituting the free response (10) into (15), we obtain

$$\Delta u = K \cdot (\overline{y} - \widetilde{y}) = K \cdot \left(\overline{y} - \overleftarrow{y} - \overleftarrow{A} \cdot \Delta \overleftarrow{u}\right), \tag{16}$$

where $K = \left(A^T \cdot A + \lambda \cdot I\right)^{-1} \cdot A^T$. Note that if Δu is calculated only for control, it is sufficient to calculate only the value of the control increment for the current instant $\Delta u_{k|k}$, which is described by the following formula:

$$\Delta u_{k|k} = K_1 \cdot \left(\overline{y} - \overleftarrow{y} - \overleftarrow{A} \cdot \Delta \overleftarrow{u}\right), \tag{17}$$

where K_1 is the 1st row of the matrix K. In this case, the value of the future control increment $\Delta u_{k|k}$ depends in the analytical DMC algorithm on the current value of the output and the past control increments. In addition, the matrix K and its individual rows remain the same in each iteration. In this case, it is sufficient to determine this matrix once in the controller design stage. As a result, a large part of the calculations are performed offline.

If one assumes that reference trajectory is constant on the prediction horizon, then the vector $\overline{y}$ from (2) becomes

$$\overline{y} = [\overline{y}_k, \ldots, \overline{y}_k] \,, \tag{18}$$

where $\overline{y}_k$ is the current setpoint value. In such a case, the following control law can be obtained:

$$\Delta u_{k|k} = \Delta u_k = r_0 \cdot e_k + \sum_{i=1}^{p_d-1} r_i \cdot \Delta u_{k-i}, \tag{19}$$

where $r_0 = \sum_{j=1}^{p} K_{1j}$, $[r_1, \ldots, r_{p_d-1}] = K_1 \cdot \overleftarrow{A}$, $K_1 = [K_{11}, \ldots, K_{1p}]$.

The output of the analytical DMC controller is the control increment. The following formula describes the control value:

$$u_{k|k} = u_{k-1} + \Delta u_{k|k} \,. \tag{20}$$

Applying an LMPC algorithm to a nonlinear process may result in unsatisfactory control performance, especially if the MPC algorithm should operate at different operating points. In such a case, the operation of the control system can be improved using an MPC algorithm based on a nonlinear model.

2.3. Efficient SSDMC Algorithm

The algorithm proposed in this article is formulated in such a way that solving the optimization task online is avoided, because, due to the assumed form of the linear approximation used to obtain the dynamic matrix and the appropriate choice of the tuning parameter λ depending on time, it is possible to simplify the control law. Let us assume that one has a static model of the process and the step response of the process. These models will be used skillfully to formulate the proposed analytical algorithm. Of course, such an algorithm will probably perform worse than an algorithm based on a well-identified model, like the one proposed, e.g., in [26,27]. However, at a relatively low cost (assuming one has a steady-state process model, which is often developed for the setpoint optimization layer), one can obtain an algorithm that should offer better control quality than the LMPC algorithm; this is especially true when the process has strong static nonlinearity.

Assume that in each iteration of the algorithm, for the current operating point, a linear approximation of the process model is obtained using the following formula:

$$y_k^L = K_k \cdot \left(\sum_{i=1}^{p_d-1} a_i \cdot \Delta u_{k-i} + a_{p_d} \cdot u_{k-p_d} \right), \tag{21}$$

where K_k is the slope of the steady-state characteristic of the process (the gain of the control plant) around the current operating point; it is also assumed that the coefficients of the step response a_i are normalized in such a way that a_{p_d} is equal to 1. Due to the form of the adopted linear approximation of the process model, the proposed algorithm is an extension of the DMC algorithm. Thus, it will be abbreviated as the SSDMC algorithm (Steady-State Model-Based DMC—DMC algorithm using the steady-state characteristic of the process). The dynamic matrix obtained in each iteration will thus be given by the following formula:

$$A_k = K_k \cdot A, \tag{22}$$

where A is described by Equation (9).

The free response is calculated using the following formula:

$$\widetilde{\boldsymbol{y}} = \overleftarrow{\boldsymbol{y}} + \overleftarrow{\boldsymbol{A}}_k \cdot \Delta\overleftarrow{\boldsymbol{u}}, \tag{23}$$

where this time, $\overleftarrow{\boldsymbol{A}}_k$ changes at each sampling instant but depends on $\overleftarrow{\boldsymbol{A}}$ as described by Equation (11):

$$\overleftarrow{\boldsymbol{A}}_k = K_k \cdot \overleftarrow{\boldsymbol{A}}. \tag{24}$$

Then, using the obtained dynamic matrix described by Equation (22) and the free response given by Equation (23), one obtains the output prediction described by the following formula:

$$\boldsymbol{y} = \widetilde{\boldsymbol{y}} + \boldsymbol{A}_k \cdot \Delta\boldsymbol{u} = \overleftarrow{\boldsymbol{y}} + \overleftarrow{\boldsymbol{A}}_k \cdot \Delta\overleftarrow{\boldsymbol{u}} + \boldsymbol{A}_k \cdot \Delta\boldsymbol{u}. \tag{25}$$

Next, the prediction given by (25) is used to formulate the quadratic optimization problem, with the following performance index:

$$J_{SSDMC} = (\widetilde{\boldsymbol{y}} + \boldsymbol{A}_k \cdot \Delta\boldsymbol{u} - \overline{\boldsymbol{y}})^T \cdot (\widetilde{\boldsymbol{y}} + \boldsymbol{A}_k \cdot \Delta\boldsymbol{u} - \overline{\boldsymbol{y}}) + \lambda_k \cdot \Delta\boldsymbol{u}^T \cdot \Delta\boldsymbol{u}. \tag{26}$$

As a result of solving the optimization task with the quadratic performance index defined in Equation (26) without constraints, the following result is obtained:

$$\Delta\boldsymbol{u} = \left(\boldsymbol{A}_k^T \cdot \boldsymbol{A}_k + \lambda_k \cdot \boldsymbol{I}\right)^{-1} \cdot \boldsymbol{A}_k^T \cdot (\overline{\boldsymbol{y}} - \widetilde{\boldsymbol{y}}). \tag{27}$$

It is important to note that in Equation (27), the dynamic matrix $\boldsymbol{A}_k$ changes at each sampling instant due to the nonlinear nature of the control plant. Therefore, an additional transformation must be made to account for these changes. Note that $\boldsymbol{A}_k^T \cdot \boldsymbol{A}_k = K_k^2 \cdot \boldsymbol{A}^T \cdot \boldsymbol{A}$. Then, after assuming the coefficient $\lambda_k = K_k^2 \cdot \lambda$ (which is crucial for obtaining a compact control law), the following relation is obtained:

$$\left(\boldsymbol{A}_k^T \cdot \boldsymbol{A}_k + \lambda_k \cdot \boldsymbol{I}\right) = K_k^2 \cdot \left(\boldsymbol{A}^T \cdot \boldsymbol{A} + \lambda \cdot \boldsymbol{I}\right). \tag{28}$$

Therefore, after substituting Equations (22)–(24) into (27), along with performing the appropriate mathematical transformations, one obtains the following result:

$$\Delta\boldsymbol{u} = \frac{1}{K_k} \cdot \boldsymbol{K} \cdot \left(\overline{\boldsymbol{y}} - \overleftarrow{\boldsymbol{y}} + K_k \cdot \overleftarrow{\boldsymbol{A}} \cdot \Delta\overleftarrow{\boldsymbol{u}}\right), \tag{29}$$

where the matrix $\boldsymbol{K} = \left(\boldsymbol{A}^T \cdot \boldsymbol{A} + \lambda \cdot \boldsymbol{I}\right)^{-1} \cdot \boldsymbol{A}^T$ has the same form as in the classical DMC algorithm. Then, as in the classical DMC algorithm, the main part of the calculations in the SSDMC algorithm can be efficiently performed once at the algorithm design stage (in the offline phase). This approach allows for a significant reduction in the computational demand required by the algorithm during its execution.

After further transformations, one obtains the following formula, which describes the current increment of the manipulated variable:

$$\Delta u_{k|k} = \frac{1}{K_k} \cdot \boldsymbol{K}_1 \cdot \left(\overline{\boldsymbol{y}} - \overleftarrow{\boldsymbol{y}} - K_k \cdot \overleftarrow{\boldsymbol{A}} \cdot \Delta\overleftarrow{\boldsymbol{u}}\right) = \frac{1}{K_k} \cdot \boldsymbol{K}_1 \cdot (\overline{\boldsymbol{y}} - \overleftarrow{\boldsymbol{y}}) - \boldsymbol{K}_1 \cdot \left(\overleftarrow{\boldsymbol{A}} \cdot \Delta\overleftarrow{\boldsymbol{u}}\right). \tag{30}$$

Then, if a constant reference trajectory as in Equation (18) is assumed, the following control law can be finally obtained:

$$\Delta u_{k|k} = \Delta u_k = r_{0,k} \cdot e_k + \sum_{i=1}^{p_d-1} r_i \cdot \Delta u_{k-i}, \tag{31}$$

where $r_{0,k} = \dfrac{1}{K_k} \cdot r_0$ and $r_0, r_1, \ldots, r_{p_d}$ are derived in the same way as in the control law presented in Equation (19) of the analytical DMC algorithm.

Although the control law obtained in the SSDMC algorithm is very close to that of the standard Dynamic Model Control algorithm, it is important to note that the SSDMC algorithm offers considerably better control quality when applied to nonlinear processes compared to its predecessor.

Tuning of the parameters of the SSDMC controller can be achieved in the same way as in the case of the DMC controller. The sampling period should be chosen in such a way that the delay or inverse response is included in the step-response model. The prediction horizon can be chosen to be equal to the dynamics horizon; tjos is the safest approach, and in the case of the SSDMC algorithm, the control law is obtained. Therefore, the length of the prediction horizon (and also the control horizon) has no influence on the online computational demand of the controller. Both horizons can thus be chosen during offline simulation experiments without any limitations. Moreover, the SSDMC algorithm was designed in such a way that the λ parameter has a similar influence on the behavior of the control system as in the case of the standard DMC algorithm.

3. Results

3.1. Control Plant

The control plant is a nonlinear, isothermal CSTR in which the van de Vusse reaction takes place—a popular benchmark with difficult dynamics, used in much research to test newly developed control algorithms (see, e.g., [26,27,44–47]) as well as in MIMO configuration, where not only concentration, but also temperature [48,49], is stabilized. Also, other CSTRs with less demanding dynamics that are controlled in the MIMO configuration can be found in the literature; see, e.g., [50,51]. The process model of the reactor is as follows [52]:

$$\begin{aligned} \tfrac{dC_A}{dt} &= -k_1 \cdot C_A - k_3 \cdot C_A^2 + \tfrac{F}{V}(C_{Af} - C_A) \ , \\ \tfrac{dC_B}{dt} &= k_1 \cdot C_A - k_2 \cdot C_B - \tfrac{F}{V} C_B \ , \end{aligned} \tag{32}$$

where C_A, C_B—the concentrations of components A and B, respectively; F—the flow rate, where it is assumed that its upper bound is equal to $F_{max} = 60$ L/h; V—the volume in which the reaction takes place (assumed constant and $V = 1$ L); and C_{Af}—the concentration of component A in the inlet flow stream ($C_{Af} = 10$ mol/L if not declared otherwise). The parameters of the model have the following values: $k_1 = 50$ L/h, $k_2 = 100$ L/h, and $k_3 = 10$ L/(h · mol). The output variable is the concentration C_B of substance B, the manipulated variable is the flow rate F, and C_{Af} is the disturbance variable.

The control plant under consideration is highly nonlinear. Its step responses obtained for different flow rate values ($F_1 = 54.3$ L/h, $F_2 = 44.3$ L/h, $F_3 = 34.3$ L/h, $F_4 = 24.3$ L/h, $F_5 = 14.3$ L/h) are shown in Figure 1. Although the difference between the subsequent values of the flow rate is the same ($\Delta F = 10$ L/h) the obtained responses are asymmetric; it is clear that the control plant has both nonlinear dynamics and statics. Moreover, inverse response is present in the step responses obtained.

The same control plant was also used during the tests in [26,27], where advanced numerical versions of the Fuzzy MPC algorithms were proposed and tested; the nonlinear steady-state characteristic of the process is depicted in Figure 2. The algorithm proposed in the current article exploits this characteristic.

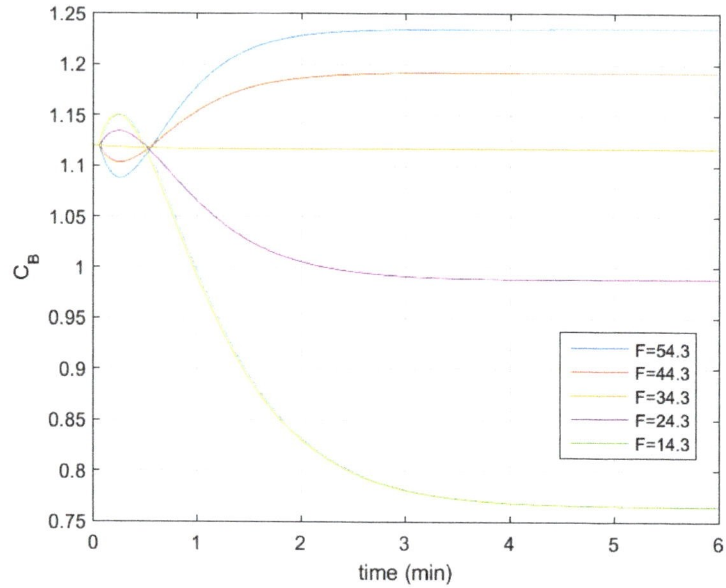

Figure 1. Step responses of control plant.

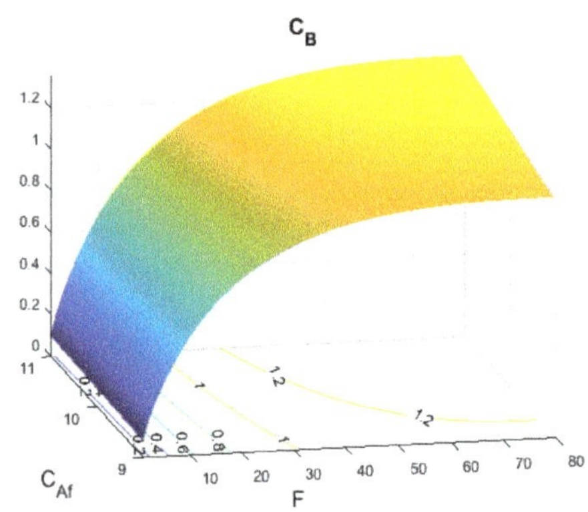

Figure 2. Steady-state characteristic of control plant.

To calculate the current gain K_k, the equation that describes the steady-state characteristic was obtained from Equation (32). The equations were rewritten for the steady-state; the constant $V = 1$ L was also taken into account. Moreover, it is important to note that all variables representing the steady-state are denoted by an overline to clearly distinguish them from their dynamic counterparts. The first equation from (32), therefore, transforms into the following equation:

$$0 = -k_1 \cdot \overline{C}_{\mathrm{A}} - k_3 \cdot \overline{C}_{\mathrm{A}}^2 + \overline{F}\left(\overline{C}_{\mathrm{Af}} - \overline{C}_{\mathrm{A}}\right) \ . \tag{33}$$

And the second one transforms into the following equation:

$$0 = k_1 \cdot \overline{C}_{\mathrm{A}} - k_2 \cdot \overline{C}_{\mathrm{B}} - \overline{F C}_{\mathrm{B}} \ . \tag{34}$$

After rewriting Equation (33), one obtains

$$-k_3 \cdot \overline{C}_A^2 - (k_1 + \overline{F})\overline{C}_A + \overline{F} \cdot \overline{C}_{Af} = 0 \ ; \tag{35}$$

and after transforming Formula (34), the following expression that describes $\overline{C}_B$ is obtained:

$$\overline{C}_B = \frac{k_1 \cdot \overline{C}_A}{k_2 + \overline{F}} \ . \tag{36}$$

After conducting the necessary and appropriate transformations, and assuming that the operating point would be positioned on the left-hand side of the steady-state characteristic curve, the following equation was obtained as a result of this analysis:

$$\overline{C}_B(\overline{F}) = \frac{k_1 + \overline{F} - \sqrt{(k_1 + \overline{F})^2 + 4 \cdot k_3 \cdot \overline{F} \cdot \overline{C}_{Af}}}{-2 \cdot k_3 \cdot \frac{k_2 + \overline{F}}{k_1}} . \tag{37}$$

Then, the approximate value of the derivative was calculated using the equation, which takes into account the change in the function's value relative to a small change in the input variable:

$$K_k = \frac{\overline{C}_B(\overline{F} + \Delta\overline{F}) - \overline{C}_B(\overline{F})}{\Delta\overline{F}} , \tag{38}$$

where $\Delta\overline{F} = 0.01$ was assumed.

3.2. Simulation Results

The performance of the SSDMC algorithm was compared with the classical DMC algorithm's performance in the chemical reactor's control system. In both algorithms, the following values of parameters were assumed: prediction horizon $p = 70$, control horizon $s = 35$, and coefficient $\lambda = 0.001$. Moreover, a constant reference trajectory on the prediction horizon was assumed. The control systems were simulated in Matlab on a PC equipped with the AMD Athlon II X3 460 processor running at 3.40 GHz. A sampling time equal to $T_s = 3.6$ s was assumed. The control plant was simulated using the Dormand–Prince method implemented in the *ode45* solver. The structure of the control system is shown in Figure 3.

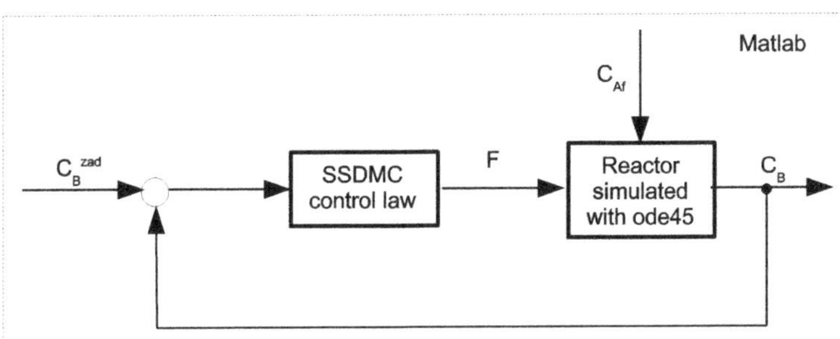

Figure 3. Structure of simulated control system.

The responses of control systems with DMC and SSDMC controllers are shown in Figure 4. The response to the change of the setpoint to $\overline{C}_{B1} = 1$ mol/L obtained in the control system with the SSDMC controller (red lines) practically does not have overshoot; therefore, the control time is slightly shorter than in the case when the DMC controller (blue lines) is used. In the case of disturbance response, the SSDMC controller does not generate overshoot, but the maximal temporary control error is slightly higher than in the control system with the DMC controller.

Moreover, the DMC controller compensates the disturbance faster. On the other hand, the control signal achieves much smaller values than with the SSDMC controller, generating the calm control signal. In the case of responses to the change of the setpoint to $\overline{C}_{B2} = 1.25\ \mathrm{mol/L}$, the SSDMC controller outperforms the DMC controller. It is significantly faster than the DMC controller and generates responses without overshoot. This time, the SSDMC controller compensates the disturbance faster than the DMC controller. However, the maximal temporary control error is slightly bigger in the control system with the SSDMC controller.

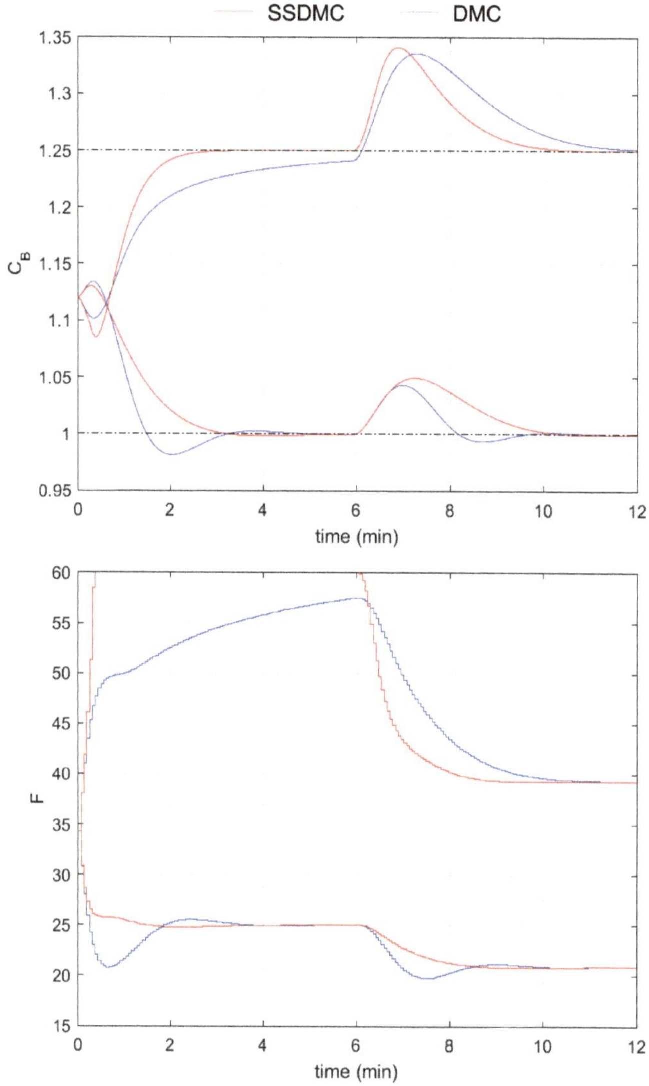

Figure 4. Responses of control system to changes in setpoint to $\overline{C}_{B1} = 1\ \mathrm{mol/L}$ and $\overline{C}_{B2} = 1.25\ \mathrm{mol/L}$ and to change in disturbance by 10% in 6th minute of experiment; $\lambda = 0.001$; SSDMC—red lines, DMC—blue lines.

To improve the operation of the SSDMC controller, experiments with decreasing λ coefficient were conducted; the results are depicted in Figure 5. Initial responses (for $\lambda = 0.001$) are drawn with red lines; the ones obtained for λ decreased 10 times—with blue lines, and for λ

decreased 100 times—with magenta lines. Decreasing λ did not influence the overshoot—it is not present at all in responses to the change of the setpoint to $\overline{C}_{B1} = 1.25$ mol/L and almost not present in responses to the change of the setpoint to $\overline{C}_{B1} = 1$ mol/L. Decreasing λ in all cases brought a decrease in the maximal temporary control error in disturbance responses. Decreasing λ 10 times visibly accelerated the control system's responses. However, the further decrease in λ to 10^{-5} almost did not influence the control time. Moreover, in the latter case and in the case of the change of the setpoint to $\overline{C}_{B1} = 1$ mol/L, oscillations of the control signal at the beginning of the experiment occurred. For the next experiment, $\lambda = 10^{-4}$ was chosen.

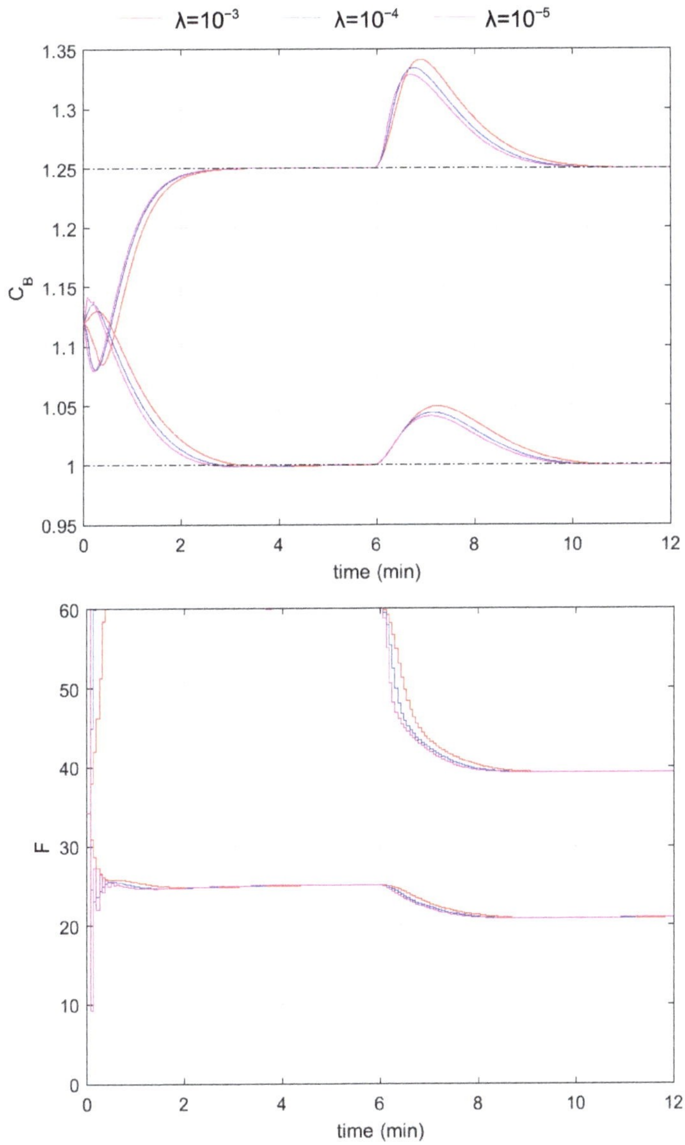

Figure 5. Responses of the control system with the SSDMC controller to changes in the setpoint to $\overline{C}_{B1} = 1$ mol/L and $\overline{C}_{B2} = 1.25$ mol/L and to the change of the disturbance by 10% in the 6th minute of the experiment. $\lambda = 10^{-3}$—red lines; $\lambda = 10^{-4}$—blue lines; $\lambda = 10^{-5}$—magenta lines.

In addition, experiments with different values of the control horizon s were performed; the results are shown in Figure 6. The control horizon gradually decreased from $s = 35$. Interestingly, the responses obtained remained unchanged even for $s = 4$ (they are drawn with the red lines). A tiny change occurred for $s = 3$ (blue lines); the response was a little slower. The further decrease in the control horizon to $s = 2$ (green lines) and $s = 1$ (black dashed lines) continued this trend; the slowest responses were obtained for $s = 1$. In this last case, the maximal temporary control error in the disturbance response near $\overline{C}_{B1} = 1$ mol/L slightly increased, and oscillations occurred in the control signal at the beginning of the experiment. However, in all cases, the response to the setpoint change to $\overline{C}_{B2} = 1.25$ mol/L remained the same.

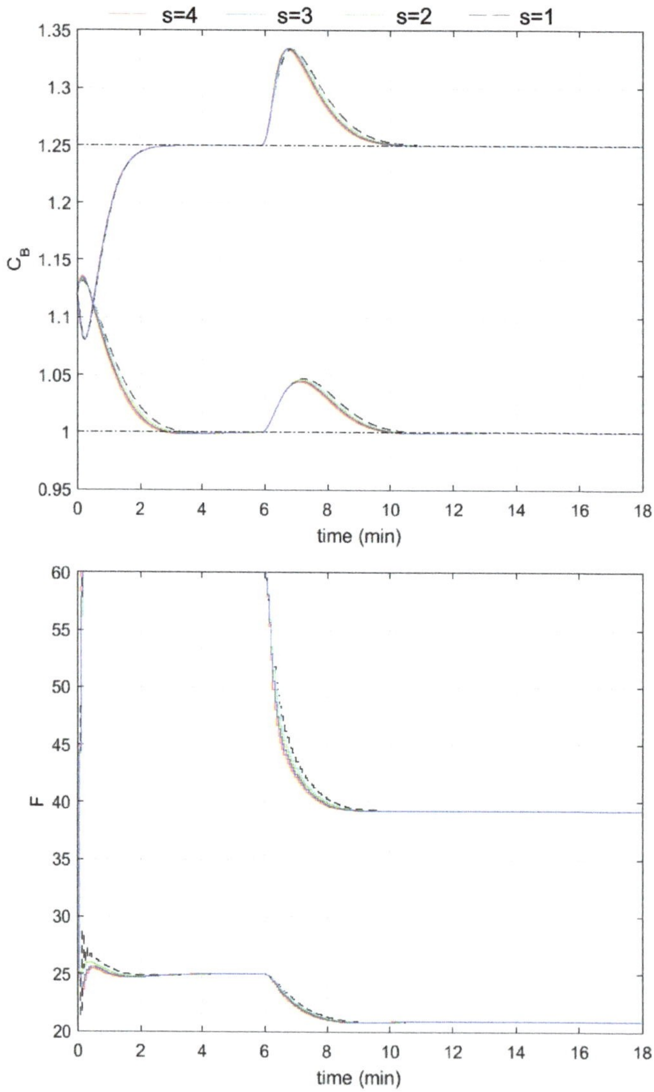

Figure 6. Responses of the control system with the SSDMC controller to changes in the setpoint to $\overline{C}_{B1} = 1$ mol/L and $\overline{C}_{B2} = 1.25$ mol/L and to the change of the disturbance by 10% in the 6th minute of the experiment. $\lambda = 10^{-4}$; s between 4 and 35—red lines; $s = 3$—blue lines; $s = 2$—green lines; $s = 1$—black dashed lines.

Experiments were also conducted to test the robustness of the proposed algorithm. In Figure 7, responses of the control system to the change in the setpoint to $\overline{C}_{B1} = 1$ mol/L and $\overline{C}_{B2} = 1.25$ mol/L and to the change in the disturbance by 10% in the 6th minute of the experiment are shown; the responses are shown when the output was subject to a delay of one sampling time that was not included in the model the algorithm was designed with (blue lines). Despite the delay not being known to the controller, it operates only slightly worse than in the ideal case. The responses to setpoint changes are slightly slower. The overshoot in the response to the setpoint change to $\overline{C}_{B1} = 1$ mol/L increased a little. The responses to the disturbance change worsened. Also, the maximal control error was larger especially when the setpoint was equal to $\overline{C}_{B2} = 1.25$ mol/L.

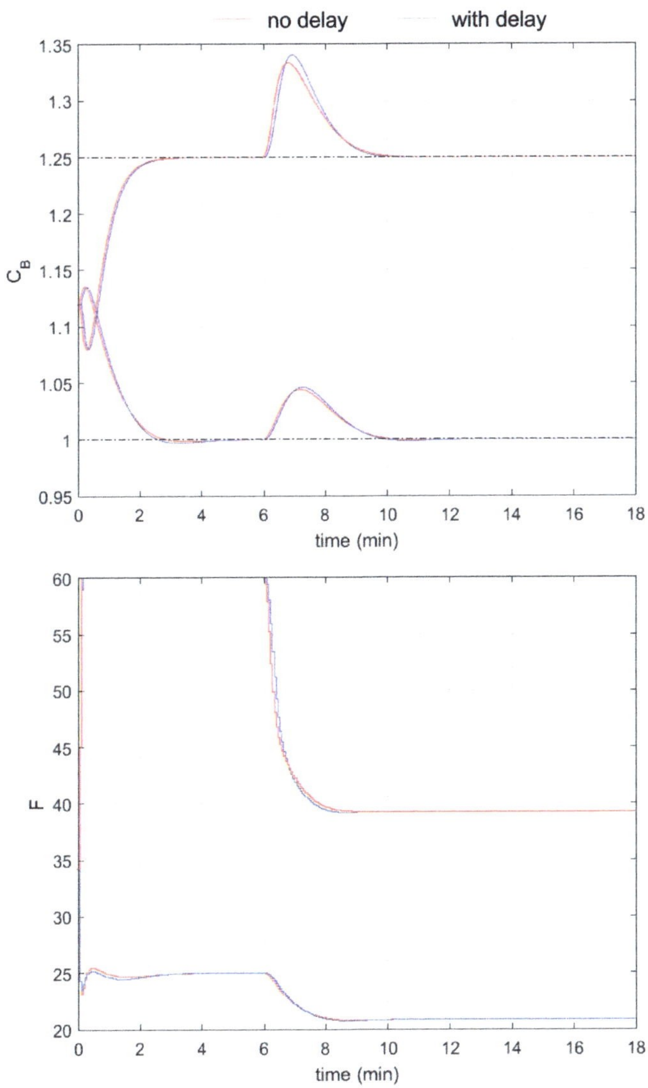

Figure 7. Responses of the control system with the SSDMC controller to changes in the setpoint to $\overline{C}_{B1} = 1$ mol/L and $\overline{C}_{B2} = 1.25$ mol/L and to the change of the disturbance by 10% in the 6th minute of the experiment; $\lambda = 10^{-4}$; $s = 4$. No measurement delay—red lines; with additional measurement delay—blue lines.

In Figure 8, responses of the control system to the change of the setpoint to $\overline{C}_{B1} = 1$ mol/L and $\overline{C}_{B2} = 1.25$ mol/L and to the change of the disturbance by 10% in the 6th minute of the experiment are shown; the responses are given when the output was subject to a measurement noise. This was simulated using random numbers from the interval $[-0.005, 0.005]$ added to the output measurement and sent to the controller. The proposed SSDMC controller copes well with the measurement noise. It achieves the setpoints without problem, even $\overline{C}_{B2} = 1.25$ mol/L though small oscillations of the control signal occurred when it hit the constraint. The change of disturbance was also compensated without problems.

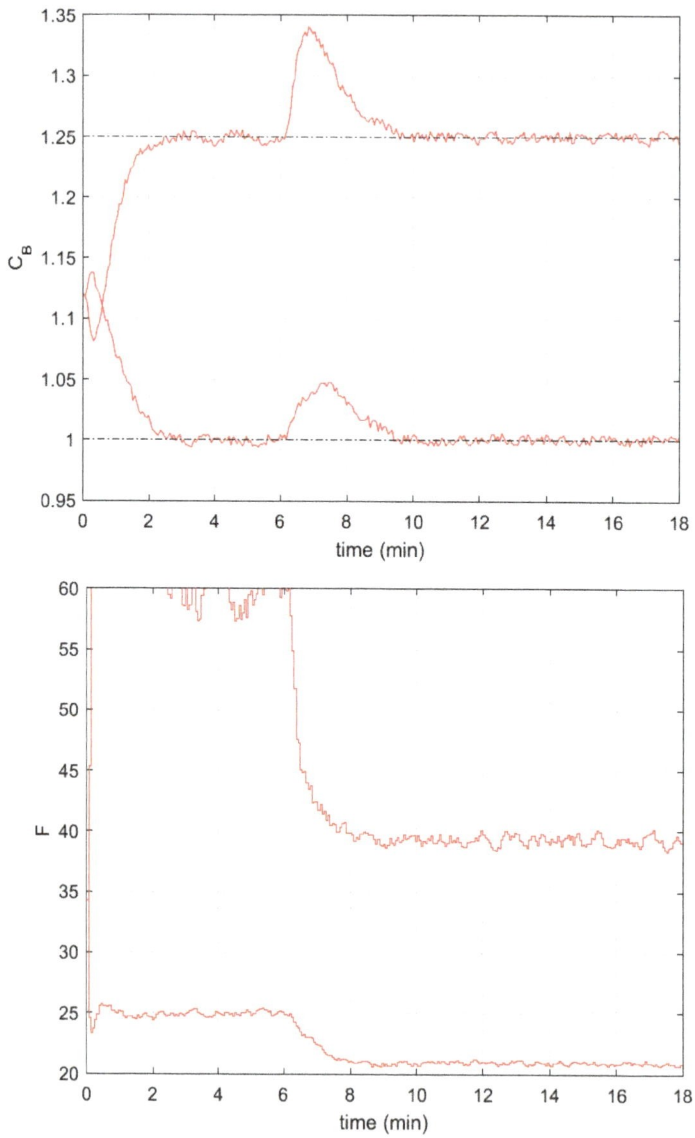

Figure 8. Responses of the control system with the SSDMC controller to changes in the setpoint to $\overline{C}_{B1} = 1$ mol/L and $\overline{C}_{B2} = 1.25$ mol/L and to the change of the disturbance by 10% in the 6th minute of the experiment; $\lambda = 10^{-4}$; $s = 4$; measurement noise added.

Experiments were also conducted with changes in values of the parameters k_1, k_2, and k_3 in the control plant model—a 10% change was made to each value so that the constraint was not active, and each change was made separately. The obtained responses of the control system to the change of the setpoint to $\overline{C}_{B1} = 1$ mol/L and $\overline{C}_{B2} = 1.25$ mol/L and to the change of the disturbance by 10% in the 6th minute of the experiment are shown in Figure 9. In all cases, the control system remains stable, though the obtained responses became worse. When $k_1 = 55$ L/h was assumed (the parameters k_2 and k_3 having nominal values), the responses drawn with the red lines were obtained. A significant overshoot occurred in the response to the setpoint change to $\overline{C}_{B2} = 1.25$ mol/L, and a small overshoot occurred in the case of the setpoint change to $\overline{C}_{B2} = 1$ mol/L. The response to the disturbance change near $\overline{C}_{B2} = 1$ mol/L did not change, and near $\overline{C}_{B2} = 1.25$ mol/L, it became better (a smaller maximal control error was obtained compared to the nominal case).

When $k_2 = 90$ L/h was assumed (k_1 and k_3 parameters having nominal values), the responses drawn with the blue lines were obtained. The biggest overshoot occurred in the response to the setpoint change to $\overline{C}_{B2} = 1.25$ mol/L, a slightly larger overshoot than that obtained in the previous case for the setpoint change to $\overline{C}_{B2} = 1$ mol/L. The responses are the slowest among all the ones depicted in Figure 9. The responses to the disturbance change are almost the same as in the case where only the k_1 parameter was changed.

When $k_3 = 9$ l/(h $\cdot$ mol) was assumed (k_1 and k_2 parameters having nominal values), the responses drawn with the magenta lines were obtained. The smallest overshoot occurred in the response to the setpoint change to $\overline{C}_{B2} = 1.25$ mol/L, as well as for the setpoint change to $\overline{C}_{B2} = 1$ mol/L. Unfortunately, in the response to the setpoint change to $\overline{C}_{B2} = 1.25$ mol/L, oscillations occurred. The response to the disturbance change near $\overline{C}_{B2} = 1$ mol/L is almost the same as in the other cases, while that near $\overline{C}_{B2} = 1$ mol/L is the worst; the maximal control error is the largest among the cases considered.

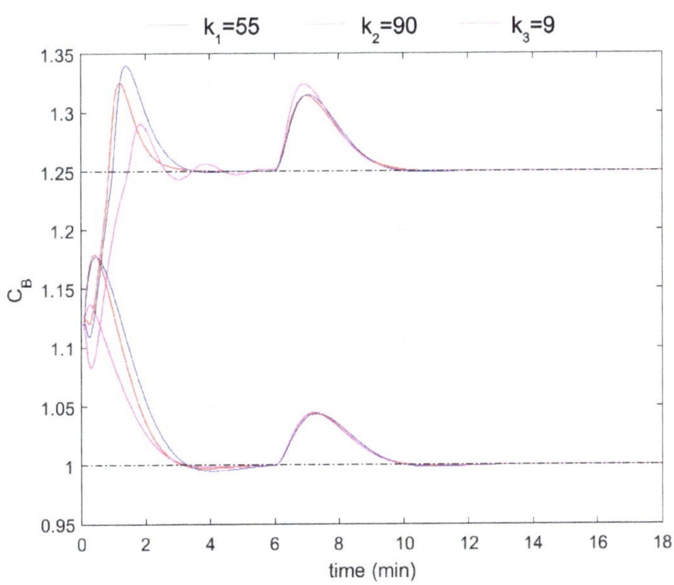

Figure 9. *Cont.*

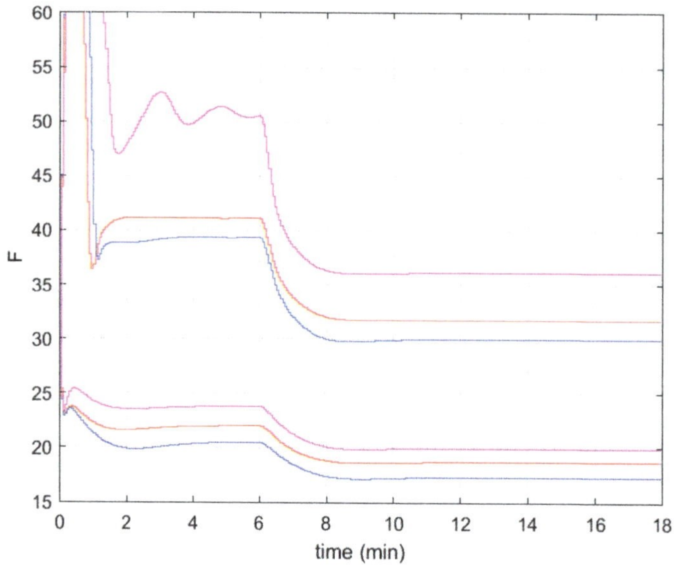

Figure 9. Responses of the control system with the SSDMC controller to changes in the setpoint to $\overline{C}_{B1} = 1$ mol/L and $\overline{C}_{B2} = 1.25$ mol/L and to the change of the disturbance by 10% in the 6th minute of the experiment. $\lambda = 10^{-4}$; $s = 4$; k_1 changed to 55 L/h ($k_2 = 100$ 1/h, $k_3 = 10$ L/(h · mol))—red lines; k_2 changed to 90 1/h ($k_1 = 50$ L/h, $k_3 = 10$ l/(h · mol))—blue lines, k_3 changed to 9 L/(h · mol) ($k_1 = 50$ L/h, $k_2 = 100$ L/h)—magenta lines.

4. Discussion and Conclusions

It is worth noting that the computational complexity of both DMC and SSDMC controllers is similar. In the SSDMC algorithm, in addition to the operations performed in the DMC algorithm, only the slope of the steady-state characteristic (the derivative of a specific function) needs to be calculated additionally, which does not significantly complicate the proposed algorithm. Moreover, in the example under consideration, determining the derivative is particularly easy due to the relative simplicity of obtaining the analytical formula for calculating it.

The main tuning parameter, λ, is still available in the SSDMC controller and has the same meaning as in the standard algorithms. It decides on the size of the penalty for the control signal changes. However, inside the algorithm, it depends on the process gain at the current operating point to obtain the compact control law.

The next main tuning parameter, the control horizon s, does not influence the responses obtained as much as the parameter λ. Moreover, its decrease slightly slows down the responses obtained, worsening the control quality. On the other hand, thanks to the formulation of the SSDMC algorithm in the form of the control law, the longer control horizon does not influence the numerical complexity of the algorithm.

An important advantage of the proposed algorithm is its robustness to measurement noise, measurement delay, and the uncertainty of process parameters. Even when the parameters of the control plant were significantly changed, the controller managed to stabilize the reactor and maintain satisfactory performance.

The use of a dynamic model in the form of the process step response and static characteristic of the process, combined in a skillful way in order to synthesize the MPC algorithm, resulted in a computationally efficient predictive control algorithm in which the main part of the calculations needed to determine the control value is performed offline as in a conventional, analytical DMC algorithm. However, note that despite the relative simplicity of the controller obtained and the relatively straightforward way of receiving it, it can offer much better control quality than the conventional DMC controller based on the linear model.

Funding: This research received no external funding.

Data Availability Statement: The data are contained within the article.

Conflicts of Interest: The author declares no conflicts of interest.

Abbreviations

The following abbreviations are used in this manuscript:

CSTR	Continuous Stirred-Tank Reactor
DMC	Dynamic Matrix Control
LMI	Linear Matrix Inequality
LMPC	Linear Model-Based Model Predictive Control
MPC	Model Predictive Control
NMPC	Nonlinear Model-Based MPC
PID	Proportional–Integral–Derivative
SISO	Single-Input Single-Output
SSDMC	Steady-State Model-Based Dynamic Matrix Control

References

1. Arteaga, M.A.; Guajardo-Benavides, E.J.; Sánchez-Sánchez, P. Stability Analysis and Experimental Validation of Standard Proportional-Integral-Derivative Control in Bilateral Teleoperators with Time-Varying Delays. *Algorithms* **2024**, *17*, 580. [CrossRef]
2. Candan, F.; Dik, O.F.; Kumbasar, T.; Mahfouf, M.; Mihaylova, L. Real-Time Interval Type-2 Fuzzy Control of an Unmanned Aerial Vehicle with Flexible Cable-Connected Payload. *Algorithms* **2023**, *16*, 273. [CrossRef]
3. Kong, W.; Zhang, H.; Yang, X.; Yao, Z.; Wang, R.; Yang, W.; Zhang, J. PID control algorithm based on multistrategy enhanced dung beetle optimizer and back propagation neural network for DC motor control. *Sci. Rep.* **2024**, *14*, 28276. [CrossRef]
4. Mao, W.-L.; Chen, S.-H.; Kao, C.-Y. Fractional-Order Fuzzy PID Controller with Evolutionary Computation for an Effective Synchronized Gantry System. *Algorithms* **2024**, *17*, 58. [CrossRef]
5. Guo, X.; Shirkhani, M.; Ahmed, E.M. Machine-Learning-Based Improved Smith Predictive Control for MIMO Processes. *Mathematics* **2022**, *10*, 3696. [CrossRef]
6. Mohammadzaheri, G.M.; Ghodsi, M. An Enhanced Smith-Predictor-based Control System for delayed MIMO Processes and its Use on a CSTR with Multiple Time-delays. In Proceedings of the 2023 28th International Conference on Automation and Computing (ICAC), Birmingham, UK, 30 August–1 September 2023; pp. 1–6
7. Camacho, E.F.; Bordons, C. *Model Predictive Control*; Springer: London, UK, 1999.
8. Maciejowski, J.M. *Predictive Control with Constraints*; Prentice Hall: Harlow, UK, 2002.
9. Nebeluk, R.; Marusak, P. Efficient MPC algorithms with variable trajectories of parameters weighting predicted control errors. *Arch. Control Sci.* **2020**, *30*, 325–363.
10. Rossiter, J.A. *Model-Based Predictive Control: A Practical Approach*; CRC Press: Boca Raton, FL, USA, 2003.
11. Sands, T. Comparison and Interpretation Methods for Predictive Control of Mechanics. *Algorithms* **2019**, *12*, 232. [CrossRef]
12. Tatjewski, P. *Advanced Control of Industrial Processes; Structures and Algorithms*; Springer: London, UK, 2007.
13. Ławryńczuk, M. *Computationally Efficient Model Predictive Control Algorithms: A Neural Network Approach*; Springer: Berlin/Heidelberg, Germany, 2014.
14. Mohamed, M.A.-E.-H.; Abbas, H.S.; Shouran, M.; Kamel, S. A Neuro-Predictive Controller Scheme for Integration of a Basic Wind Energy Generation Unit with an Electrical Power System. *Energies* **2022**, *15*, 5839. [CrossRef]
15. Mohammadzaheri, M.; Chen, L.; Mirsepahi, A.; Ghanbari, M.; Tafreshi, R. Neuro-Predictive Control of an Infrared Dryer with a Feedforward-Feedback Approach. *Asian J. Control* **2015**, *17*, 1972–1977. [CrossRef]
16. Abdelaal, M.; Schön, S. Predictive Path Following and Collision Avoidance of Autonomous Connected Vehicles. *Algorithms* **2020**, *13*, 52. [CrossRef]
17. Chen, H.; Allgöwer, F. A Quasi-Infinite Horizon Nonlinear Model Predictive Control Scheme with Guaranteed Stability. *Automatica* **1998**, *34*, 1205–1217. [CrossRef]

18. Tatjewski, P. Offset–free nonlinear model predictive control with state–space process models. *Arch. Control Sci.* **2017**, *27*, 595–615. [CrossRef]
19. Diehl, M.; Bock, H.G.; Schlöder, J.P.; Findeisen, R.; Nagy, Z.; Allgöwer, F. Real–time optimization and nonlinear model predictive control of processes governed by differential–algebraic equations. *J. Process Control* **2002**, *12*, 577–585. [CrossRef]
20. Schäfer, A.; Kühl, P.; Diehl, M.; Schlöder, J.; Bock, H.G. Fast reduced multiple shooting methods for nonlinear model predictive control. *Chem. Eng. Process.* **2007**, *46*, 1200–1214. [CrossRef]
21. Zavala, V.M.; Laird, C.D.; Biegler, L.T. A fast moving horizon estimation algorithm based on nonlinear programming sensitivity. *J. Process Control* **2008**, *18*, 876–884. [CrossRef]
22. Ławryńczuk, M. Nonlinear state–space predictive control with on–line linearisation and state estimation. *Int. J. Appl. Math. Comput. Sci.* **2015**, *25*, 833–847. [CrossRef]
23. Morari, M.; Lee, J.H. Model predictive control: Past, present and future. *Comput. Chem. Eng.* **1999**, *23*, 667–682. [CrossRef]
24. Marusak, P. Efficient model predictive control algorithm with fuzzy approximations of nonlinear models. *LNCS* **2009**, *5495*, 448–457.
25. Marusak, P. Advantages of an easy to design fuzzy predictive algorithm in control systems of nonlinear chemical reactors. *Appl. Soft Comput.* **2009**, *9*, 1111–1125. [CrossRef]
26. Marusak, P. Numerically Efficient Fuzzy MPC Algorithm with Advanced Generation of Prediction: Application to a Chemical Reactor. *Algorithms* **2020**, *13*, 143. [CrossRef]
27. Marusak, P. Advanced Construction of Dynamic Matrix in Numerically Efficient Fuzzy MPC Algorithms. *Algorithms* **2021**, *14*, 25. [CrossRef]
28. Nebeluk, R.; Ławryńczuk, M. Fast Nonlinear Predictive Control Using Classical and Parallel Wiener Models: A Comparison for a Neutralization Reactor Process. *Sensors* **2023**, *23*, 9539. [CrossRef]
29. Dominguez, L.F.; Pistikopoulos, E.N. A Novel mp-NLP Algorithm for Explicit/Multi-parametric NMPC. In Proceedings of the 8th IFAC Symposium on Nonlinear Control Systems, Bologna, Italy, 1–3 September 2010.
30. Johansen, T.A. On multi–parametric nonlinear programming and explicit nonlinear model predictive control. In Proceedings of the 41st IEEE Conf Decision and Control, Las Vegas, NV, USA, 10–13 December 2002; Volume 3, pp. 2768–2773.
31. Johansen, T.A. Approximate explicit receding horizon control of constrained nonlinear systems. *Automatica* **2004**, *40*, 293–300. [CrossRef]
32. Bemporad, A.; Borrelli, F.; Morari, M. Piecewise linear optimal controllers for hybrid systems. In Proceedings of the 2000 American Control Conference, Chicago, IL, USA, 28–30 June 2000; Volume 2; pp. 1190–1194.
33. Bemporad, A.; Morari, M.; Dua, V.; Pistikopoulos, E.N. The explicit linear quadratic regulator for constrained systems. *Automatica* **2002**, *38*, 3–20. [CrossRef]
34. Pistikopoulos, E.N.; Dua, V.; Bozinis, N.A.; Bemporad, A.; Morari, M. On–line optimization via off–line parametric optimization tools. *Comput. Chem. Eng.* **2002**, *26*, 175–185. [CrossRef]
35. Chaber, P.; Ławryńczuk, M. Fast analytical model predictive controllers and their implementation for STM32 ARMmicrocontroller. *IEEE Trans. Ind. Inform.* **2019**, *15*, 4580–4590. [CrossRef]
36. Wojtulewicz, A.; Ławryńczuk, M. Implementation of multiple–input multiple–output dynamic matrix control algorithm for fast processes using field programmable gate array. *IFAC–PapersOnLine* **2018**, *51*, 324–329. [CrossRef]
37. Bagheri, P.; Sedigh, A.K. Analytical approach to tuning of model predictive control for first-order plus dead time models. *IET Control Theory Appl.* **2013**, *7*, 1806–1817. [CrossRef]
38. Short, M. Move suppression calculations for well-conditioned MPC. *ISA Trans.* **2017**, *67*, 371–381. [CrossRef]
39. Zheng, H.; Zou, T.; Hu, J.; Yu, H. An offline optimization and online table look-up strategy of two-layer model predictive control. *IEEE Access* **2018**, *6*, 47433–47441. [CrossRef]
40. Abbas, H.S.; Hanema, J.; Tóth, R. Mohammadpour, J.; Meskin, N. An improved robust model predictive control for linear parameter-varying input-output models. *Int. J. Robust Nonlinear Control* **2018**, *28*, 859–880. [CrossRef]
41. Ding, B.; Zou, T. A synthesis approach for output feedback robust model predictive control based-on input–output model. *J. Process Control* **2014**, *24*, 60–72. [CrossRef]
42. Yan, Y.; Zhang, L. Robust Model Predictive Control with Almost Zero Online Computation. *Mathematics* **2021**, *9*, 242. [CrossRef]
43. Marusak, P. A numerically efficient fuzzy MPC algorithm with fast generation of the control signal. *Int. J. Appl. Math. Comput. Sci.* **2021**, *31*, 59–71. [CrossRef]
44. Jain, A.; Taparia, R. Laguerre function based model predictive control for van–de–vusse reactor. In Proceedings of the 2nd IEEE International Conference on Power Electronics, Intelligent Control and Energy Systems, ICPEICES 2018, Delhi, India, 22–24 October 2018; Volume 3 , pp. 1010–1015.
45. Mate, S.; Kodamana, H.; Bhartiya, S.; Nataraj, P.S.V. A Stabilizing Sub–Optimal Model Predictive Control for Quasi–Linear Parameter Varying Systems. *IEEE Control Syst. Lett.* **2020**, *4*, 402–407. [CrossRef]

46. Ribeiro, L.M.; Secchi, A.R. A methodology to obtain analytical models that reduce the computational complexity faced in real time implementation of NMPC controllers. *Braz. J. Chem. Eng.* **2019**, *36*, 1255–1277. [CrossRef]
47. Nguyen, T.S.; Hoang, N.H.; Hussain, M.A. Tracking error plus damping injection control of non-minimum phase processes. *IFAC-Papers Online* **2018**, *51*, 643–648. [CrossRef]
48. Uçak, K. A Runge–Kutta neural network-based control method for nonlinear MIMO systems. *Soft Comput.* **2019**, *23*, 7769–7803. [CrossRef]
49. Uçak, K. A Novel Model Predictive Runge–Kutta Neural Network Controller for Nonlinear MIMO Systems. *Neural Process. Lett.* **2020**, *51*, 1789–1833. [CrossRef]
50. Banerjee, S.; Khan, O.; El Mistiri, M.; Nandola, N.N.; Rivera, D.E. Data-Driven Control of Highly Interactive Systems using 3DoF Model-On-Demand MPC: Application to a MIMO CSTR. *IFAC-PapersOnLine* **2024**, *58*, 420–425. [CrossRef]
51. Mohammadzaheri, M.; Chen, L. Double-command fuzzy control of a nonlinear CSTR. *Korean J. Chem. Eng* **2010**, *27*, 19–31. [CrossRef]
52. Doyle, F.; Ogunnaike, B.A.; Pearson, R.K. Nonlinear model–based control using second–order Volterra models. *Automatica* **1995**, *31*, 697–714. [CrossRef]

algorithms

MDPI

Article

Evaluation of PID-Based Algorithms for UGVs

Tiago Gameiro [1,2,3], Tiago Pereira [1,2,3,4], Hamid Moghadaspoura [5], Francesco Di Giorgio [6], Carlos Viegas [3], Nuno Ferreira [2,4,7,*], João Ferreira [4,8], Salviano Soares [1,9,10] and António Valente [1,7]

1 Engineering Department, School of Sciences and Technology, University of Trás-os-Montes and Alto Douro (UTAD), Quinta de Prados, 5000-801 Vila Real, Portugal; tiagocostagameiro@gmail.com (T.G.); tiago.pereira@ipc.pt (T.P.); salblues@gmail.com (S.S.); antonio.luis.valente@gmail.com (A.V.)
2 GECAD—Knowledge Research Group on Intelligent Engineering and Computing for Advanced Innovation and Development of the Engineering Institute of Porto (ISEP), Polytechnic Institute of Porto (IPP), 4200-465 Porto, Portugal
3 Department of Mechanical Engineering, Association for the Development of Industrial Aerodynamics (ADAI), University of Coimbra, Rua Luís Reis Santos, Pólo II, 3030-788 Coimbra, Portugal; carlos.viegas@uc.pt
4 Coimbra Institute of Engineering (ISEC), Polytechnic Institute of Coimbra (IPC), Rua Pedro Nunes-Quinta da Nora, 3030-199 Coimbra, Portugal; ferreira@isec.pt
5 Institute of Telecommunications, Department of Electrical and Computer Engineering, University of Coimbra, 3004-531 Coimbra, Portugal; hamid.moghadas.pour@co.it.pt
6 Department of Electronics and Telecommunications, Polytechnic of Torino, Corso Duca Degli Abruzzi, 24, 10129 Torino, Italy; francescodigiorgio26@gmail.com
7 Institute for Systems and Computer Engineering-Technology and Science (INESC TEC), Rua Dr. Roberto Frias, 4200-465 Porto, Portugal
8 Institute of Systems and Robotics, Department of Electrical and Computer Engineering, University of Coimbra, Rua Silvio Lima-Polo II, 3030-290 Coimbra, Portugal
9 Institute of Electronics and Informatics Engineering of Aveiro (IEETA), University of Aveiro, 3810-193 Aveiro, Portugal
10 Intelligent Systems Associate Laboratory (LASI), University of Aveiro, 3810-193 Aveiro, Portugal
* Correspondence: nunomig@isec.pt

Abstract: The autonomous navigation of unmanned ground vehicles (UGVs) in unstructured environments, such as agricultural or forestry settings, has been the subject of extensive research by various investigators. The navigation capability of a UGV in unstructured environments requires considering numerous factors, including the quality of data reception that allows reliable interpretation of what the UGV perceives in a given environment, as well as the use these data to control the UGV's navigation. This article aims to study different PID control algorithms to enable autonomous navigation on a robotic platform. The robotic platform consists of a forestry tractor, used for forest cleaning tasks, which was converted into a UGV through the integration of sensors. Using sensor data, the UGV's position and orientation are obtained and utilized for navigation by inputting these data into a PID control algorithm. The correct choice of PID control algorithm involved the study, analysis, and implementation of different controllers, leading to the conclusion that the Vector Field control algorithm demonstrated better performance compared to the others studied and implemented in this paper.

Keywords: PID control; UGV; algorithms; real environment tests

1. Introduction

Unmanned ground vehicles (UGVs) have received significant attention due to their ability to operate in unstructured and dynamic environments where human intervention is limited or hazardous. These robotic platforms are widely used in applications for unstructured environments, such as in agriculture, where the current literature reports the application of UGVs in specific agricultural tasks [1,2]. Additionally, in forestry, although advancements are more limited compared to agriculture, the literature already highlights some progress, as demonstrated in [3,4]. The navigation of UGVs in unstructured outdoor environments has been challenging due to the presence of adversities/unpredictable factors such as lighting, shadows, obstructions, dynamic obstacles, and rugged or demanding terrains [5,6]. Given these constraints, the focus of research by many investigators in the field of mobile robotics has been on developing UGVs capable of navigating autonomously and efficiently.

Such autonomous systems in challenging environments require a computational component to enable UGVs to perform trajectory planning. The ability of a UGV to plan a trajectory that not only reaches a target destination but also avoids obstacles with time and efficiency guarantees are basic functions that UGVs must possess, regardless of the application scenario. We can identify three types of controllers commonly used in this field: classical control, referred to as Proportional, Integral, and Derivative (PID); intelligent and adaptive control (Fuzzy); and predictive control [7]. However, for the work addressed in this article, the PID controller is used.

Thus, the autonomous navigation technology of UGVs in unstructured environments involves trajectory planning and control, precise positioning, and other functions.

The current literature reveals the existence of various navigation systems, with the most commonly used being the real-time kinematic global satellite navigation system (RTK-GNSS). This type of system achieves centimeter-scale accuracy in satellite positioning, but requires a clear line of sight [8]. In addition to this navigation system, other, less predominant systems also appear in the literature, which collects different types of sensory data. These systems include GNSS/INS, which result from the combination of a Global Navigation Satellite System (GNSS) and an Inertial Navigation System (INS) [9,10]; GNSS/VISUAL/INS systems, which combine GNSSs, visual information, and INSs [11]; GNSS/VISUAL/IMU/MAP systems [12]; and others.

For the work in question, the GNSS-RTK/INS navigation system was used, which combines data from GNSS + RTK + IMU sensors to obtain the position, as well as a magnetometer to determine the heading or yaw (referring to the robot's rotation along the Z-axis of the UGV).

Thus, in this article, a set of PID control algorithms, referred to as follows, is evaluated and studied:

- ON–OFF controller;
- PID Heading controller (PID-H);
- PID Cross Track Error controller (PID-CTE);
- PID Cross Track Error + Heading controller (PID-CTE + H);
- PID Vector Field (PID-VF).

Thus, this article aims to demonstrate which of the implemented algorithms achieves the most efficient behavior for UGV navigation in unstructured environments (in this case, the unstructured environment under study consists of a forest environment).

This paper is organized as follows: Section 1 introduces the motivation behind this work. Section 2 presents topics related to the state of the art of PID controllers. Section 3 details the methodology, including a description of the robotic platform used and its integrated sensors, the PID control algorithms with a detailed explanation of each one employed, and, finally, the performance evaluation metrics. Section 4 shows the results obtained through real-time experiments and the evaluation of the proposed PID control algorithms. Section 5 concludes with an overall analysis of the work carried out.

2. Related Work

2.1. Advantages and Disadvantages of Different Control Methods

The PID controller is one of the most widely used methods in UGV control systems due to its simplicity, robustness, and effectiveness in adjusting control variables such as speed and direction. In addition to this type of control, the literature also highlights three others: the ON–OFF controller, fuzzy controller, and Model Predictive Control (MPC).

The ON–OFF controller is particularly simple and practical to implement, such that quick response capabilities can be realized in systems with on-off inputs, and thus the ON–OFF controller is widely employed for binary actuations. Despite this, it is power hungry and imprecise and therefore not suitable for applications that demand control with optimal or continuous control [13].

The PID controller, with its three parameters, can control the steady-state and transient responses nicely and provides simple yet effective control solutions for a wide range of control problems. Nowadays, they are widely used in a variety of industries because of their simple structure and intuitive understanding of the controller principle, as compared to other types of controllers. As described, the behavior of PID controllers depends on these parameters. Yet, the potential vulnerability of their robustness and simplicity can make them challenging to parameterize [14].

The fuzzy controller has significant benefits in energy consumption and convergence time. It also affords a more stable response across variable conditions in contrast to conventional approaches that may be responsive to initial torques and to inhomogeneity in friction. Despite these benefits, the fuzzy design has a number of problems, such as the accuracy being affected by the actuation deadband and the computational complexity, meaning that the design frequently needs to be simplified [15].

Model Predictive Control (MPC) is a powerful control architecture that uses dynamic models to predict and optimize control actions within a time window. It can accommodate input and output constraints, making it ideal for complex and dynamic systems, such as industrial process level control. However, the validity of MPC depends upon the validity of the system models, and the absence of this validity may lead to suboptimal behavior. Moreover, real-time optimization procedures may be computationally heavy, resulting in implementation difficulty [16].

PID controllers are widely preferred due to their simplicity, readability, and ability to handle both steady-state and transient responses. Although more sophisticated controllers such as fuzzy logic and Model Predictive Control (MPC) have specific advantages, e.g., a better energy efficiency or optimization for dynamic systems, they generally come with disadvantages, e.g., increased complexity or larger computational needs. Table 1 shows the advantages and disadvantages of each type of control.

Table 1. Advantages and Disadvantages of each type of controller.

	ON–OFF	PID	Fuzzy Logic	Predictive Control
Simplicity	√	√	×	×
Accuracy	×	√	√	√
Computational Cost	√	√	×	×
Stability	×	√	√	√
Speed	√	√	√	√
Tuning	√	×	√	√

2.2. Comparative Approaches to the Use of PID Controller Algorithms in UGVs

Several studies and reviews are available in the literature addressing UGV navigation methods, whether in structured or unstructured environments. The work conducted by Ji

Y. et al. demonstrates the application of a UGV in unstructured environments, where the A-STAR algorithm was used, enhanced with improvements in the heuristic function to achieve shorter paths [17]. In [18], the authors proposed a method involving a hierarchical adaptive control strategy for UGVs, using a PID to estimate the yaw moment and PSO optimization to handle structural uncertainties, distributing the yaw moment among the motors. Sun Y. et al. present a trajectory-following PID control design for a three-wheeled UGV, addressing lateral directional control, vector-field-based orientation, and sensor fusion using a Kalman filter [19]. In [20], the authors introduced a method based on vector differences and self-adaptive mechanisms for PID tuning, aimed at minimizing human intervention in the adjustment of PID controllers across a diverse and extensive set of problems/tasks. To achieve this, an innovative approach based on the Differential Evolution algorithm with Success-Based Particle Adaptations (DEPA) was employed. This algorithm utilizes a memory mechanism to autonomously and efficiently adapt control parameters.

Moreover, modern control techniques also stand out in complex systems such as Markov jump systems. For instance, Vijayakumar et al. [21] proposed an approach based on a Proportional–Integral Observer (PIO) and disturbance rejection techniques with IEID, as well as a Smith predictor for systems with input delays and state-dependent nonlinearities. This method employs linear matrix inequalities (LMI) and Lyapunov stability theory to ensure robust output tracking with disturbance rejection. Similarly, Song and Jin [22] presented a tracking control approach based on observers for Markov jump systems with partially known transition rates, utilizing LMI and stochastic stability theory. This method focuses on reference control and ensuring stability for systems with undefined transitions. Although this work targets specific transition rate conditions, it highlights the importance of observers in improving accuracy and stability in uncertain systems.

However, Gomathi N. et al. introduced an adaptive trajectory planning framework where a UGV equipped with LIDAR and a camera was used to monitor agricultural terrains. For trajectory planning, they proposed the HSAStar hybrid algorithm (Hybrid SLAM and A Star), which combines SLAM and A* to allow the UGV to continuously monitor the path while mapping [23]. Farag W. et al. developed a PID controller designed to improve the capability of autonomous cars to perform maneuvers on pre-calculated tracks. They proposed three approaches to design and tune the controller's hyperparameters, using the CTE as input and generating steering commands as output. Simulations on complex tracks, including sharp curves, were used to evaluate the controller's performance at different speeds [24]. In [25], the authors proposed a PID controller to address the trajectory tracking problem in mobile robots with differential kinematics. The developed method consists of a trial-and-error technique with six tuning parameters to allow the robot to follow a desired trajectory. The controller was designed to handle the non-linearity of reference trajectory tracking and adjust the speeds of the robot's DC motors.

Additionally, Akopov et al. [26] adopted an algorithmic optimization approach for autonomous systems by introducing a simulation-based optimization technique for autonomous transport systems. They implemented a Real-Coded Genetic Algorithm with Scalable Non-Uniform Mutation (RCGA-SNUM). This method was designed to minimize traffic accidents through the simulation of autonomous vehicles on an Artificial Multi-Connected Road Network (AMCRN).

Despite extensive study on PID control for UGVs, issues persist in its adaptation to dynamic and unstructured situations. These issues encompass the management of nonlinear dynamics resulting from fluctuating terrain conditions, the assurance of dependable trajectory tracking amongst external disturbances, and the achieving of real-time sensor fusion for accurate control. The design is further complicated by the need for scalability across various workloads and the minimization of latency in resource-constrained systems.

3. Methodology

3.1. System Description

The UGV used for the development of this work is an internal combustion tractor called Green Climber LV600, manufactured by MDB in Abruzzo, Italy, as illustrated in Figure 1a. This platform is equipped with a sensory box (referred to as Sentry), as shown in Figure 1b, which integrates a variety of sensors and hardware elements. This setup is connected to the tractor, thus providing a set of features for autonomous navigation in unstructured environments.

(a) (b)

Figure 1. Robotic platform (forest tractor) equipped with a sensory box: (**a**) UGV; (**b**) sensory box (Sentry) to control the UGV.

Thus, the goal is to enable the above robotic platform to perform autonomous trajectory navigation. The trajectories are defined by a set of Cartesian points, and the objective is for the robot to execute these trajectories using a PID algorithm, where the control variables are derived from a navigation system.

The adopted navigation system, which will collaborate with the PID algorithms, is based on GNSS-RTK/INS, where the PID control algorithms will receive data on the position and orientation/heading of the UGV. The position and heading values are provided by a sensor located on top of the sensory box, called Duro Inertial. The Duro Inertial system is ideal for navigation systems as it consists of sensors such as GPS, an accelerometer, a gyroscope, and a magnetometer, and through the combination/fusion of these, it is possible to obtain the position and orientation. This sensor, when connected to the RTK system, can provide a position accuracy of between 1 cm and 1.5 cm [27].

The system that inputs data into the PID controller can be seen in the diagram presented in Figure 2. The robot's position, whose origin/acquisition is based on work developed in [28], is essentially obtained by combining data from the GNSS + RTK system, which provides the latitude and longitude, along with an IMU that gives information on the robot's acceleration and velocity in three dimensions. These data are then aggregated in a Kalman filter, which allows, with some confidence, to provide the robot's x and y position. The robot's heading, which is derived from work developed in [28,29], comes from a three-dimensional magnetometer, and through the magnetic fields, it is possible to obtain the heading in Cartesian space (which, in this case, refers to the yaw of the UGV). However, before processing the magnetometer data, it undergoes a filtering process, where a Raised Cosine Moving Average (RCMA) filter is applied to minimize the noise present in these types of sensors. After filtering, these data are integrated with IMU data to compensate for inclinations in the terrain.

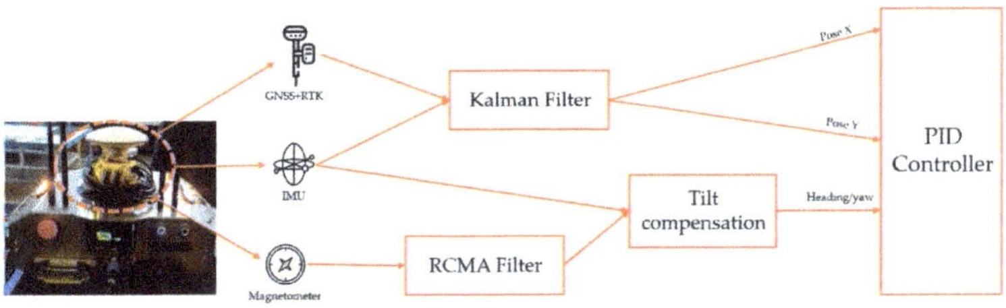

Figure 2. Process of acquiring the variables to be implemented in the algorithms of the PID control.

3.2. Control System and Controller Selection for UGV Navigation

The robot control system is a MIMO (Multiple Inputs and Multiple Outputs) system equipped with various controllers. Due to the lack of knowledge regarding the speeds of each track, its control is achieved by obtaining the position and orientation of the UGV. Through the ROS platform, it is possible to acquire both the position and orientation of the robot via various published "topics", as well as the linear and angular velocity of the robot through the "cmd_vel" topic. Since it is not possible to directly control the UGV's speed, we assume the velocities as control variables but treat them as indicators to understand the UGV's movement.

Given that we are dealing with a differential structure, it only has two axes, x and z, with the x-axis corresponding to linear velocity and the z-axis to angular velocity. To ensure system safety, software protection has been included where the sum of these two components cannot exceed 1. In other words, 1 is considered the system's maximum speed, and 0 is the minimum speed. Table 2 provides several examples illustrating how the robot should move based on the values obtained from the "cmd_vel" topic.

Table 2. Behavioral responses based on "cmd_vel" values.

Linear Velocity (v)	Angular Velocity (w)	Behavior
v = 1	w = 0	Front Linear Movement
v = −1	w = 0	Back Linear Movement
v = 0	w = 1	Rotate Anti-Clockwise
v = 0	w = −1	Rotate Clockwise
v = 0.5	w = 0.5	Circular Movement Anti-Clockwise
v = 0.5	w = −0.5	Circular Movement Clockwise

The "controller" publishes the commands, but the voltage applied to the UGV is controlled by a driver managed by the "microcontroller". The microcontroller operates as a state machine, adjusting the voltage sent to the tracks based on the "cmd_vel" topic.

Initial tests established the maximum and minimum voltage limits for the reliable operation of the solenoid valves and tracks. These tests involved gradually applying voltage and observing the effects on speed, steering, and stability. Using the results, functions were created to model how the solenoid valves and tracks respond to voltage variations. This allowed the development of rules to optimize the UGV's performance and ensure efficient operation.

The references R1 and R2 are desired values from the UGV's trajectory planning system, serving as inputs for the controllers. Errors e1 and e2 are calculated as the difference between desired and actual values. The controllers send corrections to the microcontroller, which adjusts the tracks to align the UGV's movement with the planned trajectory.

The UGV's various controllers can be selected based on the operating circumstances. For example, a controller can be activated to maximize traction and stability on inclined or slippery terrain, thereby improving safety and efficiency. Additionally, the ability to dynamically switch controllers helps reduce environmental impacts, such as choosing a gentler controller in sensitive areas where soil and vegetation preservation is critical, thereby avoiding inevitable damage to the surrounding ecosystem. The use of multiple controllers in forestry operations is a significant innovation in this context. This methodology provides technical advantages and enhances the sustainability of operations in challenging environments, showcasing the technology's ability to tackle diverse challenges while promoting more ethical and effective practices in navigating these machines.

The next section discusses different types of controllers developed for controlling the robot, such as the ON–OFF controller and various PID controllers for managing different variables.

3.3. ON–OFF Controller

The ON–OFF controller is represented in Figure 3 and operates by switching between two values, meaning that it involves an instantaneous change between two states [30].

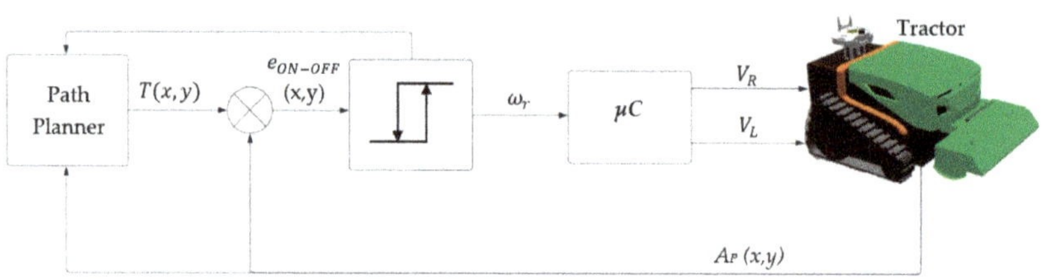

Figure 3. ON–OFF controller block diagram.

In the context of this study and analysis, several variables play crucial roles in understanding and controlling the system shown in Figure 3. The Target (T) variable defines the desired location on the map, while the Actual Position (AP) variable is the precise position relative to a reference point. The On–Off Error ($e_{\text{ON-OFF}}$) variable represents the position error, where if it exceeds a certain threshold, a new trajectory is calculated. This error is the difference between the desired position (T) and the actual position (AP) of the system. The Angular Value (ωr) variable expresses the angular value associated with rotational or curvilinear movement. The Microcontroller (μC) is the "brain" of the system, responsible for processing the values obtained from the "cmd_vel" topic to control the UGV. The Voltage Right Wheel (VR) and Voltage Left Wheel (VL) variables indicate the voltages applied to the right and left wheels, respectively, of the locomotion system, influencing the movement and direction.

Based on the desired trajectory, two parallel trajectories were created with a tolerance distance of $\pm$0.25 m. Initially, the robot aligns with the desired trajectory. If the robot's position coincides with any point of these parallel trajectories during navigation, the algorithm performs a recalculation between the current position and the destination. This action is repeated until the robot's position is within a 0.25 m radius (R) of the destination.

The algorithm is as follows (Algorithm 1):

Algorithm 1. ON–OFF controller algorithm.

```
Flag_Goal_Reached = FALSE
Flag_Rotation = TRUE
FOR coordinates in FILE:
    WHILE Flag_Goal_Reached = FALSE:
 IF detect_people = TRUE:
 V_L = 0 and V_R = 0 (STOP MACHINE)
 ELSE:
 e_{ON-OFF} = sqrt((T_x - A_Px)^2 + (T_y - A_Py)^2)
 IF e_{ON-OFF} ≤ R:
  V_L = 0 and V_R = 0 (STOP MACHINE)
  Flag_Goal_Reached = TRUE

 IF Flag_Rotation = TRUE:
  IF Rotation_Finished:
   V_L = 0 and V_R = 0 (STOP MACHINE)
   Flag_Rotation = FALSE
  ELSE:
   v = 0 and ω ≠ 0 (ROTATE MACHINE)
   IF 10_Seconds_Passed_Without_Changing_Position:
    INCREASE ROTATION (ω++)
 IF Flag_Rotation = FALSE:
  IF Not_Between_Lines:
   HeadingRotation = ActualHeading
   Flag_Rotation = TRUE
   V_L = 0 and V_R = 0 (STOP MACHINE)
  ELSE:
   GO IN FRONT (constant Vr and Vl)
```

Algorithm 1 defines a navigation process and decision-making for the UGV's movement. The system is designed to respond dynamically to environmental conditions and the proximity to the destination point. Algorithm 1 begins by setting two main flags: "Flag_Goal_Reached" and "Flag_Rotation", initially configured as true or false, respectively. The algorithm processes the coordinates until "Flag_Goal_Reached" becomes true.

The first check in the algorithm is the detection of people; if detected, the UGV will stop moving to ensure safety. If no one is detected, the algorithm evaluates whether the destination has been reached. If the goal is reached, the machine stops, and "Flag_Goal_Reached" is set to true. If there is a rotation required (i.e., "Flag_Rotation" is true), the algorithm checks whether the rotation is complete. If the rotation is finished, the machine stops, and "Flag_Rotation" is set to false. If the rotation is not completed, the machine continues rotating, and after 10 s with no position change, the rotation speed is increased.

If rotation is not needed (i.e., "Flag_Rotation" is false), the algorithm checks whether the UGV is within the desired path. If it is not, "Flag_Rotation" is reactivated, the machine stops, and the UGV realigns its orientation. If the UGV is within the accepted limits, it continues moving towards the goal, as shown in Figure 4.

3.4. PID Controller

The PID (Proportional, Integral, and Derivative) controller is widely used in linear control systems, known for its ease of implementation and effectiveness in controlling processes and variables (such as temperature, pressure, speed) to a desired value [31]. PID control involves three separate control actions, whose outputs are summed to form a single output signal. The current reading of the controlled parameter is subtracted from the command to generate an error signal. This error signal is processed by three distinct units [32]. The PID controller is commonly used in industry and automated systems due to its effectiveness and ease of implementation, as shown in Figure 5 [33].

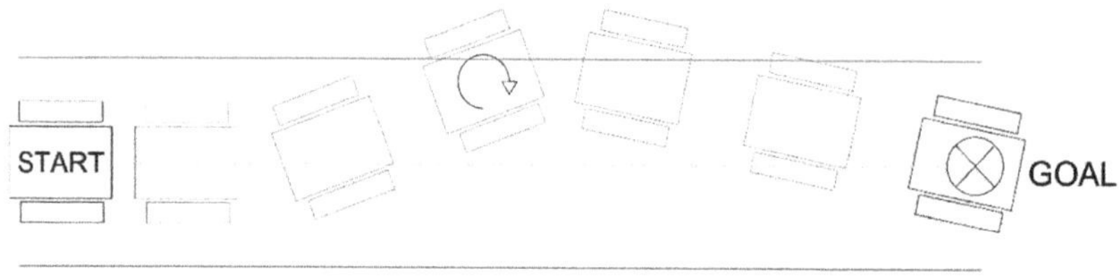

Figure 4. Trajectory with the ON–OFF algorithm.

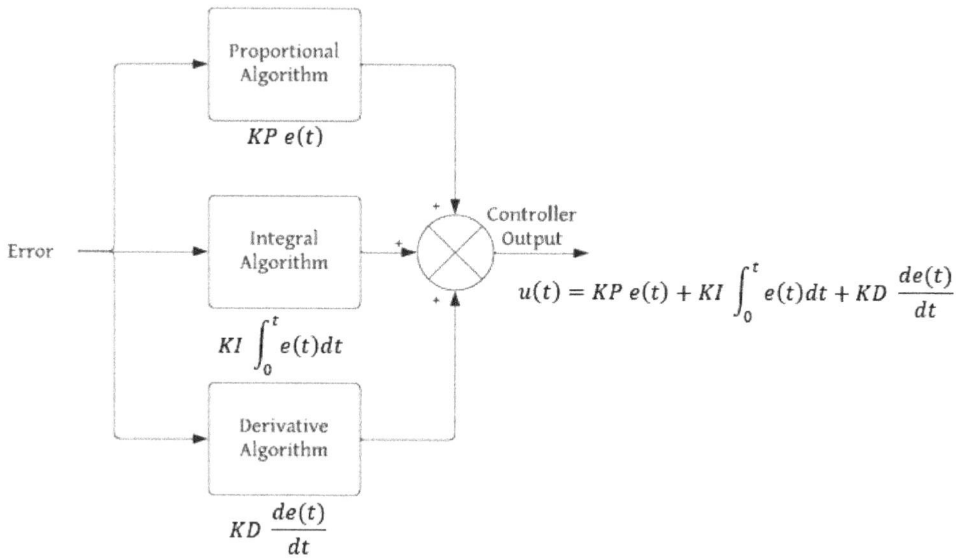

Figure 5. Basic description of the PID controller.

Proportional Action (P), also known as the proportional gain (Kp), multiplies the error between the desired value and the actual value by this coefficient. Therefore, the larger the error, the greater the correction applied by the controller. The proportional controller can correct the error, but if the gain is too high, it may cause oscillations around the desired value [34,35].

Integral Action (I) helps to eliminate the accumulated error over time. This control action, known as the integral gain (Ki), allows the controller to correct persistent errors, even if the proportional action is not sufficient to eliminate them. Additionally, the integral term is useful for eliminating steady-state error, which can occur when there is a constant disturbance in the system [36].

Derivative Action (D) predicts the rate of change of the error over time. This control action, known as the derivative gain (Kd), is useful to prevent excessive oscillations and reduces the controller's response to rapid changes in the error variable. It acts as a "damping" effect that smooths the response and improves the overall stability of the system [37,38].

The combination of these terms allows the controller to react quickly to disturbances, correct persistent errors, and keep the controlled variable close to the desired value. The tuning of the coefficients is essential to optimize system performance, minimize oscillations, and improve the response time. The PID controller represents the contribution of these different control actions. Over 95% of control problems can be solved with this type of control system, although some may only require two control actions, such as PI (Proportional–Integral) without the derivative action or PD (Proportional–Derivative) without the integral action [39].

3.4.1. PID Heading Controller

The PID Heading Controller (PID-H) aims to control both linear and angular trajectories. To achieve this, two independent PID controllers are used, as shown in Figure 6, where the initial focus is located on a line with the destination coordinates. This initial alignment adjusts the UGV relative to the destination point with a precision of up to four degrees, which is the accepted angular threshold.

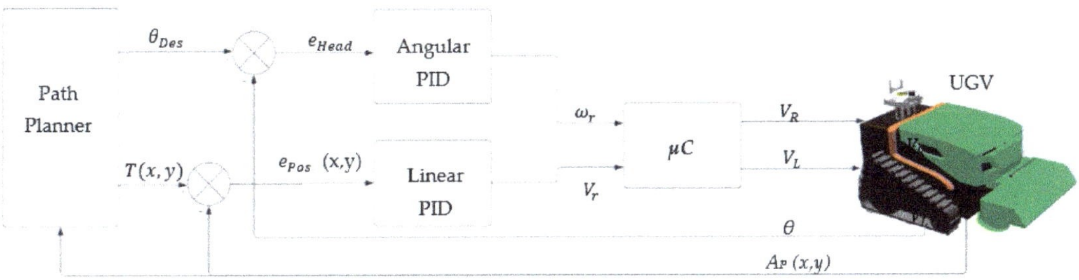

Figure 6. Controller with error associated with heading.

The error values related to the robot's orientation and its position relative to the destination are updated during the navigation process. The system thus allows for a maximum limitation of ±2 degrees within the scope of orientation error. The voltage applied to the tracks is corrected when the controller detects that this limit has been exceeded. Therefore, the UGV stays on the path between the origin and the destination. As the angular error is reduced, this effect contributes to a smooth trajectory and applies a voltage level to the robot's tracks corresponding to the calculated error. The angular error between the robot and the destination point is input as a reference into the PID controller as the robot starts its trajectory, intending to align the robot with the destination point as accurately as possible. The algorithm aims to optimize navigation, ensuring precise and smooth movement toward the destination.

In this study and analysis context, various variables play crucial roles in understanding and controlling the system shown in Figure 6.

The variable Desired Heading (θDes) represents the desired orientation or the angle to be reached or maintained by the system.

The variable Target (T) defines the desired location on the map. The variable Actual Position (AP) is the precise position relative to a reference point. The variable Heading Error (eHead) is the error between the desired angle (θDes) and the actual angle (θ) of the system. The variable Position Error (ePos) is the error between the desired position (T) and the actual position (AP) of the system. The variable Angular Value (ωr) represents the angular value associated with rotational or curvilinear movement. The variable Linear Value (Vr) represents the linear motion of the system, and the variable Actual Heading (θ) indicates the actual angle or current orientation of the system. The variable Microcontroller (μC) is the "brain" of the system, responsible for processing the values obtained from the "cmd_vel" topic to control the UGV. The variables Voltage Right Wheel (VR) and Voltage

Left Wheel (VL) indicate the voltages applied to the right and left wheels, respectively, of the locomotion system to influence movement and direction.

The algorithm is shown in the pseudocode below (Algorithm 2), aiming to move as illustrated in Figure 7. It is somewhat more complex than the previous one, as it incorporates a PID controller in its control system.

Algorithm 2. PID Heading Controller algorithm.

Flag_Goal_Reached = **FALSE**
Flag_Rotation = **TRUE**
FOR coordinates in **FILE**:
WHILE Flag_Goal_Reached = **FALSE**:
  IF detect_people = **TRUE**:
   $V_L = 0 \text{ and } V_R = 0 \text{ (STOP MACHINE)}$

  ELSE:
  IF Flag_Rotation = **TRUE**
   IF Not_Aligned **AND** 10_Seconds_Passed_Without_Changing_Position:
    $v = 0 \text{ and } \omega \neq 0 \text{ (ROTATE MACHINE)}$
   ELSE:
    Original_Position = Actual_Position
    Flag_Rotation = **FALSE**

$$e_{Position} = \sqrt{(T_x - A_{Px})^2 + (T_y - A_{Py})^2}$$

$$\theta_{Desired} = atan2(T_y - A_{Py}\,,\ T_x - A_{Px})$$

$$e_{Heading} = \theta_{Desired} - \theta_{Real}$$

IF $e_{Position} \leq R$:
 $V_L = 0 \text{ and } V_R = 0 \text{ (STOP MACHINE)}$
 Flag_Goal_Reached = **TRUE**
 Flag_Rotation = **TRUE**

IF $e_{Heading} > \Delta\theta$ and $e_{Position} > R$:
 Angular PID
 $\omega = K_p^{\theta} e_{Heading} + K_i^{\theta} \int e_{Heading}\, dt + K_d^{\theta} \frac{de_{Heading}}{dt}$
 Linear PID
 $v = K_p^{linear} e_{Position} + K_i^{linear} \int e_{Position}\, dt + K_d^{linear} \frac{de_{Position}}{dt}$

 $V_L = v - \frac{L}{2}\omega$ AND $V_R = v + \frac{L}{2}\omega$

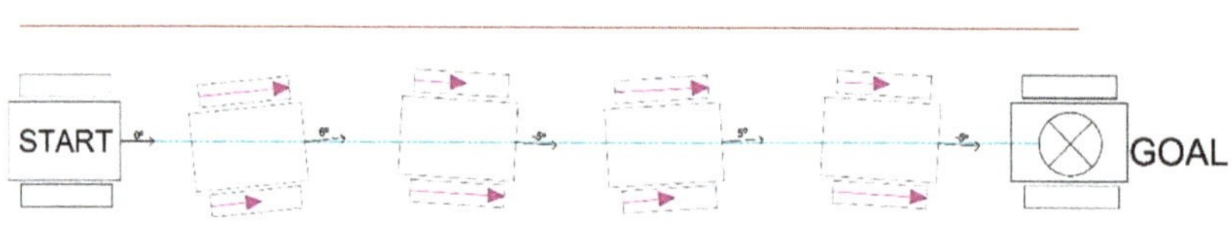

Figure 7. Trajectory with the PID Heading algorithm.

The scenario outlined by the presented pseudocode defines a highly sensitive navigation process where the UGV dynamically adapts to various circumstances. The foundation of this process relies on two flags: "Flag_Goal_Reached" and "Flag_Rotation". The first flag starts inactive, indicating that the destination has not yet been reached, while the second begins active, signaling the need for a rotation. The detection of people is a priority, leading to an immediate stop of the UGV if detected. In the absence of people, the algorithm guides the UGV according to the planned trajectory.

When a rotation is needed ("Flag_Rotation" is active), the algorithm checks whether it has been completed or if no position change has occurred after 10 s. If the rotation is completed, the machine stops, and "Flag_Rotation" is deactivated. However, if no position change occurs after 10 s, the "Flag_Rotation" is also deactivated. Otherwise, the machine is directed to perform the rotation.

When no further rotation is needed ("Flag_Rotation" is inactive), the algorithm checks whether the destination has been reached. If so, the machine stops, "Flag_Goal_Reached" is activated, and "Flag_Rotation" is reactivated to calculate the best orientation. If the destination is not reached, the algorithm calculates the distance and orientation errors relative to the destination. The linear and angular PID controllers ensure that the UGV maintains its precise trajectory, staying aligned with the destination point, as shown in Figure 7.

3.4.2. PID Heading Cross Track Error Controller

The PID CTE (Cross Track Error) controller autonomously manages both linear and angular trajectories using two separate PID controllers, as shown in Figure 8. The error values are continuously updated during the navigation process and include the robot's relative position concerning the line and its final destination. A maximum tolerance of ±10 cm is considered for the position error relative to the desired trajectory. The controller adjusts the voltage supplied to both tracks when it detects that the robot is nearing the allowed tolerance. This adjustment enables the UGV to navigate accurately, keeping it close to the planned trajectory between the origin and destination.

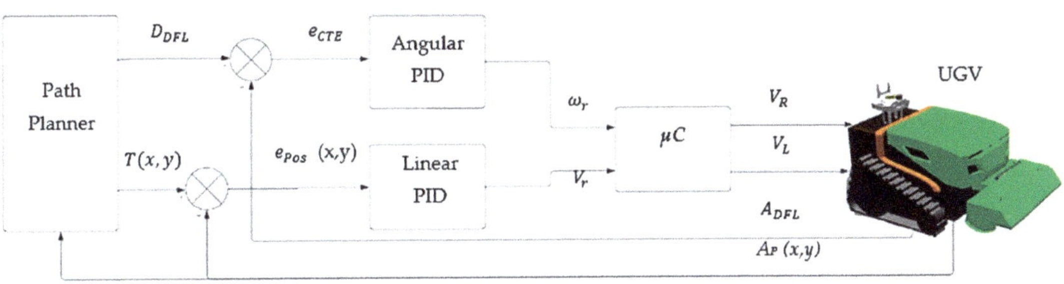

Figure 8. Controller with error associated with trajectory distance.

The position error serves as a reference, allowing the system to modify the voltage applied to the tracks depending on the proximity to the destination. This means that the voltage can either increase or decrease based on the distance, enabling the UGV to adapt to changing conditions.

In this study and analysis, several variables play crucial roles in understanding and controlling the system shown in Figure 8. These are similar to the previously mentioned variables, except for the desired distance from the line (D_DFL), the current distance from the line (A_DFL), and the error in this distance (e_CTE).

The PID CTE algorithm, as shown in the pseudocode below (Algorithm 3), aims to move the UGV as depicted in Figure 9. This algorithm is quite similar to the previous one, but the error variable used as input for the PIDs is based on the distance between the robot and the desired trajectory.

Algorithm 3. PID Cross Track Error controller.

Flag_Goal_Reached = **FALSE**
Flag_Rotation = **TRUE**
FOR coordinates in **FILE**:
WHILE Flag_Goal_Reached = **FALSE**:
  IF detect_people = **TRUE**:
  $V_L = 0 \; and \; V_R = 0 \; (STOP\ MACHINE)$

  ELSE:
  IF Flag_Rotation = **TRUE**
    IF Not_Aligned **AND** 10_Seconds_Passed_Without_Changing_Position:
$v = 0 \; and \; \omega \neq 0 \; (ROTATE\ MACHINE)$

    ELSE:
Original_Position = Actual_Position
Flag_Rotation = **FALSE**
  ELSE:
  $e_{Position} = \sqrt{(T_x - A_{Px})^2 + (T_y - A_{Py})^2}$

  $e_{CTE} = Actual_{DistanceFromLine} - Desired_{DistanceFromLine}$

    IF $e_{Position} \leq R$:
$V_L = 0 \; and \; V_R = 0 \; (STOP\ MACHINE)$
Flag_Goal_Reached = **TRUE**
Flag_Rotation = **TRUE**
    ELSE:
Angular PID
$\omega = K_p^{DFL} e_{CTE} + K_i^{DFL} \int e_{CTE}\, dt + K_d^{DFL} \frac{de_{CTE}}{dt}$
Linear PID
$v = K_p^{linear} e_{Position} + K_i^{linear} \int e_{Position}\, dt + K_d^{linear} \frac{de_{Position}}{dt}$

  $V_L = v - \frac{L}{2}\omega$ AND $V_R = v + \frac{L}{2}\omega$

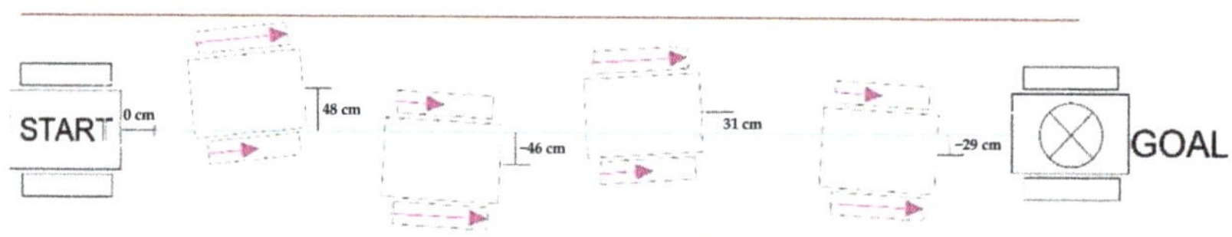

Figure 9. Trajectory with the PID CTE algorithm.

This pseudocode outlines the UGV's navigation approach, focusing on both efficiency and safety as it follows a predefined path. The flags "Flag_Goal_Reached" and "Flag_Rotation" are central to this algorithm, guiding the UGV's behavior in response to various contexts. While traversing coordinates, the algorithm prioritizes two aspects: detecting people and adjusting the trajectory. If people are detected, the UGV immediately stops to ensure safety. In the absence of detection, the focus shifts to movement precision. When rotation is necessary ("Flag_Rotation" is activated), the system checks whether the UGV is misaligned and, if there is no positional change after 10 s (indicating it is stuck), the rotation is performed. If the criteria are not met, the original position is logged, and the "Flag_Rotation" is deactivated. When no further rotation is needed ("Flag_Rotation" = FALSE), the algorithm checks whether the destination has been reached. If the goal is met, the UGV stops, the "Flag_Goal_Reached" is activated, and the movement ceases. If the goal has not been reached, errors in distance from the target and line are calculated, allowing the UGV to adjust its trajectory accurately.

3.4.3. PID CTE + H

The PID CTE + H controller autonomously manages the UGV's linear and angular trajectories using a set of two PID controllers, as depicted in Figure 10. This nonlinear controller consists of two distinct parts. Initially, the reference angle, θ, is obtained from the trajectory planning system, the "Path Planner". In the block diagram, the external loop provides feedback by comparing the robot's current trajectory with the planned trajectory provided by the "Path Planner".

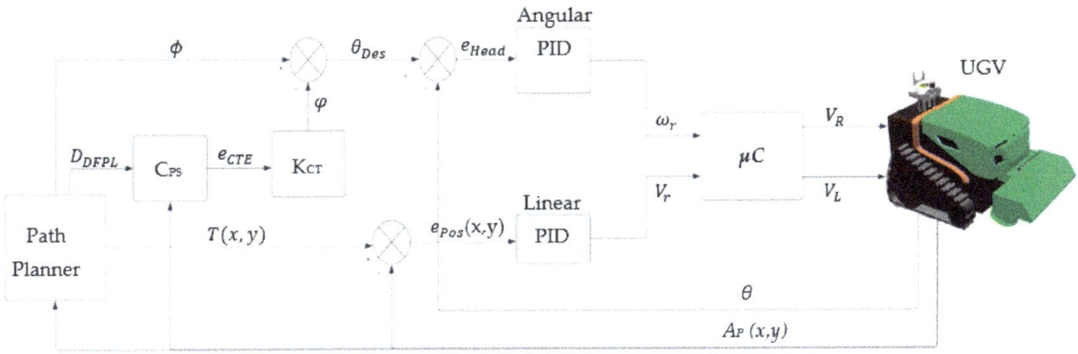

Figure 10. CTE + H controller.

The obtained value is then converted into a correction angle through a proportional controller with a gain, Kct, resulting in a correction term, φ. This correction is subtracted from the θ value to obtain the new desired θ, which will be the new reference input for the internal loop of the block diagram. This internal loop, in turn, uses the current orientation with feedback to calculate the necessary actuation effect.

In this context, several variables play crucial roles in understanding and controlling the system depicted in Figure 10. The variable "Bearing of the path" (ϕ) represents the orientation the system should follow relative to a reference point.

The "Distance from point to line" (DDFPL) measures the perpendicular distance between a specific point and the reference line. This measure helps evaluate how close the system is to the desired route and correct any deviations. The "Cross track error" (e_CTE) measures the lateral deviation of the system from the desired trajectory. It indicates how far the system is from the planned route and is used to calculate corrections. The "Gain" (KCT) is a multiplicative factor applied to certain variables or controller actions. It regulates the intensity of corrections or system responses as needed. The "Corrective turn angle" (φ) determines the angle by which the system must adjust to correct deviations from the planned trajectory, guiding the system back onto the correct route.

The "Desired Heading" (θDes) represents the desired orientation or the angle the system should achieve or maintain. The "Target" (T) defines the desired location on the map. The "Actual Position" (AP) is the precise position relative to a reference point. The "Heading Error" (e_{Head}) is the error between the desired angle (θDes) and the actual angle (θ) of the system. The "Position Error" (ePos) is the error between the desired position (T) and the actual position (AP) of the system.

The "Angular Value" (ωr) expresses the angular value associated with rotational or curvilinear motion. The "Linear Value" (Vr) represents the system's linear motion, and the "Actual Heading" (θ) indicates the current orientation or real angle of the system.

The "Microcontroller" (μC) is the system's "brain", responsible for processing the values obtained from the "cmd_vel" topic for UGV control. The "Voltage Right Wheel" (VR) and "Voltage Left Wheel" (VL) represent the voltages applied to the right and left wheels, respectively, of the locomotion system to influence movement and direction.

The CTE + H algorithm is shown in the pseudocode below (Algorithm 4) and is presented as depicted in Figure 11. It is a more complex algorithm than the previous ones because it includes both error variables from the earlier algorithms. This algorithm can be characterized as the integration of the PIDH and PIDCTE algorithms.

Algorithm 4. PID CTE + H controller.

IF No_Goals = **TRUE**
  RETURN ***FALSE***
Flag_Goal_Reached = **FALSE**
Flag_Rotation = **TRUE**
WHILE Flag_Goal_Reached = **FALSE**:
  IF detect_people = **TRUE**:
  $V_L = 0 \text{ and } V_R = 0 \text{ (STOP MACHINE)}$

  ELSE:
  IF Flag_Rotation = **TRUE**
    IF Not_Aligned **AND** 10_Seconds_Passed_Without_Changing_Position:
    $v = 0 \text{ and } \omega \neq 0 \text{ (ROTATE MACHINE)}$
    ELSE:
    Original_Position = Actual_Position
    Flag_Rotation = **FALSE**
  ELSE:
  $e_{Position} = \sqrt{(T_x - A_{Px})^2 + (T_y - A_{Py})^2}$

  $e_{CTE} = Actual_{DistanceFromLine} - Desired_{DistanceFromLine}$

  $\phi = K_{CT} * e_{CTE}$

  $\theta_{Desired} = \theta_{path} - \phi$

  $e_{Heading} = \theta_{Desired} - \theta_{Real}$

    IF $e_{Position} \leq R$:
    $V_L = 0 \text{ and } V_R = 0 \text{ (STOP MACHINE)}$
    Flag_Goal_Reached = **TRUE**
    Flag_Rotation = **TRUE**

    ELSE:
    Angular PID
    $\omega = K_p^\theta e_{Heading} + K_i^\theta \int e_{Heading}\, dt + K_d^\theta \frac{de_{Heading}}{dt}$
    Linear PID
    $v = K_p^{CTE} e_{CTE} + K_i^{CTE} \int e_{CTE}\, dt + K_d^{CTE} \frac{de_{CTE}}{dt}$

  $V_L = v - \frac{L}{2}\omega$ AND $V_R = v + \frac{L}{2}\omega$

The pseudocode outlines a systematic approach for the UGV's navigation, incorporating multiple factors to ensure effectiveness and safety. The process begins with a check for "No_Goals", returning FALSE if no goal is set, thus preventing the execution of the algorithm. Following this, two flags, "Flag_Goal_Reached" and "Flag_Rotation", are initialized, with the first set to FALSE, indicating that the goal has not yet been reached, and the second set to TRUE, signifying that rotation is required. At the core of the algorithm is a loop that continues until the goal is reached ("Flag_Goal_Reached" = FALSE).

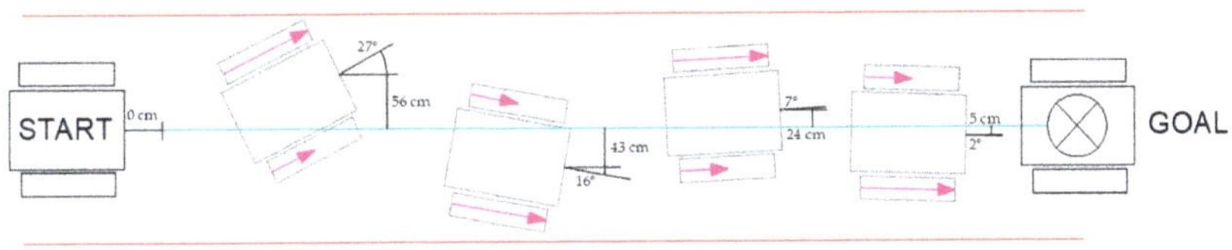

Figure 11. Trajectory with the CTE + H algorithm.

During this loop, person detection takes priority, halting the UGV immediately if someone is detected. In scenarios where rotation is necessary ("Flag_Rotation" = TRUE), the algorithm evaluates the trajectory alignment and the elapsed time without any positional change. If trajectory adjustment is needed, the UGV is directed to rotate. Otherwise, the original position is updated, and the "Flag_Rotation" is deactivated.

When no further rotation is needed ("Flag_Rotation" = FALSE), the algorithm checks whether the goal has been achieved. If the goal is met, the machine stops, and "Flag_Goal_Reached" is activated. If the goal has not been reached, a series of error calculations are performed, involving the "Cross_Track_Error" (CTE) for orientation control, the position error for linear control, and the heading error for angular control.

3.4.4. PID Vector Field

The algorithm is shown in pseudocode below (Algorithm 5) and presented in Figure 12. It is somewhat different from the others, as it also uses PID control, but its error is derived from the vector sum of the virtual forces encountered during navigation.

The pseudocode presents a dynamic strategy for the UGV's navigation, incorporating multiple checks and calculations to ensure a precise and safe trajectory. The process begins with a check for "No_Goals", which returns FALSE if no goals are defined, preventing the algorithm from proceeding without a clear purpose. Next, two flags are initialized: "Flag_Goal_Reached" and "Flag_Rotation". The first starts as FALSE, indicating that the goal has not yet been reached, while the second is initialized as TRUE, signaling the need for rotation. The core of the algorithm is a loop that continues until the goal is reached ("Flag_Goal_Reached" = FALSE). During each iteration, a priority check for person detection is performed. If a positive detection occurs, the UGV is immediately halted, prioritizing safety. In cases where rotation is required ("Flag_Rotation" = TRUE), the algorithm evaluates whether the UGV is not aligned and whether 10 s have passed without positional change. If both criteria are met, the UGV is directed to rotate. Otherwise, the original position is updated, and the "Flag_Rotation" is deactivated. When rotation is no longer needed ("Flag_Rotation" = FALSE), the algorithm checks whether the goal has been reached. If the goal is met, the machine stops, and "Flag_Goal_Reached" is activated. If the goal has not been reached, the algorithm enters a series of calculations involving the "S_Star" error (for linear trajectory control) and the "Tau_Error" (for angular orientation control).

This algorithm is based on the concept of following a trajectory by creating a vector field around the path to be followed. The vectors in this field provide orientation commands to guide the robot towards the desired trajectory.

The goal is not to follow a moving point, but rather to position the robot along the trajectory as it moves. The vectors in this field are directed toward the path that should be followed, following the desired direction of navigation [40]. These vectors act as orientation commands for the robot. As shown in Figure 13, which represents a sample of a vector field between the start and the destination (black arrows), this approach directs the robot (red arrow) along the line between points from the start of its navigation.

Algorithm 5. PID Vector Field controller.

IF No_Goals = **TRUE**
 RETURN ***FALSE***
Flag_Goal_Reached = **FALSE**
Flag_Rotation = **TRUE**
WHILE Flag_Goal_Reached = **FALSE**:
IF detect_people = **TRUE**:
 $V_L = 0$ *and* $V_R = 0$ *(STOP MACHINE)*
 ELSE:
  IF Flag_Rotation = **TRUE**
   IF Not_Aligned **AND** 10_Seconds_Passed_Without_Changing_Position:
   $v = 0$ *and* $\omega \neq 0$ *(ROTATE MACHINE)*
   ELSE:
   Original_Position = Actual_Position
   Flag_Rotation = **FALSE**
  ELSE:

$\chi^f = atan2(w2_y - w1_y\,,\, w2_x - w1_x)$

$S^* = \frac{(z-w1)^T(w2-w1)}{||w2-w1||}$

$\varepsilon = ||z - (S^* * (w2 - w1) + w1)||$

$\rho = sign((w2 - w1) * (z - w1))$

  IF $S^* \geq 1$:
  $V_L = 0$ *and* $V_R = 0$ *(STOP MACHINE)*
  Flag_Goal_Reached = **TRUE**
  Flag_Rotation = **TRUE**

  IF $S^* < 1$:
$\varepsilon = \rho * \varepsilon$

IF $|\varepsilon| > \tau$:
$\chi^d = \chi^f - \rho * \chi^e$

IF $|\varepsilon| \leq \tau$:
$\chi^d = \chi^f - \chi^e \left(\frac{\varepsilon}{\tau}\right)^k$

  Angular PID
  $\omega = K_p^\theta \chi^d + K_i^\theta \int \chi^d \, dt + K_d^\theta \frac{d\chi^d}{dt}$
  Linear PID
  $v = K_p^{linear} S^* + K_i^{linear} \int S^* \, dt + K_d^{linear} \frac{dS^*}{dt}$

$V_L = v - \frac{L}{2}\omega$ AND $V_R = v + \frac{L}{2}\omega$

The concept of vector fields, as shown in Figure 14, is comparable to that of potential fields, which have been widely used as a tool for trajectory planning. Potential fields can be applied in robot navigation for obstacle avoidance and collision prevention scenarios [41]. Vector fields differ from potential fields in that they do not always represent the gradient of a potential. Instead, the vector field simply indicates a desired direction of movement.

As we can see, the vector field force (black arrow) will guide the robot between it starting point (green dot) and its goal (red dot).

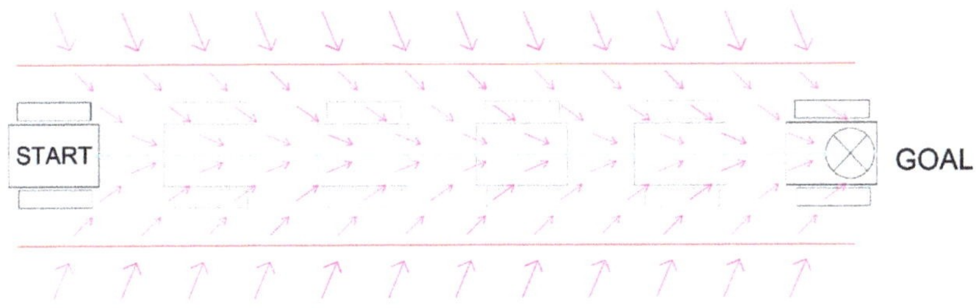

Figure 12. Trajectory with the Vector Field algorithm.

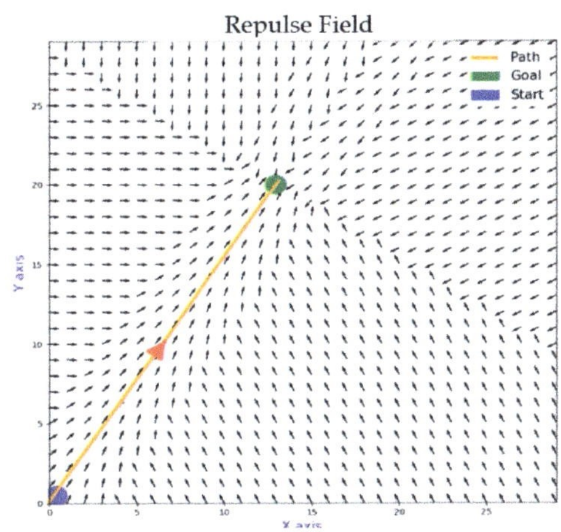

Figure 13. Typical magnetic field in navigation with the Vector Field algorithm.

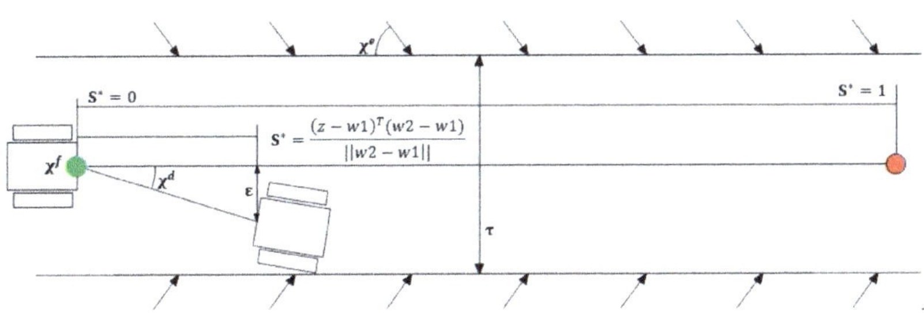

Figure 14. Representation of the variables in the Vector Field algorithm.

The following steps represent the process of the Vector Field algorithm:

1. Calculation of the Orientation Angle (χ^f): In this step, the desired orientation angle (χ^f) is calculated for the robot to move from the first waypoint ($w1$) to the second waypoint ($w2$).

$$\chi^f = atan2(w2_y - w1_y\, ,\ w2_x - w1_x) \quad (1)$$

2. Calculation of Position Along the Trajectory (S*): Here, the robot's position along the trajectory between the waypoints is determined. The vector connecting the current

position (z) and the first waypoint ($w1$) is projected onto the vector between $w1$ and $w2$, giving a measure of where the robot is along the trajectory.

$$S^* = \frac{(z - w1)^T (w2 - w1)}{||w2 - w1||} \tag{2}$$

3. Calculation of Distance to the Trajectory (ε): This step calculates the distance between the robot's actual position (z) and the closest point on the trajectory between the waypoints. This helps understand how far the robot is from the desired path.

$$\varepsilon = ||z - (S^*(w2 - w1) + w1)|| \tag{3}$$

4. Determination of the Side of the Trajectory (ρ): Here, a value (ρ) is calculated to indicate which side of the trajectory the robot is on. This is achieved using the cross product between the vector connecting the waypoints ($w2 - w1$) and the vector from the current position (z) to the first waypoint ($w1$). The sign of this value indicates whether the robot is to the left or right of the trajectory.
5. Verification of Position Relative to Waypoint 2: If the value of S^* is greater than 1, it means the robot has passed the second waypoint. In this case, the robot transitions to the next waypoint, as it has reached the destination of the current waypoint.
6. Change of Waypoint: The transition to the next waypoint in the trajectory is made.
7. Continuation of the Process: If S^* is less than 1, it means the robot is still between the waypoints, and its navigation continues.
8. Defining ε as $\rho\varepsilon$: In this step, the value of ε is updated to $\rho\varepsilon$, which represents the distance of the robot to the trajectory, considering which side of the path the robot is on.
9. Verification of Distance to the Trajectory: If the absolute value of ε is greater than a predefined threshold τ, it indicates that the robot is significantly far from the desired path.
10. Calculation of Desired Angle (χ^d): If the robot is far from the trajectory, χ^f is calculated as the difference between the reference angle χ^f and the product of ρ and χ^e, where χ^e is a correction factor.

$$\chi^d = \chi^f - \rho * \chi^e \tag{4}$$

11. Otherwise (Trajectory Distance Within the Limit): If the absolute value of ε is less than or equal to τ, it means the robot is close enough to the trajectory.
12. Calculation of Desired Angle with Correction (χ^d): In this scenario, χ^d is calculated as the difference between the reference angle χ^f and the product of χ^e, τ, and a factor k.

$$\chi^d = \chi^f - \chi^e \left(\frac{\varepsilon}{\tau}\right)^k \tag{5}$$

13. End of the Process: The process concludes here.

These steps enable the robot to follow a desired trajectory using vector fields, adjusting its orientation and position dynamically to ensure that it stays on course while accounting for any deviations.

3.5. Process of Calculating PID Coefficients

To calculate the respective gains of the controller, there are several methods, which can be divided into two categories: closed-loop and open-loop methods. Numerous methods can be implemented for PID controller tuning, such as the Ziegler–

Nichols (Z-N) method, Tyreus–Luyben (T_L), C-H-R, Cohen and Coon (C-C), Fertik, and Ciancone–Marlin (C-M) [42].

The Ziegler–Nichols (Z-N) and Cohen–Coon (C-C) controllers are simple and easy to implement. The Cohen–Coon method for PID control is an extension of the Ziegler–Nichols method. This technique improves the steady-state response, especially when there is a large delay in the process compared to the open-loop time constant [43]. To achieve this, the PID parameters are obtained through open-loop experiments, as shown in Figure 15.

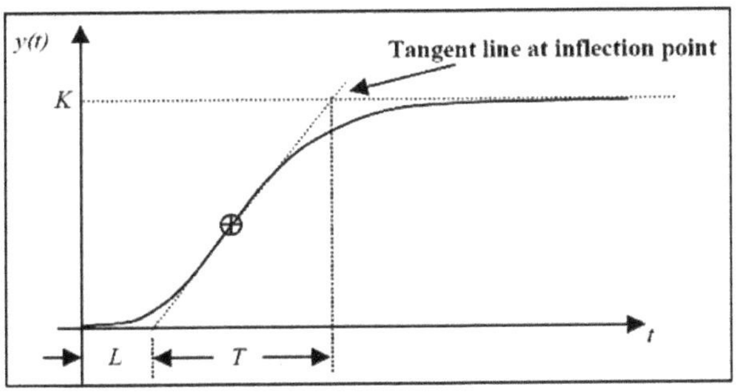

Figure 15. Open-loop reaction curve [44].

From the obtained data, it is possible to calculate the associated gains, as shown in Table 3.

Table 3. Gain calculation formulas [43].

Cohen–Coon	K_C	T_I	T_D	τ	a
PID	$\frac{1.35}{a}\left(1+\frac{0.18\tau}{1-\tau}\right)$	$\frac{2.5-2.0\tau}{1-0.39\tau} * L$	$\frac{0.37-0.37\tau}{1-0.81\tau} * L$	$\frac{L}{L+T}$	$\frac{K_{process} * L}{T}$

3.6. Evaluation Criteria for PID Control Algorithms

In the methodology for designing a PID controller, one of the most important performance criteria is the difference (error) between the system's output and the reference value. Generally, optimization functions are formulated based on error equations, with the three most common being [45]:

- Integral of the Absolute Error Magnitude (IAE);
- Integral of the Squared Error (ISE);
- Integral of the Time multiplied by the Absolute Error Magnitude (ITAE).

These are given as follows [45]:

$$\mathrm{IAE} = \int_0^{\mathrm{T}} |\mathrm{e}(\mathrm{t})|\mathrm{dt} \quad (6)$$

$$\mathrm{ISE} = \int_0^{\mathrm{T}} \left|\mathrm{e}(\mathrm{t})^2\right|\mathrm{dt} \quad (7)$$

$$\mathrm{ITAE} = \int_0^{\mathrm{T}} t|\mathrm{e}(\mathrm{t})|\mathrm{dt} \quad (8)$$

To complement the values provided by the metrics given in formulas 6–8, multi-objective optimization (MOO) techniques were used with the selection of Pareto-optimal solutions. This method, as mentioned in [46], explains that optimization aims to maximize performance with minimal resources and is divided into exact methods, which guarantee optimal solutions but have limited applicability, and meta-heuristic methods, which effectively handle complex, real-world problems. In MOO, multiple conflicting objectives are addressed simultaneously, resulting in a set of Pareto-optimal solutions where no single solution is universally better, requiring trade-offs.

A decision vector $x^* \in S$ is Pareto-optimal if no other vector $x \in S$ can improve all components without worsening at least one [47]. Mathematically, point $x^* \in S$ is Pareto-optimal only if there is no point $x \in S$ such that $f(x) \leq f(x^*)$ with at least one $fi(x) > fi(x^*)$ [46].

As noted by [48], all Pareto-optimal solutions in decision variable space form the Pareto-optimal set. Furthermore the representation of the Pareto optimal set in the objective function space is called the Pareto-optimal front [49], expressed as:

$$PF^* = \{f(x^*)|x^* \in PS^*\} \tag{9}$$

This indicates that the Pareto-optimal front (PF) is the set of objective function values for all Pareto-optimal solutions (PSs) in the decision space, showcasing the trade-offs between conflicting objectives.

In addition to the criteria mentioned, further evaluation metrics were added to complement the above criteria. These metrics consist of the mean, standard deviation, and maximum, with the scale being in meters. With these three metrics, the aim was to analyze the position error of the robot relative to the trajectory that the UGV should follow. Finally, the navigation time was also considered to determine which of the control algorithms could execute a given trajectory in the shortest possible time.

4. Experimental Results

The various control algorithms derived from the PID controller that were proposed were successfully analyzed and evaluated. It was possible to determine which control algorithms offer greater efficiency and precision. By placing the UGV on a forest terrain (i.e., unstructured) to investigate the differences between the presented controllers, real-time navigation data were collected during these practical experiments.

Thus, this section aims to present the experimental results regarding the process of tuning the PID coefficients (Kp, Ki, and Kd), followed by an analysis of the proposed control algorithms, highlighting the characteristics of each one.

4.1. Response of PID Parameters

For the PID gain calculations, the Cohen–Coon open-loop method was used. For each controller, two tests were conducted: one for the angular component and another for the linear component. In the linear component test, the UGV moved forward until reaching the requested reference of 8 m, where we observed the system's response curve for each controller. In the angular component, the UGV was asked to change its reference orientation by 45°, and we also observed the response to this movement, as shown in Table 4.

Table 4. Graphs of the responses obtained for each PID control algorithm.

	Linear Response	Angular Response
PID-H	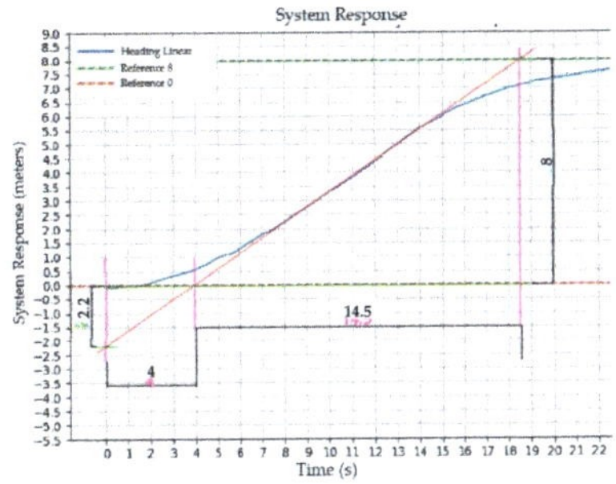	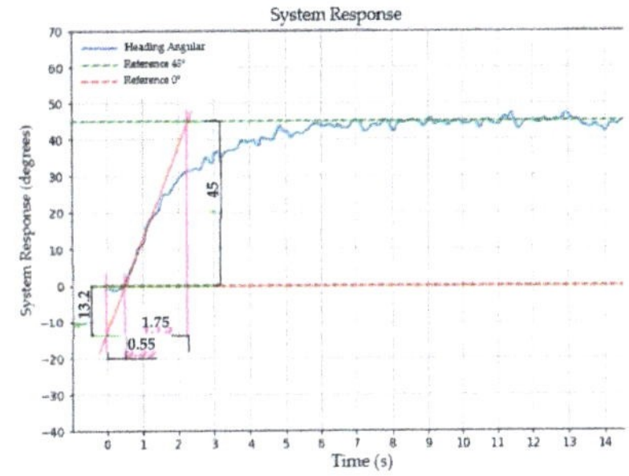

Table 4. *Cont.*

	Linear Response	Angular Response
PID-CTE	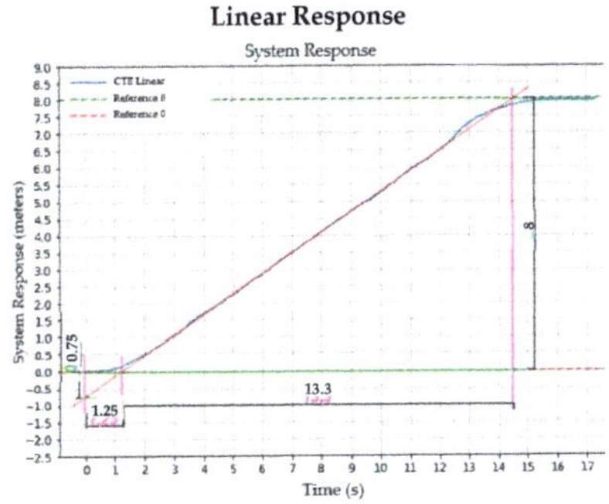	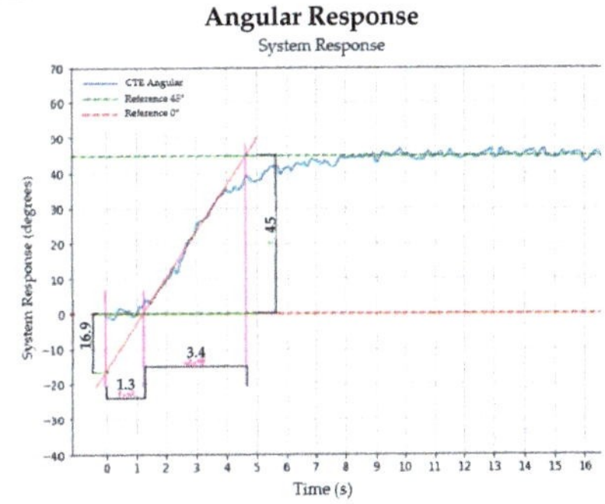
PID + CTE + H	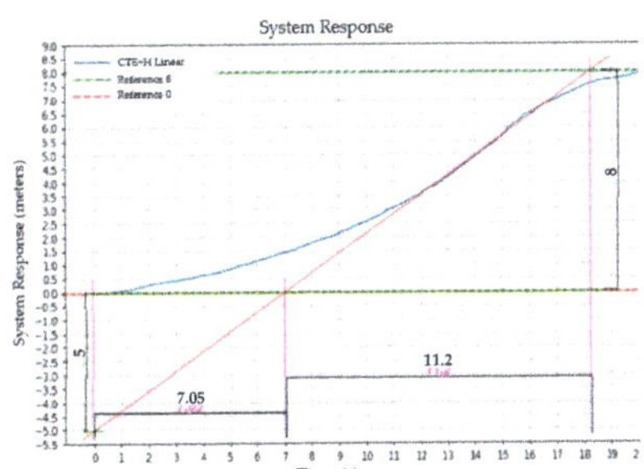	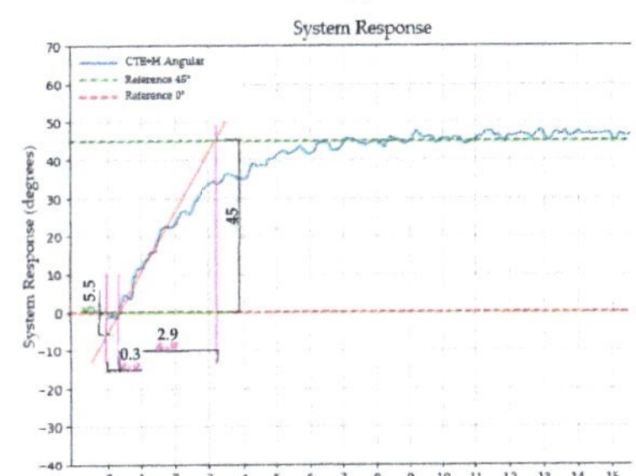
PID VF	Uses S*	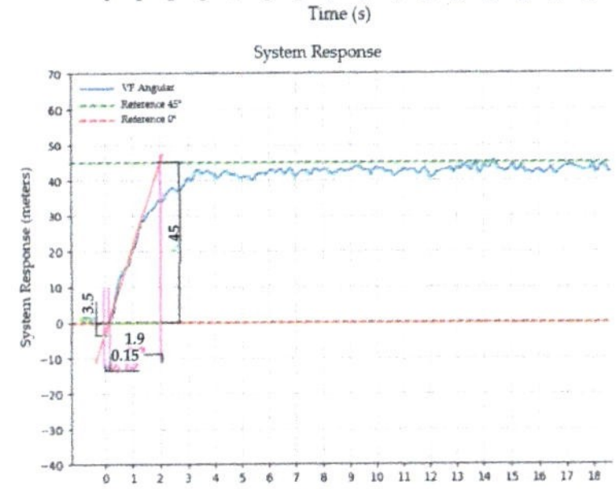

After the values were calculated, it was possible to deduce and experiment with the values. The calculated values are represented in Table 5.

Table 5. Parameters obtained for each PID control algorithm.

Controller	PID Linear Coefficient			PID Angular Coefficient		
	Kp	**Ki**	**Kd**	**Kp**	**Ki**	**Kd**
PID H	0.642	0.071	0.90	0.101	0.0054	0.0040
PID CTE	1.882	0.607	0.83	0.084	0.0295	0.0376
PID CTE + H	0.298	0.021	0.69	0.297	0.411	0.0546
PIDH (VF)		Uses S*		0.385	0.1026	0.0211

4.2. PID Algorithm's Control Performance

To visualize the data from the experiments carried out for each control system, we created a visual presentation to provide a clear and comparative perspective of the performance of each controller. This practical approach aims to provide more practical and valuable insights into the behavior and effectiveness of navigation controllers in the real world. All the tests conducted can be observed in Figure 15.

After thoroughly analyzing the results obtained from the field tests, we decided to conduct additional tests to more precisely identify the most promising methods to be incorporated into an obstacle avoidance algorithm during navigation. Through this careful analysis, we aimed to select approaches that demonstrate consistency and effectiveness in a variety of situations. Figure 16 is a visual representation of the various paths taken under different control types.

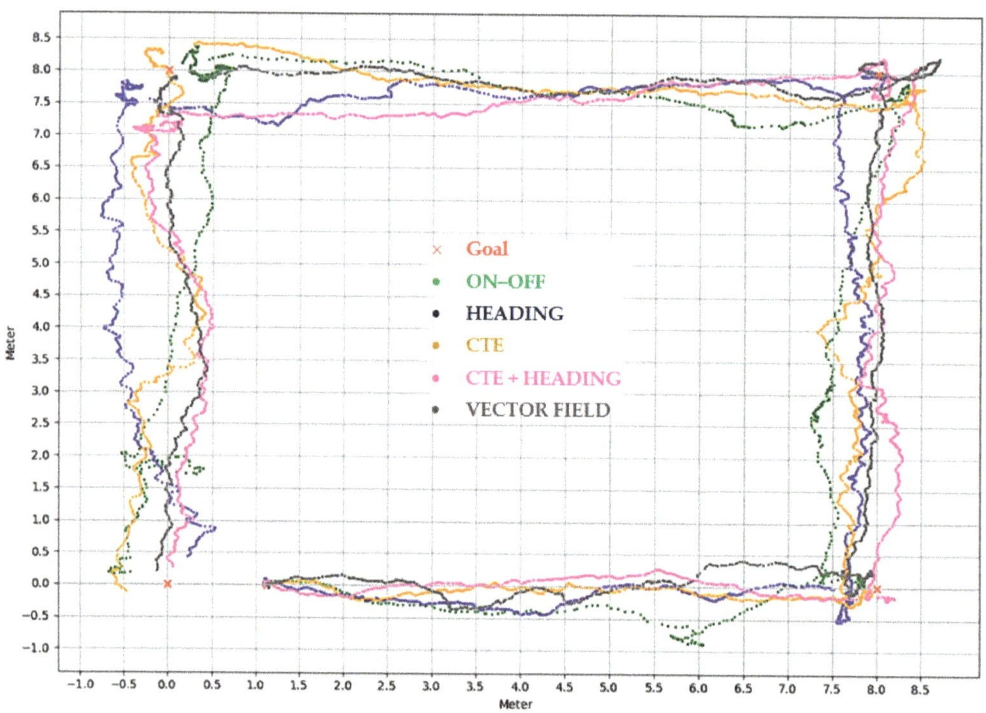

Figure 16. Tests conducted in a real environment.

We observed that the proposed destinations were successfully reached; however, since this was not an ideal environment and contained disturbances, additional comparisons were made by repeating the same trajectories for all algorithms. In our case, we considered the square movement, where the robot passed through the coordinates [(8.0, 0.0); (8.0, 8.0); (0.0, 8.0); (0.0, 0.0)], respectively. All tests started with the UGV facing east before navigation. In all tests, the robot used GPS + RTK technology, providing an accuracy of up to 2 cm. For all navigation tests, an offset of 0.2 m was considered until the destination was reached. For each of these tests, an analysis of the robot's position error relative to the trajectory it should follow was performed. That is, the mean error, maximum error, and standard deviation were calculated for each situation. In the graphs, a position translation of 1.1 m is noticeable. This means that the robot's location, instead of being at the "Sentry" point where the GPS is located, was now situated at the robot's center of rotation, affecting the observed trajectories. This occurred because the position did not start from the origin point (0,0), but from the point (1,0).

To better clarify the different paths taken by the UGV, Figure 17 shows the impacts that the robot took and moved. This visualization enables an accurate analysis by presenting the observed data with the context given in Figure 16.

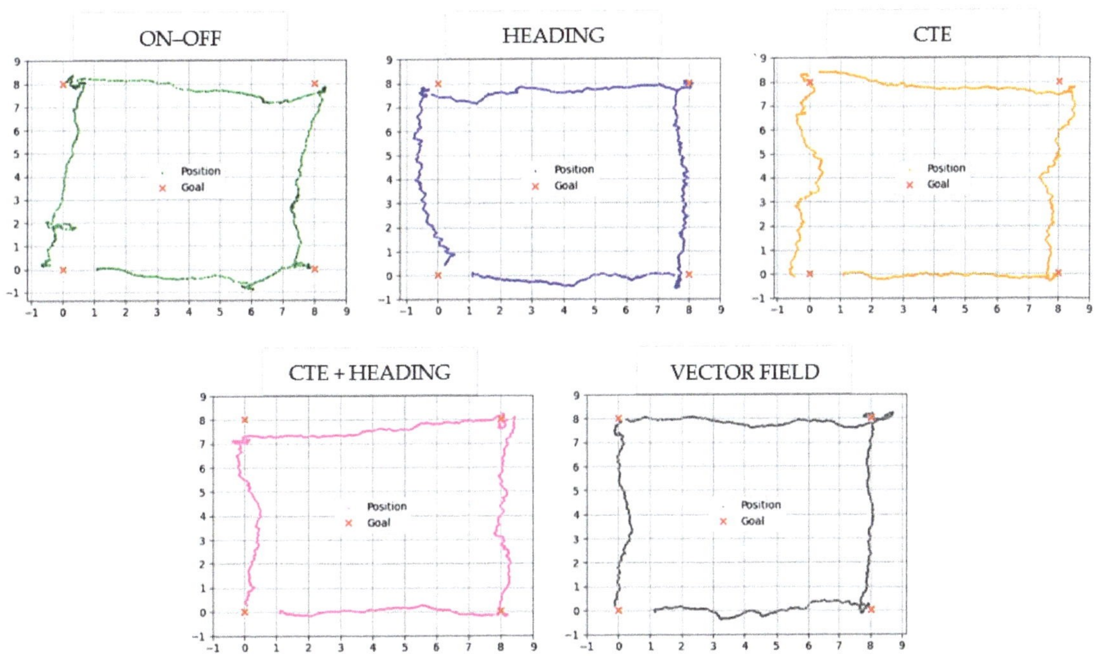

Figure 17. Final result of the trajectory of each PID control algorithm (separately).

Table 6 presents the performance evaluation criteria used to evaluate and compare the proposed algorithms, focusing on their effectiveness in terms of error reduction, routing accuracy, and navigation efficiency.

Table 6. Evaluation criteria applied to each controller during the experiments.

Algorithm	ITAE	IAE	ISE	Mean [m]	Standard Deviation [m]	Max [m]	Navigation Time [s]
ON–OFF	2815.625	118.19	46.844	0.33	0.19	0.89	103.60
Heading	1695.307	138.11	44.1836	0.21	0.18	0.85	88.90
CTE	1541.619	131.13	46.9071	0.18	0.14	0.65	86.45
CTE + H	1257.305	95.303	19.6773	0.21	0.19	0.74	93.60
Vector Field	520.9629	66.989	11.8488	0.18	0.17	0.66	82.46

The analysis of the data presented in the table reveals that the CTE (Cross Track Error) and Vector Field Control (VFC) algorithms outperform the others in terms of overall performance. In particular, the VFC algorithm exhibits the best results in key quantitative performance parameters, including ITAE (Integral Time Absolute Error), IAE (Integral Absolute Error), and ISE (Integral Square Error).

The VFC algorithm obtains the lowest values of ITAE (520.96), IAE (66.989), ISE (11.8488), indicating stability and accuracy with minimal accumulated errors over time. Moreover, the stationary error (Mean [m] = 0.18) and the mean (Standard Deviation [m]. = 0.17) show low values, indicating that a route is always closer to the correct route. During travel, the VFC is also efficient, completing the task in 82.46 s, which is the shortest among all algorithms considered.

Figure 18 illustrates the UGV navigating the 8 × 8 square path in the actual field where the PID controller algorithms were previously tuned. The figure comprises four distinct images, each capturing the robot positioned at one of the square's corners.

Figure 18. Representation of all paths taken on the terrain during the execution of the 8 × 8 m squares: (**a**) initial position; (**b**) first coordinate; (**c**) second coordinate; (**d**) third coordinate.

These results indicate that the VFC algorithm performs particularly well for applications that require high accuracy in trajectory execution and time efficiency. The potential reason for this superior performance is the ability to continuously optimize control vectors, allowing the UGV (unmanned ground vehicle) to better adapt to planned changes in direction so that it meets and resolves sliding obstructions quickly and accurately. In contrast, the ON–OFF and other algorithms exhibit the highest cumulative error (ITAE = 2815.625, IAE = 118.19, and ISE = 46.844) and the largest position error (Max [m]). = 0.89). This indicates a very basic and inefficient method of control, meaning that they are highly unsuitable for applications requiring more optimized trajectories and higher accuracy.

To complement the validity of the robustness of the obtained values, the Pareto-optimal front can be observed in Figures 19–21. These graphs demonstrate how improving one objective impacts others. In our case, the ideal focus is on minimizing each objective, highlighting that the Vector Field controller emerges as the optimal choice, dominating all other controllers.

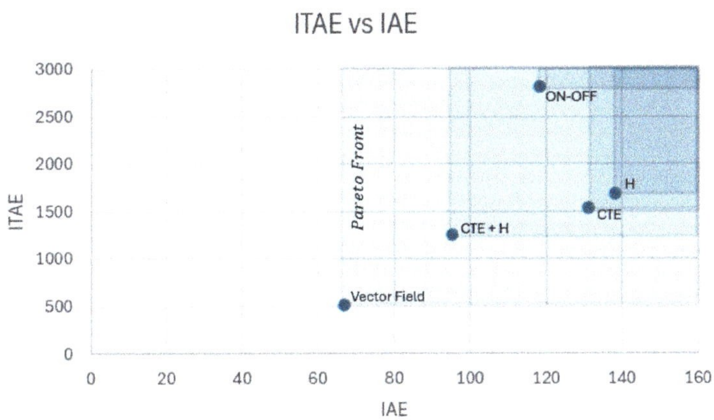

Figure 19. Pareto front between ITAE and IAE objectives.

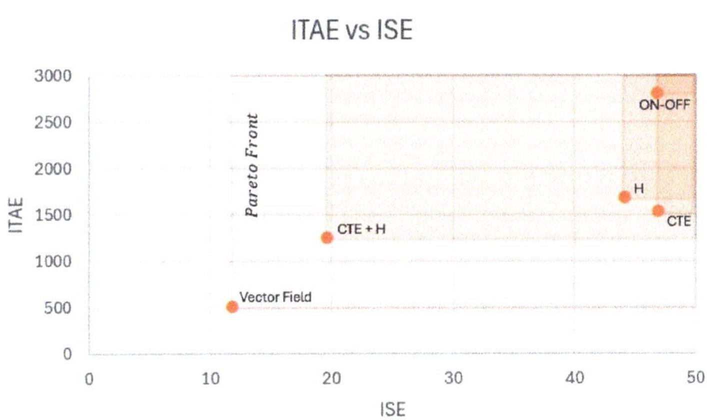

Figure 20. Pareto front between ITAE and ISE objectives.

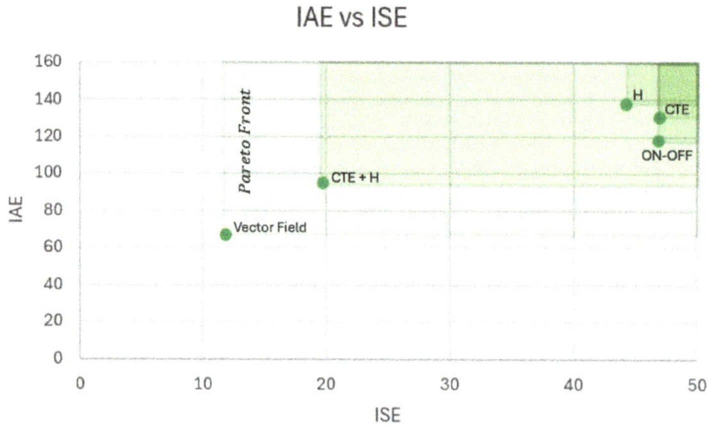

Figure 21. Pareto front between IAE and ISE objectives.

5. Conclusions

In summary, the comprehensive research on the autonomous navigation of unmanned ground vehicles (UGVs) within unstructured environments, such as those commonly encountered in agriculture and forestry, has highlighted the vital importance of various PID control algorithms in enhancing their operational effectiveness. The capability of UGVs to navigate independently in these intricate environments is not merely a technological enhancement, but an essential requirement for efficiency, safety, and sustainability in tasks that are frequently hazardous or overly labor-intensive for human operators.

The study thoroughly assessed multiple PID control algorithms, including the ON–OFF controller, PID Heading controller, PID Cross Track Error (CTE) controller, PID CTE + Heading controller, and PID Vector Field controller. Each algorithm underwent rigorous testing in real-world scenarios using a forestry tractor converted into a UGV, equipped with advanced sensors for precise data acquisition. The evaluations revealed significant variations in performance metrics among the different control strategies.

Notably, the PID Vector Field controller was identified as the optimal approach, demonstrating exceptional performance regarding navigation efficiency, trajectory tracking precision, and adaptability to the unpredictable conditions inherent in unstructured terrain. Utilizing the multi-objective optimization framework confirmed that this method properly balanced stability, adaptability, and computing efficiency. This algorithm's capacity to derive its error from the vector sum of virtual forces enabled dynamic adjustments during navigation, ensuring that the UGV could stay close to its intended path despite obstacles or irregular terrain features.

Additionally, the integration of high-accuracy GNSS-RTK positioning alongside inertial measurement units (IMUs) supplied the UGV with crucial data for the continuous real-time monitoring of its position and orientation. This confluence of technologies not only elevated the precision of the navigation system, but also fostered the formulation of reactive control strategies prioritizing safety and efficiency.

However, the performance of a PID control algorithm also depends on environmental factors. Variability in terrain conditions, such as soil, mud, or uneven surfaces, can affect the traction of the UGV, thereby complicating its navigation. Since the scope of this article focuses on unstructured environments, specifically forested areas, the presence of dense vegetation and trees may reduce the reliability of GNSS-RTK signals, potentially impacting the PID control algorithms.

The practical implications of these results are substantial. The effective adaptation of PID control algorithms for UGVs represents a significant advancement in robotics applications within sectors such as agriculture and forestry, where the demand for autonomous systems continues to grow. The capacity for UGVs to function effectively in challenging environments can reduce labor costs, lower environmental impacts, and enhance safety for human operators.

Furthermore, this research establishes a foundational framework for future progress in mobile robotics. By creating a performance evaluation framework based on criteria such as Integral of Absolute Error (IAE), Integral of Squared Error (ISE), and Integral of Time multiplied by Absolute Error (ITAE), along with metrics like mean, standard deviation, maximum position errors, and navigation time, the study allows for a thorough analysis of control algorithms. These metrics may serve as benchmarks for future research, facilitating the ongoing enhancement of UGV navigation technologies.

Author Contributions: Conceptualization, T.G., T.P. and H.M.; Methodology, T.G., T.P., F.D.G. and S.S.; Software, T.G., T.P., H.M. and F.D.G.; Validation, T.P., N.F., J.F., S.S. and A.V.; Formal analysis, F.D.G., N.F., J.F., S.S. and A.V.; Investigation, T.G., T.P., H.M. and F.D.G.; Resources, C.V. and N.F.; Writing—original draft, T.G., T.P. and N.F.; Writing—review & editing, C.V., N.F., J.F., S.S. and A.V.; Visualization, C.V.; Supervision, C.V., N.F., J.F., S.S. and A.V.; Project administration, N.F. and C.V.; Funding acquisition, N.F. and C.V. All authors have read and agreed to the published version of the manuscript.

Funding: The present work was funded in the scope of the following projects: E-Forest—Multi-agent Autonomous Electric Robotic Forest Management Framework, ref. POCI-01-0247-FEDER-047104 and by project F4F—Forest for Future, ref. CENTRO-08-5864-FSE-000031, co-financed by European Funds through the programs Compete 2020 and Portugal 2020. Also, this work was funded by the Portuguese Foundation for Science and Technology under the project grant UIDP/00760/2020 with the DOI 10.54499/UIDP/00760/2020 | https://doi.org/10.54499/UIDP/00760/2020, project LA/P/0079/2020, DOI: 10.54499/LA/P/0079/2020 | https://doi.org/10.54499/LA/P/0079/2020 and project grant UIDB/00760/2020 with the DOI 10.54499/UIDB/00760/2020 | https://doi.org/10.54499/UIDB/00760/2020.

Data Availability Statement: Data is contained within the article.

Conflicts of Interest: The authors declare no conflicts of interest.

Abbreviations

The following abbreviations are used in this manuscript:

UGVs	Unmanned Ground Vehicles
PID	Proportional, Integral, and Derivative
RTK-GNSS	Real-Time Kinematic Global Satellite Navigation System
GNSS	Global Navigation Satellite System
INS	Inertial Navigation System
PID-H	PID Heading Controller
PID-CTE	PID Cross Track Error Controller
PID-CTE + H	PID Cross Track Error + Heading Controller
PID-VF	PID Vector Field
PIO	Proportional-Integral Observer
RCMA	Raised Cosine Moving Average
MIMO	Multiple Inputs and Multiple Outputs
T	Target
AP	Actual Position
$e_{\text{ON-OFF}}$	On–Off Error
ωr	Angular Value
μC	Microcontroller
VR	Voltage Right Wheel
VL	Voltage Left Wheel

R	Radius
P	Proportional Action
Kp	Proportional Gain
I	Integral Action
Ki	Integral Gain
D	Derivative Action
Kd	Derivative Gain
PI	Proportional–Integral
PD	Proportional–Derivative
θDes	Desired Heading
eHead	Heading Error
θDes	Desired Angle
θ	Actual Angle
ePos	Position Error
Vr	Linear Value
D_DFL	Desired Distance from the Line
A_DFL	Current Distance from the Line
e_CTE	Error in this Distance
ϕ	Bearing of the Path
DDFPL	Distance from Point to Line
ωr	Angular Value
IAE	Integral of the Absolute Error Magnitude
ISE	Integral of the Squared Error
ITAE	Integral of the Time multiplied by the Absolute Error Magnitude
MOO	Multi-Objective Optimization

References

1. Fernandes, H.R.; Polania, E.C.M.; Garcia, A.P.; Barrero, O.; Albiero, D. Agricultural Unmanned Ground Vehicles: A Review from the Stability Point of View. *Rev. Cienc. Agron.* **2020**, *51*, e20207761. [CrossRef]
2. Lytridis, C.; Kaburlasos, V.G.; Pachidis, T.; Manios, M.; Vrochidou, E.; Kalampokas, T.; Chatzistamatis, S. An Overview of Cooperative Robotics in Agriculture. *Agronomy* **2021**, *11*, 1818. [CrossRef]
3. Oliveira, L.F.P.; Moreira, A.P.; Silva, M.F. Advances in Forest Robotics: A State-of-the-Art Survey. *Robotics* **2021**, *10*, 53. [CrossRef]
4. Gameiro, T.; Pereira, T.; Viegas, C.; Di Giorgio, F.; Ferreira, N.F. Robots for Forest Maintenance. *Forests* **2024**, *15*, 381. [CrossRef]
5. Wijayathunga, L.; Rassau, A.; Chai, D. Challenges and Solutions for Autonomous Ground Robot Scene Understanding and Navigation in Unstructured Outdoor Environments: A Review. *Appl. Sci.* **2023**, *13*, 9877. [CrossRef]
6. Beycimen, S.; Ignatyev, D.; Zolotas, A. A Comprehensive Survey of Unmanned Ground Vehicle Terrain Traversability for Unstructured Environments and Sensor Technology Insights. *Eng. Sci. Technol. Int. J.* **2023**, *47*, 101457. [CrossRef]
7. Ruslan, N.A.I.; Amer, N.H.; Hudha, K.; Kadir, Z.A.; Ishak, S.A.F.M.; Dardin, S.M.F.S. Modelling and Control Strategies in Path Tracking Control for Autonomous Tracked Vehicles: A Review of State of the Art and Challenges. *J. Terramechanics* **2023**, *105*, 67–79. [CrossRef]
8. Huang, G.; Du, S.; Wang, D. GNSS Techniques for Real-Time Monitoring of Landslides: A Review. *Satell. Navig.* **2023**, *4*, 5. [CrossRef]
9. Jing, Y.; Li, Q.; Ye, W.; Liu, G. Development of a GNSS/INS-Based Automatic Navigation Land Levelling System. *Comput. Electron. Agric.* **2023**, *213*, 108187. [CrossRef]
10. Yan, W.; Bastos, L.; Magalhaes, A. Performance Assessment of the Android Smartphone's IMU in a GNSS/INS Coupled Navigation Model. *IEEE Access* **2019**, *7*, 171073–171083. [CrossRef]
11. Song, J.; Li, W.; Duan, C.; Zhu, X. R^2-GVIO: A Robust, Real-Time GNSS-Visual-Inertial State Estimator in Urban Challenging Environments. *IEEE Internet Things J.* **2024**, *11*, 22269–22282. [CrossRef]
12. Bai, X.; Hsu, L.-T. GNSS/Visual/IMU/Map Integration Via Sliding Window Factor Graph Optimization for Vehicular Positioning in Urban Areas. *IEEE Trans. Intell. Veh.* 2024; 1–11, Early Access. [CrossRef]
13. Rouzegar, H.; Ghanbarisabagh, M. A Novel on–off Linear Quadratic Regulator Control Approach for Satellite Rendezvous. *Aerosp. Syst.* **2023**, *6*, 613–620. [CrossRef]
14. Khan, H.; Khatoon, S.; Gaur, P.; Abbas, M.; Saleel, C.A.; Khan, S.A. Speed Control of Wheeled Mobile Robot by Nature-Inspired Social Spider Algorithm-Based PID Controller. *Processes* **2023**, *11*, 1202. [CrossRef]

15. Bello, A.; Olfe, K.S.; Rodríguez, J.; Ezquerro, J.M.; Lapuerta, V. Experimental Verification and Comparison of Fuzzy and PID Controllers for Attitude Control of Nanosatellites. *Adv. Space Res.* **2023**, *71*, 3613–3630. [CrossRef]
16. Efheij, H.; Albagul, A.; Ammar Albraiki, N. Comparison of Model Predictive Control and PID Controller in Real Time Process Control System. In Proceedings of the 2019 19th International Conference on Sciences and Techniques of Automatic Control and Computer Engineering (STA), Sousse, Tunisia, 24–26 March 2019; IEEE: Piscataway, NJ, USA, 2019; pp. 64–69.
17. Ji, Y.; Wu, X.; Shang, Y.; Fu, H.; Yang, J.; Wu, W. Unmanned Ground Vehicle in Unstructured Environments Applying Improved A-Star Algorithm. In Proceedings of the 2024 4th International Conference on Computer, Control and Robotics (ICCCR), Shanghai, China, 19–21 April 2024; IEEE: Piscataway, NJ, USA, 2024; pp. 166–170.
18. Zhang, L.; Jiang, Y.; Chen, G.; Tang, Y.; Lu, S.; Gao, X. Heading Control of Variable Configuration Unmanned Ground Vehicle Using PID-Type Sliding Mode Control and Steering Control Based on Particle Swarm Optimization. *Nonlinear Dyn.* **2023**, *111*, 3361–3378. [CrossRef]
19. Sun, Y.-P.; Liang, Y.-C. Vector Field Path-Following Control for a Small Unmanned Ground Vehicle with Kalman Filter Estimation. *Proc. Inst. Mech. Eng. Part B J. Eng. Manuf.* **2022**, *236*, 1885–1899. [CrossRef]
20. Parque, V.; Khalifa, A. PID Tuning Using Differential Evolution With Success-Based Particle Adaptations. *IEEE Access* **2023**, *11*, 136219–136268. [CrossRef]
21. Vijayakumar, M.; Sakthivel, R.; Mohammadzadeh, A.; Karthick, S.A.; Marshal Anthoni, S. Proportional Integral Observer Based Tracking Control Design for Markov Jump Systems. *Appl. Math. Comput.* **2021**, *410*, 126467. [CrossRef]
22. Song, W.; Jin, A. Observer-Based Model Reference Tracking Control of the Markov Jump System with Partly Unknown Transition Rates. *Appl. Sci.* **2023**, *13*, 914. [CrossRef]
23. Gomathi, N.; Rajathi, K. Adaptive Path Planning for Unknown Environment Monitoring. *J. Ambient. Intell. Smart Environ.* **2023**, *15*, 287–314. [CrossRef]
24. Farag, W.; Saleh, Z. Tuning of PID Track Followers for Autonomous Driving. In Proceedings of the 2018 International Conference on Innovation and Intelligence for Informatics, Computing, and Technologies (3ICT), Sakhier, Bahrain, 18–20 November 2018; IEEE: Piscataway, NJ, USA, 2018; pp. 1–7.
25. Zangina, U.; Buyamin, S.; Abidin, M.S.Z.; Mahmud, M.S.A.; Hasan, H.S. Non-Linear PID Controller for Trajectory Tracking of a Differential Drive Mobile Robot. *J. Mech. Eng. Res. Dev.* **2020**, *43*, 255–270.
26. Akopov, A.S.; Beklaryan, L.A.; Beklaryan, A.L. Simulation-Based Optimisation for Autonomous Transportation Systems Using a Parallel Real-Coded Genetic Algorithm with Scalable Nonuniform Mutation. *Cybern. Inf. Technol.* **2021**, *21*, 127–144. [CrossRef]
27. Duro Inertial User Manual [UM-110008-02]. Available online: https://www.swiftnav.com/resource-files/Duro%20Inertial/v2/Manual/Duro%20Inertial%20User%20Manual%20[UM-110008-02].pdf (accessed on 20 January 2025).
28. Pereira, T.; Gameiro, T.; Viegas, C.; Santos, V.; Ferreira, N. Sensor Integration in a Forestry Machine. *Sensors* **2023**, *23*, 9853. [CrossRef] [PubMed]
29. Pereira, T.; Santos, V.; Gameiro, T.; Viegas, C.; Ferreira, N. Evaluation of Different Filtering Methods Devoted to Magnetometer Data Denoising. *Electronics* **2024**, *13*, 2006. [CrossRef]
30. Edamana, B.; Oldham, K. An Optimal On-off Controller with Switching Costs Using Non-Linear Binary Programming. In Proceedings of the 2009 American Control Conference, St. Louis, MO, USA, 10–12 June 2009; IEEE: Piscataway, NJ, USA, 2009; pp. 4227–4232.
31. Borase, R.P.; Maghade, D.K.; Sondkar, S.Y.; Pawar, S.N. A Review of PID Control, Tuning Methods and Applications. *Int. J. Dynam. Control* **2021**, *9*, 818–827. [CrossRef]
32. Holland, J.M. *Designing Mobile Autonomous Robots*; Elsevier Newnes: Amsterdam, The Netherlands; Boston, MA, USA, 2004; ISBN 978-0-7506-7683-0.
33. Åström, K.J.; Murray, R.M. *Feedback Systems: An Introduction for Scientists and Engineers*; Princeton University Press: Princeton, NJ, USA, 2008; ISBN 9780691135762.
34. Raj, R.; Kos, A. A Comprehensive Study of Mobile Robot: History, Developments, Applications, and Future Research Perspectives. *Appl. Sci.* **2022**, *12*, 6951. [CrossRef]
35. Rubio, F.; Valero, F.; Llopis-Albert, C. A Review of Mobile Robots: Concepts, Methods, Theoretical Framework, and Applications. *Int. J. Adv. Robot. Syst.* **2019**, *16*, 1729881419839596. [CrossRef]
36. Sathiabalan, N.A.; Lokimi, A.F.M.; Jin, O.Z.; Hasrin, N.S.M.; Zain, A.S.M.; Ramli, N.; Zakaria, H.L.; Ariffin, W.N.S.F.W.; Hashim, N.B.M.; Taib, M.H.M. Autonomous Robotic Fire Detection and Extinguishing System. *J. Phys. Conf. Ser.* **2021**, *2107*, 012060. [CrossRef]
37. Herath, D.; St-Onge, D. (Eds.) *Foundations of Robotics: A Multidisciplinary Approach with Python and ROS*; Springer Nature: Singapore, 2022; ISBN 978-981-19198-2-4.
38. Amer, N.H.; Zamzuri, H.; Hudha, K.; Kadir, Z.A. Modelling and Control Strategies in Path Tracking Control for Autonomous Ground Vehicles: A Review of State of the Art and Challenges. *J. Intell. Robot. Syst.* **2017**, *86*, 225–254. [CrossRef]

39. Chemical Process Dynamics and Controls. Available online: https://open.umich.edu/sites/default/files/downloads/chemical_process_dynamics_and_controls-book_1.pdf (accessed on 20 January 2025).
40. Nelson, D.R.; Barber, D.B.; McLain, T.W.; Beard, R.W. Vector Field Path Following for Small Unmanned Air Vehicles. In Proceedings of the 2006 American Control Conference, Minneapolis, MN, USA, 14–16 June 2006; IEEE: Piscataway, NJ, USA, 2006; p. 7.
41. Borenstein, J.; Koren, Y. The Vector Field Histogram-Fast Obstacle Avoidance for Mobile Robots. *IEEE Trans. Robot. Automat.* **1991**, *7*, 278–288. [CrossRef]
42. Berner, J.; Soltesz, K.; Hägglund, T.; Åström, K.J. An Experimental Comparison of PID Autotuners. *Control Eng. Pract.* **2018**, *73*, 124–133. [CrossRef]
43. Sen, R.; Pati, C.; Dutta, S.; Sen, R. Comparison Between Three Tuning Methods of PID Control for High Precision Positioning Stage. *Mapan* **2015**, *30*, 65–70. [CrossRef]
44. Isdaryani, F.; Feriyonika, F.; Ferdiansyah, R. Comparison of Ziegler-Nichols and Cohen Coon Tuning Method for Magnetic Levitation Control System. *J. Phys. Conf. Ser.* **2020**, *1450*, 012033. [CrossRef]
45. Almabrok, A.; Psarakis, M.; Dounis, A. Fast Tuning of the PID Controller in An HVAC System Using the Big Bang–Big Crunch Algorithm and FPGA Technology. *Algorithms* **2018**, *11*, 146. [CrossRef]
46. Sharma, S.; Kumar, V. A Comprehensive Review on Multi-Objective Optimization Techniques: Past, Present and Future. *Arch. Computat. Methods Eng.* **2022**, *29*, 5605–5633. [CrossRef]
47. Goos, G.; Hartmanis, J.; van Leeuwen, J.; Hutchison, D.; Kanade, T.; Kittler, J.; Kleinberg, J.M.; Kobsa, A.; Mattern, F.; Mitchell, J.C.; et al. *Lecture Notes in Computer Science*; Springer: Berlin/Heidelberg, Germany, 1973.
48. Deb, K. Multi-Objective Optimization Using Evolutionary Algorithms: An Introduction. In *Multi-Objective Evolutionary Optimisation for Product Design and Manufacturing*; Springer: London, UK, 2011; pp. 3–34.
49. Cui, Y.; Geng, Z.; Zhu, Q.; Han, Y. Review: Multi-Objective Optimization Methods and Application in Energy Saving. *Energy* **2017**, *125*, 681–704. [CrossRef]

algorithms

MDPI

Article

Control of a Mobile Line-Following Robot Using Neural Networks

Hugo M. Leal [1], Ramiro S. Barbosa [1,2,*] and Isabel S. Jesus [1,2]

[1] Department of Electrical Engineering, Institute of Engineering—Polytechnic of Porto (ISEP/IPP), 4249-015 Porto, Portugal; 1190660@isep.ipp.pt (H.M.L.); isj@isep.ipp.pt (I.S.J.)

[2] GECAD—Research Group on Intelligent Engineering and Computing for Advanced Innovation and Development, ISEP/IPP, 4249-015 Porto, Portugal

* Correspondence: rsb@isep.ipp.pt

Abstract: This work aims to develop and compare the performance of a line-following robot using both neural networks and classical controllers such as Proportional–Integral–Derivative (PID). Initially, the robot's infrared sensors were employed to follow a line using a PID controller. The data from this method were then used to train a Long Short-Term Memory (LSTM) network, which successfully replicated the behavior of the PID controller. In a subsequent experiment, the robot's camera was used for line-following with neural networks. Images of the track were captured, categorized, and used to train a convolutional neural network (CNN), which then controlled the robot in real time. The results showed that neural networks are effective but require more processing and calibration. On the other hand, PID controllers proved to be simpler and more efficient for the tested tracks. Although neural networks are very promising for advanced applications, they are also capable of handling simpler tasks effectively.

Keywords: AGV; robot; Raspbot; PID; LSTM; CNN; AI; deep learning; line-follower

1. Introduction

In recent years, artificial intelligence techniques, such as machine learning and deep learning, have revolutionized various fields of science and engineering, including robotics [1–4]. These techniques have shown significant potential to enhance the autonomy and intelligence of robots, enabling them to perform complex tasks with greater efficiency and precision. One of the promising fields where these techniques are currently applied is the control of mobile robots, including Autonomous Guided Vehicles (AGVs).

Traditionally, techniques such as PID control and trajectory planning algorithms have been used in mobile robot control. However, these approaches face limitations in dynamic and unstructured environments. Deep learning (DL) techniques offer a data-driven approach that can enhance the adaptability and intelligence of these control systems. Inspired by recent advances in artificial intelligence, modern alternatives like LSTM and CNN networks have emerged, offering potential solutions to these challenges.

In this context, the development of a line-following robot control algorithm using DL techniques was chosen. This practical and relevant application enables one to demonstrate the effectiveness of neural networks in robot control, providing solid validation for new control approaches. By comparing traditional and modern techniques, this work aims to identify the advantages and limitations of DL, contributing to the development of smarter and more efficient robotic systems. On the other hand, the use of DL algorithms such as LSTM and CNN does not inherently require a mathematical model of the robot for its control. The need for a mathematical model depends on the specific application and the role of neural networks in the control system. In the present case, the LSTM or CNN models are trained to predict control actions directly from sensor data, and the robot can be controlled using only the sensor inputs. This data-driven approach relies on neural networks to learn the relationships between sensor input and control output during training. Thus, LSTM is used to process sequential data, such as time series sensor readings, while CNN is used to handle spatial data such as camera images. The results obtained are very promising, showing that the quality and quantity of the training data used were sufficient to provide satisfactory control of the robot in a real scenario. Therefore, the main contributions of this work can be summarized as follows:

- Introducing the LSTM and CNN architectures for the control of a mobile robot.
- Providing detailed insights into the implementation of various control algorithms, with a particular focus on the LSTM and CNN networks.
- Comparison of artificial intelligence algorithms with the classical PID controller.
- Evaluating and comparing the performance of different control algorithms using various metrics.

The article is structured as follows. Section 2 presents the robot architecture and its main components. The control methods are described in Section 3. Section 4 discusses the details of the implementation of the three control strategies used, PID, LSTM, and CNN. The results are provided in Section 5, while Section 6 includes a discussion of the real experiments. Finally, Section 7 draws the main conclusions and outlines the future developments of the presented work.

Literature Review

In recent years, the use of artificial intelligence and deep learning for autonomous vehicle control has attracted a great deal of interest. In [5], the authors developed a Bluetooth- and vision-controlled AGV for COVID-19, capable of carrying 10 kg and following a labeled user at an optimal distance of 80 cm and a 55° detection angle. The AGV reduces contact risk, aids seniors by eliminating the need to push heavy loads, and operates via a mobile app or autonomous tracking within a 10 m range. The work by [6] introduced an AI-driven AGV for factory automation, using magnetic tape for navigation to handle goods. The limitations include misjudgment when tape breaks and an inability to change routes around obstacles. The study explored divergence-wheeled robots for smoother navigation in crowded environments. In [7], an AGV was presented for seamless indoor and outdoor navigation, utilizing a self-evolving free space detection (FSD) framework with online active machine learning and sensor data fusion. The framework outperforms DeepLabV3+ by self-learning from real-time multimodal data, reducing the need for large datasets while improving robustness in unstructured environments. In [8], an obstacle avoidance system was implemented for AGVs using deep action learning (DAL) to enhance visual navigation, object recognition, and decision-making. By integrating YOLOv4, SURF, and kNN, the system achieves real-time obstacle avoidance and navigation, meeting Industry 4.0 standards for speed, accuracy, and robustness in unstructured environments. In [9], the authors proposed an AGV obstacle avoidance system combining deep learning object detection and grid-based path planning for dynamic industrial environments. Tested in a simulated tobacco production workshop, the system achieved a 98.67% success rate in obstacle avoidance and improved task efficiency by 27.29%, offering a reliable solution for industrial AGVs. In [10], a deep-reinforcement-learning-based method for automatic PID adjustment to ensure smooth AGV movement was presented. Using the Deep Q-Learning Network (DQN), the approach transforms PID tuning into an action–value optimization problem. Simulations and tests demonstrate the method's effectiveness in achieving optimal PID settings without manual intervention. Another study [11] introduced a two-wheel

AGV platform utilizing sensor fusion and neural networks for intelligent path planning and navigation in dynamic unknown environments. The neural network processes sensor inputs to determine safe paths while avoiding arbitrarily shaped and moving obstacles, with simulations validating the approach for Industry 4.0 applications. The work in [12] reviewed recent applications of deep learning in UAVs for tasks like security, disaster rescue, and warehouse management, highlighting the key techniques, their performance, and limitations while discussing the challenges and future directions for UAV-based deep learning solutions. The work in [13] presented an AI algorithm for platform autonomy, enabling navigation without human intervention. Using cameras, LIDAR sensors, and a vision system, the platform employs convolutional neural networks for environment analysis and path optimization. Transfer learning trains the network, with the results demonstrating its effectiveness. In [14], a deep reinforcement learning approach for mapless AGV navigation using LiDAR and RGB cameras was presented. The NavACL-Q method combines curriculum learning with soft actor–critic to address challenges like sparse samples and partial observability. The results demonstrated a 40% performance gain over random starts and a 60% boost with a pre-trained feature extractor, outperforming map-based navigation.

2. System Architecture

This section describes the robot platform, its architecture, and the software tools used for the project.

2.1. Mobile Platform

The robot chosen for this study was the Raspbot AI Vision Robot Car from Yah-Boom [15]. It is equipped with the necessary sensors for implementing a line-follower, including infrared sensors and a camera. Table 1 lists a summary of the main characteristics of the Raspbot AI Vision Robot Car. It integrates vision functions based on open-source computer vision (CV) via Python programming. This enables the robot to be controlled via an app, infrared remote (IR), and the JupyterLab web interface.

Table 1. Main characteristics of Yahboom Raspbot AI Vision Robot Car.

Parameter	Yahboom
Sensors	Camera Lower and lateral infrared Ultrasound
Infrared module	4
No. of wheels	4
No. of motors	4
Microcontroller	Raspberry Pi 4B
Camera	5 Megapixels 1080P@30FPS/ 720P@60FPS/480P@90FPS interface CSI
Camera Gimbal	Yes
Ultrasound Gimbal	No

2.2. Robot Architecture

The Raspbot is equipped with interconnected components, including sensors, micro-controllers, drivers, and motors. This setup enables the robot to perform several tasks necessary for the realization of this project. Figure 1 presents a block diagram of the system's architecture, highlighting the main components of the system and their connections [15].

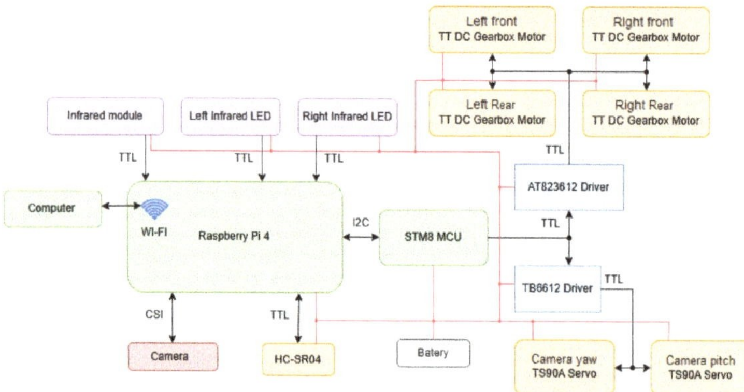

Figure 1. Block diagram of the robot architecture.

The green blocks represent the system's controllers, the main one being the Raspberry Pi 4 model B. The Raspberry will be responsible for controlling all the system's components. The robot is equipped with six motors: 4 generic TT DC gearbox motors from TTmotors in China [16] and 2 TS90A servo motors from TianKongRC, China [17]. In addition, it has a Raspberry Pi Camera Rev 1.3 [18] (Figure 2a), capable of recording still images at a resolution of 2592 × 1944 pixels. For line tracking, the robot employs a lower tracking module equipped with four tracking probes in an optimized spacing layout. The two inner probes accurately detect the black line, while the two outer ones assist the inner probes by providing additional detection and early warnings. This configuration enables the robot to navigate complex tracks, including 90° curves (Figure 2b) [15].

This setup provides remote access to the Raspberry Pi operating system through the JupyterLab environment [15].

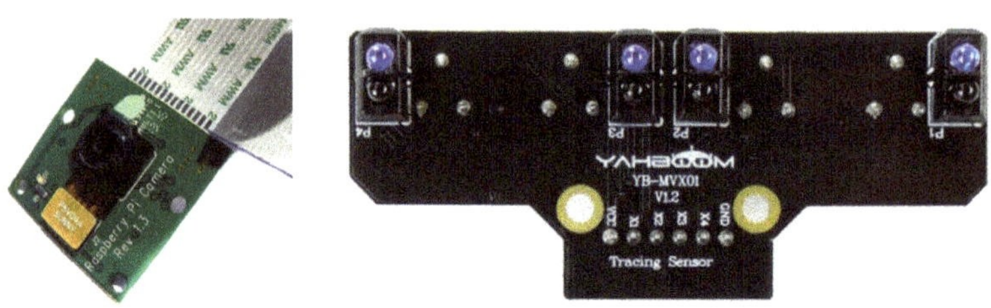

(**a**) (**b**)

Figure 2. (**a**) Raspberry Pi Camera Rev 1.3 [18] and (**b**) Yahboom's 4-channel infrared tracking sensor [15].

2.3. Software and Tools

For this work, an operating system (OS) distributed by the robot's manufacturer (based on Raspbian 5.10.63-v7l+) was used, which enables the user to connect the Raspberry Pi to a Wi-Fi network without having to connect it to a monitor or keyboard afterwards. Once connected, remote access to the system is also available through a JupyterLab 6.1.4 server (Figure 3).

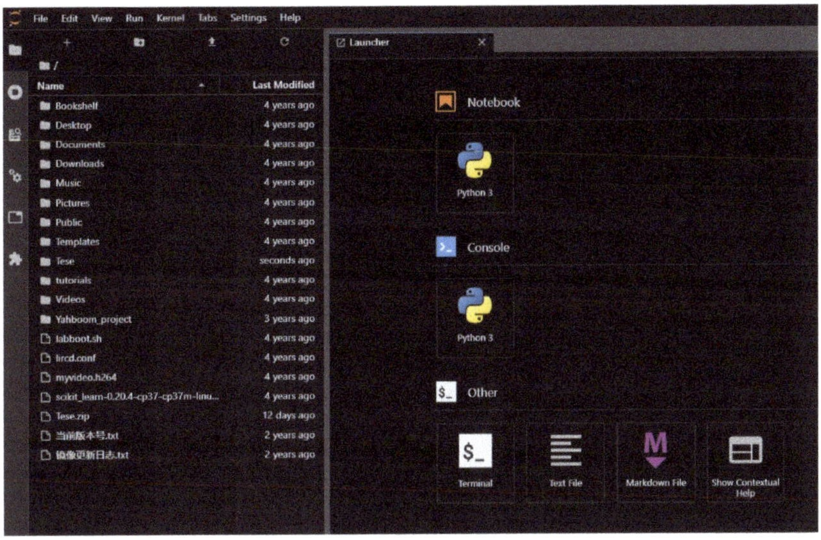

Figure 3. JupyterLab environment.

The data collected by the robot for training the neural networks were transferred to a more powerful computer equipped with an NVIDIA RTX 3060 GPU [19], a Ryzen 7 3700X AMD CPU (3.6 GHZ base clock speed) [20], and 32 GB of DDR4 RAM. This setup enabled faster neural network training and testing of different network configurations. The Python language (version 3.7.4) was selected because of the greater degree of familiarity already present and its powerful data visualization, which also helped the debugging process during the development of the work. The main tools included the Anaconda environment, the Jupyter Notebook, and libraries such as TensorFlow 1.14.0 and Keras 2.2.4 [21,22].

3. Control Strategies

The objective of this work was to develop, implement and test multiple control methods to assess their performance in the control of a line-following robot. For that purpose, classical and deep learning methods were studied. During execution, sensor data from the infrared sensors or camera are sent to the Raspberry Pi and then the controller implemented in the software will calculate the new motor speed values and send these new values to the motors, as illustrated in Figure 4. The control is created with two values, where a single value will be updated for both right motors (front and rear), and the other value will be updated for the left motors.

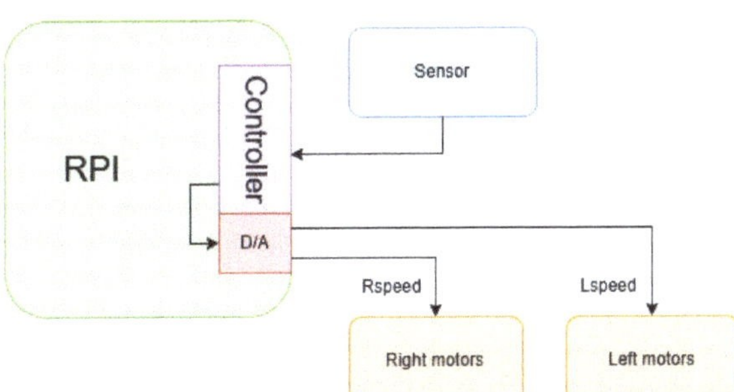

Figure 4. Schematic of the system with the software controller.

3.1. PID

For the classical methods, the PID (Proportional–Integral–Derivative) controller was selected. The PID is the most common controller in industry and is widely used in all control applications. It also represents an essential element of more sophisticated controllers [23–26]. Figure 5 presents a block diagram of a PID-controlled system [27,28].

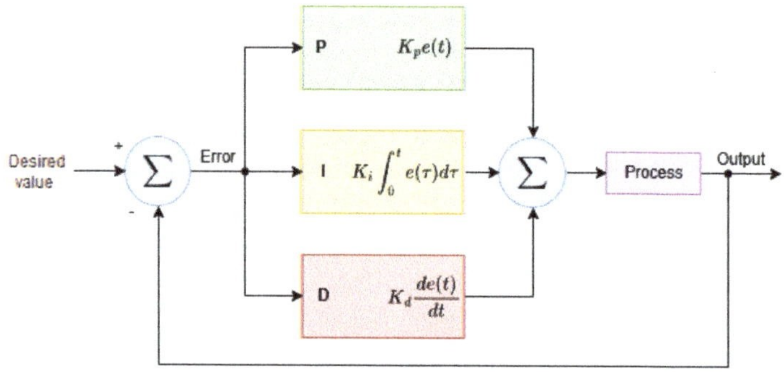

Figure 5. PID-controlled system.

The PID controller can be described as

$$u(t) = K_p\left(e(t) + \frac{1}{T_i}\int_0^t e(\tau)\,d\tau + T_d\frac{de(t)}{dt}\right) \tag{1}$$

where $u(t)$ represents the controller action output and $e(t)$ is a control error input, which is the difference between the desired reference value and the current value of the variable to be controlled. The controller output is thus the sum of three terms: the P-term (which is proportional to the error), the I-term (which is proportional to the integral of the error), and the D-term (which is proportional to the derivative of the error). The parameters K_p, T_i, and T_d are, respectively, the proportional gain, the integral time constant, and the derivative time constant [29].

The discrete PID controller can be obtained as

$$u[n] = K_p\left(e[n] + \frac{T}{T_i}\sum_{k=0}^{n} e[k] + \frac{T_d}{T}(e[n] - e[n-1])\right) \tag{2}$$

where T is the sampling period and n is the sample instant. Since T is constant ($T = 1/80$ s), the following simplified equation was used:

$$u[n] = K_p e[n] + K_i\sum_{k=0}^{n} e(k) + K_d(e[n] - e[n-1]) \tag{3}$$

where $K_i = \frac{K_p T}{T_i}$ is the integral gain and $K_d = \frac{K_p T_d}{T}$ the derivative gain.

3.2. LSTM

LSTM (Long-Short Term Memory) is an advanced type of RNN (recurrent neural network) developed by Hochreiter and Schmidhuber [30]. Traditional RNNs are characterized by using the previous output as one of the inputs of the network, similarly to PID controllers. However, RNNs have difficulty learning long-term dependencies due to the vanishing gradient problem. LSTM solves this problem by introducing a memory cell that can retain information over extended periods of time. Figure 6 shows the structure of an LSTM cell [31].

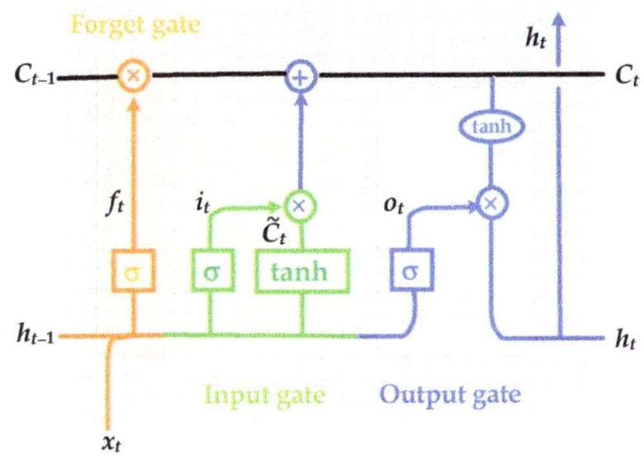

Figure 6. LSTM cell.

The equations for the forward pass of an LSTM cell are as follows:

$$\begin{aligned} f_t &= \sigma(W_f \cdot [h_{t-1}, x_t] + b_f) \\ i_t &= \sigma(W_i \cdot [h_{t-1}, x_t] + b_i) \\ \tilde{C}_t &= \tanh(W_C \cdot [h_{t-1}, x_t] + b_C) \\ C_t &= f_t * C_{t-1} + i_t * \tilde{C}_t \\ o_t &= \sigma(W_o \cdot [h_{t-1}, x_t] + b_o) \\ h_t &= o_t * \tanh(C_t) \end{aligned} \tag{4}$$

where W terms denote the weight matrices, $[h_{t-1}, x_t]$ the concatenation of the current input and the previous hidden state, the b terms denote bias vectors, σ is the sigmoid activation function, and i, f, o, and C are, respectively, the input gate, forget gate, output gate, and cell activation vectors; $*$ is the elementwise multiplication, and tanh function is the activation function.

The LSTM, by having the ability to capture long-term dependencies and process sequential data efficiently, has revolutionized many fields, including natural language processing, speech recognition, and time-series forecasting. Their advanced architecture, which incorporates memory cells and gates, enables them to learn and retain complex patterns over time, making them an essential tool in modern machine learning and artificial intelligence applications, including image classification [32].

3.3. CNN

A CNN (convolutional neural network) is a widely used discriminative deep learning architecture that learns directly from input data without the need for manual feature extraction. As a result, CNN improves on the design of traditional ANNs (artificial neural networks), such as regularized MLP (Multi-Layered Perceptron) networks. Each layer in the CNN takes into account optimal parameters to produce a meaningful output, as well as to reduce the complexity of the model [33].

They are specifically designed to handle a variety of 2D shapes, making them widely used in visual recognition, medical image analysis, image segmentation, natural language processing, and many other domains. The ability to automatically discover essential input features without human intervention makes it more powerful than a traditional network [34].

Table 2 shows the CNN LeNet (LeNet-5) architecture to classify images [22]. LeNet-5 is characterized by having a total of 7 layers (3 convolutional layers, 2 pooling layers, and 2 dense fully connected (FC) layers) and is a simple and efficient network generally used for the categorization of handwritten letters and numbers. In the present work, it was used for the classification of shapes of the black line in front of the robot. This architecture was chosen primarily for its lightweight and computationally efficient design, making it well suited for low-end hardware implementations, which is the case with respect to the Raspberry Pi utilized. It also offers several advantages, including ease of implementation, with fewer parameters than other CNNs, making it easier to train and less prone to overfitting in smaller datasets.

Table 2. LeNet-5 architecture.

Layer	Layer Type	Feature Map	Size	Kernel Size	Stride	Activation
Input	Image	1	32 × 32	-	-	-
1	Convolution	6	28 × 28	5 × 5	1	tanh
2	Average Pooling	6	14 × 14	2 × 2	2	tanh
3	Convolution	16	10 × 10	5 × 5	1	tanh
4	Average Pooling	16	5 × 5	2 × 2	2	tanh
5	Convolution	120	1 × 1	5 × 5	1	tanh
6	FC	-	84	-	-	tanh
Output	FC	-	10	-	-	softmax

4. Implementation

This section details the various control methods used for the control of the line-follower robot. The project will be divided into two experiments. The first one uses the track on the wooden floor and the infrared sensors with an LSTM network, and the second one, on a modified track, uses the camera and a CNN for robot control.

4.1. PID

The objective is to control the robot to follow a line drawn on the ground utilizing neural networks through infrared sensors. To achieve this, in order to collect and classify data to be used to train the LSTM network, a PID controller was first implemented. Therefore, whilst the robot is being controlled by the PID, the infrared sensor data and right and left speeds are saved for use in the next experiment. Figure 7 shows the main loop of the PID-controlled system. This loop is executed 80 times per second.

While the user does not interrupt the program, the algorithm will start on each loop by obtaining the new error value to be fed to the PID controller. This error is defined as the approximate distance between the central position of the infrared sensor module and the central position of the line. Consequently, the current position value is first calculated by the following equation:

$$Position = \frac{(0 \times S1) + (2750 \times S2) + (3550 \times S3) + (6300 \times S4)}{S1 + S2 + S3 + S4} \tag{5}$$

where S1 to S4 represent the binary logic values of each sensor. This estimate is completed using a weighted average of the sensor indexes multiplied by a specified value. The values used can be chosen arbitrarily, so the controller gains would need to be adjusted accordingly. However, since the four sensors are not spaced equally apart, the solution found was to match the gains to the distance between the different sensors. By measuring this distance, the values were set to 0, 2750, 3550 and 6300, with the first weight being 0, kept in the equation for clarity of the weight used for each infrared sensor of the module, as shown in Figure 8.

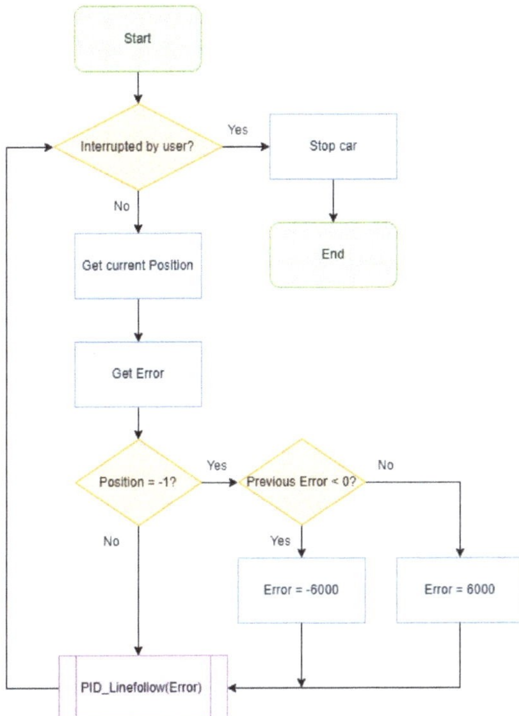

Figure 7. Main loop of the PID controller.

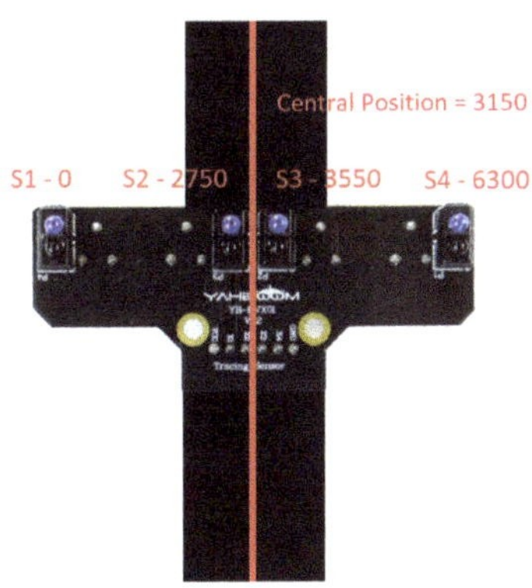

Figure 8. Diagram of the weighted average used by the system and the error calculation.

Finally, with the distance calculated, the error can be determined by subtracting the desired value (3150) from the current position, $Error = 3150 - Position$. In this way, if the error is 0, the sensor is centered with the line; if it is negative, the line is to its right; and, if it is positive, to its left. Furthermore, if the previous function returns -1, that is, the sensor 'loses' the line, the error will be adjusted taking into account the previous error. If the previous error is negative, it will be changed to −6000, and, if positive, it will be set to 6000, as described in the implementation of Figure 7.

With the error determined, this value can be used as the parameter for the function `PID_Linefollow`. Figure 9 illustrates the steps of this function:

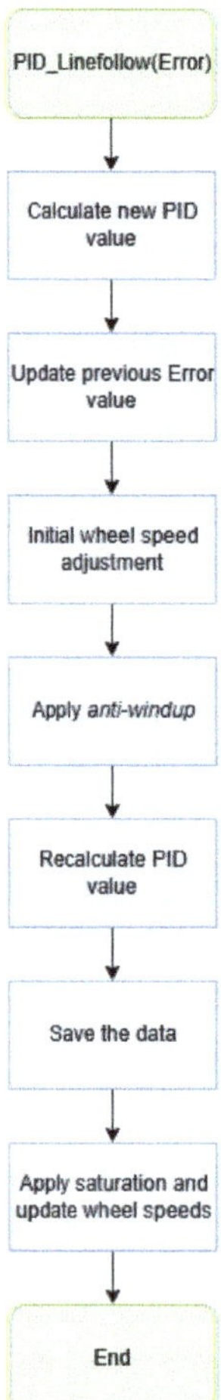

Figure 9. Steps of the PID controller.

- **Calculation of terms**: proportional ($P = error$), integrative ($I = I + error$), and derivative ($D = Error - previousError$), multiply by their respective gains, and add them to calculate the PID value.
  The gains were obtained experimentally, trying several combinations so that oscillations were minimized and responsiveness optimized. In this case, the gains are $K_p = 0.04$, $K_i = 0.00002$, and $K_d = 0.035$.
- **Initial wheel speed adjustment**: a default value is set for the motors to turn, in this case 70, called the base speed. The adjustment will add the result of the PID to the right-hand motors and subtract it from the left-hand motors so that the average value of 70 is maintained in the forward direction of the robot.
- **Apply the anti-windup** mechanism to ensure that the integrative action does not reach very high values, which could lead to the robot, when it loses the line, spinning

indefinitely, unable to get back on track. In this way, if the wheel speeds exceed the acceptable limit (less than −255 or more than +255), the amount by which these speeds exceed the limits will be added to the anti-windup value.

- **Recalculate the PID value**: due to the fact that the anti-windup changes the value of the integrative action, it is necessary to recalculate the output of the PID and the speed of the wheels.
- **Save data** for analysis, debugging, and then training the neural network.
- **Apply saturation** to the motor speeds so that they do not exceed the limits (−255 to +255), and finally apply these speeds to the motors.

The resulting scheme for the PID control is shown in Figure 10.

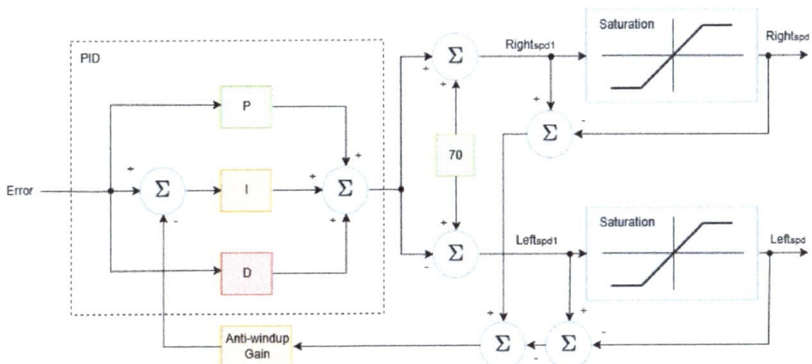

Figure 10. Block diagram of the implemented PID controller.

4.2. LSTM

With the data collected, it is now possible to train an LSTM neural network so that it can simulate the behavior of the PID controller. To accomplish this, it is necessary to choose a suitable model for this implementation.

Since the PID controller takes previous values to calculate the new output value, it is important to consider a model that has the ability to use past values to calculate new motor speeds. Therefore, an LSTM network was selected.

The implementation of an LSTM neural network involves several steps. First, the training data are prepared by organizing the CSV data, identifying the inputs and outputs, creating sequences, and splitting the data into training and test sets. The network is then defined by determining the depth, type, and size of each layer. The following step is the network training, which includes testing different configurations and depths while comparing the errors obtained in each case. Finally, the trained model is saved and can be transferred to the Raspberry Pi of the robot, where it will be used for control.

The LSTM model is designed to accurately deliver new left and right speeds to the motors, striking a balance between complexity and regularization to optimize performance while mitigating overfitting. Figure 11 illustrates the network model used in this implementation. Table 3 lists the network parameters.

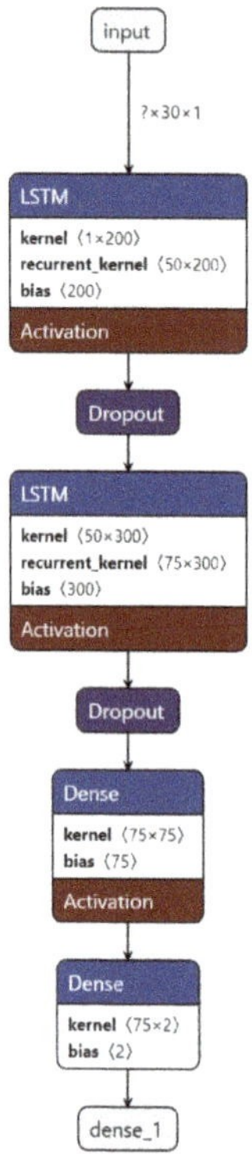

Figure 11. Diagram of the LSTM network used.

Table 3. Hyperparameters of the LSTM model.

Hyperparameter	Value
LSTM Units (Layer 1)	50
Input Shape	$(n\_steps, 1)$
Return Sequences (Layer 1)	True
Dropout (Layer 1)	0.1 (10%)
LSTM Units (Layer 2)	50
Return Sequences (Layer 2)	False
Dropout (Layer 2)	0.1 (10%)
Dense Units (Hidden)	50
Activation Function (Hidden)	ReLU
Dense Units (Output)	2
Optimizer	Adam
Loss Function	MSE (Mean Squared Error)
Batch size	32
Epochs	60
Validation Data	(X_test, y_test)

The network was trained along 60 epochs, that is, the number of times the entire training dataset is passed through the network; for that and to ensure that the model is trained correctly, the dataset was divided into training and test data, the split was configured so that 80% of the data are used for training and 20% for testing. It was observed that training with more epochs enables the model to learn better, but too many can lead to overfitting. Figure 12 shows the evolution of the model error as it is trained.

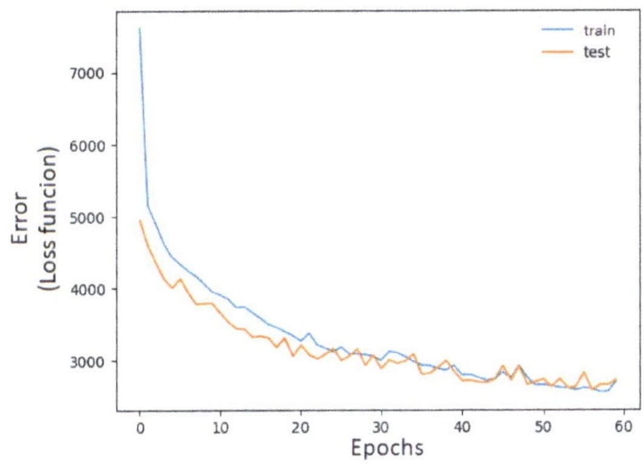

Figure 12. Evolution of the LSTM network's error during training.

The resulting controller is shown in Figure 13. Evidently, the PID controller and the anti-windup system were removed and replaced by the LSTM network.

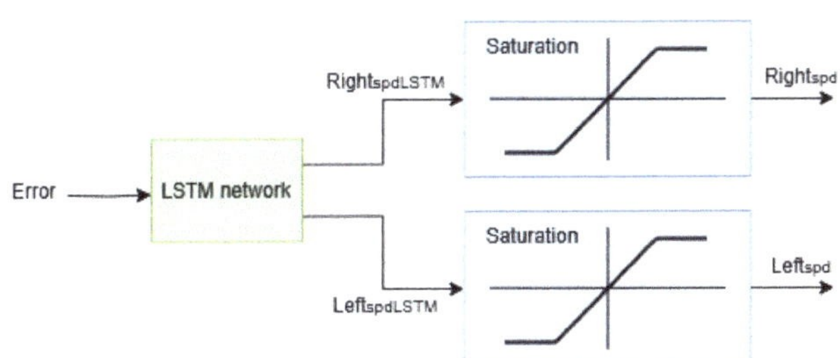

Figure 13. Block diagram of the implemented LSTM controller.

This approach enabled the robot to be controlled with a neural network using only infrared sensors as input. Its control is very similar to the PID control, which is expected, since data from that controller were used to train the neural network. However, existing similarities validate that the LSTM network was able to learn the associated patterns and temporal dependencies of the PID controller.

4.3. CNN

In the second experiment, the aim is to develop a platform for the robot to follow a line drawn on the ground using neural networks, as in the previous experiment, but using a camera. In this case, the Raspberry Pi camera mounted on the robot will point downward so that it can take successive images of the ground in front of it. These images will then be fed to a neural network that will control the robot movement along the path.

With this strategy, the use of an LSTM neural network would offer limited benefits compared to a CNN since the LSTM network was chosen for the previous experiment to simulate the behavior of the PID controller, which requires past information to calculate the new output. However, the use of real-time images to control the robot does not involve the temporal dependence found in the PID controller. However, the use of an LSTM network could easily, if configured with an incorrect number of steps for each sequence, lead to the network memorizing the path it was trained to follow, capable of causing the robot to behave abnormally or incorrectly if placed on a different track. For these reasons, a CNN was chosen.

As in the first experiment, a large amount of data is required to train the neural network. In this case, the data will be a large number of images taken by the robot itself, so it is necessary to develop a method for obtaining these images.

As mentioned, the first step is to take several images of the path and save them for use in neural network training. This will be completed following the steps outlined in the flowchart of Figure 14:

- **Camera initialization and positioning**: During initialization, the camera is configured to capture images and is positioned correctly for the task. Additionally, the positions of the servos connected to the camera are adjusted to ensure that the camera is aligned pointing straight down for accurate image capture;
- **Taking a new image**: In each iteration of the loop, a new image is captured from the camera (Figure 15). This continuous image acquisition is crucial for real-time image processing;
- **Image processing for line detection**: The process begins by converting the color image to grayscale (Figure 16), which simplifies the complexity of the image and improves the effectiveness of binary thresholding. Binary thresholding is then applied (Figure 17), where a threshold value transforms the image into a binary representation, highlighting the relevant pixels in black and white. To optimize processing, the image is then cropped to keep only the top part (Figure 18), thus reducing unnecessary areas and improving the detection of the desired line near the robot, which is essential for the control operation;
- **Save image**: After processing, the final image is saved to a file. The file path is generated dynamically and the image is saved in .jpg format.

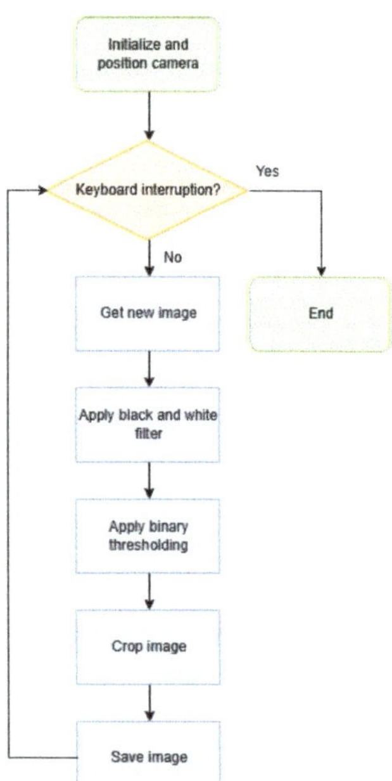

Figure 14. Process of capturing, processing, and saving images.

Figure 15. Example of a raw image.

Figure 16. Example of a grayscale image.

With this procedure, several images of the track are taken at different locations, positions, and angles to ensure that the neural network is trained to handle any situation the robot may encounter. The dataset has a size of 1800 images.

Figure 17. Example of an image with binary thresholding.

Figure 18. Example of a cropped final image.

With the dataset obtained, the next step is to classify the images so that they can be used to train the neural network. For this, each image will be assigned the action that the robot will have to complete. These actions will be divided into the categories listed in Table 4.

Table 4. Speed of the right and left motors for each category.

Category	Right Speed	Left Speed
forward	60	60
soft_left	50	70
soft_right	70	50
hard_left	30	90
hard_right	90	30
spin_left	−50	70
spin_right	70	−50
lost_line	-	-

The wheel speed values are between −255 and +255, where negative values cause the wheel to spin backward and positive values spin forward. Additionally, in the last category ('lost_line') corresponding to when the robot loses the line, the robot will move accordingly to the previous reading. So, if the vehicle was turning to the left on the previous reading, the robot, when losing the line, will spin to the left and vice versa to the right.

For the classification task, eight different folders were created, one with the name of each category, where all images taken in the previous step were manually classified. Although this classification method is simpler, it requires considerably more time. With this method, the robot will have eight different modes of operation. However, using more categories would lead to greater difficulty in classifying the *dataset* due to the greater ambiguity in distinguishing these categories.

With the dataset obtained and classified, it can finally be used to train the CNN network, as depicted in Figure 19:

- **Configure model**: In the first step, the CNN network is configured using the LeNet architecture, which is suitable for image classification tasks. The model is configured to receive 36 × 36-pixel grayscale images and classify them into one of eight categories, each representing a different driving command;
- **Load categorized images and assign labels**: The dataset containing images is loaded from the specified directories. Each image is read and resized to 36 × 36 pixels to match the input dimensions of the CNN. The images are stored in a list for further processing. The labels are derived from the directory structure: each folder corresponds to a driving command (e.g., 'forward' or 'soft_left'), which is then converted into numerical label;

- **Divide the dataset into training and test data**: To ensure a good generalization of the model, the dataset is split into training and test sets. The split is configured so that 75% of the data is used to train the model and the remaining 25% are reserved for testing. This split enables the model's performance to be assessed on data not observed after training;
- **Train the model**: The CNN is trained using the training data. To avoid overfitting, early stopping is implemented. This technique monitors validation loss and stops training if the model stops improving after a certain number of epochs, ensuring that the model does not overfit the training data and generalizes better;
- **Model evaluation**: After training, the model performance is evaluated by plotting the training and validation loss over iterations. These plots provide information on how well the model has learned to generalize. If the validation loss continues to decrease, this indicates that the model is improving;
- **Save the model**: Finally, after the model has been successfully trained, it is saved to disk. This enables the model to be used in the future.

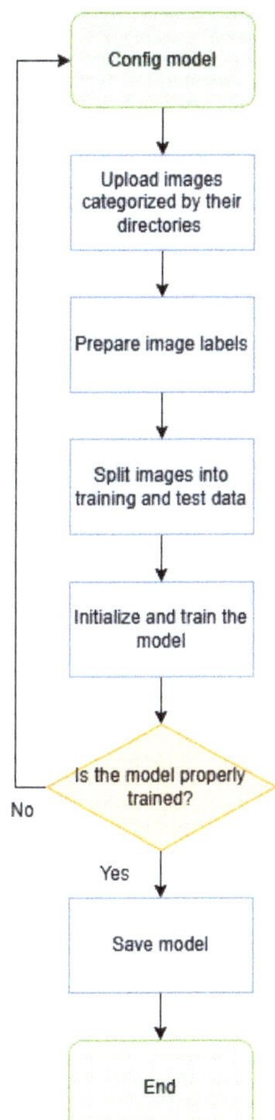

Figure 19. Process of training the CNN.

The CNN model used is shown in Figure 20, and its hyperparameters are provided in Table 5.

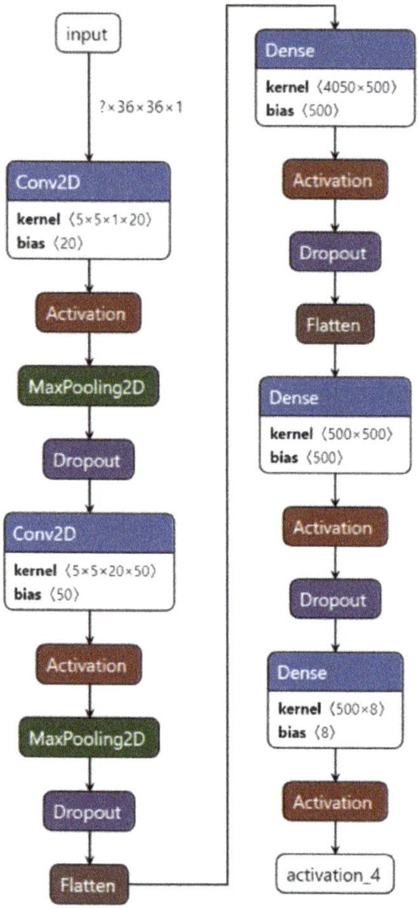

Figure 20. Structure of the CNN used.

Table 5. Hyperparameters of the LeNet model.

Hyperparameter	Value
Input Format	(height, width, depth)
Number of Convolutional Layers	2
Filters in First Convolutional Layer	20
Filters in Second Convolutional Layer	50
Filter Size (Both Convolutional Layers)	(5, 5)
Activation Function	ReLU
Pooling Size	(2, 2)
Pooling Stride	(2, 2)
Dropout (After Pooling Layers)	0.25
Dropout (Before Classification Layers)	0.5
Number of Dense Layers	2
Units in First Dense Layer	500

Table 5. *Cont.*

Hyperparameter	Value
Units in Second Dense Layer	500
Units in Output Layer	Number of classes
Output Activation Function	Softmax

As mentioned, an early stopping method has been set up during the training of the model, which will automatically evaluate the model's performance. If the validation error rises during three successive epochs, the model's training will be interrupted. The evolution of the model performance can be observed in Figure 21.

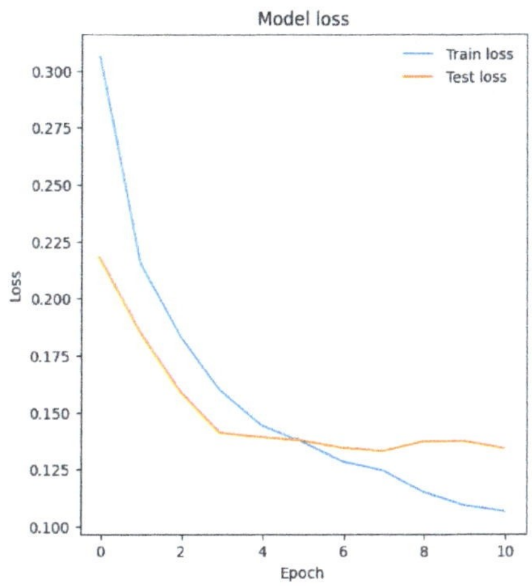

Figure 21. Evolution of the CNN error over the training.

Figure 22 shows the confusion matrix of the trained model, where each label value corresponds to the class indicated in Table 6. This shows how many times the model was able to correctly categorize the test data. Thus, the main diagonal shows the number of times the model correctly predicted the class, while the off-diagonal shows the number of times the model was incorrect, classifying one class as another. The performance of the system is satisfactory as it is able, in most cases, to correctly categorize the data with an accuracy (the ratio of correctly predicted instances (both positive and negative) to the total number of predictions) of 79.17%, precision (the ratio of correctly predicted positive observations to the total number of predicted positive observations) of 74.92%, recall (the ratio of correctly predicted positive observations to all actual positive observations) of 0.7375, and F1-score (the harmonic mean of accuracy and recall, providing a balance between the two) of 0.7360.

It should be noted that an accuracy target was not defined, as the objective was to strive for the highest accuracy possible within the scope and limitations of the project. Ultimately, the objective is that the robot is capable of navigating the track effectively and efficiently, which was met with an accuracy of 79.17%. Some ways to further improve this value would require more careful classification and a larger dataset.

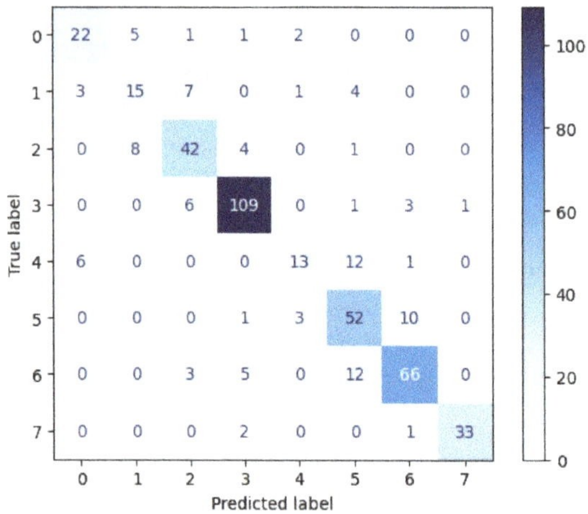

Figure 22. Confusion matrix of the CNN model.

Table 6. Number corresponding to each class of the CNN.

Class	Corresponding Label
forward	0
soft_left	1
hard_left	2
spin_left	3
soft_right	4
hard_right	5
spin_right	6
lost_line	7

5. Results

This section presents the results of the implemented control methods using pre-built tracks to assess their performance.

5.1. Tracks

For testing, experimentation, and validation of the control methods implemented, two tracks were built, as illustrated in Figure 23. Each track was built in such a way as to fit the control methods developed. Both tracks have the same length of 475 cm.

The second track (Figure 23b) was built on a white platform so that noise from the camera feed could be reduced since the use of the camera for data collection during the first experiment would be greatly affected by the dark color, texture, and shininess of the wooden floor. The attempt to use the first track (Figure 23a) resulted in noisy post-processing images, making it difficult to distinguish the black line from the image. Other more advanced filters could have been implemented in the image processing step to avoid this problem. However, adding these filters would increase the processing overhead of the control loop, increasing the control loop execution time, and thus further decreasing the sampling rate.

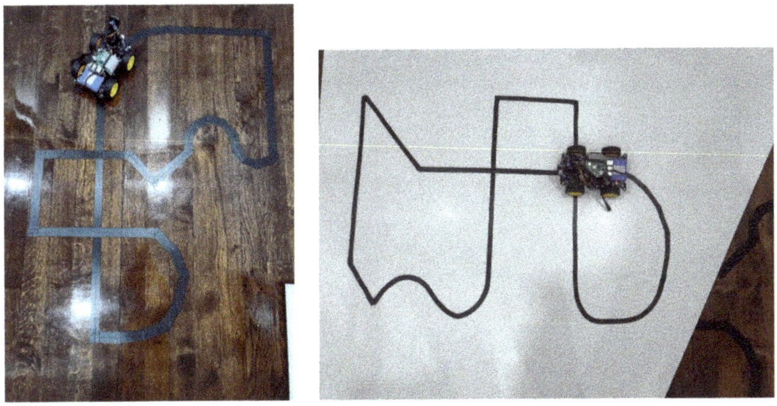

(a) (b)

Figure 23. (**a**) Track used for the first experiment and (**b**) track used for the second experiment.

5.2. PID

The performance of the PID control method is shown in Figure 24. For this experiment, the first track was used (Figure 23a). The figure illustrates the plots of the error, the output value of the PID with its terms P, I, and D, and the antiwindup effect over one lap of the track.

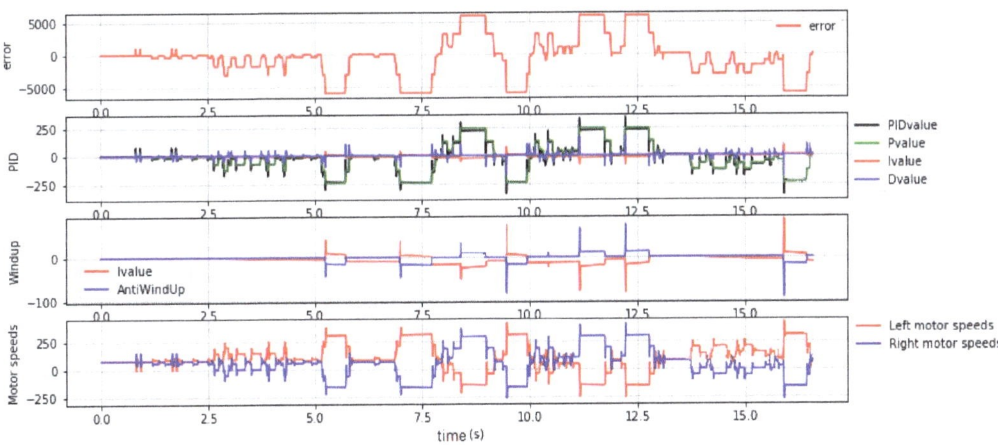

Figure 24. Plots of the error, PID terms, and corresponding output with the anti-windup scheme over one lap of the track.

5.3. LSTM

Figure 25 shows the results of the control with the LSTM network and the motor speeds on one lap of the track. The first plot displays the error in the infrared sensor readings, while the second plot shows the predictions generated by the LSTM network. Unlike the PID controller, where the new calculated value is added to or subtracted from the wheel speeds, the LSTM network directly outputs the wheel speeds. To compare the performance of both control methods, a reverse operation was performed: using the new wheel speeds, an approximate equivalent of the PID value was calculated. However, it is important to note that this approximation does not perfectly correspond to the actual PID value as the LSTM network is trained to emulate the behavior of the PID controller rather than replicate its calculations exactly. In fact, comparing the two control methods, we can see that both are quite similar, as shown in Figure 26. Although some similarities can be observed, the differences in the initial conditions and variations throughout the experiment, even when using the same path, lead to notable differences between the two experiments.

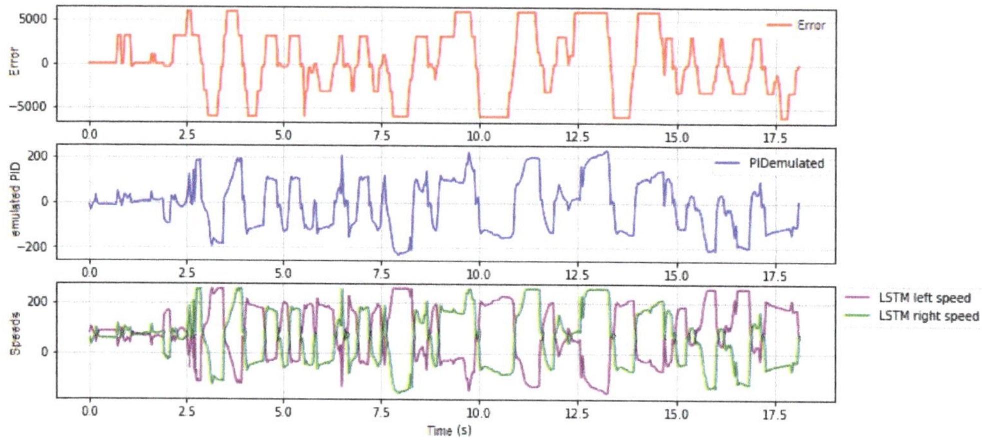

Figure 25. Plots of the control with the LSTM network and the motor speeds over one lap of the track.

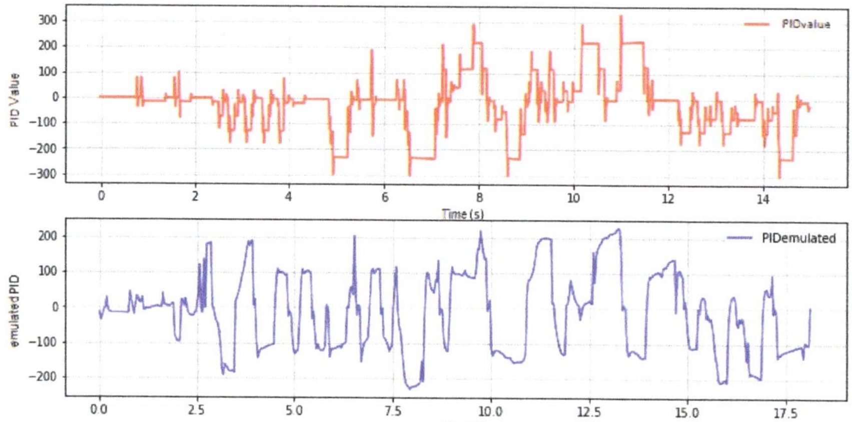

Figure 26. Comparison of the output of the PID and LSTM controllers.

5.4. CNN

The performance of the previous model was influenced by environmental and operational factors, which required adjustments to optimize behavior. One of the first changes was to replace the original track, placed on a shiny wooden floor that generated noise in the images, with a high-contrast black and white track (Figure 23b), which increased accuracy.

The lighting was also crucial because good lighting helps with track detection, but too much could cause excessive reflections. Adjusting the light intensity proved to be essential for consistent performance. Other sources of uncertainty can be attributed to the classification; as it was conducted manually, the ambiguity between classes led to some inaccuracy while classifying. The dataset could also be larger, which could result in a more accurate model with fewer errors.

Due to the high computational load of real-time image processing, the sampling rate was reduced to 24 frames per second, which required slowing down the robot to ensure that it had time to react to the track.

Figure 27 shows the graphs of the motor speeds and the CNN output over one lap of the track.

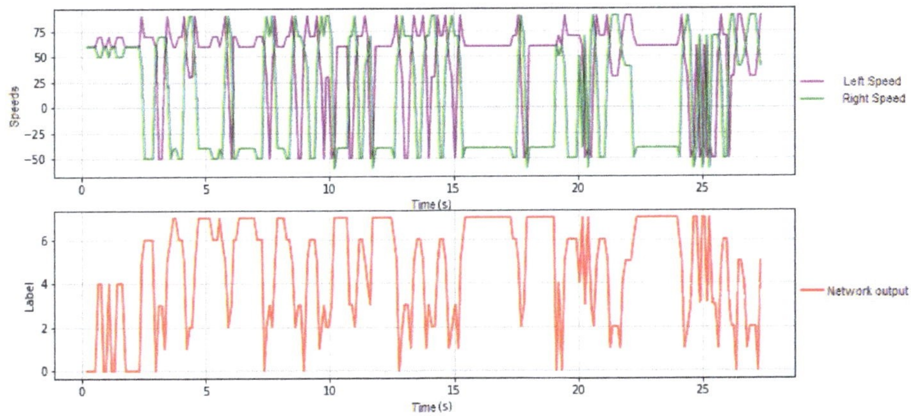

Figure 27. Plots of the motor speeds and the output of the CNN over one lap of the track.

6. Discussion

In general, all the methods used were able to efficiently control the robot along a line drawn on the ground. Consequently, both the PID controller and the LSTM and CNN networks proved to be feasible approaches for this type of control. However, due to the simple nature of the proposed line-following robot, PID control was revealed to be the most effective.

It was observed that, while the PID controller is the most efficient method, it is not perfect as it cannot overcome some obstacles on the track, such as sharp angles, which the CNN network can handle more easily. This shows that, although PID has more advantages over the other methods in the line-following experiment, neural networks and deep learning are powerful tools that can be used in more complex scenarios.

Since the control methods are quite different from each other, it is difficult to obtain common metrics to compare the performance between them. Table 7 shows the error performance indices of Mean Squared Error (MSE), Mean Absolute Error (MAE), Root Mean Squared Error (RMSE), the time taken for each method to cover one lap of the track and the robot oscillations along the path. The sign "+" indicates the level of oscillations; the higher the number of "+", the greater the oscillation. These data were obtained by running each method five times and obtaining the average values and standard deviations for each of the control methods. As the values obtained in each test run were quite consistent between each other, the somewhat arbitrary number of five test runs for each method was chosen. This value represents a fair equilibrium between the execution time required to execute each run and the variation in the standard deviation.

Table 7. Performance results.

Method	MSE	MAE	RMSE	Lap Time (s)	Oscillations
PID	10,684,111 ± 515,855	2257 ± 71	3267 ± 79	16.40 ± 0.22	+
LSTM	17,158,701 ± 1,598,305	3435 ± 242	4137 ± 192	20.53 ± 1.04	+++
CNN	21,040,166 ± 1,186,665	3857 ± 188	4585 ± 128	25.96 ± 0.29	++

As mentioned, in a central position, the error of the sensor reading is 0, while when it loses the line, the error becomes ±6000, with any value in this range defining an intermediate position value. With this approach, the error values, especially the MAE, of the PID controller are quite good compared to the other methods. Although the LSTM method exhibits higher errors, it is still satisfactory when evaluated against the other controllers.

It should be noted that the indices for the CNN method do not accurately reflect the network's performance because it does not use the infrared sensors for control that were used to calculate the error, but rather the camera, so the infrared sensors may not align with the line. In addition, as the line in the second path is less wide, in a central position, no sensor would detect the line, which will cause an increase in error.

Furthermore, the sample rate of each method was also measured, that is, how many samples each method can evaluate from the sensors and return new motor speeds. The sample rate was set to the highest value that the processor could handle. The PID method had a sample rate of 80 Hz, LSTM 25 Hz, and CNN 24 Hz.

7. Conclusions

This paper investigated the use of neural networks in the control of a mobile line-follower robot using the LSTM and CNN approaches.

Various control methods based on deep learning and PID were developed and tested on the robot, resulting in a comparative analysis between the techniques. This comparison demonstrated the advantages of neural networks for complex paths despite their greater sensitivity to factors such as lighting and computational load, which required a reduced sampling rate and limited speed.

The first approach, based on infrared sensors and using an LSTM model, proved to be efficient for simple paths, with a higher sampling rate and reduced dependence on environmental conditions. The second approach, which used a camera and a CNN, was more effective for complex paths but revealed to be sensitive to noise and reflections from the environment, requiring careful calibration. Another source of uncertainty was the classification process, which, being performed manually, is not free from biases.

Compared to the PID controller, neural networks showed better adaptation to difficult paths but with high computational complexity. PID remains practical for simple controlled paths, while neural networks offer great potential for AGVs in dynamic and unpredictable scenarios.

For future work, we can consider creating a simulation environment that allows us to test different scenarios, tracks, and configurations more quickly and under controlled conditions, thus reducing time and resources. The use of non-linear controllers over the traditional linear PID controllers could be an interesting research area. For better performance and reliability, a hybrid approach could be used that combines the neural networks of LSTM and CNN with the mathematical model of the robot. Another improvement would be the use of pre-trained networks, such as those trained on large datasets for autonomous navigation or path detection. To achieve this, the use of transfer learning (adapting an already trained network for new tasks) could significantly reduce training time and improve model accuracy under certain conditions. Testing the robot in more complex environments, simulating industrial or urban scenarios, would also make it possible to validate the robustness of the models under more realistic and demanding conditions.

Author Contributions: Conceptualization, H.M.L. and R.S.B.; methodology, H.M.L. and R.S.B.; software, H.M.L.; validation, H.M.L. and R.S.B.; formal analysis, H.M.L.; investigation, H.M.L.; writing—original draft preparation, H.M.L.; writing—review and editing, H.M.L., R.S.B. and I.S.J.; visualization, H.M.L.; supervision, R.S.B. and I.S.J. All authors have read and agreed to the published version of the manuscript.

Funding: This research received no external funding.

Data Availability Statement: The original data presented in the study are openly available from GitHub repository at https://github.com/HugoMLeal/TEDI1190660 (accessed on 13 January 2025).

Conflicts of Interest: The authors declare no conflicts of interest.

References

1. Jain, N.; Kumar, R. A Review on Machine Learning and It's Algorithms. *Int. J. Soft Comput. Eng.* **2022**, *12*, 399–406. [CrossRef]
2. Sarker, I. Deep Learning: A Comprehensive Overview on Techniques, Taxonomy, Applications and Research Directions. *SN Comput. Sci.* **2021**, *2*, 420. [CrossRef] [PubMed]
3. LeCun, Y.B. Deep learning. *Nature* **2015**, *521*, 436–444. [CrossRef] [PubMed]
4. Moshayedi, A.; Li, J.; Liao, L. AGV (automated guided vehicle) robot: Mission and obstacles in design and performance. *J. Simul. Anal. Nov. Technol. Mech. Eng.* **2019**, *12*, 5–18.
5. Wong, C.; Soon, C. A Bluetooth and Vision Controlled Automatic Guided Vehicle. *Emerg. Adv. Integr. Technol.* **2022**, *3*, 53–63. Available online: https://publisher.uthm.edu.my/ojs/index.php/emait/article/view/11856 (accessed on 12 October 2024).
6. Lin, K.; Chen, H.; Li, G.; Tu, J.; Huang, S. Automatic Guided Vehicle with Artificial Intelligence Navigation. In Proceedings of the 2019 IEEE International Conference On Consumer Electronics—Taiwan (ICCE-TW), Taiwan, China, 20–22 May 2019; pp. 1–2.
7. Roche, J.; De-Silva, V.; Kondoz, A. A Multimodal Perception-Driven Self Evolving Autonomous Ground Vehicle. *IEEE Trans. Cybern.* **2022**, *52*, 9279–9289. [CrossRef] [PubMed]
8. Aryanti, A.; Wang, M.; Muslikhin, M. Navigating Unstructured Space: Deep Action Learning-Based Obstacle Avoidance System for Indoor Automated Guided Vehicles. *Electronics* **2024**, *13*, 420. Available online: https://api.semanticscholar.org/CorpusID:267145921 (accessed on 12 October 2024). [CrossRef]
9. Li, X.; Rao, W.; Lu, D.; Guo, J.; Guo, T.; Andriukaitis, D.; Li, Z. Obstacle Avoidance for Automated Guided Vehicles in Real-World Workshops Using the Grid Method and Deep Learning. *Electronics* **2023**, *12*, 4296. Available online: https://api.semanticscholar.org/CorpusID:264328025 (accessed on 12 October 2024). [CrossRef]
10. Chen, Y.; Li, D.; Zhong, H.; Zhao, R. The Method for Automatic Adjustment of AGV's PID Based on Deep Reinforcement Learning. *J. Phys. Conf. Ser.* **2022**, *2320*, 012008. Available online: https://api.semanticscholar.org/CorpusID:251515556 (accessed on 12 October 2024). [CrossRef]
11. Simon, J.; Trojanová, M.; Hovsovská, A.; Sárosi, J. Neural Network Driven Automated Guided Vehicle Platform Development for Industry 4.0 Environment. *Teh.-Vjesn.-Tech. Gaz.* **2021**, *28*, 1936–1942. Available online: https://api.semanticscholar.org/CorpusID:243855693 (accessed on 12 October 2024).
12. Carrio, A.; Sampedro, C.; Rodriguez-Ramos, A.; Campoy, P. A Review of Deep Learning Methods and Applications for Unmanned Aerial Vehicles. *J. Sens.* **2017**, *2017*, 3296874. Available online: https://onlinelibrary.wiley.com/doi/abs/10.1155/2017/3296874 (accessed on 12 October 2024). [CrossRef]
13. Bałazy, P.; Gut, P.; Knap, P. Positioning algorithm for AGV autonomous driving platform based on artificial neural networks. *Robot. Syst. Appl.* **2021**, *1*, 41–45. Available online: https://api.semanticscholar.org/CorpusID:237210213 (accessed on 12 October 2024). [CrossRef]
14. Xue, H.; Hein, B.; Bakr, M.; Schildbach, G.; Abel, B.; Rueckert, E. Using Deep Reinforcement Learning with Automatic Curriculum earning for Mapless Navigation in Intralogistics. *arXiv* **2022**, arXiv:abs/2202.11512. Available online: https://api.semanticscholar.org/CorpusID:247058694 (accessed on 12 October 2024).
15. Raspbot Repository. Available online: http://www.yahboom.net/study/Raspbot (accessed on 20 November 2024).
16. TTmotors. Available online: https://www.ttmotor.com/10-20mm/ (accessed on 13 January 2025).
17. Einstronic. Available online: https://einstronic.com/product/sg90-micro-servo-motor/ (accessed on 13 January 2025).
18. Raspberry Pi Hardware. Available online: https://www.raspberrypi.com/products/ (accessed on 20 November 2024).
19. NVIDIA. Available online: https://www.nvidia.com/en-eu/geforce/graphics-cards/30-series/rtx-3060-3060ti/ (accessed on 13 January 2025).

20. AMD. Available online: https://www.amd.com/en/support/downloads/drivers.html/processors/ryzen/ryzen-3000-series/amd-ryzen-7-3700x.html#amd_support_product_spec (accessed on 13 January 2025).
21. Anaconda Enterprise 4 Repository. Available online: https://docs.anaconda.com/anaconda-repository/ (accessed on 18 December 2024).
22. Zhang, A.; Li, M.; Smola, A.J.; Lipton, Z. *Dive into Deep Learning*; Cambridge University Press: Cambridge, UK, 2023. Available online: https://D2L.ai (accessed on 27 November 2024).
23. Abdullahi, Z.; Danzomo, B.; Abdullahi, Z. Design and Simulation of a PID Controller for Motion Control Systems. *Iop Conf. Ser. Mater. Sci. Eng.* **2018**, *344*, 012016. [CrossRef]
24. Tehrani, K.; Mpanda, A. PID Control Theory. 2012. Available online: https://api.semanticscholar.org/CorpusID:9908243 (accessed on 13 October 2024).
25. Inc, M. AVR221: Discrete PID Controller on tinyAVR and megaAVR Devices. Available online: https://www.ni.com/docs/en-US/bundle/labview/page/fuzzy-controllers.html (accessed on 12 March 2024).
26. Jesus, I.S.; Barbosa, R.S. Genetic optimization of fuzzy fractional PD+I controllers. In *ISA Transactions*; Elsevier: Amsterdam, The Netherlands, 2015; Volume 57, pp. 220–230.
27. Dorf, R.C.; Bishop, R.H. *Modern Control Systems*, 14th ed.; Pearson Education: London, UK, 2022.
28. Aboelhassan, A.; Abdel-Geliel, M.; Zakzouk, E.; Galea, M. Design and Implementation of Model Predictive Control Based PID Controller for Industrial Applications. *Energies* **2020**, *13*, 6594. Available online: https://api.semanticscholar.org/CorpusID:230600853 (accessed on 13 October 2024). [CrossRef]
29. Åström, K.J.; Hägglund, T. *PID Controllers: Theory Design and Tuning*; ISA Press: Research Triangle Park, NC, USA, 1995.
30. Hochreiter, S.; Schmidhuber, J. Long Short-Term Memory. *Neural Comput.* **1997**, *9*, 1735–1780. Available online: https://api.semanticscholar.org/CorpusID:1915014 (accessed on 13 October 2024). [CrossRef] [PubMed]
31. colah's Blog: Understanding LSTM Networks. Available online: https://colah.github.io/posts/2015-08-Understanding-LSTMs/ (accessed on 26 December 2024).
32. Sak, H.; Senior, A.; Beaufays, F. Long short-term memory recurrent neural network architectures for large scale acoustic modeling. *arXiv* **2014**, arXiv:1402.1128.
33. Alzubaidi, L.; Zhang, J.; Humaidi, A.; Al-dujaili, A.; Duan, Y.; Al-Shamma, O.; Santamaría, J.; Fadhel, M.; Al-Amidie, M.; Farhan, L. Review of deep learning: Concepts, CNN architectures, challenges, applications, future directions. *J. Big Data* **2021**, *8*, 53. Available online: https://api.semanticscholar.org/CorpusID:232434552 (accessed on 14 October 2024). [CrossRef] [PubMed]
34. Upreti, A. Convolutional Neural Network (CNN): A comprehensive overview. *Int. J. Multidiscip. Res. Growth Eval.* **2022**, *3*, 488–493. Available online: https://api.semanticscholar.org/CorpusID:251888217 (accessed on 14 October 2024). [CrossRef]

algorithms

MDPI

Article

Stability Analysis and Experimental Validation of Standard Proportional-Integral-Derivative Control in Bilateral Teleoperators with Time-Varying Delays

Marco A. Arteaga [1], Evert J. Guajardo-Benavides [1] and Pablo Sánchez-Sánchez [2,*]

[1] Departamento de Control y Robótica, División de Ingeniería Eléctrica, Facultad de Ingeniería, Universidad Nacional Autónoma de México (UNAM), Mexico City 04510, Mexico; marteagp@unam.mx (M.A.A.); evert_guajardobds@comunidad.unam.mx (E.J.G.-B.)

[2] Departamento de Robótica y Control, Facultad de Ciencias de la Electrónica (FCE), Benemérita Universidad Autónoma de Puebla (BUAP), Puebla 72570, Mexico

* Correspondence: pablo.sanchez@correo.buap.mx

Abstract: The control of bilateral teleoperation systems with time-varying delays is a challenging problem that is frequently addressed with advanced control techniques. Widely known controllers, like Proportional-Derivative (PD) and Proportional-Integral-Derivative (PID), are seldom employed independently and are typically combined with other approaches, or at least with gravity compensation. This work aims to address a gap in the analysis of bilateral systems by demonstrating that the standard PID control law alone can achieve regulation in these systems when a human operator moves any of the robots while exchanging delayed positions. Experimental results are consistent with the theoretical analysis. Additionally, to illustrate the high degree of robustness of the standard PID, further experiments are conducted in constrained motion, both with and without force feedback.

Keywords: bilateral systems; time-varying delays; robot manipulators; PID controllers; robustness

1. Introduction

Bilateral local-remote (or master-slave) systems allow people to perform complex tasks in a remote, inaccessible, or dangerous environment [1,2]. The capabilities of a bilateral teleoperation system rely on the exchange of measured positions, velocities, and, if necessary, force data. Recent studies have addressed these challenges in bilateral teleoperation systems.

For instance, Ref. [3] introduced a teleoperation algorithm that combines delayed and undelayed position and velocity signals of the master and slave manipulators, employing an adaptation law to compensate for time-varying delays. Similarly, Ref. [4] investigated bilateral control of teleoperators with a closed architecture, proposing adaptive kinematic and dynamic controllers robust to arbitrary bounded time-varying delays. However, the local and remote manipulators are connected via a communication channel, which can result in substantial delays between the command induced by the human operator and the moment this command is received by the remote robot, not to mention that the information the latter sends back also endures a time delay [5,6].

Time-varying delays are a critical factor in many real-world teleoperation scenarios. These delays often arise from network instability, bandwidth limitations, or fluctuating latency in communication channels, which are commonly encountered in remote or hazardous environments. For example, in industrial applications, high latency may result from long-distance data transmission, while in medical or underwater teleoperation, signal interference or environmental factors can lead to variable delays. Addressing these challenges requires robust control strategies that ensure stability and performance under such uncertain conditions.

The present study incorporates time-varying delays to model these practical challenges and demonstrates how the proposed PID controller effectively handles them, as supported by [7]. Due to the inherent delay characteristics, neither exact tracking position nor transparency in teleoperation can be achieved. For this reason, many control approaches are designed to guarantee only position regulation.

The problem of bilateral systems with time-varying delays is so complex and demanding that most solutions found in the literature are based on advanced control techniques. Just to mention a few recent works as illustrative examples rather than as a deep survey, in [8], a robust adaptive nonlinear teleoperation system using an improved extended active observer, an adaptive Smith predictor, and a sliding mode control is proposed to handle time delays in the communication channel and the nonlinear robot model uncertainties. Recent studies, such as the extended dissipative analysis of affine-transformed interval type-2 (IT2) fuzzy control systems with time delay and disturbances [9], have explored advanced control techniques to address time-delay challenges. These approaches focus on enhancing system performance and robustness through sophisticated methods. While such methods provide significant improvements, they often come with increased computational complexity. In contrast, the present study validates the application of a standard PID controller, offering a simpler and more practical solution for scenarios where extreme precision is not required but robustness and simplicity are prioritized.

Furthermore, Ref. [10] analyzed the impact of sampling effects on the absolute stability of discrete-time bilateral teleoperation systems, highlighting the importance of appropriate sampling periods in maintaining system stability. Additionally, Ref. [11] proposed a position and force tracking control based on force estimation, utilizing a time-delay state observer to estimate system state variables affected by delays. The research in [12] introduced an adaptive PD control method using deep reinforcement learning to compensate for stochastic time delays in local-remote teleoperation systems. Similarly, in [13], an adaptive observer-based scaled four-channel control approach, applying damping injection for nonlinear teleoperation systems, is presented. This approach unifies the study of robotic dynamic uncertainties, operator/environment force acquisitions, and asymmetric time-varying delays. In [14], a bounded force feedback control law is introduced to improve transparency in nonlinear bilateral teleoperation systems in the presence of input saturation, asymmetric time-varying communication delays, and parametric uncertainties. The proposed controller is a nonlinear proportional plus nonlinear damping controller with the addition of an adaptive term.

Another widely employed technique is Neural Networks (NNs). For instance, in [15], an NN-based four-channel wave-based time domain passivity approach (TDPA) is proposed for a teleoperation system with time-varying delays. The applied NN is used to eliminate the system's dynamic uncertainties. Under the linearity assumption on the human and environment, the stability analysis is carried out by using the Lyapunov method.

In [16], a control scheme is developed for a teleoperation system, combining radial basis function neural networks (RBFNNs) and wave variable techniques to simultaneously compensate for the effects caused by communication delays and dynamical uncertainties. To overcome the potential instability problem in the presence of delayed communication channels, wave variables and their corrections are effectively embedded in the control system, and a Lyapunov-based analysis is performed to theoretically establish the closed-loop stability. In [17], an adaptive control architecture based on velocity feedback filters and RBFNNs is proposed to achieve stable and effective position synchronization control for bilateral systems with time-varying delays. In [18], an adaptive neural learning fixed-time control scheme incorporating an integral barrier Lyapunov function is proposed, while NNs are utilized to reconstruct environmental forces and to approximate the total uncertainty introduced by robots and the environment.

In [19], the problem of position synchronization for master-slave robots is solved by using an RBFNN together with adaptive control methods to deal with the system uncertainties. Furthermore, the design of virtual variables can effectively compensate for the effect of time-varying delays. In [20], a finite-time control method is designed on the basis of the traditional proportional damping injection control by introducing a non-integer power to the position error, velocity, and the combined error with position error and velocity. The controller also incorporates an RBFNN and an adaptive approach to compensate for unknown dynamics and external forces, thus avoiding the measurement of force signals.

Another methodology frequently used is Fuzzy Logic (FL). For instance, in [21], data-driven Type-2 Takagi-Sugeno (T-S) fuzzy modeling and control for bilateral teleoperation with dynamic uncertainties and time-varying delays is developed. The Type-2 T-S fuzzy model describes the nonlinear teleoperation system by a weighted sum of a group of linear local models. Fuzzy model-based four-channel control laws are proposed to guarantee motion synchronization and to enhance the operator's force perception of the environment when time-varying delays and large dynamic uncertainties exist.

In [22], a predictive control method for a bimanual teleoperation system without force/torque and acceleration sensors is proposed. By accurately estimating the local force, position predictors/observers are used to estimate the internal dynamics of the master and slave simultaneously, thereby avoiding the use of delayed transmitted information. An adaptive fuzzy control strategy based on linear matrix inequalities (LMIs) is proposed to evaluate and suppress system uncertainties.

In [23], a combination of a force observer using Type-2 Fuzzy Neural Network (T2FNN) and Moving Horizon Estimation (MHE) is proposed to estimate the external force/torque and simultaneously filter out disturbances in bilateral teleoperation systems. Applying the estimated forces, an external force-regulated Sliding Mode Control (SMC) strategy with the support of machine vision is proposed to enhance the adaptability of the slave robot and improve the perception of the operator about various scenarios by virtue of the detected location of the task object.

In [24], a method based on a robust adaptive fuzzy control approach is developed for nonlinear teleoperation systems with time-varying delays. It has been proven that both position tracking and force feedback problems are solved.

SMC techniques have also been applied in many works. For example, in [25,26], sliding mode-based finite-time synchronization algorithms for bilateral teleoperation systems under unsymmetrical time-varying delays and uncertainties are presented.

In [27], a position/force hybrid control strategy is proposed for a class of uncertain bilateral telerobotic systems under time-varying communication delays without using force sensors. The proposed Terminal Sliding Mode (TSM)-based force observer can estimate the human force and the environment force in a fixed time by applying a variable exponent coefficient, which effectively avoids the temporal problems of other existing force observers.

In contrast with all previous works, most basic control techniques are scarcely used in the control of bilateral systems with time-varying delays. This fact is easy to understand in view of the complexity of the problem. Despite these advancements, the application of standard Proportional-Integral-Derivative (PID) controllers in bilateral teleoperation systems with time-varying delays remains underexplored.

This study aims to fill this gap by providing a technical stability proof demonstrating that Standard Proportional-Integral-Derivative (PID) control can effectively regulate position in such systems, even in the presence of time-varying delays.

Let us recall that for a single manipulator, it is very well-known that a simple Proportional-Derivative (PD) control law is enough to achieve exact regulation if gravity terms are cancelled out. In cases where the gravity term is unknown, exact regulation can be carried out by implementing a Standard Proportional-Integral-Derivative (PID) controller [28–30].

For the case of PD controllers, the extension for bilateral systems finds a first result in [5], where a PD control law plus gravity compensation is employed to show consensus for bilateral systems with constant and symmetric time delays. An extension for time-varying delays can also be found in [31], but still, gravity compensation is necessary. The obvious solution to avoid gravity compensation is to employ PID controllers; yet, no technical proof has been established in the literature to support its use on bilateral systems with time-varying delays.

For instance, in [32], the case is analyzed but only for time-constant delays. Furthermore, the implementation requires the exchange not only of positions but also of velocities. In [33], the use of PID controllers is studied, but once again, constant time delays are considered, and instead of the highly nonlinear dynamics of robot manipulators, simple linear transfer functions are considered.

More recently, in [34], the even more complex case of consensus for networked Euler-Lagrange agents using a PID-like controller was solved. However, achieving a robust global stability result requires the use of strictly increasing linear saturation functions and some auxiliary variables. In [35], a simpler PID-like control law with observer design to solve the consensus and force reflection problems was proposed. However, the integral terms utilize a second-order sliding mode variable, and the stability result is only local.

In a recent work [36], a standard PID controller has been used for the control of a 2-DOF teleoperated manipulator; however, no stability proof is provided, and the PID gains are found by using the well-known Ziegler-Nichols approach.

This result is not surprising since, despite the lack of theoretical results, it has recently been shown that standard PID controllers exhibit strong robustness properties for nonlinear systems [37].

The main contribution of the present work is the following:

1. This work presents a novel technical proof demonstrating the closed-loop stability of PID laws in the control of bilateral systems with time-varying delays, addressing an aspect not previously established in the literature.

The proposed theoretical framework was validated using these experimental procedures:

(a) The theory is tested by setting gains according to the main theorem of this contribution, and letting a human operator move both local and remote end-effectors to constant positions.
(b) The well-known robustness properties of PID controllers are shown by carrying out experiments involving constrained motion of the remote manipulator, both with and without force feedback.

The rest of the paper is organized as follows. The system's model and some properties are given in Section 2. The main theorem about closed-loop stability of bilateral robot manipulators in free motion using standard PID control laws is stated in Section 3. Section 4 presents experimental results to validate the developed theory. The paper concludes in Section 5.

2. Dynamic Model of a Teleoperator System

Consider a bilateral robotic system, consisting of a local (l) and a remote (r) manipulator, each with n degrees of freedom (DOF), assuming for simplicity that all joints are revolute. The dynamics of the bilateral system are described by the following equation [30]:

$$\boldsymbol{H}_i(\boldsymbol{q}_i)\ddot{\boldsymbol{q}}_i + \boldsymbol{C}_i(\boldsymbol{q}_i, \dot{\boldsymbol{q}}_i)\dot{\boldsymbol{q}}_i + \boldsymbol{g}_i(\boldsymbol{q}_i) = \boldsymbol{u}_i + \boldsymbol{\tau}_{\mathrm{h}i} = \boldsymbol{u}_{\tau i}, \tag{1}$$

where, for $i = \mathrm{l}, \mathrm{r}$, $\boldsymbol{q}_i \in \mathbb{R}^n$ represents the vector of generalized joint coordinates, $\boldsymbol{H}_i(\boldsymbol{q}_i) \in \mathbb{R}^{n\times n}$ is the symmetric, positive-definite inertia matrix, $\boldsymbol{C}_i(\boldsymbol{q}_i, \dot{\boldsymbol{q}}_i)\dot{\boldsymbol{q}}_i \in \mathbb{R}^n$ represents the vector of Coriolis and centrifugal torques, and $\boldsymbol{g}_i(\boldsymbol{q}_i) \in \mathbb{R}^n$ denotes the gravitational torque vector. The control torques applied to the joints are given by $\boldsymbol{u}_i \in \mathbb{R}^n$, while $\boldsymbol{\tau}_{\mathrm{h}i} \in \mathbb{R}^n$ represents the torque applied by the human operator. Importantly, if $\boldsymbol{\tau}_{\mathrm{hl}} \neq \boldsymbol{0}$, then $\boldsymbol{\tau}_{\mathrm{hr}} \equiv \boldsymbol{0}$, and vice versa, ensuring that the human operator interacts with only one manipulator at a time. Finally, $\boldsymbol{u}_{\tau i}$ denotes the total torque applied to the system.

The largest and smallest eigenvalues of a matrix are denoted by $\lambda_{\max}(\cdot)$ and $\lambda_{\min}(\cdot)$, respectively.

By considering that only revolute joints are involved, the following properties can be established [30]:

Property 1. *It holds* $\lambda_{hi}\|\boldsymbol{x}\|^2 \leq \boldsymbol{x}^{\mathrm{T}}\boldsymbol{H}_i(\boldsymbol{q}_i)\boldsymbol{x} \leq \lambda_{Hi}\|\boldsymbol{x}\|^2 \; \forall \; \boldsymbol{q}_i \in \mathbb{R}^n, \boldsymbol{x} \in \mathbb{R}^n$, *and* $0 < \lambda_{hi} \leq \lambda_{Hi} < \infty$, *with* $\lambda_{hi} \triangleq \min_{\boldsymbol{q}_i \in \mathbb{R}^n} \lambda_{\min}\left(\boldsymbol{H}_i(\boldsymbol{q}_i)\right)$ *and* $\lambda_{Hi} \triangleq \max_{\boldsymbol{q}_i \in \mathbb{R}^n} \lambda_{\max}\left(\boldsymbol{H}_i(\boldsymbol{q}_i)\right)$. $\lambda_{\min}$ *and* $\lambda_{\max}$ *denote the minimum and maximum eigenvalues of a matrix.*

Property 2. *By using the Christoffel symbols of the first kind to compute* $\boldsymbol{C}_i(\boldsymbol{q}_i, \dot{\boldsymbol{q}}_i)$, *the matrix* $\dot{\boldsymbol{H}}_i(\boldsymbol{q}_i) - 2\boldsymbol{C}_i(\boldsymbol{q}_i, \dot{\boldsymbol{q}}_i)$ *is skew-symmetric.*

Property 3. *There exist positive constants* $0 < k_{ci} < \infty$, *such that* $\|\boldsymbol{C}_i(\boldsymbol{q}_i, \boldsymbol{x})\| \leq k_{ci}\|\boldsymbol{x}\|$ *holds* $\forall$ $\boldsymbol{x}, \boldsymbol{q}_i \in \mathbb{R}^n$.

Property 4. *The vector of the generalized gravitational torques* $\boldsymbol{g}_i(\boldsymbol{q}_i)$ *satisfies*

$$\|\boldsymbol{g}_i(\boldsymbol{q}_{i1}) - \boldsymbol{g}_i(\boldsymbol{q}_{i2})\| \leq k_{gi}\|\boldsymbol{q}_{i1} - \boldsymbol{q}_{i2}\| \quad \forall \boldsymbol{q}_{i1}, \boldsymbol{q}_{i2} \in \mathbb{R}^n, \tag{2}$$

for some positive constant k_{gi}.

The time-varying delay from the local to the remote robot is denoted by $T_l(t)$, whereas the delay in the opposite direction is represented by $T_r(t)$. The following assumptions are considered:

Assumption 1. *The initial states of* $T_l(t)$ *and* $T_r(t)$ *are assumed to be zero or small constant values, i.e.,,* $T_l(t_0) = T_r(t_0) \approx 0$. *This assumption ensures continuity in the delay dynamics, allowing for a smooth initialization of the system.*

Assumption 2. *The time-varying delay* $T_i(t)$ *is positive or zero, and it is bounded as well as its first and second derivatives,* $\dot{T}_i(t)$ *and* $\ddot{T}_i(t)$, *respectively, i.e.,,* $0 \leq T_i(t) \leq \overline{T}_i < \infty, 0 \leq |\dot{T}_i(t)| \leq T_i^* < \infty$, *and* $0 \leq |\ddot{T}_i(t)| \leq T_i^{**} < \infty$, *for* $i = l, r$. *Furthermore, the upper bound* T_i^* *is known.*

Remark 1. *Higher frequencies in the time delays result in larger bounds for their derivatives, which may, in turn, affect the stability of the closed-loop system by necessitating higher control gains to ensure stability. Nevertheless, it is typically assumed that* $T_i^* < 1$ *[38].*

The following notation is used throughout this work. The symbol $\|\boldsymbol{x}\|$ represents the standard Euclidean norm when $\boldsymbol{x}$ is a vector, whereas $\|\boldsymbol{A}\|$ denotes the induced 2-norm for a matrix $\boldsymbol{A}$. For any function $\boldsymbol{f}(t) : [t_0, \infty) \rightarrow \mathbb{R}^n$, the $\mathcal{L}_\infty$-norm is defined as

$$\|\boldsymbol{f}(t)\|_\infty = \sup_{t \geq t_0} \|\boldsymbol{f}(t)\|, \tag{3}$$

and the $\mathcal{L}_2$-norm is defined as

$$\|\boldsymbol{f}(t)\|_2 = \left(\int_{t_0}^{\infty} \|\boldsymbol{f}(t)\|^2 \mathrm{d}t\right)^{\frac{1}{2}}. \tag{4}$$

3. Main Result

3.1. Problem Statement

The standard PID controller has been employed for decades in the control of robot manipulators due to its ability to compensate for gravitational effects without the need to explicitly compute the gravitational vector. Its key properties are as follows:

(1) It can achieve position regulation, but does not ensure exact trajectory tracking.
(2) It guarantees only local stability. For detailed proofs of these properties, refer to [28,30,39].

The aforementioned characteristics do not suggest the possibility of obtaining a stronger result for bilateral systems. Therefore, the primary objective of this work is to provide a stability proof demonstrating that these properties hold for bilateral systems with time-varying delays. The key distinction is that the desired (constant) position is specified by a human operator on either of the robots.

Consider the following error definition:

$$\hat{e}_i = q_i(t) - q_j\Big(t - T_j(t)\Big), \tag{5}$$

where $i = \mathrm{l}$ implies that $j = \mathrm{r}$, and vice versa. In this expression, $q_j\Big(t - T_j(t)\Big)$ denotes the delayed position of manipulator j, taking into account a communication delay $T_j(t)$.

The PID control laws are defined as follows:

$$u_i = -K_{\mathrm{p}i}\hat{e}_i - K_{\mathrm{v}i}\dot{q}_i - K_{\mathrm{i}i}\xi_{\mathrm{u}i}, \tag{6}$$

$$\dot{\xi}_{\mathrm{u}i} = \hat{e}_i, \tag{7}$$

$$\xi_{\mathrm{u}i}(t_0) = \mathbf{0}, \tag{8}$$

where $K_{\mathrm{p}i}, K_{\mathrm{v}i}, K_{\mathrm{i}i} \in \mathbb{R}^{n\times n}$ are positive-definite diagonal matrices. The integral term $\xi_{\mathrm{u}i}$, initialized at zero, accumulates based on the relative error $\hat{e}_i$.

Note that a desired velocity of zero is assumed, simplifying the control law. However, the error definition (5) does not account for the human operator's intention to move the robots in a specific direction. Therefore, it is assumed that the torque applied by the human operator satisfies the following condition [16].

Assumption 3. *The torque exerted by the human operator can be modeled as a proportional-integral (PI) controller in the position space, i.e.,*

$$\tau_{\mathrm{h}i} = -K_{\mathrm{a}i}e_i - K_{\mathrm{i}i}\xi_{\mathrm{h}i}, \tag{9}$$

$$\dot{\xi}_{\mathrm{h}i} = A_i e_i, \tag{10}$$

$$\xi_{\mathrm{h}i}(t_0) = \mathbf{0}, \tag{11}$$

where

$$e_i = q_i - q_{\mathrm{d}}, \tag{12}$$

with $q_{\mathrm{d}} \in \mathbb{R}^n$ denoting the desired constant position specified by the operator for the i-th end-effector. In this context, $K_{\mathrm{a}i}, A_i \in \mathbb{R}^{n\times n}$ are positive-definite diagonal matrices for $i = \mathrm{l}$, while $K_{\mathrm{a}i} = A_i = O$ for $i = \mathrm{r}$, or vice versa.

Remark 2. *Assumption 3 can be viewed as a specific instance of the widely accepted assumption of human passivity [5], given that a PI control law inherently represents a passive system. It is worth noting that this assumption is not novel, as it has also been employed in [16], for example. For a more comprehensive discussion, the interested reader is referred to [16]. Some authors consider human dynamics to be represented by a PID controller [40]; however, since the operator is never intended to control the local (or remote) end-effector independently but always in conjunction with the PID controller, providing a more elaborate description of their behavior becomes unnecessary. Finally, it is important to highlight that the same integral gain $K_{\mathrm{i}i}$ is assumed for both the human operator and the PID control law. Naturally, this is impractical, and to avoid an unrealistic condition, the gain A_i has been introduced in (10) and (11), making the effective integral gain for the human equal to $K_{\mathrm{i}i}A_i$. This choice simplifies the stability analysis.*

Figure 1 presents a block diagram of the complete control scheme. It is important to note that, although the human operator is assumed to control the local end-effector, the stability analysis is not limited to this specific scenario.

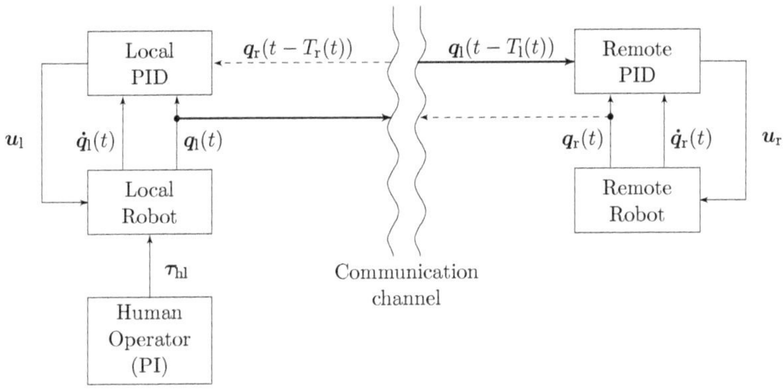

Figure 1. Teleoperation system with time-varying delays composed by two manipulators and a human operator interacting with the local robot.

3.2. Closed-Loop Dynamics and Equilibrium Points

Once the human operator generates the desired constant value $\boldsymbol{q}_{\mathrm{d}} \in \mathbb{R}^n$ for both the remote and local manipulators, the system is expected to achieve the following equilibrium:

$$\lim_{t\to\infty} \boldsymbol{q}_{\mathrm{r}}, \boldsymbol{q}_{\mathrm{l}} = \boldsymbol{q}_{\mathrm{d}}, \tag{13}$$

despite the presence of time-varying delays in the communication channel and the absence of explicit gravity compensation.

To understand how (13) can be achieved using a standard PID controller, let us assume that the manipulators exchange position data without any predetermined final value $\boldsymbol{q}_{\mathrm{d}}$. This assumption implies that the human operator is not interacting with either end-effector, i.e., $\boldsymbol{\tau}_{\mathrm{h}i} = \mathbf{0}$ for $i = \mathrm{l}, \mathrm{r}$.

Substituting (6) into (1), we obtain the following closed-loop dynamics:

$$\boldsymbol{H}_i(\boldsymbol{q}_i)\ddot{\boldsymbol{q}}_i + \boldsymbol{C}_i(\boldsymbol{q}_i, \dot{\boldsymbol{q}}_i)\dot{\boldsymbol{q}}_i + \boldsymbol{g}_i(\boldsymbol{q}_i) = -\boldsymbol{K}_{\mathrm{p}i}\hat{\boldsymbol{e}}_i - \boldsymbol{K}_{\mathrm{v}i}\dot{\boldsymbol{q}}_i - \boldsymbol{K}_{\mathrm{i}i}\boldsymbol{\xi}_{\mathrm{u}i}. \tag{14}$$

Together with (7) and (8), this describes the closed-loop dynamics of the system, whose equilibrium is characterized by $\dot{\boldsymbol{q}}_i = \hat{\boldsymbol{e}}_i = \mathbf{0}$, and the integral term satisfies:

$$\boldsymbol{\xi}_{\mathrm{u}i} = -\boldsymbol{K}_{\mathrm{i}i}^{-1}\boldsymbol{g}_i(\boldsymbol{q}_{\mathrm{c}i}), \tag{15}$$

for some constant vector $\boldsymbol{q}_{\mathrm{c}i}$. At equilibrium ($\dot{\boldsymbol{q}}_i = \mathbf{0}, \ddot{\boldsymbol{q}}_i = \mathbf{0}, \hat{\boldsymbol{e}}_i = \mathbf{0}$), the integral term of the PID controller precisely compensates for the gravitational torque $\boldsymbol{g}_i(\boldsymbol{q}_{\mathrm{c}i})$. Here, $\boldsymbol{q}_{\mathrm{c}i}$ denotes the equilibrium position of manipulator i.

To determine $\boldsymbol{q}_{\mathrm{c}i}$, consider that at equilibrium, from (5), we have:

$$\hat{\boldsymbol{e}}_i = \mathbf{0} \quad \Rightarrow \quad \boldsymbol{q}_i(t) = \boldsymbol{q}_j\Big(t - T_j(t)\Big) = \boldsymbol{q}_{\mathrm{c}i}. \tag{16}$$

From this relationship, the following conclusions can be drawn:

(1) $\boldsymbol{q}_{\mathrm{c\,l}} = \boldsymbol{q}_{\mathrm{c\,r}} \equiv \boldsymbol{q}_{\mathrm{c}}$, and
(2) $\boldsymbol{q}_{\mathrm{c}}$ is *not* unique.

As a direct consequence, an infinite number of equilibrium points exist.

The main challenge is to determine whether (13) holds when the human operator moves an end-effector to achieve the desired position $\boldsymbol{q}_{\mathrm{d}}$. Since $\boldsymbol{q}_{\mathrm{c}i} = \boldsymbol{q}_{\mathrm{c}}$ is identical for both manipulators, the error definition $\boldsymbol{e}_i$, as presented in (12), can be applied with the specific desired value $\boldsymbol{q}_{\mathrm{c}} = \boldsymbol{q}_{\mathrm{d}}$. By substituting this relationship into (5), the expression is rewritten as:

$$\begin{aligned} \hat{\boldsymbol{e}}_i(t) &= \boldsymbol{q}_i(t) - \boldsymbol{q}_{\mathrm{d}} - \boldsymbol{q}_j\Big(t - T_j(t)\Big) + \boldsymbol{q}_{\mathrm{d}} \\ &= \boldsymbol{e}_i(t) - \boldsymbol{e}_j\Big(t - T_j(t)\Big). \end{aligned} \tag{17}$$

This equation redefines $\hat{\boldsymbol{e}}_i(t)$ in terms of the human-induced error, as defined in (12), and the delayed error, described in (5). This reformulation enables an analysis of the interaction between the errors of both manipulators while explicitly accounting for communication delays. From (17), it follows that if $\boldsymbol{e}_i \to \boldsymbol{0}$ and $\boldsymbol{e}_j \to \boldsymbol{0}$ for $i, j = \mathrm{l}, \mathrm{r}$, then $\hat{\boldsymbol{e}}_i \to \boldsymbol{0}$ as well.

To facilitate the analysis, we define the delayed error as:

$$\bar{\boldsymbol{e}}_j = \boldsymbol{e}_j\Big(t - T_j(t)\Big), \tag{18}$$

and note that the time derivative of $\bar{\boldsymbol{e}}_j$ can be expressed as:

$$\dot{\bar{\boldsymbol{e}}}_j = \Big(1 - \dot{T}_j(t)\Big)\,\dot{\boldsymbol{e}}_j\Big(t - T_j(t)\Big). \tag{19}$$

This expression is obtained by applying the chain rule to the time-shifted error $\bar{\boldsymbol{e}}_j = \boldsymbol{e}_j(t - T_j(t))$. Specifically, differentiating $\bar{\boldsymbol{e}}_j$ with respect to time introduces the factor $\Big(1 - \dot{T}_j(t)\Big)$ due to the time-varying delay $T_j(t)$. This term accounts for the effect of the delay's rate of change on the overall error dynamics.

Since $\boldsymbol{q}_{\mathrm{d}}$ is a constant vector, we can rewrite (6)–(8) as:

$$\boldsymbol{u}_i = -\boldsymbol{K}_{\mathrm{p}i}\boldsymbol{e}_i - \boldsymbol{K}_{\mathrm{v}i}\dot{\boldsymbol{e}}_i - \boldsymbol{K}_{\mathrm{i}i}\boldsymbol{\xi}_{\mathrm{u}i} + \boldsymbol{K}_{\mathrm{p}i}\bar{\boldsymbol{e}}_j, \tag{20}$$

$$\dot{\boldsymbol{\xi}}_{\mathrm{u}i} = \boldsymbol{e}_i - \bar{\boldsymbol{e}}_j, \tag{21}$$

$$\boldsymbol{\xi}_{\mathrm{u}i}(t_0) = \boldsymbol{0}. \tag{22}$$

The term $\dot{\boldsymbol{\xi}}_{\mathrm{u}i}$ accumulates the difference between the instantaneous error $\boldsymbol{e}_i$ and the delayed error $\bar{\boldsymbol{e}}_j$. Initially, $\boldsymbol{\xi}_{\mathrm{u}i}$ is set to zero at t_0, ensuring that the integral term builds up over time based on the dynamics of the errors.

We now include the assumed dynamics of the human operator given by (9)–(11), resulting in a combined control law:

$$\boldsymbol{u}_{\mathrm{T}i} = \boldsymbol{u}_i + \boldsymbol{\tau}_{\mathrm{h}i} = -\boldsymbol{K}_{\mathrm{p}i}\boldsymbol{e}_i - \boldsymbol{K}_{\mathrm{a}i}\boldsymbol{e}_i - \boldsymbol{K}_{\mathrm{v}i}\dot{\boldsymbol{e}}_i - \boldsymbol{K}_{\mathrm{i}i}\boldsymbol{\xi}_i + \boldsymbol{K}_{\mathrm{p}i}\bar{\boldsymbol{e}}_j, \tag{23}$$

$$\dot{\boldsymbol{\xi}}_i = \dot{\boldsymbol{\xi}}_{\mathrm{u}i} + \dot{\boldsymbol{\xi}}_{\mathrm{h}i} = \boldsymbol{e}_i - \bar{\boldsymbol{e}}_j + \boldsymbol{A}_i\boldsymbol{e}_i, \tag{24}$$

$$\boldsymbol{\xi}_i(t_0) = \boldsymbol{0}. \tag{25}$$

The total torque applied to the system, $\boldsymbol{u}_{\mathrm{T}i}$, encompasses the contributions from the PID controller, $\boldsymbol{u}_i$, and the torque applied by the human operator, $\boldsymbol{\tau}_{\mathrm{h}i}$. The dynamics of $\boldsymbol{\xi}_i$ incorporate the integral terms associated with both the controller, $\dot{\boldsymbol{\xi}}_{\mathrm{u}i}$, and the human operator, $\dot{\boldsymbol{\xi}}_{\mathrm{h}i}$. This combined behavior captures the interaction between the system's internal feedback mechanisms and the external inputs provided by the operator.

Note that the equilibrium point of (1) in closed loop with (23) and (24) is characterized by:

$$\boldsymbol{q}_i = \boldsymbol{q}_{\mathrm{d}} \tag{26}$$

$$\dot{\boldsymbol{q}}_i = \boldsymbol{0} \tag{27}$$

$$\boldsymbol{\xi}_i = -\boldsymbol{K}_{\mathrm{i}i}^{-1}\boldsymbol{g}_i(\boldsymbol{q}_{\mathrm{d}}). \tag{28}$$

At equilibrium, the integral term ξ_i compensates exactly for the gravitational torque $g_i(q_\mathrm{d})$, ensuring that the system remains stationary at the desired position q_d.

For the stability analysis, a similar approach to that described in [39] can be employed, which requires defining:

$$s_i = \dot{e}_i + \Lambda_i B_i e_i - \Lambda_i \bar{e}_j, \tag{29}$$

where s_i represents a composite variable combining the tracking error dynamics $\dot{e}_i$, the delayed error term $\bar{e}_j$, and the proportional error term e_i scaled by B_i, with:

$$B_i = I + A_i. \tag{30}$$

This formulation consolidates the key dynamic components into a single variable, simplifying the stability analysis.

This selection renders (23) and (24) equivalent to the following system dynamics:

$$u_{\tau i} = -K_{\mathrm{v}i} s_i - K_{\omega i}\omega_i + K_{\omega i}\bar{e}_j, \tag{31}$$

$$\dot{\omega}_i = s_i, \tag{32}$$

$$\omega_i(t_0) = 0, \tag{33}$$

where ω_i serves as an auxiliary variable introduced to track the evolution of s_i.

The dynamics of ω_i, as defined by (32) and (33), facilitate the design and analysis of the system's stability properties. Specifically, $\dot{\omega}_i = s_i$ establishes a direct relationship between the auxiliary variable and the composite tracking error s_i, while $\omega_i(t_0) = 0$ ensures a consistent initial condition for the analysis.

The equivalence described above holds provided that the following parameter relationships are satisfied:

$$K_{\mathrm{i}i} = K_{\omega i}\Lambda_i, \tag{34}$$

$$K_{\mathrm{a}i} = K_{\mathrm{v}i}\Lambda_i A_i, \tag{35}$$

$$K_{\mathrm{p}i} = K_{\mathrm{v}i}\Lambda_i + K_{\omega i}. \tag{36}$$

These parameter relationships, defined in (34)–(36), ensure a consistent interaction between the controller gains and the system dynamics. By linking the integral gain $K_{\mathrm{i}i}$, the proportional gain $K_{\mathrm{p}i}$, and the dynamic contributions introduced by Λ_i and A_i, these relationships guarantee that the closed-loop system achieves stability under the specified conditions.

Furthermore, the presence of $K_{\omega i}$ in (31) highlights its role in shaping the system's response through the auxiliary dynamics ω_i, which provides an additional layer of control to enhance stability and performance.

Remark 3. *Given any arbitrary set of gains $K_{\mathrm{p}i}$, $K_{\mathrm{v}i}$, and $K_{\mathrm{i}i}$, it is not always feasible to determine an equivalent set of gains Λ_i and $K_{\omega i}$ that satisfy (34)–(36). Therefore, it is necessary to select Λ_i and $K_{\omega i}$ first, ensuring that the corresponding values of $K_{\mathrm{p}i}$, $K_{\mathrm{v}i}$, and $K_{\mathrm{i}i}$ can be derived accordingly for implementation.*

The previous analysis shows that the system described by (1), when in closed loop with (31)–(33), achieves equilibrium at $e_i = s_i = 0$ and $\omega_i = -K_{\omega i}^{-1} g_i(q_\mathrm{d})$. This is equivalent to $\dot{q}_i = \hat{e}_i = 0$, meaning that the tracking error vanishes and the desired position q_d is maintained. Additionally, the integral term ω_i compensates precisely for the gravitational torque $g_i(q_\mathrm{d})$, as indicated in (28).

This equilibrium can be verified by substituting (31) into (1), which yields:

$$H_i(q_i)\dot{s}_i + C_i(q_i, \dot{q}_i)s_i + K_{\mathrm{v}i}s_i + K_{\omega i}\omega_i + g_i(q_i) = \phi_{\mathrm{a}i}, \tag{37}$$

where:

$$\phi_{ai} = H_i(q_i)\Lambda_i(B_i\dot{e}_i - \dot{\bar{e}}_j) + C_i(q_i, \dot{e}_i)\Lambda_i(B_ie_i - \bar{e}_j) + K_{\omega i}\bar{e}_j. \quad (38)$$

The term ϕ_{ai} encapsulates additional dynamic effects arising from delayed communication and system interaction. Specifically, it accounts for the dynamic coupling between the manipulators, incorporating contributions from the inertia matrix $H_i(q_i)$, Coriolis and centrifugal forces $C_i(q_i, \dot{e}_i)$, and delayed error dynamics $\bar{e}_j$. The factors B_i and Λ_i introduce proportional and scaling adjustments, ensuring alignment with the controller design.

Furthermore, the assumption $\dot{q}_d = \ddot{q}_d = 0$ simplifies the formulation by eliminating variations in the desired trajectory. Together with (32)–(33), these equations describe the closed-loop system dynamics. This formulation integrates the auxiliary dynamics of ω_i, which track the evolution of s_i, ensuring the system achieves stability and tracks the desired trajectory under the effects of communication delays and gravitational torques.

Define now the state vector as:

$$y = \begin{bmatrix} \omega_l^T & e_l^T & s_l^T & \omega_r^T & e_r^T & s_r^T \end{bmatrix}^T, \quad (39)$$

where ω_l and ω_r are auxiliary variables introduced to track the evolution of the composite error dynamics s_l and s_r, respectively. The variables e_l and e_r represent the position tracking errors for the local and remote manipulators. With this definition, the closed-loop dynamics of the system can be expressed as:

$$\dot{y} = \begin{bmatrix} s_l \\ -\Lambda_l B_l e_l + s_l + \Lambda_l \bar{e}_r \\ -H_l^{-1}\{C_l s_l + K_{vl} s_l - \phi_{al} + K_{\omega l}\omega_l + g_l\} \\ s_r \\ -\Lambda_r B_r e_r + s_r + \Lambda_r \bar{e}_l \\ -H_r^{-1}\{C_r s_r + K_{vr} s_r - \phi_{ar} + K_{\omega r}\omega_r + g_r\} \end{bmatrix}. \quad (40)$$

In (40), the terms $\Lambda_i B_i e_i$ and $\Lambda_i \bar{e}_j$ capture the proportional and delayed error corrections, while ϕ_{ai} encapsulates dynamic effects such as inertia, Coriolis forces, and delayed errors.

The arguments for H_i, C_i, and g_i have been omitted for simplicity. The equilibrium point of (40) is clearly given by $e_i = s_i = 0$ and $\omega_i = -K_{\omega i}^{-1} g_i(q_d)$, as previously determined. This equilibrium reflects the condition where tracking errors vanish, and the gravitational torques are fully compensated by the integral terms.

Consider the following change of coordinates:

$$x_1 = \omega_l + K_{\omega l}^{-1} g_l(q_d), \quad (41)$$

$$x_4 = \omega_r + K_{\omega r}^{-1} g_r(q_d). \quad (42)$$

These coordinate transformations center the auxiliary variables ω_l and ω_r around their equilibrium values, simplifying the analysis by ensuring the equilibrium corresponds to $x_1 = x_4 = 0$.

Under this change of coordinates, the system becomes:

$$\dot{x} = \begin{bmatrix} s_l \\ -\Lambda_l B_l e_l + s_l + \Lambda_l \bar{e}_r \\ -H_l^{-1}\{C_l s_l + K_{vl} s_l - \phi_{al} + K_{\omega l} x_1 + g_l(q_l) - g_l(q_d)\} \\ s_r \\ -\Lambda_r B_r e_r + s_r + \Lambda_r \bar{e}_l \\ -H_r^{-1}\{C_r s_r + K_{vr} s_r - \phi_{ar} + K_{\omega r} x_4 + g_r(q_r) - g_r(q_d)\} \end{bmatrix}, \quad (43)$$

where

$$\begin{aligned} x &= \begin{bmatrix} x_1^{\mathrm{T}} & x_2^{\mathrm{T}} & x_3^{\mathrm{T}} & x_4^{\mathrm{T}} & x_5^{\mathrm{T}} & x_6^{\mathrm{T}} \end{bmatrix}^{\mathrm{T}} \\ &\equiv \begin{bmatrix} x_1^{\mathrm{T}} & e_1^{\mathrm{T}} & s_1^{\mathrm{T}} & x_4^{\mathrm{T}} & e_{\mathrm{r}}^{\mathrm{T}} & s_{\mathrm{r}}^{\mathrm{T}} \end{bmatrix}^{\mathrm{T}}. \end{aligned} \tag{44}$$

In the equivalent system defined in (43), the equilibrium point simplifies to $x = \mathbf{0}$, confirming its uniqueness. This reduction facilitates the stability analysis by consolidating all dynamic terms into a unified representation.

The region of interest for stability analysis can be defined as:

$$\mathcal{D} = \left\{ x \in \mathbb{R}^{6n} \backslash \|x\| \leq \epsilon \right\}, \tag{45}$$

where $\mathcal{D}$ represents a bounded region around the equilibrium within which stability can be studied. The parameter $\epsilon > 0$ defines the radius of this region, reflecting the inherent local asymptotic stability properties of PID control.

To facilitate the stability analysis and account for the dynamic interactions within the closed-loop system, the matrix K_{vi} is defined as the sum of two diagonal positive-definite matrices:

$$K_{vi} = K_{vi1} + K_{vi2}, \tag{46}$$

where $K_{vi1}, K_{vi2} \in \mathbb{R}^{n \times n}$. This decomposition provides additional flexibility in the tuning of the control gains, allowing K_{vi1} and K_{vi2} to be adjusted independently to address distinct aspects of the system's behavior. For instance, K_{vi1} may be selected to enhance damping characteristics, while K_{vi2} can be tailored to counteract specific dynamic effects or improve robustness under varying conditions.

Moreover, this formulation aligns with the composite structure of the system, as it allows for separate consideration of contributions from intrinsic manipulator dynamics and external influences such as time delays or human interaction. As a result, the gain matrix K_{vi} can be systematically tuned to ensure stability and performance across a broad range of operating scenarios.

Assumption 4. *There exist constants $\alpha_j, \beta_j \geq 1$ for $j = \mathrm{l}, \mathrm{r}$, such that the following inequalities hold:*

$$\left(\int_{t_0}^{t} \|e_j(\theta - T_j(\theta))\|^2 \, \mathrm{d}\theta \right)^{\frac{1}{2}} \leq \alpha_j \left(\int_{t_0}^{t} \|e_j(\theta)\|^2 \, \mathrm{d}\theta \right)^{\frac{1}{2}}, \tag{47}$$

$$\left(\int_{t_0}^{t} \|\dot{e}_j(\theta - T_j(\theta))\|^2 \, \mathrm{d}\theta \right)^{\frac{1}{2}} \leq \beta_j \left(\int_{t_0}^{t} \|\dot{e}_j(\theta)\|^2 \, \mathrm{d}\theta \right)^{\frac{1}{2}}, \tag{48}$$

for all $t \geq t_0$.

Remark 4. *Conditions (47) and (48) are relatively uncommon, warranting a thorough analysis of the scenarios in which they are satisfied. First, assume that $x(t) \equiv \mathbf{0}$ for all $t < t_0$ (see (50)) and consider the state definition in (44).*

Under these assumptions, it follows that $e_\mathrm{l}(t) = e_\mathrm{r}(t) = \mathbf{0}$ for $t < t_0$. Additionally, since $s_\mathrm{l}(t) = s_\mathrm{r}(t) = \mathbf{0}$ for $t < t_0$, (29) implies that $\dot{e}_\mathrm{l}(t) = \dot{e}_\mathrm{r}(t) = \mathbf{0}$ for $t < t_0$ as well.

Given this, consider rewriting (47) in the equivalent form:

$$\int_{t_0}^{t} \|e_j(\theta - T_j(\theta))\|^2 \, \mathrm{d}\theta \leq \alpha_j^2 \int_{t_0}^{t} \|e_j(\theta)\|^2 \, \mathrm{d}\theta, \tag{49}$$

where $\alpha_j \geq 1$.

If $T_j(t) \equiv T_j$ is constant, it is evident that (49) holds with $\alpha_j = 1$, and thus, (47) is satisfied as well. Intuitively, a delay of the form $T_j(t) = T_j + f_{\mathrm{d}j}(t)$, where $f_{\mathrm{d}j}(t)$ is a high-frequency signal of small magnitude, should also satisfy (47) with a similar value of α_j. Indeed, simulation results consistently indicate that (47) and (48) hold for finite values of α_j and β_j, often without requiring large values.

Therefore, we assert that (47) and (48) are not ad hoc conditions but instead are satisfied by a wide range of commonly encountered time delay scenarios. However, assuming that α_j and β_j are known a priori is less realistic. Developing a methodology to calculate these parameters remains an open area for future research. In the experimental results presented, the values $\alpha_j = \beta_j = 1$ were simply assumed for $j = \mathrm{l}, \mathrm{r}$.

The central contribution of this study is formalized in the following theorem.

Theorem 1. *Let us consider the PID control law defined by (6)–(8), combined with the assumed human dynamics given in (9)–(11). Assume, without loss of generality, that $\boldsymbol{A}_{\mathrm{r}} = \boldsymbol{O}$ and $\boldsymbol{K}_{\mathrm{ar}} = \boldsymbol{O}$, where $\boldsymbol{O}$ denotes the null matrix of appropriate dimensions, and that the parameter relationships specified in (34)–(36) are satisfied.*

Under these conditions, the variables $\hat{\boldsymbol{e}}_i$, $\dot{\boldsymbol{q}}_i$, $\boldsymbol{e}_i$, and $\boldsymbol{\xi}_i$ defined in (24)–(25) remain bounded for all $t \geq t_0$, and the following convergence properties hold:

$$\hat{\boldsymbol{e}}_i, \dot{\boldsymbol{q}}_i, \boldsymbol{e}_i \to \boldsymbol{0}, \tag{50}$$

$$\boldsymbol{\xi}_i \to -\boldsymbol{K}_{\mathrm{ii}}^{-1} \boldsymbol{g}_i(\boldsymbol{q}_{\mathrm{d}}), \tag{51}$$

as $t \to \infty$, provided that:

1. *Assumptions 2 and 4 are satisfied.*
2. *The equivalent closed-loop system dynamics in (43) satisfy the following conditions:*

$$\boldsymbol{x}(t) \equiv \boldsymbol{0}, \qquad \forall t < t_0, \tag{52}$$

$$\|\boldsymbol{x}(t_0)\| < \sqrt{\frac{\lambda_1}{\lambda_2}} \epsilon = \delta, \tag{53}$$

and the following additional constraints hold:

$$\lambda_{\min}(\boldsymbol{\Lambda}_{\mathrm{r}}) \geq \delta_{\mathrm{er}} + 3, \tag{54}$$

$$\lambda_{\min}(\boldsymbol{\Lambda}_{\mathrm{l}}) \geq \delta_{\mathrm{el}} + 3, \tag{55}$$

$$\lambda_{\min}(\boldsymbol{K}_{\mathrm{vr2}}) \geq \delta_{\dot{\mathrm{e}}\mathrm{r}} + 3, \tag{56}$$

$$\lambda_{\min}(\boldsymbol{K}_{\mathrm{vl2}}) \geq \delta_{\dot{\mathrm{e}}\mathrm{l}} + 2 + \beta_{\mathrm{l}}^2 \left(1 + T_{\mathrm{l}}^*\right)^2 \left(\frac{\lambda_{\max}\left(\boldsymbol{\Lambda}_{\mathrm{r}}^2\right) \lambda_{\max}\left(\boldsymbol{K}_{\mathrm{vr2}}^2\right)}{\lambda_{\min}\left(\boldsymbol{\Lambda}_{\mathrm{r}}^2\right) \lambda_{\min}\left(\boldsymbol{K}_{\mathrm{vr2}}\right)} \right), \tag{57}$$

$$\begin{aligned} \lambda_{\min}(\boldsymbol{B}_{\mathrm{l}}) \geq{} & \frac{1}{\lambda_{\min}\left(\boldsymbol{\Lambda}_{\mathrm{l}}\right)} \left(\delta_{\mathrm{el}} + 2\right) + \frac{\left(\frac{1}{4}\left[\alpha_{\mathrm{r}} \lambda_{\max}\left(\boldsymbol{\Lambda}_{\mathrm{l}}\right) + \alpha_{\mathrm{l}} \lambda_{\max}\left(\boldsymbol{\Lambda}_{\mathrm{r}}\right)\right]^2\right)}{\lambda_{\min}\left(\boldsymbol{\Lambda}_{\mathrm{l}}\right)} \\ & + \frac{\beta_{\mathrm{r}} \lambda_{\max}\left(\boldsymbol{K}_{\mathrm{vl2}}\right) \lambda_{\max}\left(\boldsymbol{\Lambda}_{\mathrm{l}}\right) \left(1 + T_{\mathrm{r}}^*\right)}{\lambda_{\min}\left(\boldsymbol{\Lambda}_{\mathrm{l}}\right) \sqrt{\lambda_{\min}\left(\boldsymbol{K}_{\mathrm{vl2}}\right)}}, \end{aligned} \tag{58}$$

$$\lambda_{\min}(\boldsymbol{K}_{\text{vl1}}) \geq \delta_{\text{sl}} + \frac{1}{4}\left(1+k_{\text{gl}}\right)^2 + \frac{1}{4}\alpha_{\text{r}}^2\lambda_{\max}(\boldsymbol{K}_{\omega\text{l}})^2 + \frac{1}{4}\left[\beta_{\text{r}}\lambda_{\text{Hl}}\lambda_{\max}\left(\boldsymbol{\Lambda}_{\text{l}}\right)\left(1+T_{\text{r}}^*\right)\right]^2$$
$$+\frac{1}{4}\left(\lambda_{\text{Hl}}\lambda_{\max}\left(\boldsymbol{\Lambda}_{\text{l}}\right)\lambda_{\max}\left(\boldsymbol{B}_{\text{l}}\right) + \lambda_{\max}\left(\boldsymbol{\Lambda}_{\text{l}}\right)k_{\text{cl}}\left[\lambda_{\max}\left(\boldsymbol{B}_{\text{l}}\right)\epsilon + \epsilon\right]\right)^2, \quad (59)$$

$$\lambda_{\min}(\boldsymbol{K}_{\text{vr1}}) \geq \delta_{\text{sr}} + \frac{1}{4}\alpha_{\text{l}}^2\lambda_{\max}\left(\boldsymbol{K}_{\omega\text{r}}\right)^2 + \frac{1}{4}\left[\lambda_{\text{Hr}}\lambda_{\max}\left(\boldsymbol{\Lambda}_{\text{r}}\right) + 2\lambda_{\max}\left(\boldsymbol{\Lambda}_{\text{r}}\right)k_{\text{cr}}\epsilon\right]^2$$
$$+\frac{1}{4}\left(1+k_{\text{gr}}\right)^2 + \frac{1}{4}\left[\beta_{\text{l}}\lambda_{\text{Hr}}\lambda_{\max}\left(\boldsymbol{\Lambda}_{\text{r}}\right)\left(1+T_{\text{l}}^*\right)\right]^2, \quad (60)$$

where ϵ is defined in (45), and δ_{el}, δ_{er}, $\delta_{\dot{\text{e}}\text{l}}$, $\delta_{\dot{\text{e}}\text{r}}$, δ_{sl}, and δ_{sr} are positive constants. Moreover,

$$\lambda_1 = \frac{1}{2}\min\left\{\lambda_{\min}\left(\boldsymbol{K}_{\omega\text{l}}\right), \lambda_{\text{hl}}, \lambda_{\min}\left(\boldsymbol{K}_{\omega\text{r}}\right), \lambda_{\text{hr}}, 1\right\}, \quad (61)$$

$$\lambda_2 = \max\left\{\frac{1}{2}\lambda_{\max}\left(\boldsymbol{K}_{\omega\text{l}}\right), \frac{1}{2}\lambda_{\max}\left(\boldsymbol{K}_{\omega\text{r}}\right), \frac{1}{2} + \lambda_{\max}\left(\boldsymbol{K}_{\text{vl2}}\boldsymbol{\Lambda}_{\text{l}}\boldsymbol{B}_{\text{l}}\right) + \lambda_{\max}\left(\boldsymbol{K}_{\text{vr2}}\boldsymbol{\Lambda}_{\text{r}}\right),\right.$$
$$\frac{1}{2}\lambda_{\text{Hl}}, \frac{1}{2}\lambda_{\text{Hr}}, 2\lambda_{\max}\left(\boldsymbol{K}_{\text{vl2}}\boldsymbol{\Lambda}_{\text{l}}\right) + 2\lambda_{\max}\left(\boldsymbol{K}_{\text{vr2}}\boldsymbol{\Lambda}_{\text{r}}\right), \frac{1}{2} + \lambda_{\max}\left(\boldsymbol{K}_{\text{vr2}}\boldsymbol{\Lambda}_{\text{r}}\right)$$
$$\left.+\lambda_{\max}\left(\boldsymbol{B}_{\text{l}}^{-1}\boldsymbol{K}_{\text{vl2}}\boldsymbol{\Lambda}_{\text{l}}\right)\right\}. \quad (62)$$

Here, k_{gl}, k_{gr}, k_{cl}, k_{cr}, λ_{Hl}, λ_{Hr}, T_{l}^*, and T_{r}^* are parameters defined in Section 2 and in Assumption 2.

The detailed proof of Theorem 1 is provided in Appendix A.

Remark 5. *The definition of the region $\mathcal{D}$ in (45) a priori facilitates the proof of Theorem 1, and is based on the definition of uniform stability in the sense of Lyapunov, which establishes that the equilibrium is uniformly stable if for each $\epsilon > 0$, there exists a $\delta(\epsilon) > 0$ independent of t_0 such that:*

$$\|\boldsymbol{x}(t_0)\| < \delta(\epsilon) \;\Rightarrow\; \|\boldsymbol{x}(t)\| < \epsilon,\; \forall t \geq t_0. \quad (63)$$

This condition holds as stated in [41]. This means that ϵ is a given value, while $\delta(\epsilon)$ has to be found as a function of it, mirroring what is carried out in (53) with $\delta(\epsilon) = \sqrt{\frac{\lambda_1}{\lambda_2}}\epsilon$, although $\|\boldsymbol{x}(t)\| \leq \epsilon$ is used to define $\mathcal{D}$.

However, it is very important to emphasize that Theorem 1 does not state uniform stability, but merely that $\hat{\boldsymbol{e}}_i$, $\dot{\boldsymbol{q}}_i$, $\boldsymbol{e}_i$, and $\boldsymbol{\xi}_i$ are bounded and tend to the equilibrium point. Uniform stability could be proven as outlined in [39], but it is not a mandatory step for the present work. On the other hand, the use of $\mathcal{D}$ eliminates the need to assume that the manipulators' joints are revolute; they could alternatively be prismatic as well. However, for simplicity, this assumption is maintained.

Remark 6. *Theorem 1 relies on Assumption 3, but at the same time, it introduces a second assumption, i.e., there is only a human operator on one side, while on the other side, there is no one holding the robot. However, including another human operator modeled also as a PI controller as given in Assumption 3 would barely alter the proof of Theorem 1. This leads to the logical conclusion that a PID controller plus a PI control law yields a stable closed-loop system.*

It is possible to utilize this fact to address the scenario where one of the robots interacts with its environment, requiring slight modifications to (6)–(8). First of all, change notation in (1) as

$\boldsymbol{\tau}_{\mathrm{h}i} = \boldsymbol{\tau}_i$, because one of the external forces is not generated by a human operator (say, the remote side), and consider the following modifications to (6)–(8):

$$\boldsymbol{u}_i = -\boldsymbol{K}_{\mathrm{p}i}\hat{\boldsymbol{e}}_i - \boldsymbol{K}_{\mathrm{v}i}\dot{\boldsymbol{q}}_i - \boldsymbol{K}_{\mathrm{i}i}\boldsymbol{\xi}_{\mathrm{u}i} \pm \boldsymbol{\tau}_j(t - T_j(t)) \mp \boldsymbol{K}_{\mathrm{f}i}\Delta\boldsymbol{p}_i, \tag{64}$$

$$\dot{\boldsymbol{\xi}}_{\mathrm{u}i} = \hat{\boldsymbol{e}}_i, \tag{65}$$

$$\boldsymbol{\xi}_{\mathrm{u}i}(t_0) = \boldsymbol{0}, \tag{66}$$

$$\Delta\boldsymbol{p}_i = \int_0^t (\boldsymbol{\tau}_i - \boldsymbol{\tau}_j(t - T_j(t)))\mathrm{d}t, \tag{67}$$

$$\Delta\boldsymbol{p}_i(t_0) = \boldsymbol{0}, \tag{68}$$

with $\Delta\boldsymbol{p}_i \in \mathbb{R}^n$ and $\boldsymbol{\tau}_j(t - T_j(t)) \in \mathbb{R}^n$ representing the external delayed torque transmitted from one robot to the other.

In closed loop, the introduced modifications represent PI force/torque control schemes on both sides of the bilateral system, where $\boldsymbol{K}_{\mathrm{f}i} \in \mathbb{R}^{n\times n}$ is a diagonal positive-definite matrix for each robot that represents the integral gain, and the positive sign (+) corresponds to $i = \mathrm{l}$, and the negative sign (-) corresponds to $i = \mathrm{r}$. Note that Assumption 3 is no longer required.

4. Experimental Results

The theory developed in the previous section assumes that the human operator behaves as a PI controller to provide a desired position for one manipulator (Assumption 3). This assumption is justified in Remark 2, but it is unrealistic to claim that a person can be *tuned* as required by Theorem 1. Consequently, it might be perceived that this result lacks practical utility.

To demonstrate its practicality, five experiments have been carried out:

1. Two PID controllers, as described in (6)–(8), along with a PI control law for the local side, were tuned following the guidelines provided by Theorem 1.
2. The PI control law was subsequently removed, and a human operator manually controlled the robot-first on the local side and then on the remote side. This experiment aimed to show that the gains derived in the previous step maintain the stability of the closed-loop system.
3. The well-known PD controller combined with gravity compensation, as presented in [31], was implemented to serve as a baseline for comparison.
4. To evaluate robustness, the remote end-effector was brought into contact with its environment.
5. Finally, to enhance transparency, a force control term was incorporated into the basic position PID controller.

The experimental testbed consists of two five-DOF *Geomagic Touch* haptic devices, depicted in Figure 2. Both robots were simplified to three-DOF manipulators, since actuation is limited to the first three joints [30].

The remote robot is connected via Ethernet, while the local one is connected via USB to a PC. The sampling time for data acquisition and control was set to $\mathrm{T} = 2\,\mathrm{ms}$ (the fastest possible rate achieved). The software environment employed was VisualStudio 2022 using C++ alongside the *OpenHaptics* library for communication between the manipulators and the PC to exchange commands and data.

For this configuration, time delays are insignificant under normal circumstances. However, to create a more challenging scenario, time-varying delays were artificially introduced. Specifically, the mean delays for the local and remote robots were set to $T_\mathrm{l} = 0.675\,\mathrm{s}$ and $T_\mathrm{r} = 0.625\,\mathrm{s}$, respectively, with a variance of 0.05 s.

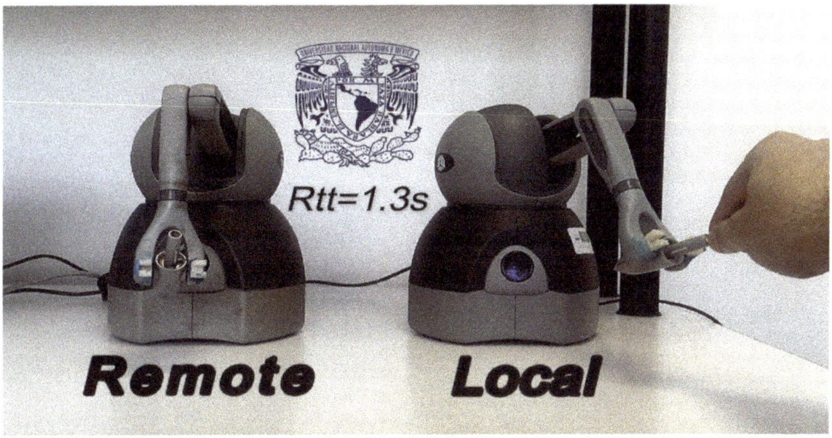

Figure 2. Teleoperation system composed of two *Geomagic Touch* haptic devices.

This resulted in a combined delay of $1.25\,\mathrm{s} \leq \mathrm{T_l}(t) + \mathrm{T_r}(t) \leq 1.35\,\mathrm{s}$, as shown in Figure 3. Under these conditions, the round-trip time (RTT) was measured to be approximately 1.3 s.

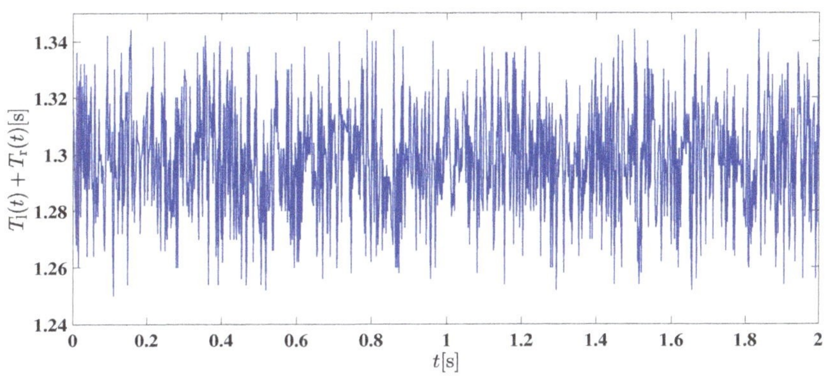

Figure 3. Typical round-trip time delay (RTT).

4.1. Gain Tuning

The initial step involves tuning the PID controllers and the PI control law according to the conditions given in Theorem 1. As a starting point, the bounds $\lambda_{\mathrm{h}i}$, $\lambda_{\mathrm{H}i}$, $k_{\mathrm{c}i}$, and $k_{\mathrm{g}i}$ must be obtained. To this end, an experimental approach was implemented, consisting of recording position and velocity data from both robots while performing random movements that span the entire task space. This information was saved in a data file. Once the data acquisition was completed, the recorded information was processed to calculate the bounds of the dynamics according to Properties 1, 3, and 4:

$$\lambda_{\mathrm{h}i} = \min_{\boldsymbol{q}_i \in \mathbb{R}^n} \lambda_{\min}\Big(\boldsymbol{H}_i(\boldsymbol{q}_i)\Big), \tag{69}$$

$$\lambda_{\mathrm{H}i} = \max_{\boldsymbol{q}_i \in \mathbb{R}^n} \lambda_{\max}\Big(\boldsymbol{H}_i(\boldsymbol{q}_i)\Big), \tag{70}$$

$$k_{\mathrm{c}i} = \max_{\boldsymbol{q}_i, \dot{\boldsymbol{q}}_i \in \mathbb{R}^n \setminus \{0\}} \frac{\|\boldsymbol{C}_i(\boldsymbol{q}_i, \dot{\boldsymbol{q}}_i)\|}{\|\dot{\boldsymbol{q}}_i\|}, \tag{71}$$

$$k_{\mathrm{g}i} = \max_{\boldsymbol{q}_i \in \mathbb{R}^n} \|\boldsymbol{g}_i(\boldsymbol{q}_i)\|. \tag{72}$$

It is important to highlight that having prior knowledge of the system model is a prerequisite. In this case, the model for both robots was obtained from [30]. The resulting parameter values are summarized in Table 1.

Table 1. System parameter values and their respective units.

Variable	Value	Unit
λ_{hl}	5.75×10^{-4}	N·s/m
λ_{hr}	5.42×10^{-4}	N·s/m
λ_{Hl}	0.0070	N·s/m
λ_{Hr}	0.0050	N·s/m
k_{cl}	0.0031	N/m
k_{cr}	0.0021	N/m
k_{gl}	0.1086	N/m
k_{gr}	0.1317	N/m

These parameter values represent the lightweight and compact design of the robotic manipulators, evident from their low inertia, damping, and gravitational terms. The values were experimentally derived by analyzing the system dynamics across its operational workspace. The small values of k_{cl} and k_{cr} indicate minimal Coriolis and centrifugal effects, which is consistent with the manipulators' limited mass and low-speed operation. These parameters were essential to determine the appropriate control gains, ensuring stability and performance under time-varying delays.

The controller gains were determined following the tuning guidelines established in the previous section. First, the derivatives of time delays were assumed to be bounded by $T_{\mathrm{l}}^* = T_{\mathrm{r}}^* = 1$. The parameters α_i and β_i were set as $\alpha_{\mathrm{l}} = \alpha_{\mathrm{r}} = \beta_{\mathrm{l}} = \beta_{\mathrm{r}} = 1$, representing constant time delays. By defining $\delta_{\mathrm{el}} = \delta_{\mathrm{er}} = 1$, from (54) and (55), it was obtained that $\lambda_{\min}(\boldsymbol{\Lambda}_{\mathrm{l}}), \lambda_{\min}(\boldsymbol{\Lambda}_{\mathrm{r}}) \geq 4$. Through trial and error, the following gains were selected: $\boldsymbol{\Lambda}_{\mathrm{l}} = \boldsymbol{\Lambda}_{\mathrm{r}} = 11\boldsymbol{I}$ to enhance damping and improve performance. Similarly, setting $\delta_{\dot{e}i}$ and $\delta_{\mathrm{s}}i$ to $\delta_{\dot{e}\mathrm{l}} = \delta_{\dot{e}\mathrm{r}} = \delta_{\mathrm{sl}} = \delta_{\mathrm{sr}} = 1$ resulted in $\lambda_{\min}(\boldsymbol{K}_{\mathrm{vr2}}) \geq 4$ according to (56). Thus, a value of $\boldsymbol{K}_{\mathrm{vr2}} = 19\boldsymbol{I}$ was chosen based on (57). This allowed for the definition of $\boldsymbol{B}_{\mathrm{l}} = 20\boldsymbol{I}$ as per (58). By assigning $\boldsymbol{K}_{\omega\mathrm{l}} = \boldsymbol{K}_{\omega\mathrm{r}} = 30\boldsymbol{I}$ and $\epsilon = 10$, the resulting gains were calculated as $\boldsymbol{K}_{\mathrm{vl1}} = 245.22\boldsymbol{I}$ and $\boldsymbol{K}_{\mathrm{vr1}} = 226.39\boldsymbol{I}$. Consequently, the overall gains are $\boldsymbol{K}_{\mathrm{vl}} = 264.22\boldsymbol{I}$ and $\boldsymbol{K}_{\mathrm{vr}} = 230.39\boldsymbol{I}$, following the computations in (46). Finally, the parameters were further refined based on (30) and (34)–(36), yielding the following results: $\boldsymbol{A}_{\mathrm{l}} = 19\boldsymbol{I}$, $\boldsymbol{K}_{\mathrm{pl}} = 2936\boldsymbol{I}$, $\boldsymbol{K}_{\mathrm{pr}} = 2564\boldsymbol{I}$, $\boldsymbol{K}_{\mathrm{il}} = \boldsymbol{K}_{\mathrm{ir}} = 330\boldsymbol{I}$, and $\boldsymbol{K}_{\mathrm{al}} = 5.5195 \times 10^4\boldsymbol{I}$. For the remote side, assuming that the human operator controls the local manipulator, $\boldsymbol{A}_{\mathrm{r}}$ and $\boldsymbol{K}_{\mathrm{ar}}$ were both set to zero matrices ($\boldsymbol{O}$).

4.2. Experiment 1: Emulated Human Dynamics

In the first experiment, the interaction of a human operator with the local robot is emulated using a PI control law, as described in (9)–(11). Standard PID controllers are implemented on both robots in accordance with (6)–(8) and the tuning rules outlined in Section 4.1. Both robots begin with the same initial conditions: $\dot{\boldsymbol{q}}_i(0) = \boldsymbol{0}[^\circ/\mathrm{s}]$, $\boldsymbol{q}_i(0) = [0^\circ, 30^\circ, -90^\circ]^{\mathrm{T}}$.

The desired position is defined as:

$$\boldsymbol{q}_{\mathrm{d}} = \begin{bmatrix} 50^\circ & 15^\circ & -40^\circ \end{bmatrix}^{\mathrm{T}}. \quad (73)$$

The induced RTT for this experiment is depicted in Figure 3. Figure 4 illustrates the tracking error $\hat{\boldsymbol{e}}_{\mathrm{l}}$.

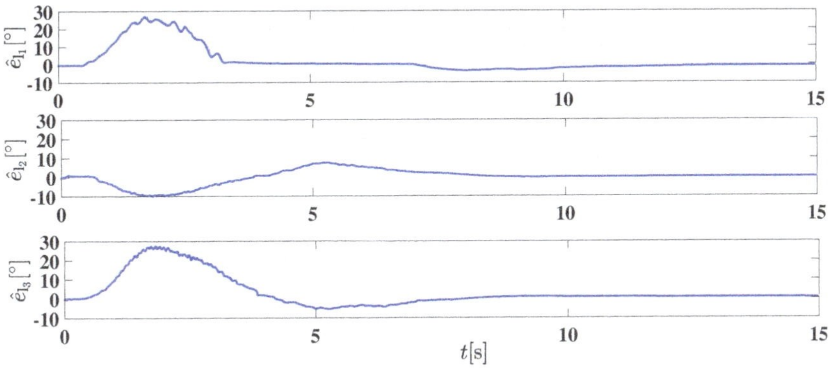

Figure 4. Experiment 1. Position tracking with emulated human dynamics: $\hat{e}_l = q_l(t) - q_r(t - T_r(t))$ (—).

Despite the considerable RTT, the tracking error converges to zero, indicating that both manipulators achieve the desired positions. It is worth noting that, although the tracking error for the first joint becomes zero at approximately $t \approx 4$ s, it does not remain constant but increases slightly before converging to zero again.

This transient behavior occurs because the remote robot's position continues to change, affecting the local manipulator's desired position. Ultimately, however, all tracking errors converge to zero and remain stable, as expected.

To quantify the system's performance, the Root Mean Square Errors (RMSEs) were calculated using the following metric:

$$\text{RMSE}(e) = \sqrt{\frac{1}{m}\sum_{k=1}^{m} e(k)^2}, \quad (74)$$

where m denotes the sample size and e represents the tracking error of interest. Table 2 presents the performance indices obtained for this experiment.

Table 2. Experiment 1: RMSE for position tracking $\hat{e}_l$ under emulated human dynamics.

Joint	RMSE [°]
1	8.4560
2	4.3047
3	9.4689

The RMSE values in Table 2 demonstrate the effectiveness of the PID controllers under emulated human dynamics. Joint 3 shows the highest RMSE, which is likely due to its larger range of motion and sensitivity to communication delays.

These results highlight the need for precise gain tuning to address time delay effects and ensure stable performance. Overall, the error values validate the theoretical tuning guidelines provided earlier.

These results experimentally validate the tuning rules provided in Theorem 1. However, they do not confirm the feasibility of replacing the PI control law with an actual human operator. Addressing this question is the focus of the second experiment.

Remark 7. *Rather than directly supplying the desired position q_d to the PI control law, fifth-order polynomials were programmed. This approach better emulates the behavior of a human operator while protecting the experimental testbed.*

4.3. Experiment 2: Human Interaction

The second experiment aims to demonstrate that the gain tuning rules provided in Theorem 1 are applicable to real teleoperation scenarios involving time-varying delays and a human operator controlling either robot. For this purpose, the PID controllers used in the previous experiment were retained, while the PI control law emulating human dynamics was removed.

In this setup, the human operator first moves the local end-effector, while the remote manipulator tracks the delayed position of the local robot.

At approximately $t \approx 43\,\mathrm{s}$, the operator brings the system to a desired position. The results are depicted in Figure 5.

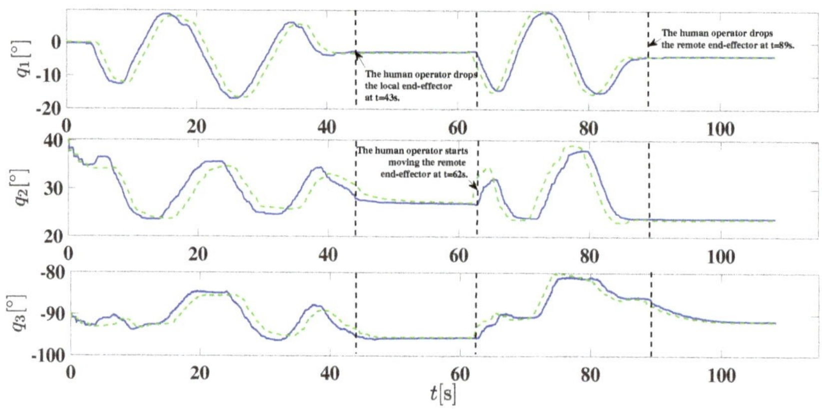

Figure 5. Experiment 2. Position tracking with human interaction: $q_l(t)$ (—), $q_r(t)$ (- - -).

As shown in (24), both the human operator and the integral term of the PID controller prevent the local end-effector from falling due to gravity. When the operator releases the end-effector, it briefly descends before the system reaches consensus, and neither end-effector falls to the ground. At $t \approx 62\,\mathrm{s}$, the operator moves the remote end-effector until it is brought to a stable position and released at approximately $t \approx 89\,\mathrm{s}$. As in the first instance, the remote end-effector initially descends slightly but stabilizes shortly thereafter, compensating for gravitational effects.

A video of Experiments 2 and 5 can be viewed at https://www.youtube.com/watch?v=GBkOU9fDd98 (accessed on 21 October 2024).

Table 3 provides the RMSE values for this experiment, which can be compared with those from Table 2. The results indicate that human interaction yields better performance. This improvement is expected, as the operator moves the end-effectors more slowly than the programmed trajectory used to emulate human dynamics.

Table 3. Experiment 2: position tracking RMSE with human interaction.

Joint	RMSE [°]
1	2.7470
2	2.1181
3	1.5224

These RMSE values reflect a marked improvement when the human operator interacts with the system compared to the emulated dynamics. For Joint 1, the RMSE is reduced by over 60%, indicating the human operator's ability to adapt to environmental variations and system delays. The results confirm that the PID tuning methodology is robust and effective in real-world teleoperation scenarios.

4.4. Experiment 3: PD + Gravity Compensation

This experiment evaluates the performance of the standard PID controller compared to an alternative control scheme, namely PD with gravity compensation [31]. Although simpler, this scheme requires prior knowledge of the robot manipulators' dynamics.

As a common and reliable approach, PD with gravity compensation provides a valid baseline for assessing the suitability of the PID controller in bilateral systems with time-varying delays. The operator attempts to reproduce the same experiment performed with the PID controllers, although exact replication is inherently difficult. The results are shown in Figure 6.

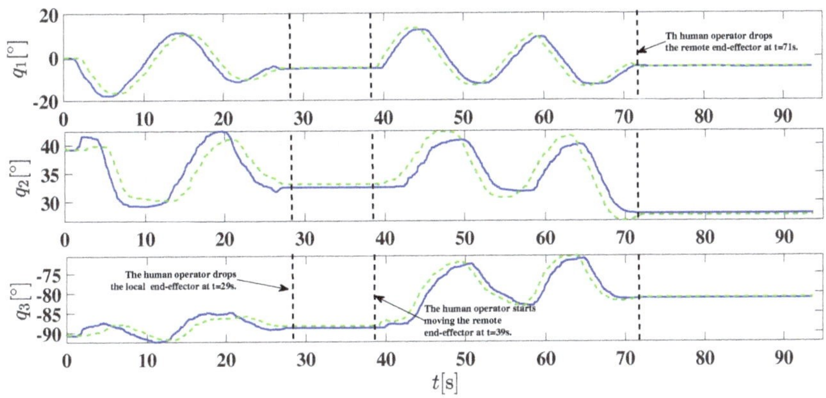

Figure 6. Experiment 3: position tracking using PD + gravity compensation [31]: $q_l(t-T_l)$ (—), $q_r(t)$ (- - -).

While the results are not directly equivalent to those in Figure 5, they can be compared objectively through Tables 3 and 4.

Table 4. Experiment 3: position tracking RMSE with human interaction using PD + gravity compensation.

Joint	RMSE [°]
1	2.8800
2	1.9506
3	1.1187

The RMSE values in this table show that the PD controller with gravity compensation performs slightly better than the PID controller, particularly in Joint 3. This difference is attributed to the instantaneous compensation for gravity effects provided by the PD approach, whereas the PID controller requires some time for the integral term to adjust. Nonetheless, the PID controller achieves comparable performance while offering greater robustness and less reliance on precise system modeling.

The PD + gravity compensation scheme performs slightly better than the PID controller, especially for the third joint. This behavior can be explained by the fact that when the human operator releases the end-effector with the PID controller, it falls momentarily until the integrator compensates for gravity. In contrast, the PD + gravity compensation approach cancels gravity effects instantaneously, eliminating this drawback. Despite this, the performance of the standard PID controller remains acceptable for comparison purposes.

4.5. Experiment 4: Constrained Motion

One of the key strengths of the PID control law is its robustness, which makes it particularly suitable for applications involving constrained motion in bilateral systems.

While the stability proof in Section 3 focuses on free motion, it is essential to test the system's robustness when the remote robot interacts with its environment. In this experiment, the remote robot contacts a book and an aluminum plate, as shown in Figure 7.

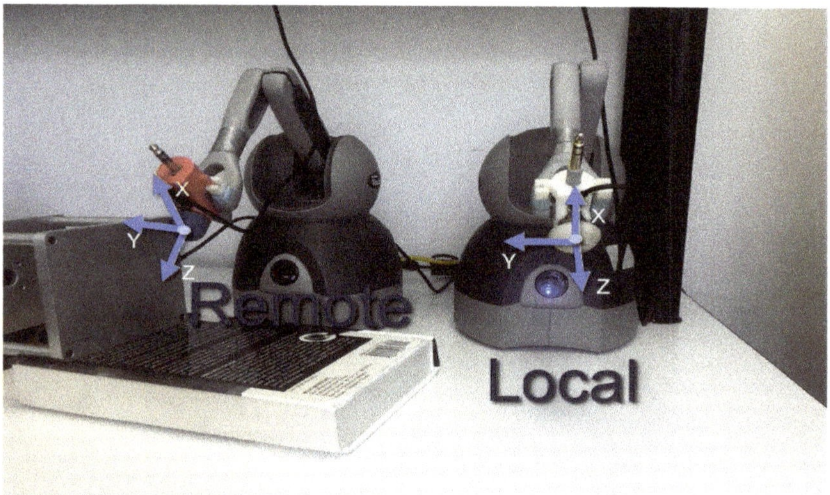

Figure 7. Experiment 4: surfaces used for constrained motion testing.

The book, being slightly deformable and subject to friction effects, poses a modeling challenge. Conversely, the aluminum plate is rigid, with lower but measurable friction. This complexity makes the experiment a robust test of the controller's capabilities. Force sensors attached to both end-effectors measure the forces applied during contact.

The experiment involves moving the remote end-effector to exert force on the book along the z-axis and later on the aluminum plate along the y-axis.

Force measurements are displayed in Figure 8.

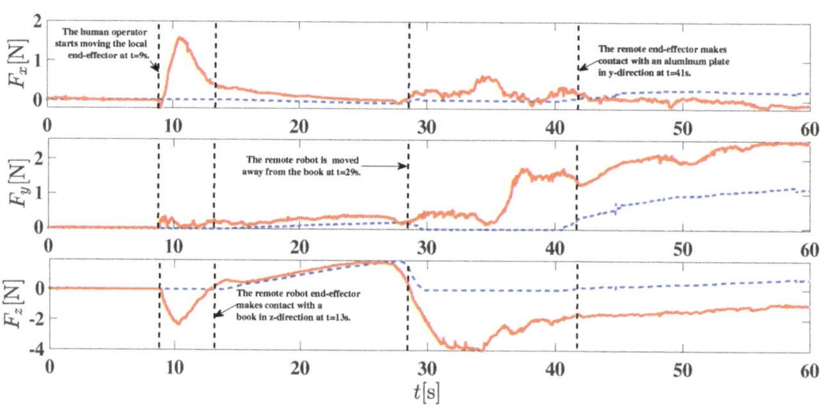

Figure 8. Experiment 4: constrained motion. Force measurements: $F_e(t)$(- - -), $F_h(t - T_l(t))$(—).

Force measurements on the local side reflect the corresponding delays, as observed on the remote side.

The results show that forces on both sides are not directly related, indicating that the human operator applies higher forces when the local end-effector is unconstrained than when motion is restricted. For instance, this can be observed before contact with the book at $t \approx 9$ s.

Figure 9 shows the position tracking $q_l(t)$ versus $q_r(t - T_r(t))$. During intervals when the remote robot contacts its environment, the local position becomes constant but no longer matches the remote position, as occurs during free motion.

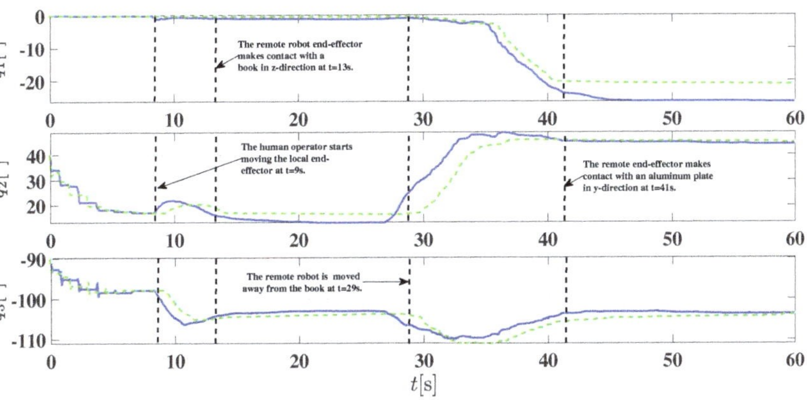

Figure 9. Experiment 4: constrained motion. Position tracking: $q_l(t)$ (—), $q_r(t - T_r(t))$ (- - -).

This behavior indicates that the operator cannot move the local end-effector in the direction constrained by the environment. Despite these challenges, the PID controller maintains the stability of the closed-loop system under perturbations.

The force tracking errors remain bounded, as indicated in Table 5.

Table 5. Experiment 4: constrained motion. Force tracking RMSE.

Component	RMSE [N]
x	0.3449
y	1.7693
z	1.8941

The RMSE values in this table demonstrate that the force tracking errors remain bounded during constrained motion scenarios. The higher RMSE values in the y and z directions are consistent with the increased difficulty of maintaining precise force control when interacting with deformable and rigid surfaces, such as the book and aluminum plate used in the experiment.

Despite these challenges, the PID controller effectively handles the dynamic perturbations introduced by environmental constraints. In addition, the PID controller effectively ensures position tracking stability during constrained motion, as evidenced by the position tracking RMSE values in Table 6.

Table 6. Experiment 4: constrained motion. Position tracking RMSE.

Joint	RMSE [°]
1	3.1200
2	3.9702
3	1.4177

The position tracking RMSE values indicate that the PID controller maintains stability and acceptable performance even under constrained motion conditions. The slightly higher errors compared to free motion experiments can be attributed to the physical restrictions imposed by environmental interaction.

These results further highlight the robustness of the PID controller, as it successfully stabilizes the system without compromising overall tracking accuracy.

4.6. Experiment 5: Force Reflection

The previous experiment demonstrated the robust performance of PID controllers in constrained motion scenarios. Nevertheless, the results presented in Figure 8 reveal a lack of force matching, which limits the system's transparency.

To overcome this limitation, the concept of delayed kinematic correspondence, as outlined in [35], is utilized. Force feedback is incorporated using controllers (64)–(68) with the parameter $\boldsymbol{K}_{fi} = 1350\boldsymbol{I}$.

This control strategy relies on torque measurements, derived through the relationship $\boldsymbol{\tau}_i = \boldsymbol{J}_i^{\mathrm{T}}(\boldsymbol{q}_i)\boldsymbol{F}_i$ [30], where $\boldsymbol{J}_i(\boldsymbol{q}_i)$ denotes the geometric Jacobian, and $\boldsymbol{F}_i$ corresponds to the measured forces.

The principle of delayed kinematic correspondence ensures minimal position errors on the local side and accurate force tracking errors on the remote side. This mechanism allows the operator to experience the remote environment as if it were directly reproduced locally.

Unlike Experiment 4, the operator maneuvers the local end-effector to bring the remote end-effector into contact with the book. Subsequently, a circular motion is performed on the book, followed by contact with the aluminum plate, where a linear motion is executed. Finally, the end-effector is returned to its initial position.

Figure 10 presents the force tracking results, demonstrating acceptable performance during contact with the book (from $t \approx 7$ s to $t \approx 24$ s) and the aluminum plate (from $t \approx 29$ s to $t \approx 44$ s). These results indicate that the remote manipulator accurately applies the forces commanded by the operator.

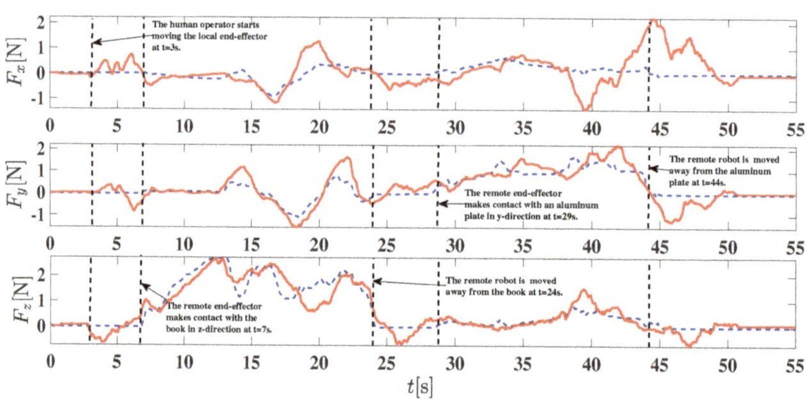

Figure 10. Experiment 5: force reflection. Force tracking: $\boldsymbol{F}_{\mathrm{e}}(t)$(- - -), $\boldsymbol{F}_{\mathrm{h}}(t - T_1(t))$(—).

The RMSE values for force tracking are presented in Table 7, demonstrating significant improvements compared to Table 5. These results highlight the effectiveness of incorporating force feedback in enhancing system performance.

The force tracking RMSE values in Table 5 reveal that the addition of the force feedback term enhances transparency during teleoperation. The lower RMSE in the x and z directions highlights the effectiveness of force control in providing the human operator with a more accurate perception of the remote environment. This improvement demonstrates the ability of the PID controller with force feedback to handle dynamic interactions while preserving stability and robustness. Position tracking performance during force reflection is shown in Figure 11.

Table 7. Experiment 5: force reflection. Force tracking RMSE.

Component	RMSE $[N]$
x	0.5545
y	0.3855
z	0.3308

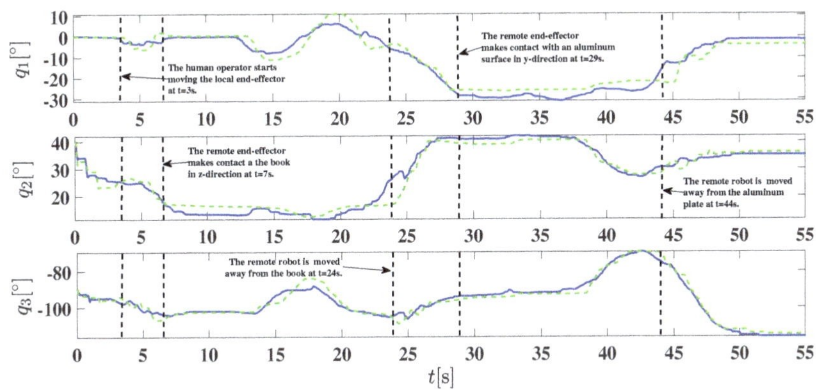

Figure 11. Experiment 5: force reflection. Position tracking: $q_l(t)$ (—), $q_r(t - T_r(t))$ (- - -).

The RMSE values, provided in Table 8, confirm that the PID controller maintains precise tracking throughout the experiment, even under varying force conditions.

Table 8. Experiment 5: force reflection. Position tracking RMSE.

Joint	RMSE [°]
1	3.2540
2	2.2470
3	2.1648

The position tracking RMSE values in this table show a slight improvement compared to constrained motion experiments without force feedback. This enhancement reflects the synergistic effect of force feedback on position control, as the human operator benefits from increased transparency when manipulating the local end-effector. These results validate the proposed PID controller's adaptability and effectiveness in scenarios requiring both position and force control.

This level of position tracking performance is particularly critical during constrained motion scenarios. Since both robots share identical kinematic configurations, the operator perceives the remote environment as being directly reproduced locally [35]. The round trip time (RTT), with a mean value of 1.3 s, remains a key metric for evaluating bilateral system performance. As noted in [42], this RTT value represents superior performance for the standard PID controller compared to most alternative algorithms, as detailed in Table 3 of the reference. In conclusion, the standard PID controller demonstrates acceptable performance across all test scenarios. For further performance enhancements, more advanced control methodologies may be considered.

To summarize the results of the experiments presented, Figure 12 provides a comparative analysis of the RMSE values for position tracking across different scenarios. This figure highlights the improvement in performance from uncontrolled systems to controlled configurations, including PID- and MRAC-based approaches. The synthesis underscores the robustness and practicality of the PID control strategy under varying conditions, particularly when computational simplicity is prioritized. The comparison of RMSE values for position tracking across different experiments is depicted in Figure 12.

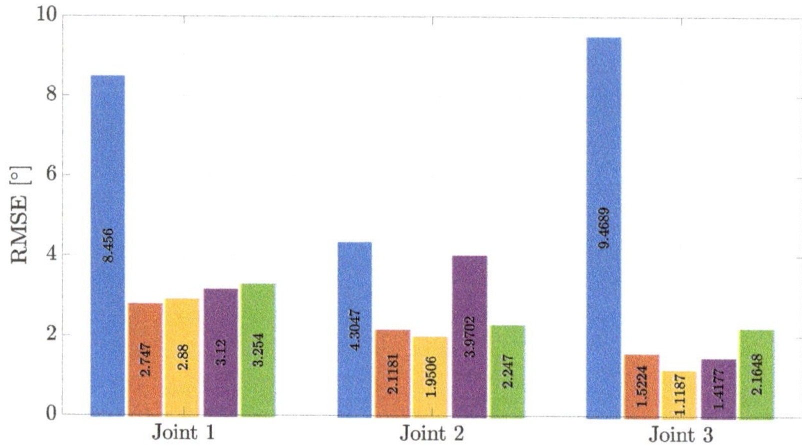

Figure 12. RMSE comparison for position tracking. Emulated dynamics, human interaction, PD + gravity compensation, constrained motion, and force reflection.

5. Conclusions

This study provides a comprehensive theoretical and experimental analysis of the application of the standard Proportional-Integral-Derivative (PID) controller to bilateral systems consisting of robot manipulators with time-varying delays. Through a detailed closed-loop stability proof, it is demonstrated that PID control ensures the convergence of both manipulators to the desired position specified by the human operator on either side of the system.

The stability proof provided does not rely on traditional Lyapunov theory or passivity assumptions, but instead employs $\mathcal{L}_2$ and $\mathcal{L}_\infty$ norms alongside Barbalat's Lemma. While it is assumed that human dynamics can be approximated by a simple PI control law, experimental results confirm that this assumption does not limit practical implementation. The derived tuning rules for the PID controllers yield consistent and robust performance, even when a human operator directly controls either of the two robots.

Additionally, a comparison with the well-known PD + gravity compensation scheme demonstrates that PID controllers achieve comparable performance, making them a viable option for bilateral systems with time-varying delays. Experimental scenarios, including free motion, environmental contact, and force feedback, highlight the robustness and reliability of the PID control strategy, as well as its ability to maintain system stability and achieve a good degree of transparency. The main advantage of employing a standard PID controller in this context lies in its simplicity and robustness. Unlike advanced control techniques, which often require extensive computational resources or detailed system modeling, the PID controller provides a practical and reliable solution for systems where achieving stability under time-varying delays is more critical than attaining extreme precision. This study rigorously validates the application of a standard PID controller in bilateral teleoperation systems with time-varying delays, demonstrating that, for applications where simplicity, reliability, and robustness are prioritized, PID controllers represent an effective and practical choice. As illustrated in Figure 12, the standard PID controller achieves comparable performance to more complex control schemes, showcasing its viability as a practical and robust solution for teleoperated systems with time-varying delays.

The primary contribution of this work lies in validating the applicability of standard PID control for systems where high precision or computational complexity is not required. In such contexts, the simplicity and inherent robustness of PID controllers make them the preferred choice, as they can handle delays and challenging environments without significant modifications to the controller architecture.

Finally, while it is acknowledged that PID control cannot compete with more advanced techniques in terms of maximum performance, this work demonstrates that its application in bilateral systems with time-varying delays constitutes a practical and effective solution. This makes standard PID controllers a valuable tool for industrial and research applications in teleoperated robotics, especially where simplicity, reliability, and robustness are prioritized. However, for scenarios requiring extreme performance, the use of advanced control methodologies remains essential.

While the results presented demonstrate the robustness and stability of the proposed standard PID control strategy in bilateral teleoperation systems with time-varying delays, certain limitations must be acknowledged. First, the theoretical stability proof assumes idealized conditions, such as bounded time delays and linearized system dynamics, which may not fully capture the complexities of highly nonlinear or uncertain real-world environments. Second, the experiments were conducted using simplified 3-DOF manipulators, which, while effective for validation, may not generalize directly to systems with higher degrees of freedom or more complex operational requirements.

Future work could explore extending the stability proof to account for more general cases, such as unbounded or stochastic time delays and interactions with more dynamic and unpredictable environments. Additionally, integrating advanced control techniques, such as adaptive or learning-based methods, may further enhance performance and adaptability in highly nonlinear systems. Expanding the experimental validation to include higher-DOF manipulators and more diverse scenarios, such as teleoperation in unstructured or hazardous environments, would provide greater insight into the practical applicability of the proposed approach.

Author Contributions: Conceptualization, M.A.A.; Data curation, E.J.G.-B.; Formal analysis, M.A.A.; Funding acquisition, P.S.-S.; Methodology, M.A.A.; Resources, P.S.-S.; Validation, E.J.G.-B.; Writing—original draft, M.A.A. and P.S.-S.; Writing—review and editing, P.S.-S. All authors have read and agreed to the published version of the manuscript.

Funding: This research was funded by the **DGAPA-UNAM** under grant **IN102723** and **CONACyT** under grant **Estancias Posdoctorales por México: Proceso de Renovación 2023**.

Data Availability Statement: No new data were created or analyzed in this study. Data sharing is not applicable to this article.

Conflicts of Interest: The authors declare no conflicts of interest.

Abbreviations

The following abbreviations are used in this manuscript:

FL	Fuzzy Logic
LMI	Linear matrix inequality
MHE	Moving Horizon Estimation
NN	Neural Network
RBFNN	Radial basis function neural network
SMC	Sliding Mode Control
TDPA	Time domain passivity approach
T-S	Takagi-Sugeno
T2FNN	Type-2 Fuzzy Neural Network
TSM	Terminal Sliding Mode
PD	Proportional-Derivative
PID	Proportional-Integral-Derivative

Appendix A

To establish the proof of Theorem 1, it is essential to rely on two widely recognized lemmas:

Lemma A1 ([43]). *Let $\boldsymbol{x}(t) : [t_0, \infty) \to \mathbb{R}^n$ be a state vector such that $\boldsymbol{x}(t) \in \mathcal{L}_2 \cap \mathcal{L}_\infty$ and $\dot{\boldsymbol{x}}(t) \in \mathcal{L}_\infty$. Then, the following holds:*

$$\lim_{t \to \infty} \boldsymbol{x}(t) = \boldsymbol{0}. \tag{A1}$$

Lemma A2. ***Barbalat's Lemma*** ([44]). *Consider a differentiable function $\boldsymbol{x}(t)$ defined over $[t_0, \infty)$ such that it remains bounded and converges to a finite limit as $t \to \infty$. If $\dot{\boldsymbol{x}}(t)$ is uniformly continuous, then the time derivative satisfies $\dot{\boldsymbol{x}}(t) \to \boldsymbol{0}$ as $t \to \infty$.*

The proof is developed through the following steps:

1. Given that $\boldsymbol{q}_\mathrm{d}$ is assumed to remain constant, the PID control laws (6)–(8), in combination with the assumed human dynamics described in (9)–(11), are mathematically equivalent to the formulation in (23)–(25) by applying the relationships in (17)–(18) and the condition given by (12). Furthermore, under the definition (29), the control law presented in (23)–(25) can also be expressed equivalently as (31)–(33), provided that the conditions in (34)–(36) are satisfied.
As a result, the closed-loop system dynamics described by (43) are equivalent to those obtained by substituting the PID control laws (6)–(8) and the human dynamics in (9)–(11) directly into the system equations in (1). From this equivalence, the following conclusions can be drawn:

$$\boldsymbol{x} = \boldsymbol{0} \quad \Rightarrow \quad \hat{\boldsymbol{e}}_i = \boldsymbol{0},\ \dot{\boldsymbol{q}}_i = \boldsymbol{0}, \tag{A2}$$

$$\boldsymbol{e}_i = \boldsymbol{0}, \tag{A3}$$

$$\boldsymbol{\xi}_i = -\boldsymbol{K}_{\mathrm{I}i}^{-1} \boldsymbol{g}_i(\boldsymbol{q}_\mathrm{d}). \tag{A4}$$

These results hold because, by applying the conditions in (34)–(36), if $\boldsymbol{x} = \boldsymbol{0}$, then it follows from (24), (29), (30), (32)–(33), (41), and (42) that:

$$\boldsymbol{w}_i \ = \ \boldsymbol{\Lambda}_i \int_0^t (\boldsymbol{e}_i - \bar{\boldsymbol{e}}_j + \boldsymbol{A}_i \boldsymbol{e}_i) \mathrm{d}t = \boldsymbol{\Lambda}_i \boldsymbol{\xi}_i = -\boldsymbol{K}_{\omega i}^{-1} \boldsymbol{g}_i(\boldsymbol{q}_\mathrm{d}). \tag{A5}$$

It is important to note that this does not represent a change of coordinates. Thus, there is no diffeomorphism between the variables $\hat{\boldsymbol{e}}_i$, $\dot{\boldsymbol{q}}_i$, $\boldsymbol{e}_i$, $\boldsymbol{\xi}_i$, and the state vector $\boldsymbol{x}$. The equivalence established in this step, which connects the PID control laws (6)–(8) and the human dynamics (9)–(11) to the closed-loop system formulation in (23)–(25) and ultimately (43), ensures that the dynamics of the system are well-defined and consistent under the given conditions. This equivalence lays the groundwork for introducing a positive definite candidate function in the subsequent analysis, enabling the examination of the stability properties of the system.
2. To establish that $\boldsymbol{x} \to \boldsymbol{0}$ as $t \to \infty$, let us analyze the following positive definite function $V_i(\boldsymbol{x})$, which, although not a Lyapunov function, is constructed with respect to the state variables of system (43):

$$V_i(\boldsymbol{x}) = \frac{1}{2}\boldsymbol{x}_k^\mathrm{T} \boldsymbol{K}_{\omega i} \boldsymbol{x}_k + \frac{1}{2}\boldsymbol{e}_i^\mathrm{T} \boldsymbol{e}_i + \frac{1}{2}\boldsymbol{s}_i^\mathrm{T} \boldsymbol{H}_i(\boldsymbol{q}_i) \boldsymbol{s}_i + (\boldsymbol{B}_i \boldsymbol{e}_i - \bar{\boldsymbol{e}}_j)^\mathrm{T} \boldsymbol{B}_i^{-1} \boldsymbol{K}_{\mathrm{v}i2} \boldsymbol{\Lambda}_i (\boldsymbol{B}_i \boldsymbol{e}_i - \bar{\boldsymbol{e}}_j), \tag{A6}$$

where $i = \mathrm{l}, \mathrm{r}$ and $k = 1$ for $i = \mathrm{l}$ or $k = 4$ for $i = \mathrm{r}$. The positive definite function $V_i(\boldsymbol{x})$ is chosen because it encapsulates the energy-like properties of the system, combining contributions from $\boldsymbol{e}_i$, $\boldsymbol{s}_i$, and $\dot{\boldsymbol{e}}_i$. This facilitates the derivation of a well-structured inequality for $\dot{V}_i(\boldsymbol{x})$, which is central to analyzing the system's stability. The positive definite function $V_i(\boldsymbol{x})$ is selected based on standard Lyapunov candidate

functions, ensuring that its gradient satisfies the conditions for stability as outlined in Theorem 1. This approach guarantees that the stability proof aligns with the principles of Lyapunov theory while maintaining the robustness required for the system's dynamics.
Using Property 2, the following relationship is established:

$$-s_i^{\mathrm{T}} K_{vi2} s_i = -\dot{e}_i^{\mathrm{T}} K_{vi2} \dot{e}_i - 2\dot{e}_i^{\mathrm{T}} K_{vi2} \Lambda_i \left(B_i e_i - \bar{e}_j\right) - \left(B_i e_i - \bar{e}_j\right)^{\mathrm{T}} \Lambda_i K_{vi2} \Lambda_i \left(B_i e_i - \bar{e}_j\right), \quad \text{(A7)}$$

derived from (29) and (46). Substituting (A7) into the derivative of (A6), we obtain:

$$\begin{aligned}\dot{V}_i(x) \le & -\lambda_{\min}(\Lambda_i)\lambda_{\min}(B_i)\|e_i\|^2 + \|e_i\|\|s_i\| + \lambda_{\max}(\Lambda_i)\|e_i\|\|\bar{e}_j\| - \lambda_{\min}(K_{vi1})\|s_i\|^2 \\ & -\lambda_{\min}(K_{vi2})\|\dot{e}_i\|^2 + k_{gi}\|s_i\|\|e_i\| + \lambda_{Hi}\lambda_{\max}(\Lambda_i)\|s_i\|\left(\lambda_{\max}(B_i)\|\dot{e}_i\| + \|\dot{\bar{e}}_j\|\right) \\ & +\lambda_{\max}(\Lambda_i)k_{ci}\|s_i\|\|\dot{e}_i\|\left(\lambda_{\max}(B_i)\|e_i\| + \|\bar{e}_j\|\right) + \lambda_{\max}(K_{\omega i})\|s_i\|\|\bar{e}_j\| \\ & -\lambda_{\min}(\Lambda_i^2)\lambda_{\min}(K_{vi2})\|B_i e_i - \bar{e}_j\|^2 + 2\frac{\lambda_{\max}(K_{vi2})\lambda_{\max}(\Lambda_i)}{\lambda_{\min}(B_i)}\|\dot{\bar{e}}_j\|\|B_i e_i - \bar{e}_j\|. \end{aligned} \quad \text{(A8)}$$

Next, assuming $\|x(t_0)\| < \epsilon$, where ϵ is defined in (45), and considering that $T_j(t) \geq 0$ for $j = l, r$ (by Assumption 2), the state variables remain bounded within a region $\mathcal{D}$. Substituting these bounds into (A8), the following refined inequality is obtained:

$$\begin{aligned}\dot{V}_i(x) \le & -\lambda_{\min}(\Lambda_i)\lambda_{\min}(B_i)\|e_i\|^2 + \|e_i\|\|s_i\| + \lambda_{\max}(\Lambda_i)\|e_i\|\|\bar{e}_j\| - \lambda_{\min}(K_{vi1})\|s_i\|^2 \\ & -\lambda_{\min}(K_{vi2})\|\dot{e}_i\|^2 + k_{gi}\|s_i\|\|e_i\| + \lambda_{Hi}\lambda_{\max}(\Lambda_i)\|s_i\|\left(\lambda_{\max}(B_i)\|\dot{e}_i\| + \|\dot{\bar{e}}_j\|\right) \\ & -\lambda_{\min}(\Lambda_i^2)\lambda_{\min}(K_{vi2})\|B_i e_i - \bar{e}_j\|^2 + 2\frac{\lambda_{\max}(K_{vi2})\lambda_{\max}(\Lambda_i)}{\lambda_{\min}(B_i)}\|\dot{\bar{e}}_j\|\|B_i e_i - \bar{e}_j\| \\ & +\lambda_{\max}(\Lambda_i)k_{ci}\|s_i\|\|\dot{e}_i\|(\lambda_{\max}(B_i)\epsilon + \epsilon) + \lambda_{\max}(K_{\omega i})\|s_i\|\|\bar{e}_j\|. \end{aligned} \quad \text{(A9)}$$

Next, the inequality (A9) refines (A8) by incorporating the assumption that $\|x(t_0)\| < \epsilon$. This ensures that $x(t)$ remains within $\mathcal{D}$, maintaining the boundedness of terms such as $\|\bar{e}_j\|$ and $\|\dot{\bar{e}}_j\|$. These bounds are critical in demonstrating that $\dot{V}_i(x)$ remains negative definite for all $x \neq \mathbf{0}$.
Finally, since $\dot{V}_i(x) < 0$, it follows that $V_i(x)$ is a strictly decreasing function. Combined with the positive definiteness of $V_i(x)$, this guarantees that $x(t)$ asymptotically approaches $\mathbf{0}$ as $t \to \infty$, completing the proof of stability for this subsystem.

3. Since any of the robots can be considered as local and the other one as remote, without loss of generality, it is assumed that $A_r = O$ and $B_r = I$, according to (30), while $A_l > O$. Consequently, the following positive definite function for the entire system is defined:

$$V(x) = V_l(x) + V_r(x), \quad \text{(A10)}$$

where $V_l(x)$ and $V_r(x)$ represent the positive definite functions associated with the local and remote robots, respectively.
The derivative of (A10) satisfies, based on (A9):

$$\begin{aligned}\dot{V}(x) \leq & -\lambda_{\min}(\mathbf{\Lambda}_{\mathrm{l}})\lambda_{\min}(\mathbf{B}_{\mathrm{l}})\|e_{\mathrm{l}}\|^2 + \|e_{\mathrm{l}}\|\|s_{\mathrm{l}}\| + \lambda_{\max}(\mathbf{\Lambda}_{\mathrm{l}})\|e_{\mathrm{l}}\|\|\bar{e}_{\mathrm{r}}\| - \lambda_{\min}(\mathbf{K}_{\mathrm{vl1}})\|s_{\mathrm{l}}\|^2 \\ & - \lambda_{\min}(\mathbf{K}_{\mathrm{vl2}})\|\dot{e}_{\mathrm{l}}\|^2 + k_{\mathrm{gl}}\|s_{\mathrm{l}}\|\|e_{\mathrm{l}}\| + \lambda_{\mathrm{Hl}}\lambda_{\max}(\mathbf{\Lambda}_{\mathrm{l}})\lambda_{\max}(\mathbf{B}_{\mathrm{l}})\|s_{\mathrm{l}}\|\|\dot{e}_{\mathrm{l}}\| \\ & + \lambda_{\mathrm{Hl}}\lambda_{\max}(\mathbf{\Lambda}_{\mathrm{l}})(1+T_{\mathrm{r}}^*)\|s_{\mathrm{l}}\|\|\dot{e}_{\mathrm{r}}(t-T_{\mathrm{r}}(t))\| + \lambda_{\max}(\mathbf{K}_{\omega\mathrm{l}})\|s_{\mathrm{l}}\|\|\bar{e}_{\mathrm{r}}\| \\ & + \lambda_{\max}(\mathbf{\Lambda}_{\mathrm{l}})k_{\mathrm{cl}}\|s_{\mathrm{l}}\|\|\dot{e}_{\mathrm{l}}\|(\lambda_{\max}(\mathbf{B}_{\mathrm{l}})\epsilon+\epsilon) - \lambda_{\min}(\mathbf{\Lambda}_{\mathrm{l}}^2)\lambda_{\min}(\mathbf{K}_{\mathrm{vl2}})\|\mathbf{B}_{\mathrm{l}}e_{\mathrm{l}} - \bar{e}_{\mathrm{r}}\|^2 \\ & + \left(2\frac{\lambda_{\max}(\mathbf{K}_{\mathrm{vl2}})\lambda_{\max}(\mathbf{\Lambda}_{\mathrm{l}})(1+T_{\mathrm{r}}^*)}{\lambda_{\min}(\mathbf{B}_{\mathrm{l}})}\right)\left(\|\dot{e}_{\mathrm{r}}(t-T_{\mathrm{r}}(t))\|\|\mathbf{B}_{\mathrm{l}}e_{\mathrm{l}} - \bar{e}_{\mathrm{r}}\|\right) \\ & - \lambda_{\min}(\mathbf{\Lambda}_{\mathrm{r}})\|e_{\mathrm{r}}\|^2 + \|e_{\mathrm{r}}\|\|s_{\mathrm{r}}\| + \lambda_{\max}(\mathbf{\Lambda}_{\mathrm{r}})\|e_{\mathrm{r}}\|\|\bar{e}_{\mathrm{l}}\| - \lambda_{\min}(\mathbf{K}_{\mathrm{vr1}})\|s_{\mathrm{r}}\|^2 \\ & - \lambda_{\min}(\mathbf{K}_{\mathrm{vr2}})\|\dot{e}_{\mathrm{r}}\|^2 + 2\lambda_{\max}(\mathbf{\Lambda}_{\mathrm{r}})k_{\mathrm{cr}}\|s_{\mathrm{r}}\|\|\dot{e}_{\mathrm{r}}\|\epsilon + \lambda_{\max}(\mathbf{K}_{\omega\mathrm{r}})\|s_{\mathrm{r}}\|\|\bar{e}_{\mathrm{l}}\| \\ & + k_{\mathrm{gr}}\|s_{\mathrm{r}}\|\|e_{\mathrm{r}}\| + \lambda_{\mathrm{Hr}}\lambda_{\max}(\mathbf{\Lambda}_{\mathrm{r}})\|s_{\mathrm{r}}\|\|\dot{e}_{\mathrm{r}}\| - \lambda_{\min}(\mathbf{\Lambda}_{\mathrm{r}}^2)\lambda_{\min}(\mathbf{K}_{\mathrm{vr2}})\|e_{\mathrm{r}} - \bar{e}_{\mathrm{l}}\|^2 \\ & + \left(2\lambda_{\max}(\mathbf{K}_{\mathrm{vr2}})\lambda_{\max}(\mathbf{\Lambda}_{\mathrm{r}})(1+T_{\mathrm{l}}^*)\right)\left(\|\dot{e}_{\mathrm{l}}(t-T_{\mathrm{l}}(t))\|\|e_{\mathrm{r}} - \bar{e}_{\mathrm{l}}\|\right) \\ & + \lambda_{\mathrm{Hr}}\lambda_{\max}(\mathbf{\Lambda}_{\mathrm{r}})(1+T_{\mathrm{l}}^*)\|s_{\mathrm{r}}\|\|\dot{e}_{\mathrm{l}}(t-T_{\mathrm{l}}(t))\|, \end{aligned} \tag{A11}$$

The positive definite function $V(x)$ is constructed as the summation of the local and remote components, ensuring the stability properties of the individual subsystems are preserved in the analysis of the coupled system.

The transition from (A9) to (A11) follows naturally from combining the bounded properties of $V_{\mathrm{l}}(x)$ and $V_{\mathrm{r}}(x)$, under the assumptions that $\mathbf{A}_{\mathrm{r}} = \mathbf{O}$ and $\mathbf{B}_{\mathrm{r}} = \mathbf{I}$. This simplification maintains generality while allowing any robot to assume the role of the local or remote subsystem.

Cross terms such as $\|e_{\mathrm{r}}\|\|s_{\mathrm{r}}\|$ and $\|\dot{e}_{\mathrm{l}}(t-T_{\mathrm{l}}(t))\|\|e_{\mathrm{r}} - \bar{e}_{\mathrm{l}}\|$ are appropriately bounded using the matrix norm properties $\lambda_{\min}$ and $\lambda_{\max}$. This ensures that $\dot{V}(x)$ remains negative definite for all $x \neq \mathbf{0}$. Consequently, $\dot{V}(x)$ demonstrates that $V(x)$ decreases monotonically over time, leading to $x \to \mathbf{0}$ as $t \to \infty$, thereby proving the global stability of the coupled system.

4. Instead of showing that $\dot{V}(x) \leq 0$, $\dot{V}(x)$ will be integrated. However, prior to performing this integration, the following aspects must be considered:

   (a) By applying the Cauchy-Schwarz inequality, which states that for any vector signals $a(\theta)$ and $b(\theta)$, the following holds:

$$\int_0^t a^{\mathrm{T}}(\theta)b(\theta)\mathrm{d}\theta \leq \left[\int_0^t \|a(\theta)\|^2\mathrm{d}\theta\right]^{\frac{1}{2}}\left[\int_0^t \|b(\theta)\|^2\mathrm{d}\theta\right]^{\frac{1}{2}}, \tag{A12}$$

   the following relationships can be established:

$$\int_{t_0}^{t} \|s_i(\theta)\|\|e_i(\theta)\|\mathrm{d}\theta \leq \left(\int_{t_0}^{t} \|s_i(\theta)\|^2\mathrm{d}\theta\right)^{\frac{1}{2}}\left(\int_{t_0}^{t} \|e_i(\theta)\|^2\mathrm{d}\theta\right)^{\frac{1}{2}}, \tag{A13}$$

   Additionally, by leveraging the results from equations (47)—(48), the following inequality is derived:

$$\int_{t_0}^{t} \|e_i(\theta)\|\|\bar{e}_j(\theta)\|\mathrm{d}\theta \leq \alpha_j\left(\int_{t_0}^{t} \|e_i(\theta)\|^2\mathrm{d}\theta\right)^{\frac{1}{2}}\left(\int_{t_0}^{t} \|e_j(\theta)\|^2\mathrm{d}\theta\right)^{\frac{1}{2}}, \tag{A14}$$

   Similarly, applying the same inequality in the context of delayed signals yields:

$$\int_{t_0}^{t} \|s_i(\theta)\| \|\dot{e}_j(\theta - T_j(\theta))\| \mathrm{d}\theta \leq \beta_j \left(\int_{t_0}^{t} \|s_i(\theta)\|^2 \mathrm{d}\theta \right)^{\frac{1}{2}} \left(\int_{t_0}^{t} \|\dot{e}_j(\theta)\|^2 \mathrm{d}\theta \right)^{\frac{1}{2}}. \tag{A15}$$

These inequalities, valid for $i, j = \mathrm{l}, \mathrm{r}$, are essential for bounding cross-product terms such as $\|s_i\| \|e_i\|$, $\|e_i\| \|\bar{e}_j\|$, and $\|s_i\| \|\dot{e}_j(\theta - T_j(\theta))\|$, which arise in the derivative $\dot{V}(x)$. The absence of arguments in the final integrals reflects the omission of delays for simplicity and clarity. These bounds make the integration of $\dot{V}(x)$ both mathematically rigorous and computationally tractable.

(b) The studies in (A13)–(A15) represent specific examples of norm products that appear in (A11). While these inequalities are illustrative, they are not exhaustive. Other norm product terms in (A11) can similarly be bounded using analogous approaches, ensuring consistency across the entire analysis.

(c) The following compact notation will be employed (compare with (4)):

$$\|f(t)\|_{\tilde{2}} = \left(\int_{t_0}^{t} \|f(t)\|^2 \mathrm{d}t \right)^{\frac{1}{2}}. \tag{A16}$$

The notation $\| \cdot \|_{\tilde{2}}$, introduced in (A16), compactly represents the integrals of squared norms over the interval $[t_0, t]$. This simplifies the manipulation of terms involving $\dot{V}(x)$ and provides a consistent framework for expressing bounds.

The transition from Step 3 to Step 4 involves shifting the focus from analyzing $\dot{V}(x)$ directly to integrating it over a specified time interval. This approach builds upon the boundedness established in Step 3 and leverages the inequalities outlined above to ensure the integral remains well-defined and finite.

5. Keeping the previous item in mind, the integral of (A11) satisfies for $t \in [t_0, t_\epsilon]$:

$$\begin{aligned}
\int_{t_0}^{t} \dot{V} \mathrm{d}\theta = V(x(t)) - V(x(t_0)) \leq & -\lambda_{\min}(\Lambda_\mathrm{l})\lambda_{\min}(B_\mathrm{l})\|e_\mathrm{l}\|_{\tilde{2}}^2 + \|e_\mathrm{l}\|_{\tilde{2}}\|s_\mathrm{l}\|_{\tilde{2}} - \lambda_{\min}(K_{\mathrm{vl1}})\|s_\mathrm{l}\|_{\tilde{2}}^2 \\
& + \alpha_\mathrm{r}\lambda_{\max}(\Lambda_\mathrm{l})\|e_\mathrm{l}\|_{\tilde{2}}\|e_\mathrm{r}\|_{\tilde{2}} - \lambda_{\min}(K_{\mathrm{vl2}})\|\dot{e}_\mathrm{l}\|_{\tilde{2}}^2 + k_{\mathrm{gl}}\|s_\mathrm{l}\|_{\tilde{2}}\|e_\mathrm{l}\|_{\tilde{2}} \\
& + \lambda_{\mathrm{Hl}}\lambda_{\max}(\Lambda_\mathrm{l})\lambda_{\max}(B_\mathrm{l})\|s_\mathrm{l}\|_{\tilde{2}}\|\dot{e}_\mathrm{l}\|_{\tilde{2}} + \alpha_\mathrm{r}\lambda_{\max}(K_{\omega\mathrm{l}})\|s_\mathrm{l}\|_{\tilde{2}}\|e_\mathrm{r}\|_{\tilde{2}} \\
& + \beta_\mathrm{r}\lambda_{\mathrm{Hl}}\lambda_{\max}(\Lambda_\mathrm{l})(1 + T_\mathrm{r}^*)\|s_\mathrm{l}\|_{\tilde{2}}\|\dot{e}_\mathrm{r}\|_{\tilde{2}} + \alpha_\mathrm{l}\lambda_{\max}(\Lambda_\mathrm{r})\|e_\mathrm{r}\|_{\tilde{2}}\|e_\mathrm{l}\|_{\tilde{2}} \\
& + \lambda_{\max}(\Lambda_\mathrm{l})k_{\mathrm{cl}}(\lambda_{\max}(B_\mathrm{l})\epsilon + \epsilon)\|s_\mathrm{l}\|_{\tilde{2}}\|\dot{e}_\mathrm{l}\|_{\tilde{2}} - \lambda_{\min}(\Lambda_\mathrm{r})\|e_\mathrm{r}\|_{\tilde{2}}^2 \\
& - \lambda_{\min}(\Lambda_\mathrm{l}^2)\lambda_{\min}(K_{\mathrm{vl2}})\|B_\mathrm{l}e_\mathrm{l} - \bar{e}_\mathrm{r}\|_{\tilde{2}}^2 + \|e_\mathrm{r}\|_{\tilde{2}}\|s_\mathrm{r}\|_{\tilde{2}} - \|\bar{e}_\mathrm{l}\|_{\tilde{2}}^2 \\
& + \left(2\frac{\beta_\mathrm{r}\lambda_{\max}(K_{\mathrm{vl2}})\lambda_{\max}(\Lambda_\mathrm{l})(1 + T_\mathrm{r}^*)}{\lambda_{\min}(B_\mathrm{l})}\right)\left(\|\dot{e}_\mathrm{r}\|_{\tilde{2}}\|B_\mathrm{l}e_\mathrm{l} - \bar{e}_\mathrm{r}\|_{\tilde{2}}\right) \\
& - \lambda_{\min}(K_{\mathrm{vr1}})\|s_\mathrm{r}\|_{\tilde{2}}^2 - \lambda_{\min}(K_{\mathrm{vr2}})\|\dot{e}_\mathrm{r}\|_{\tilde{2}}^2 + k_{\mathrm{gr}}\|s_\mathrm{r}\|_{\tilde{2}}\|e_\mathrm{r}\|_{\tilde{2}} \\
& + \lambda_{\mathrm{Hr}}\lambda_{\max}(\Lambda_\mathrm{r})\|s_\mathrm{r}\|_{\tilde{2}}\|\dot{e}_\mathrm{r}\|_{\tilde{2}} + \beta_\mathrm{l}\lambda_{\mathrm{Hr}}\lambda_{\max}(\Lambda_\mathrm{r})(1 + T_\mathrm{l}^*)\|s_\mathrm{r}\|_{\tilde{2}}\|\dot{e}_\mathrm{l}\|_{\tilde{2}} \\
& + 2\lambda_{\max}(\Lambda_\mathrm{r})k_{\mathrm{cr}}\epsilon\|s_\mathrm{r}\|_{\tilde{2}}\|\dot{e}_\mathrm{r}\|_{\tilde{2}} + \alpha_\mathrm{l}\lambda_{\max}(K_{\omega\mathrm{r}})\|s_\mathrm{r}\|_{\tilde{2}}\|e_\mathrm{l}\|_{\tilde{2}} \\
& + \left(2\beta_\mathrm{l}\lambda_{\max}(K_{\mathrm{vr2}})\lambda_{\max}(\Lambda_\mathrm{r})(1 + T_\mathrm{l}^*)\right)\left(\|\dot{e}_\mathrm{l}\|_{\tilde{2}}\|e_\mathrm{r} - \bar{e}_\mathrm{l}\|_{\tilde{2}}\right) \\
& - \lambda_{\min}(\Lambda_\mathrm{r}^2)\lambda_{\min}(K_{\mathrm{vr2}})\|e_\mathrm{r}\|.
\end{aligned} \tag{A17}$$

Gains are chosen as in (54)–(60), and the relationship

$$-\left(a - \frac{1}{2}\gamma b\right)^2 = -a^2 + \gamma ab - \frac{1}{4}\gamma^2 b^2, \tag{A18}$$

for any $\gamma, a, b \in \mathbb{R}$ and make some straightforward but long manipulations to show that (A17) satisfies:

$$\begin{aligned}\int_{t_0}^{t} \dot{V} \mathrm{d}\theta = \; & V(\boldsymbol{x}(t)) - V(\boldsymbol{x}(t_0)) \\ \leq & - \beta_1^2 (1 + T_1^*)^2 \frac{\lambda_{\max}(\boldsymbol{\Lambda}_r^2)\lambda_{\max}(\boldsymbol{K}_{vr2}^2)}{\lambda_{\min}(\boldsymbol{\Lambda}_r^2)\lambda_{\min}(\boldsymbol{K}_{vr2})} \|\dot{\boldsymbol{e}}_1\|_2^2 - \frac{\beta_r \lambda_{\max}(\boldsymbol{K}_{vl2})\lambda_{\max}(\boldsymbol{\Lambda}_1)(1+T_r^*)}{\sqrt{\lambda_{\min}(\boldsymbol{K}_{vl2})}} \|\boldsymbol{e}_1\|_2^2 \\ & - \lambda_{\min}(\boldsymbol{\Lambda}_r^2)\lambda_{\min}(\boldsymbol{K}_{vr2}) \|\boldsymbol{e}_r - \bar{\boldsymbol{e}}_1\|_2^2 - \lambda_{\min}(\boldsymbol{\Lambda}_1^2)\lambda_{\min}(\boldsymbol{K}_{vl2}) \|\boldsymbol{B}_1 \boldsymbol{e}_1 - \bar{\boldsymbol{e}}_r\|_2^2 - \delta_{el} \|\boldsymbol{e}_1\|_2^2 \\ & + \left(2\frac{\beta_r \lambda_{\max}(\boldsymbol{K}_{vl2})\lambda_{\max}(\boldsymbol{\Lambda}_1)(1+T_r^*)}{\lambda_{\min}(\boldsymbol{B}_1)} \right) \left(\|\dot{\boldsymbol{e}}_r\|_2 \|\boldsymbol{B}_1 \boldsymbol{e}_1 - \bar{\boldsymbol{e}}_r\|_2 - \|\dot{\boldsymbol{e}}_r\|_2^2 \right) - \delta_{sl} \|\boldsymbol{s}_1\|_2^2 \\ & + \left(2\beta_1 \lambda_{\max}(\boldsymbol{K}_{vr2})\lambda_{\max}(\boldsymbol{\Lambda}_r)(1+T_1^*) \right) \left(\|\dot{\boldsymbol{e}}_1\|_2 \|\boldsymbol{e}_r - \bar{\boldsymbol{e}}_1\|_2 \right) - \delta_{\dot{e}l} \|\dot{\boldsymbol{e}}_1\|_2^2 - \delta_{er} \|\boldsymbol{e}_r\|_2^2 \\ & - \delta_{sr} \|\boldsymbol{s}_r\|_2^2 - \delta_{\dot{e}r} \|\dot{\boldsymbol{e}}_r\|_2^2 \end{aligned} \quad \text{(A19)}$$

The term

$$- \frac{\beta_r \lambda_{\max}(\boldsymbol{K}_{vl2})\lambda_{\max}(\boldsymbol{\Lambda}_1)(1+T_r^*)}{\sqrt{\lambda_{\min}(\boldsymbol{K}_{vl2})}} \|\boldsymbol{e}_1\|_2^2 \quad \text{(A20)}$$

appears to be unnecessary in (A19) since it could be included in δ_{el}. Indeed it helps little on its own and it could be dropped in (A19), but its usefulness can be understood by considering that it comes from the factor

$$\frac{\beta_r \lambda_{\max}(\boldsymbol{K}_{vl2})\lambda_{\max}(\boldsymbol{\Lambda}_1)(1+T_r^*)}{\lambda_{\min}(\boldsymbol{\Lambda}_1)\sqrt{\lambda_{\min}(\boldsymbol{K}_{vl2})}} \quad \text{(A21)}$$

in (58) and its inclusion makes the relationship

$$\frac{\beta_r \lambda_{\max}(\boldsymbol{K}_{vl2})\lambda_{\max}(\boldsymbol{\Lambda}_1)(1+T_r^*)}{\lambda_{\min}(\boldsymbol{B}_1)} \leq \lambda_{\min}(\boldsymbol{\Lambda}_1)\sqrt{\lambda_{\min}(\boldsymbol{K}_{vl2})} \quad \text{(A22)}$$

hold, so that (A19) satisfies for all $t \in [t_0, t_\epsilon]$

$$V(\boldsymbol{x}(t)) + \delta_L + \delta_R \leq V(\boldsymbol{x}(t_0)). \quad \text{(A23)}$$

where

$$\delta_L = \delta_{el} \|\boldsymbol{e}_1\|_2^2 + \delta_{sl} \|\boldsymbol{s}_1\|_2^2 + \delta_{\dot{e}l} \|\dot{\boldsymbol{e}}_1\|_2^2 \quad \text{(A24)}$$

$$\delta_R = \delta_{er} \|\boldsymbol{e}_r\|_2^2 + \delta_{sr} \|\boldsymbol{s}_r\|_2^2 + \delta_{\dot{e}r} \|\dot{\boldsymbol{e}}_r\|_2^2. \quad \text{(A25)}$$

6. Consider now that $V(\boldsymbol{x})$ in (A10) satisfies

$$\lambda_1 \|\boldsymbol{x}\|^2 \leq V(\boldsymbol{x}), \quad \text{(A26)}$$

$\forall\, t \geq t_0$ and $\forall\, \boldsymbol{x} \in \mathbb{R}^{6n}$, where λ_1 is given in (61). On the other hand, recall that from Assumption 2, $T_j(t) \geq 0$ for $j = 1, \mathrm{r}$. Thus, from condition (52), one must have either $\bar{\boldsymbol{e}}_j(t_0) = \boldsymbol{0}$ for $T_j(t_0) > 0$ or $\bar{\boldsymbol{e}}_j(t_0) = \boldsymbol{e}_j(t_0)$ for $T_j(t_0) = 0$. Consequently, for (A10), the following holds:

$$
\begin{aligned}
V(\boldsymbol{x}(t_0)) \leq\ & \frac{1}{2}\lambda_{\max}(\boldsymbol{K}_{\omega \mathrm{l}})\|\boldsymbol{x}_1(t_0)\|^2 + \frac{1}{2}\|\boldsymbol{e}_\mathrm{l}(t_0)\|^2 + \frac{1}{2}\lambda_{\mathrm{Hl}}\|\boldsymbol{s}_\mathrm{l}(t_0)\|^2 + \lambda_{\max}(\boldsymbol{K}_{\mathrm{vl2}}\boldsymbol{\Lambda}_\mathrm{l}\boldsymbol{B}_\mathrm{l})\|\boldsymbol{e}_\mathrm{l}(t_0)\|^2 \\
& + 2\lambda_{\max}(\boldsymbol{K}_{\mathrm{vl2}}\boldsymbol{\Lambda}_\mathrm{l})\|\boldsymbol{e}_\mathrm{l}(t_0)\|\|\boldsymbol{e}_\mathrm{r}(t_0)\| + \lambda_{\max}(\boldsymbol{B}_\mathrm{l}^{-1}\boldsymbol{K}_{\mathrm{vl2}}\boldsymbol{\Lambda}_\mathrm{l})\|\boldsymbol{e}_\mathrm{r}(t_0)\|^2 + \frac{1}{2}\|\boldsymbol{e}_\mathrm{r}(t_0)\|^2 \\
& + \frac{1}{2}\lambda_{\max}(\boldsymbol{K}_{\omega \mathrm{r}})\|\boldsymbol{x}_4(t_0)\|^2 + \frac{1}{2}\lambda_{\mathrm{Hr}}\|\boldsymbol{s}_\mathrm{r}(t_0)\|^2 + \lambda_{\max}(\boldsymbol{K}_{\mathrm{vr2}}\boldsymbol{\Lambda}_\mathrm{r})\|\boldsymbol{e}_\mathrm{r}(t_0)\|^2 \\
& + 2\lambda_{\max}(\boldsymbol{K}_{\mathrm{vr2}}\boldsymbol{\Lambda}_\mathrm{r})\|\boldsymbol{e}_\mathrm{r}(t_0)\|\|\boldsymbol{e}_\mathrm{l}(t_0)\| + \lambda_{\max}(\boldsymbol{K}_{\mathrm{vr2}}\boldsymbol{\Lambda}_\mathrm{r})\|\boldsymbol{e}_\mathrm{l}(t_0)\|^2 \\
\leq\ & \lambda_2\|\boldsymbol{x}(t_0)\|^2,
\end{aligned}
\tag{A27}
$$

where λ_2 is given in (62), and $\lambda_{\mathrm{H}i}$ is specified in Property 1 for $i = \mathrm{l}, \mathrm{r}$. Furthermore, it is considered that $\boldsymbol{B}_\mathrm{r} = \boldsymbol{I}$. Combining (A23)–(A26) and (A27) results in the inequality:

$$
\|\boldsymbol{x}(t)\| \leq \sqrt{\frac{\lambda_2}{\lambda_1}}\|\boldsymbol{x}(t_0)\|, \tag{A28}
$$

for $t \in [t_0, t_\epsilon]$. In order for (A23) and (A28) to hold for all $t \geq t_0$, the following condition must be satisfied:

$$
\sqrt{\frac{\lambda_2}{\lambda_1}}\|\boldsymbol{x}(t_0)\| < \epsilon \quad \Rightarrow \quad \|\boldsymbol{x}(t_0)\| < \sqrt{\frac{\lambda_1}{\lambda_2}}\epsilon, \tag{A29}
$$

which justifies (53).
The value of ϵ is necessary to set $\lambda_{\min}(\boldsymbol{K}_{\mathrm{vl1}})$ in (59) and $\lambda_{\min}(\boldsymbol{K}_{\mathrm{vr1}})$ in (60). However, these bounds are not directly used in (61)–(62), allowing ϵ to be made arbitrarily large and independently of these conditions.

7. Since it has been shown that $\|\boldsymbol{x}\| < \epsilon$ for all $t \geq t_0$ whenever (53) holds, then (A23) also holds for all $t \geq t_0$, which means that the following becomes valid:

$$
V(\boldsymbol{x}(\infty)) + \delta_{\mathrm{el}}\|\boldsymbol{e}_\mathrm{l}\|_2^2 + \delta_{\mathrm{sl}}\|\boldsymbol{s}_\mathrm{l}\|_2^2 + \delta_{\dot{e}l}\|\dot{\boldsymbol{e}}_\mathrm{l}\|_2^2 + \delta_{\mathrm{er}}\|\boldsymbol{e}_\mathrm{r}\|_2^2 + \delta_{\mathrm{sr}}\|\boldsymbol{s}_\mathrm{r}\|_2^2 + \delta_{\dot{e}r}\|\dot{\boldsymbol{e}}_\mathrm{r}\|_2^2 \leq V(\boldsymbol{x}(t_0)). \tag{A30}
$$

This equation establishes an upper bound on the system's energy at infinity in terms of its initial energy, ensuring that all terms contributing to $V(\boldsymbol{x})$ remain finite. The coefficients $\delta_{\mathrm{el}}, \delta_{\mathrm{sl}}, \delta_{\dot{e}l}, \delta_{\mathrm{er}}, \delta_{\mathrm{sr}}, \delta_{\dot{e}r}$ determine the decay rates of specific state variables.

8. Relationship (A30), together with (29), (A6) and (A26), guarantees that:

    i. $\boldsymbol{x}_1, \boldsymbol{e}_\mathrm{l}, \dot{\boldsymbol{e}}_\mathrm{l}, \boldsymbol{s}_\mathrm{l}, \boldsymbol{x}_4, \boldsymbol{e}_\mathrm{r}, \dot{\boldsymbol{e}}_\mathrm{r}, \boldsymbol{s}_\mathrm{r} \in \mathcal{L}_\infty$,
    ii. $\boldsymbol{e}_\mathrm{l}, \dot{\boldsymbol{e}}_\mathrm{l}, \boldsymbol{s}_\mathrm{l}, \boldsymbol{e}_\mathrm{r}, \dot{\boldsymbol{e}}_\mathrm{r}, \boldsymbol{s}_\mathrm{r} \in \mathcal{L}_2$.

    By using Lemma A1, it is concluded that:

    iii. $\boldsymbol{e}_\mathrm{l}, \boldsymbol{e}_\mathrm{r} \to \boldsymbol{0}$.

    The application of Lemma A1 ensures that the system's error states converge to zero as time approaches infinity, affirming asymptotic stability. Moreover, the membership of the state variables in $\mathcal{L}_\infty$ guarantees boundedness, while their inclusion in $\mathcal{L}_2$ confirms energy dissipation.

9. To establish that $\dot{\boldsymbol{e}}_\mathrm{l}, \dot{\boldsymbol{e}}_\mathrm{r}, \boldsymbol{s}_\mathrm{l}, \boldsymbol{s}_\mathrm{r}$ converge to zero, it is necessary to demonstrate that their derivatives are bounded. Instead of relying on (43), it is more effective to use (29), whose first derivative is expressed as:

$$
\dot{\boldsymbol{s}}_i = \ddot{\boldsymbol{e}}_i + \boldsymbol{\Lambda}_i\boldsymbol{B}_i\dot{\boldsymbol{e}}_i - \boldsymbol{\Lambda}_i(1 - \dot{T}_j(t))\dot{\boldsymbol{e}}_j(t - T_j(t)), \tag{A31}
$$

where (19) has been applied.
As previously shown, $\dot{\boldsymbol{e}}_i \in \mathcal{L}_\infty$ for $i = \mathrm{l}, \mathrm{r}$, implying that $\dot{\boldsymbol{e}}_j(t - T_j(t)) \in \mathcal{L}_\infty$. Moreover, $\dot{T}_j(t)$ is bounded by Assumption 2. Therefore, $\dot{\boldsymbol{s}}_i \in \mathcal{L}_\infty$ provided that $\ddot{\boldsymbol{e}}_i \in \mathcal{L}_\infty$.

Since $\ddot{e}_i \equiv \ddot{q}_i$ under the assumption that q_d remains constant, it follows that $u_{\tau i}$ in (31) must also be bounded. This can be verified by considering (41)–(42) and the fact that $x_1, x_4 \in \mathcal{L}_\infty$.

Therefore, from (1) and Property 1, $\ddot{q}_i \in \mathcal{L}_\infty$ and, as a consequence, $\ddot{e}_i, \dot{s}_i \in \mathcal{L}_\infty$. Note that the boundedness of $\dot{q}_i = \dot{e}_i$ had already been shown. Therefore, by taking into account *i.* and *ii.*, Lemma A1 can be used again to conclude:

iv. $\dot{e}_\mathrm{l}, \dot{e}_\mathrm{r}, s_\mathrm{l}, s_\mathrm{r} \to \mathbf{0}$.

This conclusion demonstrates that all higher-order derivatives of the error and synchronization variables decay to zero over time, ensuring smooth convergence of the system's dynamics. The boundedness of the inputs and intermediate terms guarantees the validity of the assumptions used throughout the proof.

10. To demonstrate that x_1 and x_4 converge to zero, observe that from (43), $x_1 \to \mathbf{0}$ if $\dot{s}_\mathrm{l} \to \mathbf{0}$, and similarly, $x_4 \to \mathbf{0}$ if $\dot{s}_\mathrm{r} \to \mathbf{0}$. The first derivative of (A31) yields:

$$\ddot{s}_i = e_i^{(3)} + \Lambda_i B_i \ddot{e}_i + \Lambda_i \ddot{T}_j(t)\dot{e}_j(t - T_j(t)) - \Lambda_i(1 - \dot{T}_j(t))^2 \ddot{e}_j(t - T_j(t)), \tag{A32}$$

where $e_i^{(3)} = \dfrac{\mathrm{d}^{(3)}}{\mathrm{d}t^{(3)}} e_i$. By applying Assumption 2 and the previous analysis, it follows that $\ddot{s}_i \in \mathcal{L}_\infty$ if $e_i^{(3)} \in \mathcal{L}_\infty$, which holds if $q_i^{(3)} \in \mathcal{L}_\infty$. From (1), the expression for $q_i^{(3)}$ is:

$$q_i^{(3)} = H_i^{-1}(q_i)\Big\{\dot{u}_{\tau i} - \dot{H}_i(q_i, \dot{q}_i)\ddot{q}_i - \dot{g}_i(q_i) - C_i(q_i, \dot{q}_i)\ddot{q}_i - \dot{C}_i(q_i, \dot{q}_i, \ddot{q}_i)\dot{q}_i\Big\}. \tag{A33}$$

Considering that revolute joints are used, it follows that the vectors $\dot{H}_i(q_i, \dot{q}_i)\ddot{q}_i$, $C_i(q_i, \dot{q}_i)\ddot{q}_i$, $\dot{C}_i(q_i, \dot{q}_i, \ddot{q}_i)\dot{q}_i$, and $\dot{g}_i(q_i)$ are bounded.

Consequently, $q_i^{(3)} \in \mathcal{L}_\infty$ if $\dot{u}_{\tau i} \in \mathcal{L}_\infty$. From (31)–(33), it follows that:

$$\dot{u}_{\tau i} = -K_{vi}\dot{s}_i - K_{\omega i}s_i + K_{\omega i}(1 - \dot{T}_j(t))\dot{e}_j(t - T_j(t)), \tag{A34}$$

demonstrating that $\dot{u}_{\tau i}$ is indeed bounded.

The derivation of (A34) follows from substituting the auxiliary dynamics defined in (A30)–(A32) into the closed-loop system's stability analysis. Starting from the composite variable:

$$s_i = \dot{e}_i + \Lambda_i B_i e_i - \Lambda_i e_j, \tag{A35}$$

the time derivative $\dot{s}_i$ can be expressed as:

$$\dot{s}_i = \ddot{e}_i + \Lambda_i B_i \dot{e}_i - \Lambda_i \dot{e}_j. \tag{A36}$$

Using the error dynamics and substituting $\ddot{e}_i = -K_{vi}s_i - K_{\omega i}\omega_i + K_{\omega i}e_j\Big(t - T_j(t)\Big)$, the dynamics of $\dot{s}_i$ are rewritten as:

$$\dot{s}_i = -K_{vi}s_i - K_{\omega i}\omega_i + K_{\omega i}\Big(1 - \dot{T}_j(t)\Big)e_j\Big(t - T_j(t)\Big) + \Lambda_i B_i \dot{e}_i - \Lambda_i \dot{e}_j. \tag{A37}$$

Subsequently, the control law $u_{\tau i}$ is defined as:

$$u_{\tau i} = -K_{vi}s_i - K_{\omega i}\omega_i + K_{\omega i}e_j\Big(t - T_j(t)\Big). \tag{A38}$$

Combining these equations and considering the bounded nature of the delay terms $T_j(t)$, $\dot{T}_j(t)$, and $\ddot{T}_j(t)$, Equation (A34) is derived. For clarity, the derivation assumes bounded and smooth trajectories for the delayed terms $e_j\Big(t - T_j(t)\Big)$ and their time derivatives, consistent with the assumptions outlined earlier in the proof.

In summary, it has been shown that $s_i \to 0$ and that $\dot{s}_i$ is both bounded and uniformly continuous, as $\ddot{s}_i$ is also bounded. By invoking Lemma A2 (Barbalat's Lemma), it follows that $\dot{s}_i \to 0$ for $i = \mathrm{l}, \mathrm{r}$. Therefore, from (43), it can be concluded that:

v. $x_1, x_4 \to 0$.

because ϕ_{ai} in (38) vanishes at the origin.

References

1. Passenberg, C.; Peer, A.; Buss, M. A survey of environment-, operator-, and task-adapted controllers for teleoperation systems. *Mechatronics* **2010**, *20*, 787–801. [CrossRef]
2. Liu, Y.C.; Chopra, N. Control of semi-autonomous teleoperation system with time delays. *Automatica* **2013**, *49*, 1553–1565. [CrossRef]
3. Islam, S.; Liu, P.X.; Saddik, A.E.; Yang, Y.B. Bilateral Control of Teleoperation Systems With Time Delay. *IEEE/ASME Trans. Mechatron.* **2015**, *20*, 1–12. [CrossRef]
4. Wang, H.; Li, Y.; Jiang, T. Bilateral Control of Teleoperators with Closed Architecture and Time-Varying Delay. *arXiv* **2021**, arXiv:2106.12470.
5. Nuño, E.; Ortega, R.; Barabanov, N.; Basañez, L. A Globally Stable PD Controller for Bilateral Teleoperators. *IEEE Trans. Robot.* **2008**, *24*, 753–758. [CrossRef]
6. Zhang, M.; Saberi, A.; Stoorvogel, A. Synchronization in the presence of unknown, nonuniform and arbitrarily large communication delay. *Eur. J. Control* **2017**, *38*, 63–72. [CrossRef]
7. Wang, C.; Luo, R.; Whitney, J.P.; Padir, T. Practical Approaches Towards Transparent and Stable Bilateral Teleoperation Under Time-Varying Network Delay. *Int. J. Soc. Robot.* **2024**, *16*, 123–137. [CrossRef]
8. Chan, L.; Liu, Y.; Huang, Q.; Wang, P. Robust Adaptive Observer-Based Predictive Control for a Non-Linear Delayed Bilateral Teleoperation System. *IEEE Access* **2022**, *10*, 52294–52305. [CrossRef]
9. Kavikumar, R.; Sakthivel, R.; Lee, S.H. Extended dissipative analysis of affine-transformed IT2 fuzzy control systems with time delay and disturbances. *J. Frankl. Inst.* **2023**, *360*, 10917–10941. [CrossRef]
10. Aminzadeh Ghavifekr, A.; Chehraghi, S.; De Rossi, G. An Analysis of Sampling Effect on the Absolute Stability of Discrete-time Bilateral Teleoperation Systems. *arXiv* **2020**, arXiv:2008.10439.
11. Wu, Y.; Liu, X.; Yang, Y. Position and Force Control of Bilateral Teleoperation Systems With Time-varying Delays Based on Force Estimation. *Int. J. Control Autom. Syst.* **2024**, *22*, 276–287. [CrossRef]
12. McCutcheon, L.; Fallah, S. Adaptive PD Control using Deep Reinforcement Learning for Local-Remote Teleoperation with Stochastic Time Delays. *arXiv* **2023**, arXiv:2305.16979.
13. Chan, L.; Huang, Q.; Wang, P. Adaptive-observer-based robust control for a time-delayed teleoperation system with scaled four-channel architecture. *Robotica* **2022**, *40*, 1385–1405. [CrossRef]
14. Pourseifi, M.; Rezaei, S. Adaptive control for position and force tracking of uncertain teleoperation with actuators saturation and asymmetric varying time delays. *Int. J. Nonlinear Sci. Numer. Simul.* **2023**, *24*, 3113–3132. [CrossRef]
15. Sun, D.; Naghdy, F.; Du, H. Neural network-based passivity control of teleoperation system under time-varying delays. *IEEE Trans. Cybern.* **2017**, *47*, 1666–1680. [CrossRef]
16. Yang, C.; Wang, X.; Li, Z.; Li, Y.; Su, C.Y. Teleoperation control based on combination of wave variable and neural networks. *IEEE Trans. Syst. Man Cybern.* **2017**, *47*, 2125–2136. [CrossRef]
17. Chen, K.; Zhang, H. Design of Synchronization Tracking Adaptive Control for Bilateral Teleoperation System with Time-Varying Delays. *Sensors* **2022**, *22*, 7798. [CrossRef] [PubMed]
18. Li, L.; Liu, Z.; Ma, Z.; Huang, P. Adaptive neural learning fixed-time control for uncertain teleoperation system with time-delay and time-varying output constraints. *Int. J. Robust Nonlinear Control* **2022**, *32*, 8912–8931. [CrossRef]
19. Su, S.; Ji, Y. Fixed-time adaptive neural network synchronization control for teleoperation system with position error constraints and time-varying delay. *Nonlinear Dyn.* **2023**, *111*, 13053–13072. [CrossRef]
20. Zhang, H.; Fu, L.; Zhang, A. A Novel Adaptive Finite-Time Position Tracking Control Strategy for Teleoperation System with Varying Communication Delays. *Mathematics* **2023**, *11*, 1486. [CrossRef]
21. Sun, D.; Liao, Q.; Ren, H. Type-2 fuzzy modeling and control for bilateral teleoperation system with dynamic uncertainties and time-varying delays. *IEEE Trans. Ind. Electron.* **2017**, *65*, 447–459. [CrossRef]
22. Lu, Z.; Huang, P.; Liu, Z. Predictive Approach for Sensorless Bimanual Teleoperation Under Random Time Delays with Adaptive Fuzzy Control. *IEEE Trans. Ind. Electron.* **2018**, *65*, 2439–2448. [CrossRef]
23. Sun, D.; Liao, Q.; Stoyanov, T.; Kiselev, A.; Loutfi, A. Bilateral telerobotic system using Type-2 fuzzy neural network based moving horizon estimation force observer for enhancement of environmental force compliance and human perception. *Automatica* **2019**, *106*, 358–373. [CrossRef]
24. Bouteraa, Y.; Alattas, K.A.; Peng, T.; Fekih, A.; Rahmani, R.; Mobayen, S. Design of robust adaptive fuzzy control for uncertain bilateral teleoperation systems based on backstepping approach. *IET Control Theory Appl.* **2023**, *17*, 800–813. [CrossRef]

25. Islam, S.; Sunda-Meya, A. Robust Sliding Mode Based Finite-time Bilateral Shared Teleoperation System with Unsymmetrical Time-Varying Delay. In Proceedings of the IECON 2022-48th Annual Conference of the IEEE Industrial Electronics Society, Brussels, Belgium, 17–20 October 2022; pp. 1–6. [CrossRef]
26. Islam, S. NTSM Based Adaptive Finite-Time Synchronization for Bilateral Teleoperators with Asymmetrical Delay and Disturbances. In Proceedings of the 2023 IEEE International Conference on Industrial Technology (ICIT), Orlando, FL, USA, 4–6 April 2023; pp. 1–6. [CrossRef]
27. Yang, Y.; Guo, F.; Li, J.; Luo, X. New delay-dependent position/force hybrid controller design for uncertain telerobotics without force sensors. *Trans. Inst. Meas. Control* **2023**, *46*, 01423312231167916. [CrossRef]
28. Kelly, R.; Santibáñez, V.; Loria, A. *Control of Robot Manipulators in Joint Space*; Springer: London, UK, 2005.
29. Siciliano, B.; Khatib, O. *Springer Handbook of Robotics*; Springer: Berlin/Heidelberg, Germany, 2008.
30. Arteaga, M.A.; Gutiérrez-Giles, A.; Pliego-Jiménez, J. *Local Stability and Ultimate Boundedness in the Control of Robot Manipulators*; Springer: Cham, Switzerland, 2022. [CrossRef]
31. Nuño, E.; Arteaga, M.; Espinosa-Pérez, G. Control of bilateral teleoperators with time delays using only position measurements. *Int. J. Robust Nonlinear Control* **2018**, *28*, 808–824. [CrossRef]
32. Forouzantabar, A.; Talebi, H.A.; Sedigh, A.K. Bilateral control of master-slave manipulators with constant time delay. *ISA Trans.* **2012**, *51*, 74–80. [CrossRef] [PubMed]
33. Alfi, A.; Bakhshi, A.; Yousefi, M.; Talebi, H.A. Design and Implementation of Robust-Fixed Structure Controller for Telerobotic Systems. *J. Intell. Robot. Syst.* **2016**, *83*, 253–269. [CrossRef]
34. Hernández-Guzmán, V.M.; Orrante-Sakanassi, J. Model-independent consensus control of Euler-Lagrange agents with interconnecting delays. *Int. J. Robust Nonlinear Control* **2019**, *29*, 4069–4096. [CrossRef]
35. Arteaga, M.A.; López, M.; Nuño, E.; Hernández-Ortiz, O. On the delayed kinematic correspondence with variable time delays for the control of the bilateral teleoperation of robots. *Int. J. Control* **2021**, *94*, 2353–2368. [CrossRef]
36. Mohsen, M.; Mohamed, A.M.; Ahmed, S.; Ibrahim, K. Bilateral Control of a 2-DOF Teleoperated Manipulators Using UDP Scheme. *Ain Shams Eng. J.* **2023**, *14*, 102065. [CrossRef]
37. Zhao, G.; Guo, L. Towards a theoretical foundation of PID control for uncertain nonlinear systems. *Automatica* **2022**, *142*, 110360. [CrossRef]
38. Hashemzadeh, F.; Tavakoli, M. Position and force tracking in nonlinear teleoperation systems under varying delays. *Robotica* **2015**, *33*, 1003–1016. [CrossRef]
39. Arteaga, M.A. An alternative proof to the asymptotic stability of PID controllers for regulation of robot manipulators. *IFAC J. Syst. Control* **2019**, *9*, 100066. [CrossRef]
40. Rodríguez-Ángeles, A.; Arteaga, M.A.; Portillo-Vélez, R.; Cruz-Villar, C. Transparent Bilateral Master-Slave Control Based on Virtual Surfaces: Stability Analysis and Experimental Results. *Int. J. Robot. Autom.* **2015**, *30*, 128–139. [CrossRef]
41. Khalil, H.K. *Nonlinear Systems*, 3rd ed.; Prentice-Hall: Upper Saddle River, NJ, USA, 2002.
42. Hernández-Ortiz, O.; Arteaga, M.A. A simple approach for the force control of bilateral teleoperated manipulators with variable time delays. *Control Eng. Pract.* **2020**, *102*, 104564. [CrossRef]
43. Nuño, E.; Basañez, L.; López-Franco, C.; Arana-Daniel, N. Stability of nonlinear teleoperators using PD controllers without velocity measurements. *J. Frankl. Inst.* **2014**, *351*, 241–258. [CrossRef]
44. Slotine, J.J.E.; Li, W. *Applied Nonlinear Control*; Prentice-Hall: Englewood Cliffs, NJ, USA, 1991.

algorithms

MDPI

Article

Fuzzy Modelling Algorithms and Parallel Distributed Compensation for Coupled Electromechanical Systems

Christian Reyes [1], Julio C. Ramos-Fernández [2], Eduardo S. Espinoza [1,3] and Rogelio Lozano [1,*]

[1] Center for Research and Advanced Studies of the National Polytechnic Institute, Av. Instituto Politécnico Nacional 2508, San Pedro Zacatenco, Mexico City 07360, Mexico; christian.reyes@cinvestav.mx (C.R.); eduardo.espinoza@cinvestav.mx (E.S.E.)

[2] Dirección de Investigación, Innovación y Posgrado, Universidad Politécnica de Pachuca, Hidalgo 43830, Mexico; jramos@upp.edu.mx

[3] National Council of Humanities, Sciences and Technologies, Mexico City 03940, Mexico

* Correspondence: rogelio.lozano@cinvestav.mx; Tel.: +52-(55)-5747-3800

Abstract: Modelling and controlling an electrical Power Generation System (PGS), which consists of an Internal Combustion Engine (ICE) linked to an electric generator, poses a significant challenge due to various factors. These include the non-linear characteristics of the system's components, thermal effects, mechanical vibrations, electrical noise, and the dynamic and transient impacts of electrical loads. In this study, we introduce a fuzzy modelling identification approach utilizing the Takagi–Sugeno (T–S) structure, wherein model and control parameters are optimized. This methodology circumvents the need for deriving a mathematical model through energy balance considerations involving thermodynamics and the non-linear representation of the electric generator. Initially, a non-linear mathematical model for the electrical power system is obtained through the fuzzy c-means algorithm, which handles both premises and consequents in state space, utilizing input–output experimental data. Subsequently, the Particle Swarm Algorithm (PSO) is employed for optimizing the fuzzy parameter m of the c-means algorithm during the modelling phase. Additionally, in the design of the Parallel Distributed Compensation Controller (PDC), the optimization of parameters pertaining to the poles of the closed-loop response is conducted also by using the PSO method. Ultimately, numerical simulations are conducted, adjusting the power consumption of an inductive load.

Keywords: fuzzy c-means; PDC controller; power generation

1. Introduction

Electric Power Generation Systems (PGSs) based on Internal Combustion Engines (ICEs) in combination with an electric generator are widely used in industrial and commercial applications due to their low maintenance and ease of operation under several environmental conditions. However, the low energy efficiency of ICEs reduces the performance of the whole power generation system. In recent years, many researches have proposed new strategies to optimize the results of this type of power generation systems. Such research includes the development of new fuels and explosion chamber systems with new materials for ICE operation, electrical generators with new architectures to maximize fuel efficiency, and voltage and power regulation systems with control algorithms using hybrid automatic identification and control techniques [1].

In order to optimize these systems, different strategies have been addressed, such as the use of innovative control techniques [2,3] or the study of the compartmentalization of electric power generation systems with different topologies of artificial neural networks to predict and be efficient in the complicated characteristics of various types of engine with different fuels [4].

The authors in [5] reviewed typical applications of machine learning (ML) and data-driven control (DDC) at the level of monitoring, control, optimization, and fault detection of power generation systems, with a particular focus on finding out how these methods can be used to evaluate, counteract, or withstand the effects of the associated uncertainties. The benefits of ML and DDC techniques are accordingly interpreted in terms of visibility, manoeuvrability, flexibility, profitability, and safety. The authors in [6] provide an overview of artificial-intelligence (AI) applications for power electronic systems. The applications of four categories of AI are discussed, which are expert system, fuzzy logic, metaheuristic method (like PSO), and machine learning. In [7], the authors discussed the design choices and parameters that affect the system performance, the closed-loop stability, and the controller robustness. Moreover, they presented the solvers and control platforms that can be employed for the real-time implementation of Model Predictive Control (MPC) algorithms. Furthermore, in [8], a comprehensive review is conducted on artificial-intelligence applications in regards to optimization system configuration and energy control strategy, along with the applicability of different energy storage technologies.

Most of the control techniques used for voltage regulation require a mathematical model of the ICE coupled to the electric generator. However, obtaining a complete mathematical model is a challenging task due to the interrelation between all the system components and the corresponding determination of its parameters. In order to deal with this issue, the authors in [9] proposed the use of a non-linear mathematical model, as well as the combination of the first principle of thermodynamics, physical laws, and steady state data of the engine mass air flow, obtained empirically. This type of approach typically results in inaccurate models due to unmodelled system dynamics and, in addition, the resulting complex mathematical models are not suitable to be used to derive voltage regulation control laws.

One of the major potential areas of application of this type of power generator system is autonomous vehicles. For instance, the authors in [10] developed an unmanned military action vehicle, which uses a power generator system composed of a gasoline engine together with an electric generator and a lithium iron phosphate cell. Similarly, the American company Top Flight created the Airborg H8 10k [11], a hybrid powered UAV with eight rotors and an estimated flight time of two hours with a 4 kg payload or one hour of flight with a 10 kg payload, with a maximum speed of 40 mph. In addition, Sullivan UV is one of the leading companies that develop power generator systems in the expanding market of unmanned aerial vehicles [12].

1.1. Related Work

Techniques based on machine learning have proven to be effective approaches for modelling and controlling ICEs, due to their robustness, which allows compensating variations in the electrical load and whose approach guarantees stability [3]. Nevertheless, artificial-intelligence techniques require significant amounts of data to achieve a good model; in addition, they are merely black boxes, in the sense of interpreting the system's parameters and its mathematical structure. This contrasts with fuzzy models and controllers, such as Mamdani linguistic systems, where an expert in the physical system dictates the basis of operation rules, which are not optimal, but rather based on human experience. On the other hand, the fuzzy modelling and control technique proposed by Takagi–Sugeno (T–S) can be complemented with optimal parameter identification algorithms, as well as with different control techniques. In the Mamdani fuzzy model, both the antecedent and the consequent are fuzzy propositions, which are chosen by experts on the system to be modelled or by an expert in fuzzy modelling, while in the T–S fuzzy modelling, the antecedent is a fuzzy proposition and the consequent is a mathematical function, which can have a polynomial state-space architecture [13]. This represents a strength for the modelling of complex systems and control based on submodels represented in state space. For instance, the authors in [14] presented a fuzzy logic-based control and power management strategy for unmanned aerial vehicles, in which they developed a set of fuzzy rules for controlling and effectively dividing the power between the two power sources: electric generator and ICE. Similarly, the authors in [15] used a fuzzy logic controller to improve the performance of the traditional perturb and observe algorithm for power generation using a photovoltaic system. The proposed fuzzy logic controller with a rule base collection of 25 rules outperformed the controller using the traditional perturb and observe algorithm due to its adaptive step size, enabling the fuzzy logic controller to adapt the photovoltaic system faster to changing environment conditions.

However, the selection of the fuzzy parameter m of the fuzzy c-means algorithm is a crucial aspect in the implementation of this type of techniques. The authors in [16] found that the value of m must be greater than $n/(n-2)$ (where n is the total number of data objects in the data set) viewed from the perspective of the algorithm convergence. More recently, the authors in [17] proposed, based in their experience, a range of $1.1 \leq m \leq 5$, whereas [18] proposed a new guideline for m selection based on robust fuzzy c-means analysis. They suggested to define m in the range [1.5–4]. The authors in [19] proposed a method for the selection of the optimal m value using four cluster validity indices, obtaining an optimal m value in the interval [2.5–3]. The authors in [20] analyzed the use of soft computing techniques based on the c-means fuzzy classification algorithm and the T–S type fuzzy rule structure in research developed in the field of ICE for the generation of electric power. In [21], the authors proposed a novel semi-supervised fuzzy c-means clustering algorithm using multiple fuzzification coefficients instead of an auxiliary matrix to adjust the membership grade of the data elements, aiming to make the proposed fuzzy c-means algorithm a semi-supervised machine-learning method. The authors demonstrated the convergence of the algorithm and validated the efficiency of the method through a numerical example and derived a supervised approach to determine the parameter m of the c-means algorithm.

In our previous work [22], we used the fuzzy T–S technique to estimate the remaining battery energy in an autonomous vehicle. We used the fuzzy c-means algorithm for the assumptions and the consequents were obtained using linear polynomials, while the m parameter used in the fuzzy c-means algorithm was found by implementing the Particle Swarm Optimization (PSO) algorithm. The PSO metaheuristic algorithm has been previously used in several research works in combination with fuzzy logic techniques; for example, the authors in [23] developed a time-delay network control model to predict the output of the control system. In order to deal with the problem of falling into local optimality, they proposed a non-linear fitting formula to obtain the PSO algorithm parameters based on the number of iterations and using the T–S algorithm to obtain a global optimal solution. Similarly, the authors in [24] employed a fuzzy logic control structure for load frequency control of a dual-area power system, in addition to the PSO method to improve its performance.

In the present research work, the technique proposed by Takagi–Sugeno and Tanaka is used to identify a power generation system based on an internal combustion engine–generator scheme controlled using a fuzzy strategy that allows the regulation of the voltage generated by the system. With this strategy, it is sought to avoid the need to derive a complex mathematical model. The contribution of the proposed strategies is not in the development of a new fuzzy control law, but rather in the development of system identification and control algorithms for a specific application to a power generation system.

1.2. Contributions

The main contributions of this research work are summarized in the development of the following two algorithms:

A1. An algorithm that uses input–output data corresponding to the control signal sent to the Internal Combustion Engine (ICE) and the voltage signal acquired from the electric generator. This algorithm aims to identify offline a T–S type fuzzy model of the power generation system, where the consequent consists of four state-space fuzzy rules. The model consists of four linear submodels, which represent the input–output operation within the learning space. In order to derive the fuzzy model, the consequents are established using the fuzzy data clustering technique, namely the fuzzy c-means algorithm. This method enables an optimal search for the premises of the fuzzy rules. In this technique, an open problem is to determine the fuzzy parameter m, which allows classification of the data into groups with fuzzy affinity. In the present paper, we propose to employ the Particle Swarm Optimization (PSO) method to identify the optimal value of the fuzzy parameter m from within the search space.

A2. An algorithm that uses Parallel Distributed Compensation (PDC) to regulate the output voltage, whose gains are determined through the combination of pole placement and PSO methods. This control technique, rooted in the T–S fuzzy model, leverages the premises of the rules and adjusts the consequents using state feedback.

The remainder of the article is organized as follows: In Section 2, the description of the power generation system is presented. In Section 3, the T–S fuzzy modelling algorithm with the assumptions in the form of clustering and linear consequents, as well as the construction of the fuzzy system, applied to the power generation system, are derived. The PDC controller for the voltage regulation of the system is shown in Section 4. Finally, the conclusions and future directions of this research work are presented in Section 5.

2. Simulation Platform

To obtain the required experimental data, the system is considered an open-loop Power Generation System (PGS) in series configuration with an electric generator powered by an Internal Combustion Engine (ICE) [25]. In this configuration, the generated voltage is measured in open loop to first identify a fuzzy model of the power generation system and then design a Parallel Distributed Compensation Controller (PDC) that regulates the generated voltage in closed loop.

The PGS is composed of a myRIO-1900 device from National Instruments used for data acquisition and processing. Both the generator/electric motor and the electric motor used as an electrical load are U12 II (120 KV) brushless motors, while the Electronic Speed Controller (ESC) is a 100 Amp Flame HV, all from T-Motor. The servomotor is a DS3230MG, which is 30 kg/cm. The three-phase diode rectifier is 100 amps and 1600 volts. The ICE used is the Stihl-2MIX model, which is a 1.1 HP/0.8 kW and 22.2 cm^3 single-cylinder engine, whose operation is two-stroke. We used a resistive voltage sensor to measure the output voltage of the PGS.

A connection diagram of the proposed power generation system is shown in Figure 1, where $r(k)$ is the desired voltage, k_r is a precompensation gain, $e(k)$ is the voltage error, $u(k)$ is the obtained control signal, and $VG(k)$ represents the generated voltage, and the variable load block corresponds to an inductive load used to produce a richer system behaviour in open loop in order to improve the off-line identification process.

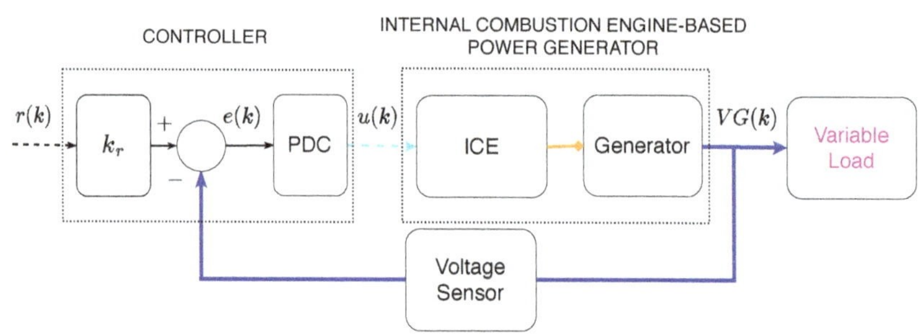

Figure 1. Connection diagram of the power generator system.

3. T–S Fuzzy Modelling

Two main topics of research and application for the development of fuzzy systems, known as Mamdani and Takagi–Sugeno, are highlighted in the bibliography [26]. The

If–Then fuzzy rules contain two fundamental parts, which are the premises and the consequents. In this work, we demonstrate a fuzzy algorithm with the T–S fuzzy system, where the premises are extracted with the clustering technique, which consists of grouping the learning data into subsets based on their similarity to each other. Since the fuzzy c-means algorithm was developed for pattern recognition by [16], it has been of great technical value for the fuzzy modelling and control of non-linear dynamic systems, as presented in this work. We use the c-means clustering algorithm to extract the premises or firing degrees of the fuzzy T–S rules, because it is effective and feasible in the search for the best prototypes of the membership values; Equation (1).

The iterative fuzzy c-means algorithm is applied to find the clustering centres, c_i, which are the prototypes of the membership functions and the membership values, $\mu_{ik} \in [0,1]$, in the learning phase [27].

$$J(\mathbf{Z};\mathbf{U},\mathbf{C}) = \sum_{i=1}^{c}\sum_{k=1}^{N} (\mu_{ik})^m \|z_k - c_i\|_I^2. \tag{1}$$

where N is the pairs of input–output data used in order to perform learning, c is the number of clusters proposed by the expert designer using a certain heuristic rule (in this paper, we set $c = 3$ to illustrate the example of the fuzzy identification, modelling, and control algorithm), $\mathbf{Z} = \{z_1, z_2, \ldots, z_N\}$ is the learning matrix, which can be a time series of input–output measurements, $\mathbf{U} = [\mu_{ik}]$ is the fuzzy partition matrix, with $i = 1, 2, \ldots, c$ and $k = 1, 2, \ldots, N$, and $\mathbf{C} = [c_1, c_2, \ldots, c_c]$ is the vector of centres to identify. Normally, the parameter fuzzy $m > 1$ defines the fuzziness, adjusted heuristically or with some genetic algorithm, and has an important relevance for the representation of the premises in the fuzzy rules. Here, we propose the PSO algorithm to find the best prototypes of the membership functions within the learning space.

Several classification and modelling problems in hard sciences and in different topics have been solved efficiently using the fuzzy c-means algorithm and its different variants. In [27], the authors detail the steps to follow in order to implement the c-means algorithm; the Euclidean distances of each sample of the data to be classified from the centres is as follows:

$$D_{ikI}^2 = \|z_k - c_i\|_I^2 = (z_k - c_i)^T I (z_k - c_i), \tag{2}$$

where I is the identity matrix. In the learning phase, the solution of Equation (1) for the membership functions of each cluster is given by Equations (3) and (4) and is, iteratively:

$$\mu_{ik} = \frac{1}{\sum_{j=1}^{c} \left(\frac{D_{ikI}}{D_{jkI}}\right)^{(2/m-1)}} \tag{3}$$

$$c_i = \frac{\sum_{k=1}^{N} (\mu_{ik})^m z_k}{\sum_{k=1}^{N} (\mu_{ik})^m}, \tag{4}$$

where μ_{ik} is the firing value of the i-th cluster for the k-th sample, with $1 \le i \le c$, $1 \le k \le N$.

The construction of the T–S fuzzy model from experimental data was solved in two steps: (1) the structure identification and (2) the estimation of parameters [28]. In step (1), the structure of the model is proposed, using expert knowledge and observations of the response of the system to be modelled.

Based on the model structure already defined, the learning matrix is defined for the learning matrix for parameter estimation, using time sequences of the input–output $X \in \mathbb{R}^{N\times n}$, where n is the number of state-space variables, as follows,

$$X = \begin{bmatrix} x_{11} & x_{12} & \cdots & x_{1n} \\ x_{21} & x_{22} & \cdots & x_{2n} \\ \vdots & \vdots & \cdots & \vdots \\ x_{N1} & x_{N2} & \cdots & x_{Nn} \end{bmatrix}$$

and the output vector $Y \in \mathbb{R}^{N\times 1}$, $Y = [y_1, \ldots, y_N,]^T$; using Equation (5), the solution of the weighted average least squares, the identification of the linear consequent parameters $\hat{\theta}_i$ for each i-th rule,

$$\hat{\theta}_i = \left[X^T \Gamma_i X\right]^{-1} X^T \Gamma_i Y, \tag{5}$$

is defined by the matrix $\Gamma_i = \text{diag}\ (\mu_{ik}) \in \mathbb{R}^{N\times N}$, which contains in its main diagonal the firing value of the i-th fuzzy rule, which gives it a weighting due to the membership values of each rule $(i = 1, \ldots, c)$ and each instant $(k = 1, \ldots, N)$. A fuzzy T–S model is proposed (6), based on 4 dynamic linguistic response labels within the discourse universe: *low*, *zero*, *medium*, and *high*, $R_i, i = 1, 2, 3, 4$ rules. The premises are represented by clustering centres; a discrete-time of the state-space model is proposed [29]:

$$\mathrm{R}_i : \text{If } z_k \text{ is } c_i \text{ then } \begin{cases} x^i(k+1) = A_i x(k) + B_i u(k) \\ y^i(k) = C_i x(k) \end{cases} \tag{6}$$

where $x^i(k+1)$ is the state vector at time $(k+1)$, $A_i \in \mathbb{R}^{n\times n}$ is the state matrix of the system, $x(k) \in \mathbb{R}^n$ is the state vector at time (k), $B_i(k) \in \mathbb{R}^{n\times m}$ is the input matrix of the system, $C_i(k) \in \mathbb{R}^{q\times n}$ is the output matrix, $u(k) \in \mathbb{R}^m$ is the input vector of the system, and $y^i(k) \in \mathbb{R}^q$ is the output vector. The overall output of the fuzzy rule base (defuzzification) is the weighted sum of the firing values of the fuzzy rules [28], given as:

$$x(k+1) = \frac{\sum_{i=1}^{c} \mu_{ik}\{A_i x(k) + B_i u(k)\}}{\sum_{i=1}^{c} \mu_{ik}}. \tag{7}$$

3.1. Fuzzy Identification of a Second-Order System

It is well known that any real-time system identification technique is commonly affected by uncertainties and identification errors. In fact, if multiple runs of an identification process applied to exactly the same model were performed, we would end up obtaining similar but slightly different results [30]. For this reason, we decided to use fuzzy logic to determine a model that was sufficiently close to the physical system and that would allow us to perform the desired voltage regulation despite the inherent errors and uncertainties.

Since the central axis of the modelling with fuzzy logic lies in the knowledge base of the system to be modelled, we rely on the observation of the operation of the power generation system of this research work, and the experimental measurements of the input–output, to propose four fuzzy rules.

Thus, the grouping of the power generator operation dynamics was divided into four clusters, using the learning data $Z = [VG(k-1); VG(k); u(k)]$. These clusters correspond to the time series of the voltage measurements of the electrical generator and the excitation of the system, which are respectively in variables of state x_1 and x_2 and the input signal $u(k)$.

The centroids of the prototype membership functions were determined using the c-means algorithm. Table 1 presents the 4 coordinates of the centroids, which were obtained in Matlab® using the *fcm()* function inside the search loop for the best parameter m with Algorithm 1. These values correspond to the time series of the measurements of the voltage of the electric generator and the PWM excitation, which are, respectively, in the identification of the states x_1, x_2, and $u(k)$ control signal, as shown in Figure 1.

Table 1. Centres of the prototype membership functions.

Centroids	x_1	x_2	u
1	45.5960	45.5858	0.7158
2	38.8837	38.8710	0.6258
3	21.2521	21.2416	0.3369
4	25.3004	23.9919	0.4860

Algorithm 1 Fuzzy system identification and m parameter optimization.

```
VG, u ← Load open_loop_experimental_data.mat
Z ← [VG(k − 1), VG(k), u(k)]
c ← 4                                          ▷ Number of rules or clusters
N ← Total number of data
function FUZZY C-MEANS(Z, c)
    Calculate the centroids c
end function
return c
for i ← 1 to c do                              ▷ Obtaining of consequents
    A_i, B_i ← Equation (5)                    ▷ Least squares
end for
return A_i, B_i
function PSO ALGORITHM                         ▷ Open Loop System
    for m ← 1.1 to 3 do                        ▷ Fuzzy Parameter m
        Optimize m using Equation (10)         ▷ Objective function
    end for
end function
return m
```

Four clusters and their corresponding fuzzy rules, which map fuzzy linear subspaces, were proposed. Each clustering operation is defined by locally mapping the system of equations into state-space variables; Equation (6). The global model is the defuzzification of the rules, which infers the non-linear response. The non-linearities of the ICE driver are represented within the ensemble of the four T–S fuzzy rules; Equation (7).

Figure 2 shows the dynamics of operation, due to the excitation input and the response in the state variables, as well as the clustering centres.

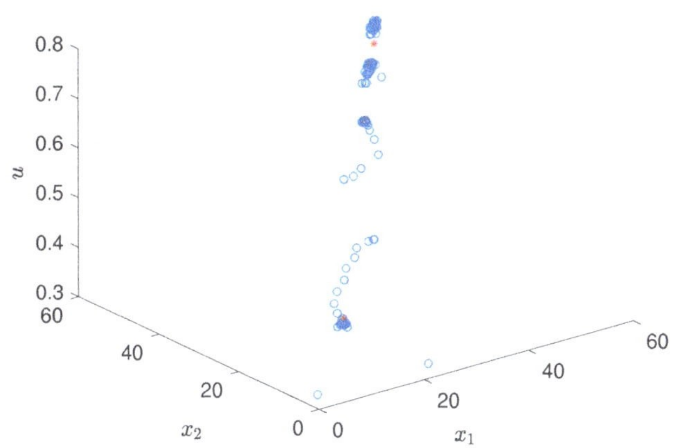

Figure 2. Measurements of the excitation input and state variable responses, characterised with groups by clustering centres identified as *.

The proposed state-space structure, Equation (8), for each of the four rules locally does not represent all the effects acting on the system, but globally the rule base integrates the non-linearity of the identified system.

$$\begin{bmatrix} x_1^i(k+1) \\ x_2^i(k+1) \end{bmatrix} = \underbrace{\begin{bmatrix} 0 & 1 \\ a_2^i & a_1^i \end{bmatrix}}_{A_i} \begin{bmatrix} x_1(k) \\ x_2(k) \end{bmatrix} + \underbrace{\begin{bmatrix} 0 \\ b^i \end{bmatrix}}_{B_i} u(k) \quad (8)$$

where a_1^i, a_2^i, and b^i are the linear parameters that are identified with the weighted least squares algorithm. Table 2 shows the obtained values of A_i and B_i for the four identified discrete systems.

Table 2. Resulting values for A_i and B_i.

A_1		B_1	A_2		B_2
0	1	0	0	1	0
0.8465	−0.0828	14.9186	1.0667	−0.1268	3.7456
A_3		B_3	A_4		B_4
0	1	0	0	1	0
0.9635	−0.07516	7.0516	0.9589	−0.1102	9.4053

In order to obtain the required data to conduct the system identification, we conducted open-loop experiments under different scenarios. Figure 3 depicts the open-loop system response in contrast to the output obtained from the identified fuzzy system (identified voltage) with a multiple step input. The identified voltage is smooth with respect to the actual signal from the electrical generator (generated voltage), mainly due to the linear nature of the fuzzy rule consequents, as shown in Equation (6).

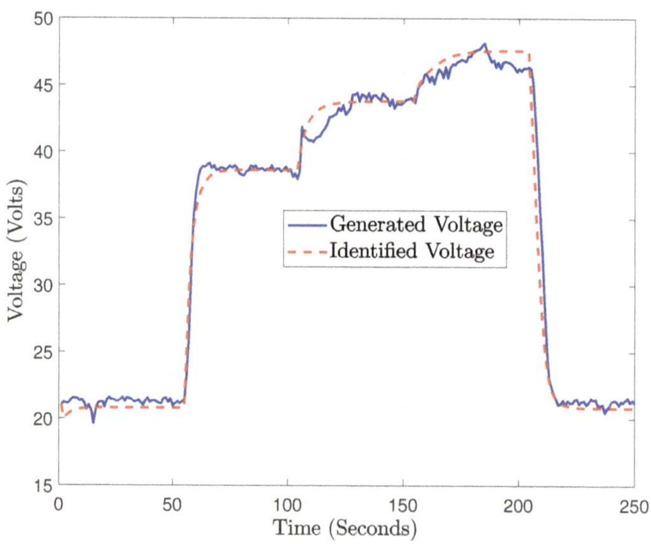

Figure 3. Open-loop generated voltage and output of the identified fuzzy model.

Figure 4 depicts the open-loop system response in contrast to the output obtained from the identified fuzzy system with a constant input and an inductive load used to produce a richer system behaviour in open loop in order to improve the off-line identification process.

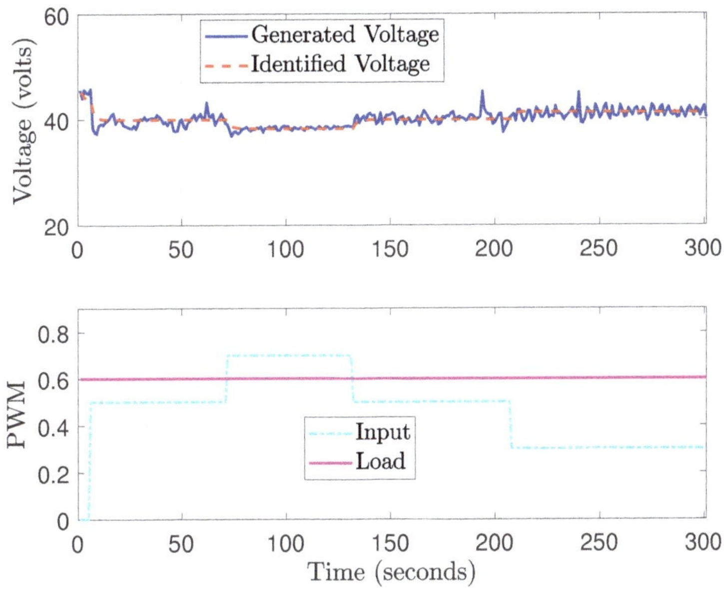

Figure 4. Open-loop generated voltage and output of the identified fuzzy model under an inductive load, where - - -, Input, is the pwm signal sent to the servomotor used to moves the throttle of the combustion engine, and ——, Load, is the pwm signal sent to the brushless motor used as an inductive load.

To validate the discordance of the model, the Quality of Fit (QoF) was calculated by dividing the Mean Squared Error (MSE) of the identified model by the Mean Squared Output (MSO) (9), which must be much smaller than 1 [31], resulting in a QoF $= 6.1264 \times 10^{-4}$

$$\frac{MSE}{MSO} = \frac{\frac{1}{N}||\theta X - Y||^2}{\frac{1}{N}||Y||^2} \tag{9}$$

3.2. Optimization of the Fuzzy Parameter *m*

To improve the approximation of the T–S fuzzy rule base with the input–output learning data, it is proposed to use the PSO algorithm for the optimal search of the m parameter of the c-means fuzzy algorithm. In addition, the PSO algorithm is also used for the optimal selection of the poles of the closed-loop system of the fuzzy rules defined in Equation (6), with a state feedback control structure for each of the fuzzy rules. In this search for the best parameters within the learning space with the input–output measurements, the PSO algorithm was used, as shown in [32,33].

The proposed cost functions for the optimization problem should be defined according to the characteristics of the system one intends to work with. In our experiment, the cost function of Algorithm 1 is proposed in order to minimise the error of the system identification. On the other hand, the corresponding number of clusters in Algorithm 1 was defined based on the open-loop response of the PGS. Since it presented four operational set points, as depicted in Figure 3, we decided to use four clusters in order to capture most of the system behaviour. This behaviour in the PGS is due to the hysteresis phenomena introduced by the servomotor used to control the ICE's accelerator.

In Algorithm 2, the cost function was defined based on the desired transient response. In this sense, the system poles of the considered electromechanical system were defined in the positive real axis inside the unite circle, since the desired system response should be similar to the response of a first-order system. For a different system, the location of the desired closed-loop poles and the number of clusters/rules will depend on the characteristics of the system, as well as on the desired system response.

Algorithm 2 Pole placement optimization and PDC control.

```
function PSO ALGORITHM                                   ▷ Close Loop System
    for p_i ← 0.01 to 0.9 do                                       ▷ Poles p_i
        Optimize p_i using Equation (12)                  ▷ Objective function
    end for
end function
return p_i
Calculate K_i for each c_i using pole assignment
function PDC CONTROL(A_i, B_i, c, c, K_i, m, x_1(0), x_2(0))
    for i ← 1 to N do
        Calculate Euclidean distances using (2)
        Calculate the membership degrees using (3)
        Calculate the strategy control using (14)
        Perform defuzzification using (7)
    end for
end function
```

The cost function employed in the PSO to optimize the parameter m, shown in Equation (3), in Algorithm 1 is based on the RMSE between the measurement obtained from the PGS and the output of the identified fuzzy model, and is given as follows:

$$\text{RMSE} = \sqrt{\frac{\sum_{k=1}^{N}(VG(k) - x_2(k))^2}{N}} \tag{10}$$

where $VG(k)$ is the value of the physical system output and $x_2(k)$ is the output (state variable) of the system identified through fuzzy modelling. Table 3 shows the values used in the PSO algorithm, as well as the search values assigned to the m parameter and the obtained optimal value of m.

Table 3. Parameters used in the PSO algorithm and obtained value for the parameter m.

Optimal Value m	Bounds	# of Particles	Inertia Coefficient ω	ς_1, ς_2	# of Iterations
2.97	[1.1, 3]	300	0.0917	0.5959	100

To obtain the value of the constants ς_1 and ς_2, parameter ξ is calculated as:

$$\xi = \frac{2\kappa}{\left|2 - \phi - \sqrt{\phi^2 - 4\phi}\right|} \tag{11}$$

where $\phi = \phi_1 + \phi_2$. The constants ϕ_1 and ϕ_2 are bounded as $\phi \geq 4$ and $\leq \kappa \leq 1$, whose values are defined in [34] for the PSO algorithm. Thus, ς_1 and ς_2 are obtained as $\varsigma_1 = \xi\phi_1$ and $\varsigma_2 = \xi\phi_2$.

Algorithm 1 shows the procedure used to obtain the parameter m as well as to obtain the identified system based on the number of defined clusters/rules.

3.3. Closed-Loop System Poles Optimization

For the optimization process of the poles of the closed-loop system, we used the following cost function:

$$\text{RMSE} = \sqrt{\frac{\sum_{k=1}^{N}(r(k) - x_2(k))^2}{N}} \tag{12}$$

where $r(k)$ is the desired voltage reference and $x_2(k)$ is the state variable, which approximates in a fuzzy way the voltage generated in closed loop. As explained before, in order to obtain the best poles that minimises the system response guaranteeing that the poles remain on the real axis inside the unit circle, the search limits were proposed in the interval $[0.01, 0.9]$. Table 4 shows the values used in the PSO algorithm, as well as the values obtained for the closed-loop poles.

Table 4. Parameters used in the PSO algorithm and obtained values for the poles.

Optimal Poles	Bounds	# of Particles	Inertia Coefficient ω	ς_1, ς_2	# of Iterations
$0.3, 0.8$	$[0.01, 0.9]$	300	0.3820	0.9549	100

In order to highlight the advantages in the implementation of the proposed PSO algorithms, we used the index errors based on the Integral of the Squared Error (ISE), the Integral of the Absolute Value of the Error (IAE), and the Integral of the Absolute Value of the Error multiplied by Time (ITAE). Table 5 depicts the obtained values from the three indexes applied to the simulation scenarios when the PSO algorithm was used and when it was not employed.

Table 5. Error indexes using the algorithm PSO and without the algorithm PSO.

	ISE	IAE	ITAE
	$\sum_{k=0}^{N} e^2(k) T_s$	$\sum_{k=0}^{N} \lvert e(k) \rvert T_s$	$\sum_{k=0}^{N} k \lvert e(k) \rvert T_s$
With PSO	2.6677×10^3	51.6501	8.02×10^5
Without PSO	6.9970×10^6	2.6452×10^3	2.1061×10^9

Where $N = 301$ is the total number of samples, $T_s = 1$ s is the sampling time, and $e(k)$ is the system output tracking error.

From Table 5, we can see that the error indexes are bigger when the PSO algorithm is not used. This is due the fact that the value of the fuzzy parameter has to be proposed based on the designer expertise at the time of conducting the fuzzy modelling by trial and error. Furthermore, since the optimal location of the system poles is obtained with the PSO algorithm, the system performance is improved

4. PDC Fuzzy Control

To achieve the regulation of the T–S system, the control technique based on the distributed parallel compensator was used. In this control strategy, the consequent of each fuzzy rule of the model (6) is replaced by a control law with the form of linear state feedback ([29,35]). In the PDC approach with pole assignment, the eigenvalues of $(A_i - B_i K_i)$ are proposed. The consequent for each PDC fuzzy rule is given by:

$$u_i(k) = -K_i x(k) \tag{13}$$

The global output of the PDC, in other words, the fuzzy aggregation of all control rules, has the following form:

$$u(k) = \frac{\sum_{i=1}^{c} \mu_{ik} u_i(k)}{\sum_{i=1}^{c} \mu_{ik}} \tag{14}$$

where K_i is the vector of gains of the i-th rule, as shown in Table 6, and $k_r = 1.38$ is a precompensation gain, as shown in Figure 1. For obtaining the PDC gains, the method by pole assignment was used, as obtained by the PSO algorithm.

Table 6. Defined gain values for each submodel.

Gains	Values
K_1	$0.0448, -0.0559$
K_2	$0.2130, -0.2118$
K_3	$0.0529, -0.0632$
K_4	$0.0720, -0.0809$

Figure 5 shows the simulation results of the voltage regulation at different reference values, in which it can be seen that the PDC controller regulates the generated voltage, defined by reference steps of 30, 40, and 25 volts. These reference values are typical voltage values in applications that employs LiPo batteries. In such applications, 25, 40, and 30 volts are nominal voltages of LiPo batteries with different numbers of cells.

Furthermore, Figure 5 shows the control signal applied to the PGS, which is bounded to values in a range of $[0, 1]$. This variable regulates the amount of gasoline in the explosion chamber by manipulating the throttle unit (carburettor) with a servomotor. It is seen that the PDC fuzzy controller regulates the voltage in the simulation test to the reference voltage value.

Algorithm 2 describes the required steps for the optimization of the controller's gains as well as the implementation of the PDC controller. The fuzzy model tracking of the closed-loop power generation system achieves a QoF $= 3.4763 \times 10^{-4}$, given by Equation (9). The QoF is much less than 1, even though the PGS is subjected to noise in its generated voltage, natural dead zones of the control actuator in the throttle body (carburettor servo motor), and non-linear dynamically varying electrical disturbances (load).

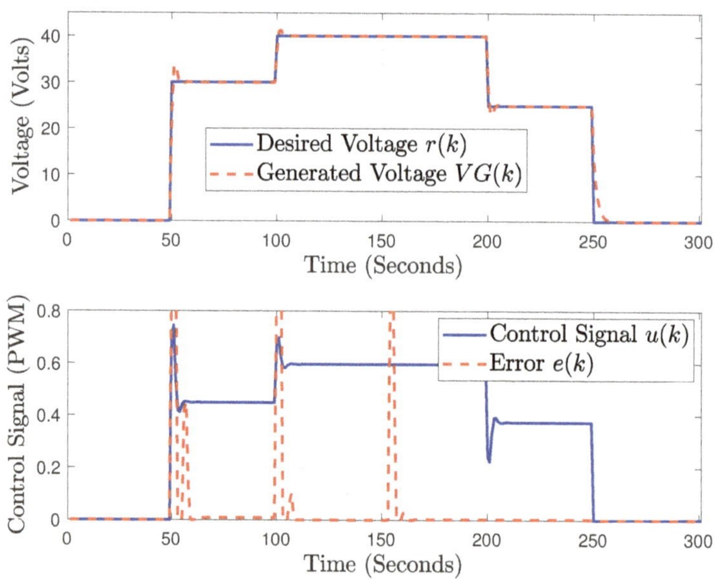

Figure 5. Simulation results of the voltage regulation using the obtained model of the power generator system.

Comparison of Implementing a PDC vs. PD Controller

In order to highlight the advantages of using the proposed strategies, we simulated a classic PD controller and compared its performance with the one obtained with the PDC strategy. We can see from Figure 6 that the PD controller is not able to reach the desired voltages at different step inputs due to the fact that its gains can only be tuned for a specific region of operation. When the desired voltage is defined at a different region of operation, the proposed PDC controller uses the obtained firing value μ_{ik} from the fuzzy strategy to modify the corresponding controller's gains. It is worth mentioning that this type of electromechanical systems has different regions of operation due to its intrinsic characteristics. These characteristics are given by the non-linear nature and complexity of the system due to its different components, such as dead zones stemming from the actuator utilized in the internal combustion engine's accelerator, voltage fluctuations, and non-linearities within the electric load and its associated electronic speed controller.

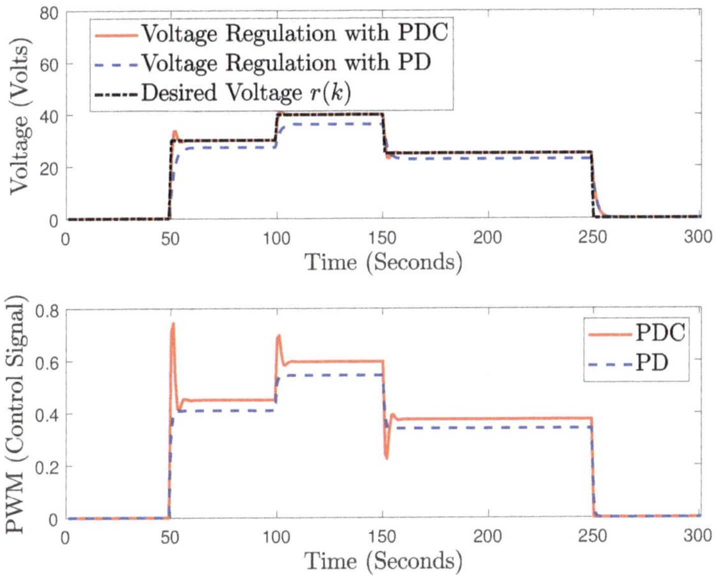

Figure 6. Comparison between the PDC strategy and a classic PD controller.

5. Conclusions

The proposed algorithms based on the fuzzy c-means technique, along with the PDC controller and the PSO metaheuristic optimization method, demonstrated effectiveness in modelling, identifying, and controlling a complex system. This capability was verified through numerical tests conducted on the obtained power generator system model.

Taking advantage of experimental data from the open-loop plant, the optimization strategy utilizing the PSO algorithm enabled the determination of the optimal fuzzy parameter m for the c-means algorithm. It was demonstrated that, by optimizing the value of m, the learning data pertaining to the premises of fuzzy rules are classified with greater similarity. This leads to an enhanced interpretation and reduced approximation error of the fuzzy model. Additionally, it facilitated the selection of poles within the unit circle for each closed-loop rule's consequent, aiding in the fine-tuning of fuzzy controllers via state feedback.

By utilizing input and output data, the process of identifying a fuzzy model for the power generation system bypasses the necessity to derive and identify a mathematical model through conventional techniques. This is particularly advantageous given the significant challenge posed by the complexity of the entire system, which encompasses both an internal combustion engine and a mechanically coupled electric generator.

The comparison of the proposed control strategies with a classical control law demonstrated that classical controllers are not able to reach the desired voltages at different step inputs due to the controller's gains only being tuned for a certain region of operation. However, when the desired voltage is required to be defined at a different region of operation, the proposed PDC controller modifies the corresponding controller's gains thorough the obtained firing value, μ_{ik}, from the fuzzy logic strategy.

In our upcoming research work, we aim to deploy the developed algorithms onto a physical power generation system. This step is crucial to validate their efficacy in addressing the inherent complexities characteristic of such systems. These complexities include dead zones stemming from the actuator utilized in the internal combustion engine's accelerator, voltage fluctuations, and non-linearities within the electric load and its associated electronic speed controller.

The obtained quality-of-fit indexes between the regulated voltage and the identified voltage are $QoF = 3.4763 \times 10^{-4}$ and $QoF = 6.1264 \times 10^{-4}$, respectively. For this index, values much smaller than 1 are considered a good performance.

Author Contributions: Conceptualization, C.R. and E.S.E.; methodology, C.R., J.C.R.-F. and E.S.E.; simulations, C.R., J.C.R.-F. and E.S.E.; dynamics modelling and control, C.R., J.C.R.-F. and E.S.E.; investigation, C.R., J.C.R.-F. and E.S.E.; writing—original draft preparation, C.R., E.S.E. and J.C.R.-F.; writing—review and editing, C.R., J.C.R.-F., R.L. and E.S.E.; supervision, E.S.E., J.C.R.-F. and R.L.; project administration, E.S.E. All authors have read and agreed to the published version of the manuscript.

Funding: This work was partially supported by the Mexican National Council for Humanities, Sciences, and Technologies through Project: Laboratorio Nacional en Vehículos Autónomos y Exoesqueletos.

Data Availability Statement: The raw data supporting the conclusions of this article will be made available by the authors on request.

Acknowledgments: Christian Reyes thanks Conahcyt in recognition of the invaluable support provided throughout his PhD studies at the Center for Research and Advanced Studies of the National Polytechnic Institute Zacatenco, Mexico.

Conflicts of Interest: The authors declare no conflicts of interest.

Abbreviations

The following abbreviations are used in this manuscript:

ICE	Internal Combustion Engine
MSE	Mean Square Error
MSO	Mean Square Output
PDC	Parallel Distributed Controller
PGS	Power Generation System
PSO	Particle Swarm Optimization
QoF	Quality of Fit
T–S	Takagi–Sugeno

References

1. Zaccone, R.; Campora, U.; Martelli, M. Optimisation of a diesel-electric ship propulsion and power generation system using a genetic algorithm. *J. Mar. Sci. Eng.* **2021**, *9*, 587. [CrossRef]
2. Xie, Y.; Savvaris, A.; Tsourdos, A. Fuzzy logic based equivalent consumption optimization of a hybrid electric propulsion system for unmanned aerial vehicles. *Aerosp. Sci. Technol.* **2019**, *85*, 13–23. [CrossRef]
3. Aliramezani, M.; Koch, C.R.; Shahbakhti, M. Modeling, diagnostics, optimization, and control of internal combustion engines via modern machine learning techniques: A review and future directions. *Prog. Energy Combust. Sci.* **2022**, *88*, 100967. [CrossRef]
4. Bhatt, A.N.; Shrivastava, N. Application of artificial neural network for internal combustion engines: A state of the art review. *Arch. Comput. Methods Eng.* **2022**, *29*, 897–919. [CrossRef]

5. Sun, L.; You, F. Machine learning and data-driven techniques for the control of smart power generation systems: An uncertainty handling perspective. *Engineering* **2021**, *7*, 1239–1247. [CrossRef]
6. Zhao, S.; Blaabjerg, F.; Wang, H. An overview of artificial-intelligence applications for power electronics. *IEEE Trans. Power Electron.* **2020**, *36*, 4633–4658. [CrossRef]
7. Karamanakos, P.; Liegmann, E.; Geyer, T.; Kennel, R. Model predictive control of power electronic systems: Methods, results, and challenges. *IEEE Open J. Ind. Appl.* **2020**, *1*, 95–114. [CrossRef]
8. Abdalla, A.N.; Nazir, M.S.; Tao, H.; Cao, S.; Ji, R.; Jiang, M.; Yao, L. Integration of energy storage system and renewable energy sources based on artificial intelligence: An overview. *J. Energy Storage* **2021**, *40*, 102811. [CrossRef]
9. Di Giovine, G.; Mariani, L.; Di Battista, D.; Cipollone, R.; Fremondi, F. Modeling and experimental validation of a triple-screw pump for internal combustion engine cooling. *Appl. Therm. Eng.* **2021**, *199*, 117550. [CrossRef]
10. Amoiralis, E.I.; Tsili, M.A.; Spathopoulos, V.; Hatziefremidis, A. Energy efficiency optimization in uavs: A review. In Proceedings of the Materials Science Forum, Xi'an, China, 8–9 August 2014; Trans Tech Publications Ltd.: Stafa-Zurich, Switzerland, 2014; Volume 792, pp. 281–286.
11. Technologies, T.F. Hybrid VTOL: Increased Energy Density for Increased Payload and Endurance. 2017. Available online: https://vtol.org/files/dmfile/24-TVF2018-Debitetto-TopFlight-Jan191.pdf (accessed on 4 March 2024).
12. Sullivan UV. Acutronic Power Systems. 2019. Available online: https://www.sullivanuv.com/ (accessed on 10 April 2024).
13. Babuška, R. *Fuzzy Modeling for Control*; Springer: Dordrecht, The Netherlands, 1998. [CrossRef]
14. Zhang, X.; Liu, L.; Dai, Y. Fuzzy state machine energy management strategy for hybrid electric UAVs with PV/fuel cell/battery power system. *Int. J. Aerosp. Eng.* **2018**, *2018*, 1–16. [CrossRef]
15. Remoaldo, D.; Jesus, I. Analysis of a Traditional and a Fuzzy Logic Enhanced Perturb and Observe Algorithm for the MPPT of a Photovoltaic System. *Algorithms* **2021**, *14*, 24. [CrossRef]
16. Bezdek, J.C. A physical interpretation of fuzzy ISODATA. In *Readings in Fuzzy Sets for Intelligent Systems*; Elsevier: Amsterdam, The Netherlands, 1993; pp. 615–616. [CrossRef]
17. Bezdek, J.C. *Pattern Recognition with Fuzzy Objective Function Algorithms*; Springer Science & Business Media: New York, NY, USA, 2013.
18. Wu, K.L. Analysis of parameter selections for fuzzy c-means. *Pattern Recognit.* **2012**, *45*, 407–415. [CrossRef]
19. Zhou, K.; Fu, C.; Yang, S. Fuzziness parameter selection in fuzzy c-means: The perspective of cluster validation. *Sci. China Inf. Sci.* **2014**, *57*, 1–8. [CrossRef]
20. Shrivastava, N.; Khan, Z.M. Application of soft computing in the field of internal combustion engines: A review. *Arch. Comput. Methods Eng.* **2018**, *25*, 707–726. [CrossRef]
21. Khang, T.D.; Tran, M.K.; Fowler, M. A Novel Semi-Supervised Fuzzy C-Means Clustering Algorithm Using Multiple Fuzzification Coefficients. *Algorithms* **2021**, *14*, 258. [CrossRef]
22. Manjarrez, L.H.; Ramos-Fernández, J.C.; Espinoza, E.S.; Lozano, R. Estimation of Energy Consumption and Flight Time Margin for a UAV Mission Based on Fuzzy Systems. *Technologies* **2023**, *11*, 12. [CrossRef]
23. You, D.; Lei, Y.; Liu, S.; Zhang, Y.; Zhang, M. Networked Control System Based on PSO-RBF Neural Network Time-Delay Prediction Model. *Appl. Sci.* **2022**, *13*, 536. [CrossRef]
24. Shouran, M.; Alsseid, A. Particle swarm optimization algorithm-tuned fuzzy cascade fractional order PI-fractional order PD for frequency regulation of dual-area power system. *Processes* **2022**, *10*, 477. [CrossRef]
25. Benevieri, A.; Carbone, L.; Cosso, S.; Kumar, K.; Marchesoni, M.; Passalacqua, M.; Vaccaro, L. Series Architecture on Hybrid Electric Vehicles: A Review. *Energies* **2021**, *14*, 7672. [CrossRef]
26. Takagi, T.; Sugeno, M. Fuzzy identification of systems and its applications to modeling and control. *IEEE Trans. Syst. Man Cybern.* **1985**, *SMC-15*, 116–132. [CrossRef]
27. Nayak, J.; Naik, B.; Behera, H. Fuzzy C-Means (FCM) Clustering Algorithm: A Decade Review from 2000 to 2014. In Proceedings of the Computational Intelligence in Data Mining, Bhubaneswar, India, 5–6 December 2015; Springer: New Delhi, India, 2014; Volume 2, pp. 133–149.
28. Setnes, M.; Babuska, R.; Verbruggen, H.B. Rule-based modeling: Precision and transparency. *IEEE Trans. Syst. Man Cybern. Part C (Appl. Rev.)* **1998**, *28*, 165–169. [CrossRef]
29. Lilly, J.H. *Fuzzy Control and Identification*; John Wiley & Sons: Hoboken, NJ, USA, 2010. [CrossRef]
30. Rubio, I.; Guijarro, G.; Garcia, L.; Hespanha, J.; Xie, J. Translational Model Identification and Robust Control for the Parrot Mambo UAS. In Proceedings of the IEEE GLOBECOM 2019 Workshop on Computing-Centric Drone Networks, Waikoloa, HI, USA, 9–14 December 2019; IEEE: Piscataway, NJ, USA, 2019; pp. 1–6. [CrossRef]
31. Hespanha, J.P. Advanced Undergraduate Topics in Control Systems Design. 2023. Available online: https://web.ece.ucsb.edu/~hespanha/published/allugtopics-20230402.pdf (accessed on 13 January 2024).
32. Hashim, H.A.; El-Ferik, S.; Abido, M.A. A fuzzy logic feedback filter design tuned with PSO for L1 adaptive controller. *Expert Syst. Appl.* **2015**, *42*, 9077–9085. [CrossRef]
33. Praseeda, C.; Shivakumar, B. Fuzzy particle swarm optimization (FPSO) based feature selection and hybrid kernel distance based possibilistic fuzzy local information C-means (HKD-PFLICM) clustering for churn prediction in telecom industry. *SN Appl. Sci.* **2021**, *3*, 613. [CrossRef]

34. Clerc, M.; Kennedy, J. The particle swarm-explosion, stability, and convergence in a multidimensional complex space. *IEEE Trans. Evol. Comput.* **2002**, *6*, 58–73. [CrossRef]
35. Wang, H.O.; Tanaka, K. *Fuzzy Control Systems Design and Analysis: A Linear Matrix Inequality Approach*; John Wiley & Sons: New York, NY, USA, 2004. [CrossRef]

algorithms

MDPI

Article

Fractional-Order Fuzzy PID Controller with Evolutionary Computation for an Effective Synchronized Gantry System

Wei-Lung Mao, Sung-Hua Chen * and Chun-Yu Kao

Department of Electrical Engineering, Graduate School of Engineering Science and Technology, National Yunlin University of Science and Technology, Yunlin 64002, Taiwan; wlmao@gemail.yuntech.edu.tw (W.-L.M.); m10812068@yuntech.edu.tw (C.-Y.K.)

* Correspondence: chenhua@yuntech.edu.tw

Abstract: Gantry-type dual-axis platforms can be used to move heavy loads or perform precision CNC work. Such gantry systems drive a single axis with two linear motors, and under heavy loads, a high driving force is required. This can generate a pulling force between the drive shafts in the coupling mechanism. In these situations, when a synchronization error becomes too large, mechanisms can become deformed or damaged, leading to damaged equipment, or in industrial settings, an additional power consumption. Effectively and accurately acquiring the synchronized movement of the platform is important to reduce energy consumption and optimize the system. In this study, a fractional-order fuzzy PID controller (FOFPID) using Oustaloup's recursive filter is used to control a synchronous X–Y gantry-type platform. The optimized controller parameters are obtained by the measurement of control errors in a simulated environment. Four optimization methods are tested and compared: particle swarm optimization, invasive weed optimization, a gray wolf optimizer, and biogeography-based optimization. The systems were tested and compared in order to optimize the control parameters. Each of the four algorithms is simulated on four contour shapes: a circle, bow, heart, and star. The simulations and control scheme of the experiments are implemented using MATLAB, and the reference paths were planned using non-uniform rational B-splines (NURBS). After running the simulations to determine the optimal control parameters, each set of acquired control parameters is also tested and compared in the experiments and the results are recorded. Both the simulations and experiments show good results, and the tracking of the X–Y platform showed improved performance. Two performance indices are used to determine and validate the relative performance of the models and results.

Keywords: synchronized gantry stage; PMLSM; fractional-order PID controller; fuzzy PID controller; particle swarm optimization (PSO); invasive weed optimization (IWO); grey wolf optimizer (GWO); biogeography-based optimization (BBO); non-uniform rational B-splines (NURBS); contour tracking

1. Introduction

Biaxial gantry systems are often found in industrial settings because of their high-speed and high-precision planar motions. Applications include CNC machines, automotive assembly lines, material handling, surface chip mounters, and positioning stages. To provide accurate Cartesian movement information to a multiple-axis configuration, the control stage must be managed in a synchronous manner, especially when carrying heavy loads. Conventional control methods use independent axis control, regardless of the other axes. Synchronous errors cannot be reduced effectively through independent axis control, and this leads to decreased precision in use. Design of a servo control system with synchronous motion techniques [1–4] is critical for high-precision gantry systems, especially where heavy loads could lead to process safety issues or damage to equipment.

Parallel synchronous control schemes are often driven by two linear motors. Without any mechanical transmission, such as lead screws or gears, the payload can be directly driven. The design in this paper uses a permanent magnet linear synchronous motor (PMLSM) [5] for its compact structure, rapid response, and high force density. Several other approaches to the multi-axis de-synchronization problem have been proposed, such as a master–slave motion control arrangement and cross-coupled controls. In [6], the authors applied a nonlinear feedback control scheme to control the PMLSM position, and overcome inherent nonlinear functions and parametric uncertainties. In [7], a synchronous control was developed on a platform with only one axis, which is actuated by servo motors and dual parallel ball screws. In addition, an identification method was proposed to build a coupled system model. The cross-coupled synchronous control method [8,9] reduced the contouring error in the gantry system. An optimized cross-coupled synchronizing control [8] was proposed to improve synchronization accuracy in dual-feed drives. The performance index includes the synchronous error, which is to be minimized. A cross-coupled synchronous control system was also combined with a complementary sliding mode control [9], to simultaneously converge position tracking and synchronous errors for the gantry position stages with uncertainties. In this study, the authors designed a PID control scheme for an X–Y-type gantry. Since a conventional PID control cannot overcome problems associated with speed changes, load disturbances, and steady-state errors, a fractional-order fuzzy PID (FOFPID) is incorporated for more flexible parameter tuning than that of integer order.

In recent years, fractional order differentiation and integration have become more commonly used in control design [10–13]. Since the calculus orders are not necessarily to be integers, the dynamic models can be described more adequately. Also, a controller with fractional orders is often more suitable than one using integer orders. A parameter tuning approach for fractional order PD controllers was proposed [14] for a class of second-order systems. This method can increase the robustness by fulfilling the given gain phase margin and crossover frequency. A temperature control with a digital fractional order controller has been demonstrated [15]. Furthermore, the practical application and improvement of PID controllers using fractional order have also been shown [16–18]. Another fractional-order fuzzy PID controller design [19] considered tuning the orders in the fuzzy controller, and then used a genetic algorithm to optimize the controller by minimizing error indices.

Although fractional order differ-integrations make the controller adapt to the plant more adequately, tuning the parameters becomes difficult. To improve the effectiveness of the controller design, several optimization algorithms have been used to adjust the parameters, such as particle swarm optimization (PSO) [20], invasive weed optimization (IWO) [21], gray wolf optimization (GWO) [22], biogeography-based optimization (BBO) [23], and genetic algorithms (GAs). In [13,24], the PSO algorithm was used for the adjustment of the fractional order PID controller parameters. The results showed the parameters given by the PSO led to a precise and strong anti-disturbance control. Another work used a modified firefly algorithm (MFA)–PSO-based fractional order PID controller [25] for an effective torque and speed regulation strategy for a BLDC motor. Other optimization algorithms, such as the IWO [26] and GWO [27], were also applied to fractional order controllers to improve their performance.

In this research, the fractional order fuzzy controller is implemented in a synchronized gantry-type X–Y platform. Several optimization algorithms, namely PSO, IWO, BBO, and GWO, are integrated with the FOFPID for precision trajectory tracking control, and their relative performances are compared. The integral of the time-weighted absolute error (ITAE) is an index for the optimization of the controller parameters. Two PMLSMs set up in parallel on the Y-axis rails move a beam simultaneously, while another PMLSM moves the head set up on the beam along the X-axis. A MATLAB system ID toolbox is used to find the parameters of the PMLSM transfer functions. The simulation and experimental results for the different reference contours are demonstrated to reveal the effectiveness of the proposed controller, with improved tracking performance.

This paper is organized as follows: Section 2 presents the system dynamics and model identification. Section 3 describes the fractional-order fuzzy PID controller. The PSO optimization algorithm used in this work is introduced in Section 4. The simulation and experimental results are demonstrated in Section 5, and Section 6 presents the conclusions drawn from the results.

2. System Model and Identification

2.1. PMLSM Model

The PMLSMs are used as the actuators in the gantry system and the mathematical model is derived below. The dynamic model [2] in the *d*–*q* reference frame is represented by

$$\begin{aligned} v_d &= Ri_d + L_d\frac{di_d}{dt} - \frac{\pi}{\tau}v_P L_d i_q \\ v_q &= Ri_q + L_q\frac{di_q}{dt} + \frac{\pi}{\tau}v_P L_q i_d + \sqrt{\frac{2}{3}}\frac{\pi}{\tau}\lambda_{\max} v_P \end{aligned} \tag{1}$$

where v_d and v_q denote the d-axis and q-axis voltages, L_d and L_q are the d-axis and q-axis inductances, i_q and i_d are the q-axis and d-axis currents, respectively, τ is the pole pitch, v_P and R are the velocity and resistance of the mover, and $\lambda_{\max}$ denotes the maximum of sinusoidal flux linkage. By (1), the derivative of these currents can be obtained as

$$\begin{bmatrix} \frac{di_d}{dt} \\ \frac{di_q}{dt} \end{bmatrix} = \begin{bmatrix} -\frac{R}{L_d} & -\frac{\pi}{\tau}v_P\frac{L_q}{L_d} \\ -\frac{\pi}{\tau}v_P\frac{L_d}{L_q} & -\frac{R}{L_q} \end{bmatrix}\begin{bmatrix} i_d \\ i_q \end{bmatrix} + \begin{bmatrix} \frac{v_d}{L_d} \\ \frac{1}{L_q}\left(v_q - \sqrt{\frac{2}{3}}\frac{\pi}{\tau}\lambda_{\max} v_P\right) \end{bmatrix} \tag{2}$$

The dynamic equation of the mechanical part is expressed as

$$F_e = M\dot{v}_P + Bv_P + F_L = M\ddot{x} + B\dot{x} + F_L \tag{3}$$

where M, B, and x are the mass, viscous friction coefficient, and displacement of the stage, respectively, F_L denotes the external loading, and F_e represents the electromagnetic force, which is given by

$$F_e = \frac{3\pi}{2\tau}\left[(L_d - L_q)i_d i_q + \lambda_{\max} i_q\right] \tag{4}$$

Since the PMLSM exhibits a uniform air gap on the stator surface, the condition $L_d = L_q = L$ can be assumed and reduces (4) to

$$F_e = \frac{3\pi}{2\tau}\lambda_{\max} i_q = k_t i_q \tag{5}$$

where $k_t = \frac{3\pi}{2\tau}\lambda_{\max}$ is the force constant. Let v_{dr} and v_{qr} be the *d*- and *q*-axis voltage commands and remove the coupled terms, then the derivative of the currents shown in (2) can be rewritten:

$$\begin{bmatrix} \frac{di_d}{dt} \\ \frac{di_q}{dt} \end{bmatrix} = -\frac{R}{L}\begin{bmatrix} i_d \\ i_q \end{bmatrix} + \frac{1}{L}\begin{bmatrix} v_{dr} \\ v_{qr} \end{bmatrix} \tag{6}$$

From (5), the q-axis current i_q produces the motor driving force F_e. Integrating (3), (5), and (6), and then applying a Laplace transform, provides the transfer function from the voltage command $V(s)$ to the displacement $X(s)$:

$$\frac{X(s)}{V(s)} = \frac{K_t}{MLs^3 + (MR + BL)s^2 + BRs} \tag{7}$$

Figure 1 shows the model block diagram of the PMLSM system.

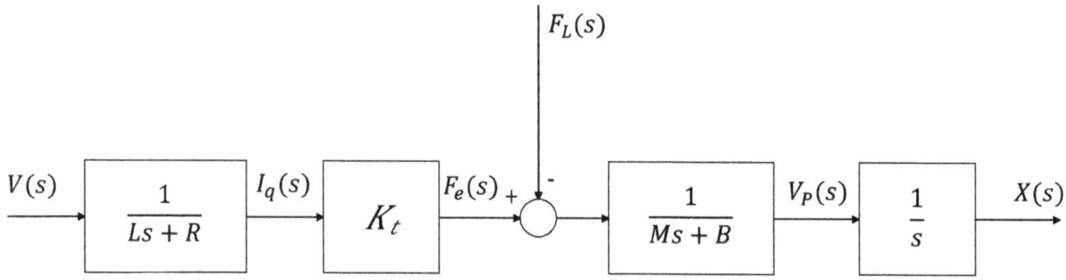

Figure 1. The PMLSM equivalent model.

2.2. Mechanical Coupling Model and System Identification

A linear motor is set up on the X-axis of the gantry platform, while the Y-axis consists of two parallel linear motors. Thus, mechanical coupling is inevitable. The displacements on the X- and Y-axis are feedbacked by optical encoders. Figure 2 shows the experimental setup of the gantry system, and the block diagram of the gantry platform is shown in Figure 3. To address the coupling effect, here we adopt the coupled parallel linear servo scheme [9] to build the Y-axis model. The transfer function $T_X(s)$ represents the X-axis PMLSM, while $T_{M\_M}(s)$, $T_{S\_S}(s)$, $T_{M\_S}(s)$, and $T_{S\_M}(s)$ model the Y-axis structure. $T_{M\_M}(s)$ and $T_{S\_S}(s)$ are the respective master and slave PMLSM models, and $T_{M\_S}(s)$ and $T_{S\_M}(s)$ describe the models of the coupling effects Y_S/V_M and Y_M/V_S.

To identify the Y-axis coupling, first, a unit step voltage input V_M is given to the master axis linear motor to drive the coupling system, while the slave axis retains its movement freely. Therefore, the slave axis is moved passively by the master axis, revealing the effect of coupling. From the measured displacements of the slides Y_M and Y_S, it is possible to build approximations of the transfer functions $T_{M\_M}(s)$ and $T_{M\_S}(s)$, which are composed of the form shown in (7). The same process can be used to identify $T_{S\_S}(s)$ and $T_{S\_M}(s)$ by giving a unit step input V_S to the slave motor and measuring both the position outputs of the slides Y_M and Y_S. Since the responses are presumed to be third-degree models, as in (7), from the collection of the output position and input voltage data, the model coefficients can be identified by using the MATLAB Toolbox. The third-order transfer functions describe the gantry platform with coupling on the Y-axis, and are described by

$$T_X(s) = \frac{1.41 \times 10^7}{s^3 + 76.1s^2 + 144.73s} \tag{8}$$

$$T_{M\_M}(s) = \frac{1.032 \times 10^9}{s^3 + 676.71s^2 + 1.0681 \times 10^5 s} \tag{9}$$

$$T_{M\_S}(s) = \frac{5.541 \times 10^9}{s^3 + 1565.4s^2 + 5.6787 \times 10^5 s} \tag{10}$$

$$T_{S\_S}(s) = \frac{1.804 \times 10^9}{s^3 + 862.93s^2 + 1.862 \times 10^5 s} \tag{11}$$

$$T_{S\_M}(s) = \frac{6.957 \times 10^9}{s^3 + 1735.1s^2 + 7.156 \times 10^5 s} \tag{12}$$

where $T_X(s)$ is the X-axis dynamic model, and $T_{M\_M}(s)$, $T_{M\_S}(s)$, $T_{S\_S}(s)$, and $T_{S\_M}(s)$ represent the model for the Y-axis.

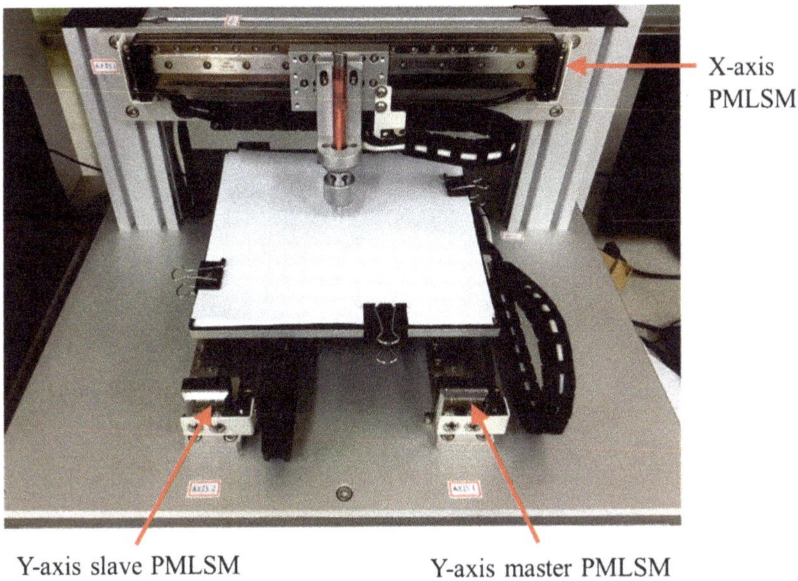

Figure 2. The two-axis gantry platform.

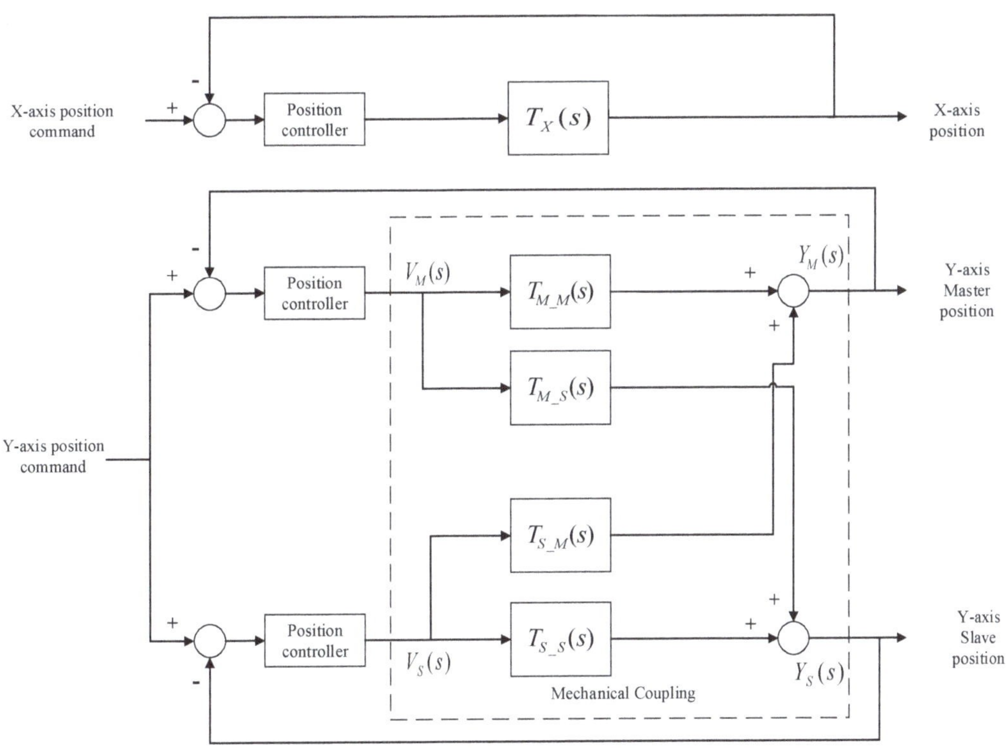

Figure 3. Block diagram of the gantry platform.

3. Control Design

3.1. Fractional Order Fuzzy PID Controller

The control scheme of the FOFPID shown in Figure 4 is a combination of fuzzy PI, and fuzzy PD controllers [19,28], taking K_e and K_{de} as the input scaling factors, and α and β as output factors. In addition, the differentiation and integration for D and I control can be of fractional orders, such that the control system can be tailored to fulfill the performance requirements.

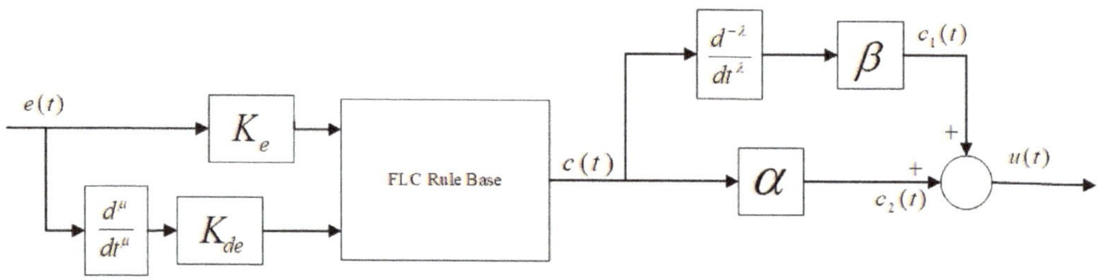

Figure 4. The block diagram of the fractional order fuzzy PID controller.

The parameters K_e, K_{de}, α, and β are the PID controller gains, while μ and λ are the orders of differentiation and integration, respectively. The two inputs of the fuzzy logic controller are from the PD control in the front part of this scheme. One is the gain K_e multiplied by the control error $e(t)$, and the other is K_{de}, multiplied by the derivative $\frac{d^\mu e}{dt^\mu}$. The fuzzy controller output $c(t)$ is subsequently input to the PI control in the rear part. Then the control of the FOFPID can be obtained by

$$u(t) = \alpha \cdot c(t) + \beta \cdot \int_0^t c(\tau) d\tau^\lambda \tag{13}$$

where $u(t)$ is the control output. The controller parameters K_e, K_{de}, α, β, μ, and λ need tuning for precise tracking. However, it is hard to tune these gains, especially when using fractional order values. The parameter tuning in this study utilizes an evolutionary computation algorithm, discussed in the next chapter.

In the fuzzy inference system [19], the input and output signals are transformed into fuzzy linguistic variables: PVB (Positive Very Big), NVB (Negative Very Big), PB (Positive Big), NB (Negative Big), PM (Positive Medium), NM (Negative Medium), PS (Positive Small), NS (Negative Small), and Z (Zero), respectively. The membership functions and rule base are shown in Figure 5 and Table 1. The triangular-shaped membership functions are chosen for the input variables, and singleton functions for the output. The two-dimensional linear rule base shown in Table 1 is used in the fuzzy controller. The inference mechanism is based on the Mamdani algorithm [19] and the rules are expressed by

$$\text{IF } e(t) \text{ is } \mathrm{A^i} \text{ AND } \frac{d^\mu e}{dt^\mu} \text{ is } \mathrm{B^i}, \text{ THEN } c(t) \text{ is } \mathrm{C^i} \tag{14}$$

where $\mathrm{A^i}$, $\mathrm{B^i}$, and $\mathrm{C^i}$ are the linguistic labels of these linguistic variables $e(t)$, $\frac{d^\mu e}{dt^\mu}$ and $c(t)$, and are characterized by membership functions for each variable. Here the max–min composition is used, and a fuzzy set $u(F)$ can be inferred from the following relation:

$$u(F_i) = \bigcup_{i=1}^{K} \left(u^{\mathrm{i}}(\mathrm{A}) \cap u^{\mathrm{i}}(\mathrm{B}) \right) \tag{15}$$

where K denotes the number of fuzzy output sets, and $u^{\mathrm{i}}(\mathrm{A})$ and $u^{\mathrm{i}}(\mathrm{B})$ are the MFs of the fuzzy sets A and B, respectively. $\cap$ and $\cup$ denote the min function (T-norm) and max function (T-conorm), respectively. F_i represents the value of the i-th output MF, and $u(F_i)$ is its membership value at the i-th quantization level. The center-average defuzzification is utilized here to obtain the output $c(t)$, as follows:

$$c(t) = \frac{\sum_{i=1}^{K} F_i u(F_i)}{\sum_{i=1}^{K} u(F_i)} \tag{16}$$

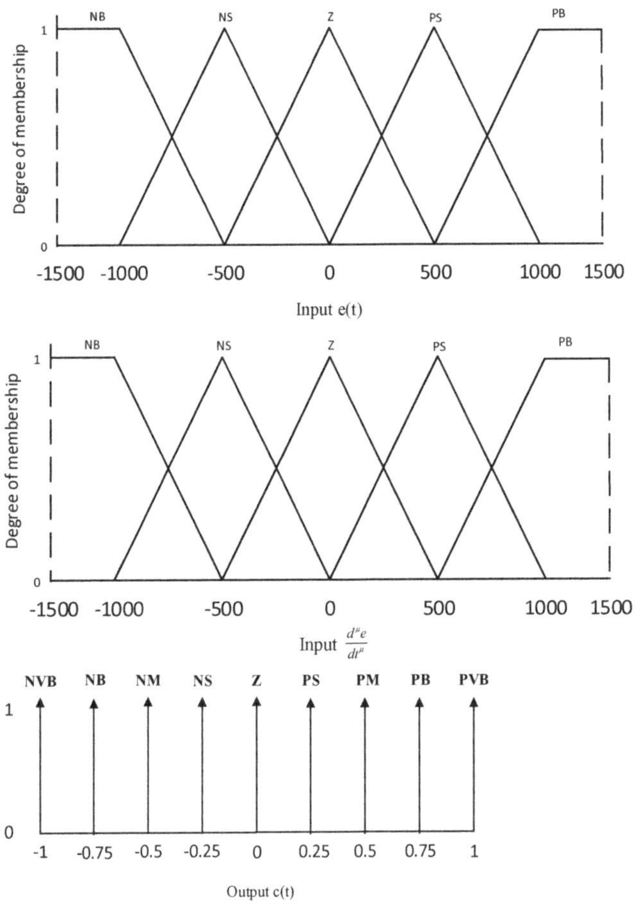

Figure 5. Membership functions of the fuzzy logic controller.

Table 1. Rule base of the fuzzy logic controller.

c(t)		e(t)				
		NB	**NS**	**Z**	**PS**	**PB**
$\frac{d^\mu e}{dt^\mu}$	NB	NVB	NB	NM	NS	Z
	NS	NB	NM	NS	Z	PS
	Z	NM	NS	Z	PS	PM
	PS	NS	Z	PS	PM	PB
	PB	Z	PS	PM	PB	PVB

Oustaloup's recursive filter [29] is utilized here to implement the fractional-order elements s^{λ} ($\lambda \in [-1, 1] \subseteq \Re$). The filter is given by

$$G_f(s) = s^{\lambda} = K \prod_{k=-N}^{N} \frac{s + \omega'_k}{s + \omega_k} \tag{17}$$

where the poles and zeros can be recursively evaluated by

$$\omega_k\prime = \omega_b \left(\frac{\omega_h}{\omega_b}\right)^{\frac{k+N+\frac{1}{2}(1-\lambda)}{2N+1}}, \ \omega_k = \omega_b \left(\frac{\omega_h}{\omega_b}\right)^{\frac{k+N+\frac{1}{2}(1+\lambda)}{2N+1}}, \ K = \omega_h^{\lambda} \tag{18}$$

The output of this filter is an approximation of a fractionally diff-integrated signal. λ is the order of the differ-integration, $[\omega_b, \ \omega_h]$ is the preset frequency range (rad/s), and N is the order of the approximate integer-order transfer function. The selected parameters for Oustaloup's recursive filter used in this work are $\omega_b = 0.001, \ \omega_h = 100, \ N = 3$.

3.2. The Objective Function

Figure 6 shows the FOFPID control scheme. It consists of two subsystems: one is the X-axis control loop, and the other is the Y-axis control loop, which possesses a mechanical coupling effect. The design of this control scheme is to reduce X- and Y-axis tracking errors, and also reduce the synchronous error in the Y-axis. To achieve this purpose with an optimization algorithm, a fitness function containing these error terms should be minimized. The ITAE performance criterion [30] is used to be the fitness function and is expressed as

$$\text{ITAE} = \int_0^T t|e(t)|dt \tag{19}$$

where $e(t)$ denotes the tracking error at instant t.

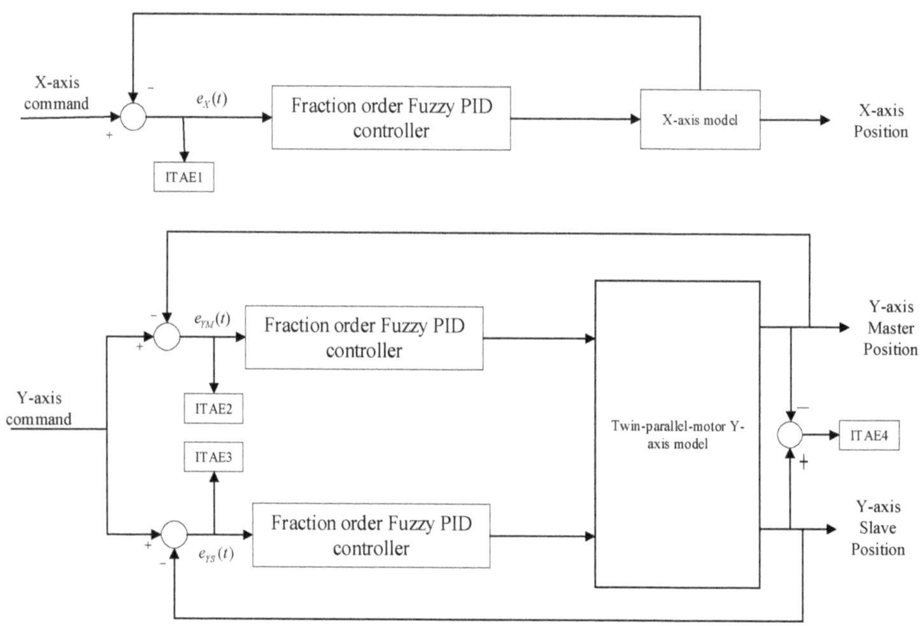

Figure 6. The proposed FOFPID synchronous control architecture.

In the control design, compared to the IAE (integral of the absolute error) and ISE (integral square error) indices, the ITAE performance index has smaller oscillations and overshoots. There are eighteen tuning parameters in the control scheme: (1) K_e, K_{de}, α, β, μ, and λ for the X-axis, (2) K_{e1}, K_{de1}, α_1, β_1, μ_1, and λ_1 for the master Y-axis, and (3) K_{e2}, K_{de2}, α_2, β_2, μ_2, and λ_2 for the slave Y-axis. To find appropriate parameters for the controller scheme, optimization algorithms can be used. For the gantry system described in Figure 4, the optimization problem is to minimize the system ITAE index. The ITAE of the whole system should consider the tracking errors for X-axis $e_X(t)$, master Y-axis $e_{YM}(t)$, and slave Y-axis $e_{YS}(t)$, and the synchronous error, which is the difference of two Y-axes $e_{YM}(t)$. Thus, the ITAE is given as

$$\text{ITAE} = \frac{1}{4}\left(\sum_{r=1}^{4}\text{ITAE}_r\right) \tag{20}$$

with $\text{ITAE}_1 = \int_0^T t|e_X(t)|dt$, $\text{ITAE}_2 = \int_0^T t|e_{YM}(t)|dt$, $\text{ITAE}_3 = \int_0^T t|e_{YS}(t)|dt$, $\text{ITAE}_4 = \int_0^T t|e_{YMS}(t)|dt$.

4. Optimization Algorithms

To choose the controller parameters, four evolutionary computations are tested and compared: particle swarm optimization (PSO), invasive weed optimization (IWO), a gray wolf optimizer (GWO), and biogeography-based optimization (BBO). The objective functions for the optimal algorithms can be formulated with the aim of minimizing the ITAE index. The time multiplication term in the ITAE index helps to reduce the settling time, for the penalty increases with time.

4.1. Grey Wolf Optimizer (GWO) Algorithm

A grey wolf optimizer [22] is an intelligent group optimization algorithm proposed by Mirjalili et al. of Griffith University, Australia, in 2014. The algorithm is an optimized search method inspired by the behavior of gray wolves when they hunt prey. The levels of the gray wolf social hierarchy are separated into α, β, δ, and ω from top to bottom. Wolf α represents the fittest solution, whereas the second and third best solutions are β and δ, respectively. The remaining wolves, ω, are candidate solutions. The GWO procedure has three steps: encircling, hunting, and attacking. The encircling behavior is modeled by the following equations:

$$\vec{D} = \left|\vec{C}\cdot\vec{X}_p(t) - \vec{X}(t)\right| \tag{21}$$

$$\vec{X}(t+1) = \vec{X}_p(t) - \vec{A}\cdot\vec{D} \tag{22}$$

where t denotes the current iterations, $\vec{X}$ is the position vector of a grey wolf, $\vec{X}_p$ is the position vector of the prey, and $\vec{A}$ and $\vec{C}$ are coefficient vectors calculated by

$$\vec{A} = 2\vec{a}\cdot\vec{r_1} - \vec{a} \tag{23}$$

$$\vec{C} = 2\cdot\vec{r_2} \tag{24}$$

where $\vec{a}$ is the convergence factor, decreasing linearly from 2 to 0 in the iterative process, and $\vec{r_1}$ and $\vec{r_2}$ are random vectors on the range [0, 1]. The outcome of these equations is that the random vectors $\vec{r_1}$ and $\vec{r_2}$ allow wolves to reach any position around the prey.

In the hunting stage, the first three best solutions obtained so far are saved, and other wolves are forced to update their positions according to the best agent. The position update equations are as follows:

$$\vec{D_\alpha} = \left|\vec{C_1}\cdot\vec{X_\alpha} - \vec{X}\right|,\ \vec{D_\beta} = \left|\vec{C_2}\cdot\vec{X_\beta} - \vec{X}\right|,\ \vec{D_\delta} = \left|\vec{C_3}\cdot\vec{X_\delta} - \vec{X}\right| \tag{25}$$

$$\vec{X_1} = \vec{X_\alpha} - \vec{A_1}\cdot\left(\vec{D_\alpha}\right),\ \vec{X_2} = \vec{X_\beta} - \vec{A_2}\cdot\left(\vec{D_\beta}\right),\ \vec{X_3} = \vec{X_\delta} - \vec{A_3}\cdot\left(\vec{D_\delta}\right) \tag{26}$$

$$\vec{X}(t+1) = \frac{\vec{X_1} + \vec{X_2} + \vec{X_3}}{3} \tag{27}$$

The final stage of hunting is to "attack the prey" (obtain the optimal solution). As iterations progress, the value of $\vec{a}$ decreases from 2 to 0, pushing the wolves to approach the prey. Note that the range of $\vec{A}$ is related to the value of $\vec{a}$. When $|A| < 1$, the wolves are forced to attack toward the prey.

With the GWO algorithm, the optimal control parameters of the proposed FOFPID controller can be found. The procedure is described as follows:

(1) Initialize the wolf group ($\alpha,\ \beta, \delta, \omega$) and select the GWO algorithm parameters.
(2) Design the appropriate parameters (K_e, K_{de}, α, β, μ, λ, K_{e1}, K_{de1}, α_1, β_1, μ_1, λ_1, K_{e2}, K_{de2}, α_2, β_2, μ_2, λ_2), and let the initial populations be feasible candidate solutions.
(3) Conduct the tracking process for all contours on the X–Y gantry system, calculate the ITAE, and then calculate the fitness function with (20).
(4) Set the iteration counter as one and the initial wolf group (α) as the best solution.
(5) Update the positions for the wolf group by (25)–(27) to obtain the new estimated prey position.
(6) Again, perform all contour tracking for the X–Y gantry system, compute the ITAE, and calculate the fitness value according to the new wolf group (α) position.
(7) Check whether the new fitness value is smaller than the best one. If the new fitness value is smaller, then replace the new position with it.
(8) Update the wolf group position and the corresponding fitness values.
(9) If the iteration limit is not reached, increase the iteration counter and return to Step (5).

These steps can also be represented as a flow chart as shown in Figure 7.

4.2. Other Optimization Algorithms

To investigate the effects of different optimization algorithms on the proposed FOFPID controller, three other optimization algorithms are tested for comparison: IWO, PSO, and BBO. In the experimental results, the comparisons of the four algorithms are demonstrated.

IWO is an effective global optimization algorithm proposed by A. Mehrabian and C. Lucas [21] in 2006. It is a numerical stochastic optimization algorithm evolved from the principle of the rapid reproduction and growth of weeds in nature. The IWO process first initializes the growth and reproduction of weeds, then updates the best fitness of weeds with a distribution equation, and finally runs a number of iterations.

The PSO algorithm is a modem heuristic algorithm developed by Kennedy and Eberhart in 1995 [20]. It formulates the optimization problems as bird flocking behavior. In the PSO algorithm, each particle in the search space stands for a solution to the optimization problem. Each particle possesses a fitness value and velocity to determine the distance and direction of its movement. Then the particles follow the particle with the best fitness values to search in the solution space. To implement this method, initialize a population of particles, then update the particle locations, and iterate to produce an optimal solution.

The BBO approach was published by Dan Simon [23] in 2008. It uses the distribution of species between neighboring islands to construct a mathematical model for species extinction and migration. The process of optimization is as follows: initialize a habitat, update that optimal habitat's suitability using given migration and mutation rates, and then iterate and update the process to obtain a solution.

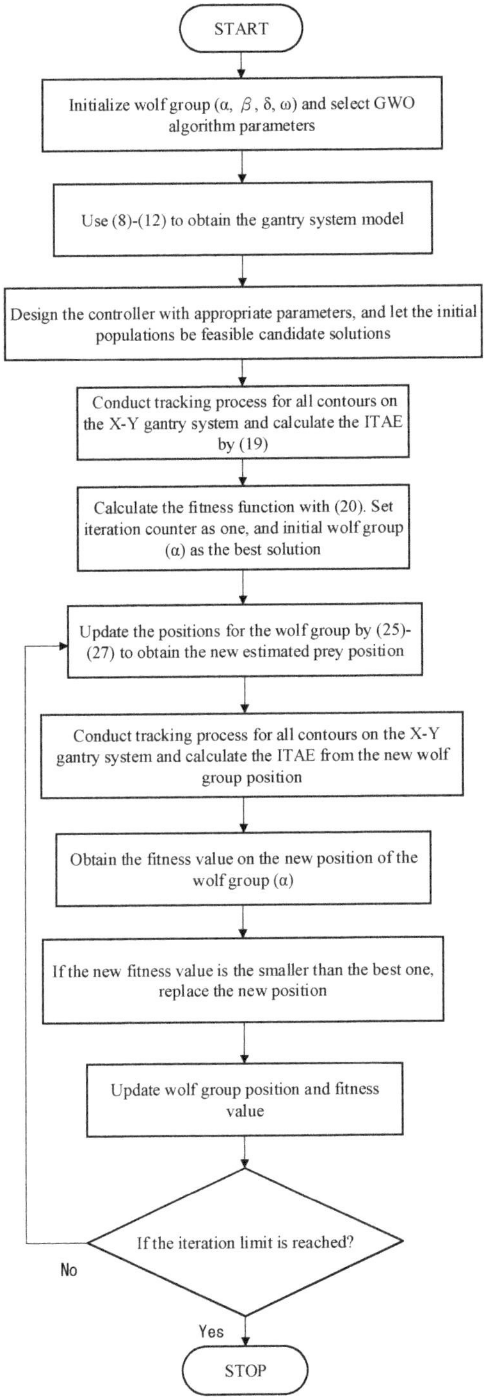

Figure 7. FOFPID flow chart controller design using the GWO algorithm.

5. Experimental Results

The setup of the gantry-type platform is shown in Figure 2. The PMLSMs are CPC-CLS-PM4 from Chieftek Precision Co., Ltd. and are actuated by the COR-5/230, which is a PWM digital servo driver manufactured by Elmo Motion Control. The peak and continuous force of the PMLSM are 74 N and 18.5 N. Its magnetic pole pitch and continuous current are 15 mm and 5 A, respectively. The platform consists of two parallel motors on the Y-axis and another one on the X-axis. A mechanical coupling happens on the Y-axis for these two motors. Optical encoder sensors provide the measurement of the displacement on each axis. The signals are transferred with an encoder card for position feedback while a D/A converter card charges for control. The optical encoders are set up to measure the displacements with the resolution of 1 μm. The sampling rate of the practical controller is 1 KHz. Both the X- and Y-axes possess a stroke of 225 mm.

5.1. Contour Planning

The contours in the simulations and experiments are planned by the non-uniform rational B-spline (NURBS), which is a parametric curve composed of parameters such as control point, knot vector, degree of curve, and weight [31–33]. The NURBS curves can be modified by adjusting the weights and control points, or by changing the basis function generated by the recursive calculation through different spacing of the elements in the node vector. This means a NURBS-generated curve can be divided into a string of multi-interval fitted splines. The equation for defining a NURBS curve is

$$C(u) = \frac{\sum_{i=0}^{n} B_{i,d}(u) W_i P_i}{\sum_{i=0}^{n} B_{i,d}(u) W_i} = \sum_{i=0}^{n} R_{i,d}(u) P_i \tag{28}$$

where P_i denotes the control point, $R_{i,d}(u)$ is the rational basis function, $B_{i,d}(u)$ is the basis function, W_i is the weight, and d and u are the degree and parameter of the NURBS curve, respectively. Table 2 shows the NURBS parameters of each contour. As shown in Figure 8a, the star NURBS can be designed with 12 control points. Figure 8b–d shows the NURBS control points for a circle, a bow, and a heart, respectively.

Table 2. NURBS parameters for the four contours.

Trajectory Type	NURBS Parameters
Circle	d = 2, P = [(0,0),(0, 25,000), (−50,000, 25,000),(−50,000, 0), (−50,000, −25,000), (0, −25,000), (0, 0)], k = [0, 0, 0, 0.25, 0.5, 0.5, 0.75, 1, 1, 1], w = [1, 0.5, 0.5, 1, 0.5, 0.5, 1]
Heart	d = 2, P = [(0,0), (−30,000, 20,000), (−20,000, 50,000), (0, 36,000), (20,000, 50,000), (30,000, 10,000), (0,0)], k = [0, 0, 0, 0.25, 0.5, 0.5, 0.75, 1, 1, 1], w = [1, 1, 1, 1, 1, 1, 1]
Bow	d = 2, P = [(0, 0), (−15,000, −15,000), (−15,000, 1.5), (0, 0), (15,000, −15,000), (15,000, 150,000), (0, 0)], k = [0, 0, 0, 0.25, 0.5, 0.5, 0.75, 1, 1, 1], w = [1, 2.5, 2.5, 1, 2.5, 2.5, 1]
Star	d = 2, P = [(0, 30,000), (−2500, −30,000), (−7500, 20,000), (−20,000, 20,000), (−1000, 10,000), (−12,500, 0), (0, 7500),(12,500, 0),(10,000, 10,000), (20,000, 20,000), (7500, 20,000),(2500, 30,000),(0, 30,000)], k = [0, 0, 0, 0.1, 0.1, 0.2, 0.3, 0.4, 0.5, 0.6, 0.7, 0.8, 0.8, 1, 1, 1], w = [1, 1, 1, 1, 1, 1, 1, 1, 1, 1, 1, 1, 1]

5.2. Optimization and Performance Indices

MATLAB and Simulink are used to complete the simulations. Simulations are conducted based on the identified dynamic model (8)–(12), which represents the gantry platform. All four optimization methods are tested: (1) PSO, (2) IWO, (3) GWO, and (4) BBO. These optimization algorithms are employed to tune the parameters in the FOFPID controller based on the ITAE criterion. To evaluate the ITAE for the four contour types, the average is calculated by

$$\text{ITAE} = \frac{\text{ITAE}_\text{C} + \text{ITAE}_\text{B} + \text{ITAE}_\text{S} + \text{ITAE}_\text{H}}{4} \tag{29}$$

where the subscripts of $ITAE_X$ denote the contour types circle, bow, star, and heart, respectively. The number of iterations for each scheme is limited to 200. Table 3 shows the parameters used in the optimization process.

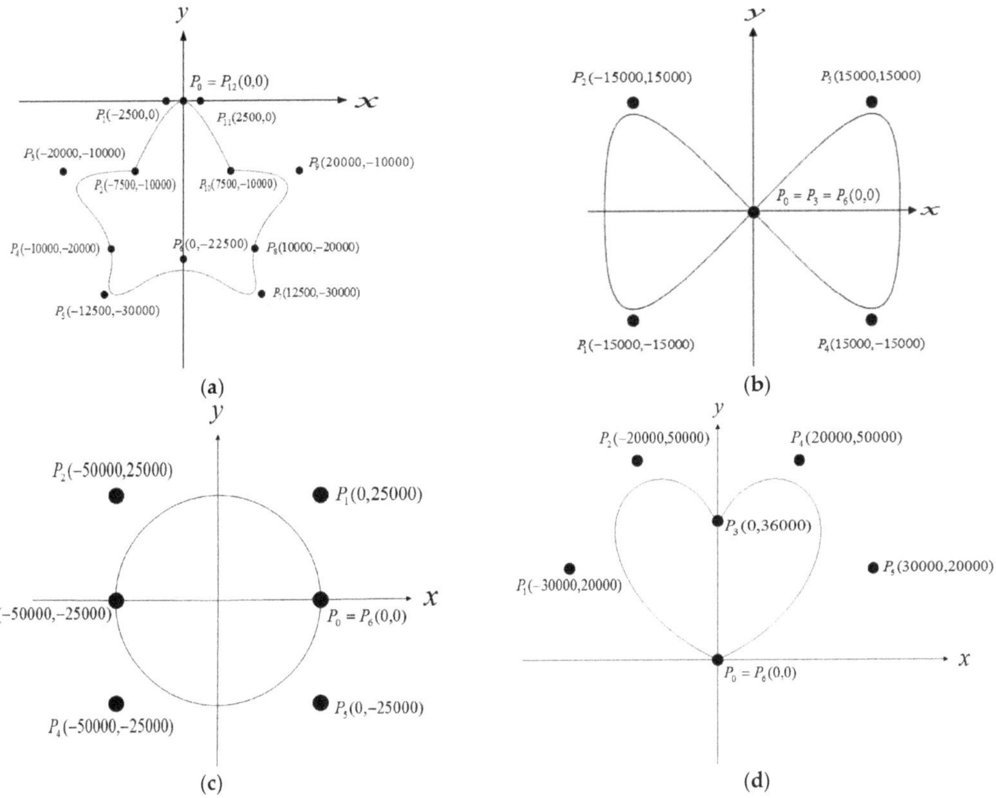

Figure 8. Reference contours: (**a**) star, (**b**) bow, (**c**) circle, and (**d**) heart (μm).

Table 3. Parameters of the optimization algorithms.

Optimization Algorithm	Parameters
PSO	population size: $N = 30$ leaning parameters: $c_1 = 1.2, c_2 = 1.2$ upper/lower bounds of the random velocity weight: $v^j_{max} = 0.72, v^j_{min} = -0.72$ upper/lower bound of the position: $x^j_{max} = 1.9, x^j_{max} = 0.1$
IWO	population size: $N = 30$ maximum group size $iter_{max} = 30$ nonlinear harmonic parameter $n = 2$ initial standard deviation $\sigma_i = 0.5$ final standard deviation $\sigma_i = 0.001$ upper/lower bound of weed seeds: 1.9/0.1
GWO	population size: $N = 30$ upper/lower bound of wolf group(alpha): 1.9/0.1
BBO	number of habitats: $N = 30$ max/min migration rates: $E = I = 1$, $m_{max} = 0.1$ upper/lower bound of habitat species: 1.9/0.1

Two indexes, the tracking error standard deviation (TESD) and average tracking error (ATE) are employed to evaluate the performances of both the simulations and experiments. These indexes are defined by

(1) ATE:

$$m = \sum_{k=1}^{n} \frac{e(k)}{n} \tag{30}$$

with $e(k) = \sqrt{e_x^2(k) + e_y^2(k)}$ where $e_x(k)$ and $e_y(k)$ are the tracking errors in the X- and Y-axis. As there are two slides on the Y-axis, the tracking error becomes $e_y(k) = \frac{e_{ym}(k)+e_{ys}(k)}{2}$, and n denotes the number of all contour points.

(2) TESD:

$$T_s = \sqrt{\frac{\sum_{k=1}^{n}(T(k) - m)^2}{n}} \tag{31}$$

The ATE and TESD indices are often used to measure contour tracking performance. The former is used to measure the capability of trajectory tracking, while the latter can evaluate the oscillation.

5.3. Simulation Results

Figure 9 shows the curves of ITAE in the iterations of optimization for the four methods. Among them, PSO has the fastest decline, but IWO eventually approaches a lower value. Table 4 shows the optimal learning parameters corresponding to the PSO, IWO, BBO, and GWO methods. Common optimal parameters are employed in each simulation result, and the tracking errors are compared and summarized. Table 5 shows the comparison of the simulation results for the optimization algorithms. Taking an average of all four contours, the IWO method achieved a higher accuracy, with an ATE of 1.7852 µm, TESD of 6.4548 µm, and ITAE of 692.6948.

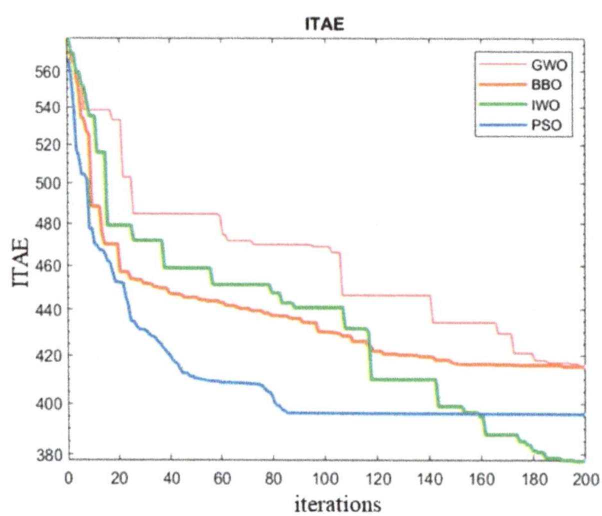

Figure 9. The learning curves of four optimization searches for one trajectory tracking.

Table 4. Optimal scaling factor parameters for all trajectory types.

value	K_e	μ	K_{de}	λ	β	α
PSO	1.8931	0.1097	0.4520	1.5940	1.9000	0.9726
IWO	1.8237	0.2757	1.8330	1.6256	1.4351	1.1889
BBO	1.8980	0.1006	1.8914	1.6927	1.9000	0.6967
GWO	1.3132	0.1285	1.8970	1.6103	1.8326	1.0344
value	K_{e1}	μ_1	K_{de1}	λ_1	β_1	α_1
PSO	0.4488	0.1000	1.9000	1.4877	1.9000	0.8245
IWO	1.8866	0.1012	1.6841	1.5311	1.8837	0.7184
BBO	1.7297	0.4819	0.7888	1.4647	1.6594	0.8007
GWO	1.8825	0.1085	1.4989	1.3023	1.8645	1.4217
value	K_{e2}	μ_2	K_{de2}	λ_2	β_2	α_2
PSO	1.2828	0.142	1.9000	1.4889	1.4156	0.6118
IWO	1.8302	0.1000	1.7325	1.5320	1.9000	0.7267
BBO	1.8914	0.4146	1.1917	1.4872	1.3578	0.6606
GWO	1.8992	0.2610	1.7539	1.3435	1.8493	1.3241

Table 5. The simulation results of all trajectories.

Method	**ATE (μm)**	**TESD (μm)**	**ITAE**
	Circle		
PSO	1.4719	3.2174	728.4400
IWO	0.9100	1.6635	689.4438
BBO	1.5367	3.0456	732.9247
GWO	1.1919	1.4536	732.1176
	Heart		
PSO	1.3767	7.3135	687.1533
IWO	1.2314	5.5600	662.0899
BBO	1.4962	7.7701	706.2485
GWO	1.2854	4.7161	716.1556
	Star		
PSO	2.9381	9.7067	758.2886
IWO	2.9195	6.0844	732.7888
BBO	2.9834	9.8334	822.2761
GWO	2.8224	6.8502	800.8768
	Bow		
PSO	6.2185	30.6246	726.3240
IWO	2.0803	12.5113	686.4565
BBO	5.9139	27.0573	778.0170
GWO	5.0548	18.6534	795.2960
	Average		
PSO	3.0013	12.7156	725.0515
IWO	1.7852	6.4548	692.6948
BBO	2.9826	11.9266	759.8666
GWO	2.5886	7.9183	761.1115

5.4. Experimental Results

The real-time control experiments are conducted to verify the performance of the proposed method. Figures 10 and 11, respectively, show the star position error trajectories using the GWO and IWO algorithms. The controller parameters are obtained from the optimization process in the simulations. Figures 10a and 11a illustrate the tracking errors on the X-axis, Figures 10b and 11b show the tracking errors of the master and slave Y-axes together, and Figures 10c and 11c show the synchronization errors, which are within 20 μm and decay gradually. Figures 10d and 11d demonstrate the contour trajectories. The smooth trajectories and small steady-state error can be seen in the results. The circle contour tracking results using the GWO and IWO algorithms are shown in Figures 12 and 13, respectively. Figures 12c and 13c show the synchronization errors, which are always within 40 μm. Figures 14 and 15 are the position error trajectories of the bow tie with GWO and IWO, respectively. Figures 14c and 15c show that the synchronization errors are within 12 μm and 15 μm, respectively. The heart contour tracking results are shown in Figures 16 and 17. The synchronization errors are shown in Figures 16c and 17c, and are within 40 μm and 15 μm, respectively.

The ATE and TESD tracking indices for the star, circle, bow, and heart contours are displayed in Table 6. From the average ATE and TESD indices in the experimental results, it can be seen that GWO exhibited better tracking performance than IWO. Although IWO has better tracking performance than the other algorithms in the simulations, the experimental results are worse than the others. This situation may be due to an undetected difference between the simulation and experimental setup. GWO has the best experimental performance and the second-best simulation results; thus, it is concluded that a FOFPID controller with a GWO parametric solution performs better than the same controller with either IWO, BBO, or PSO.

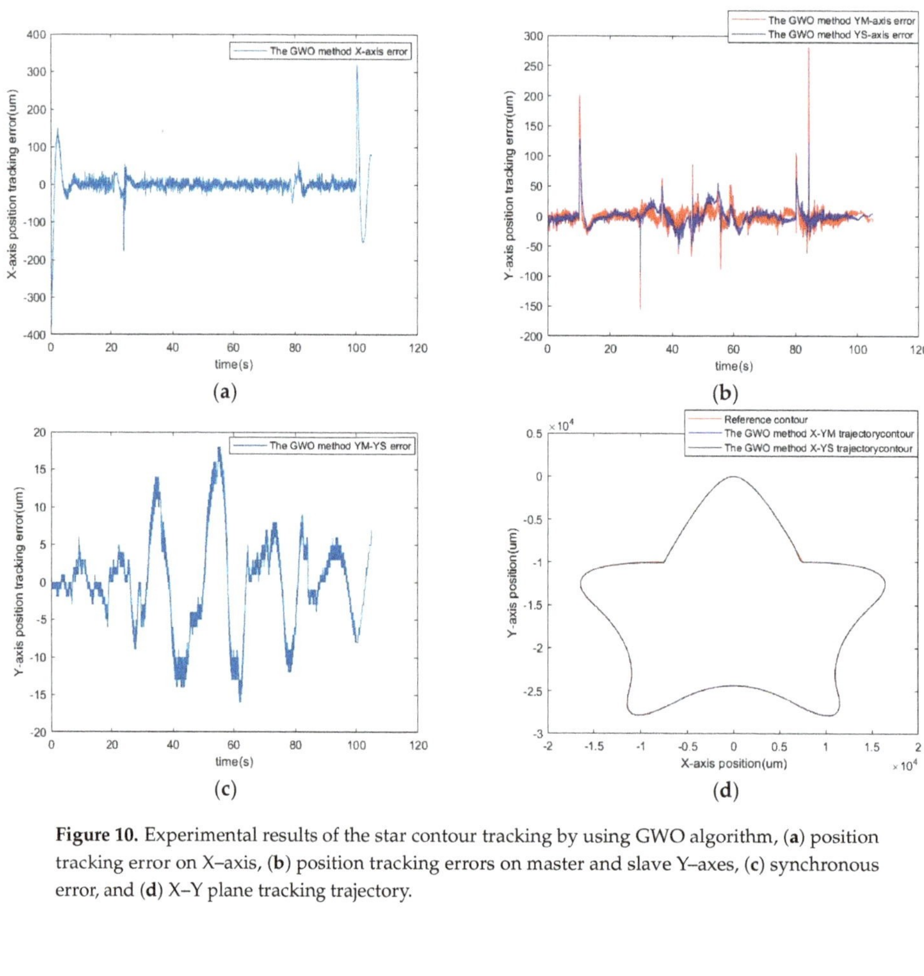

Figure 10. Experimental results of the star contour tracking by using GWO algorithm, (**a**) position tracking error on X–axis, (**b**) position tracking errors on master and slave Y–axes, (**c**) synchronous error, and (**d**) X–Y plane tracking trajectory.

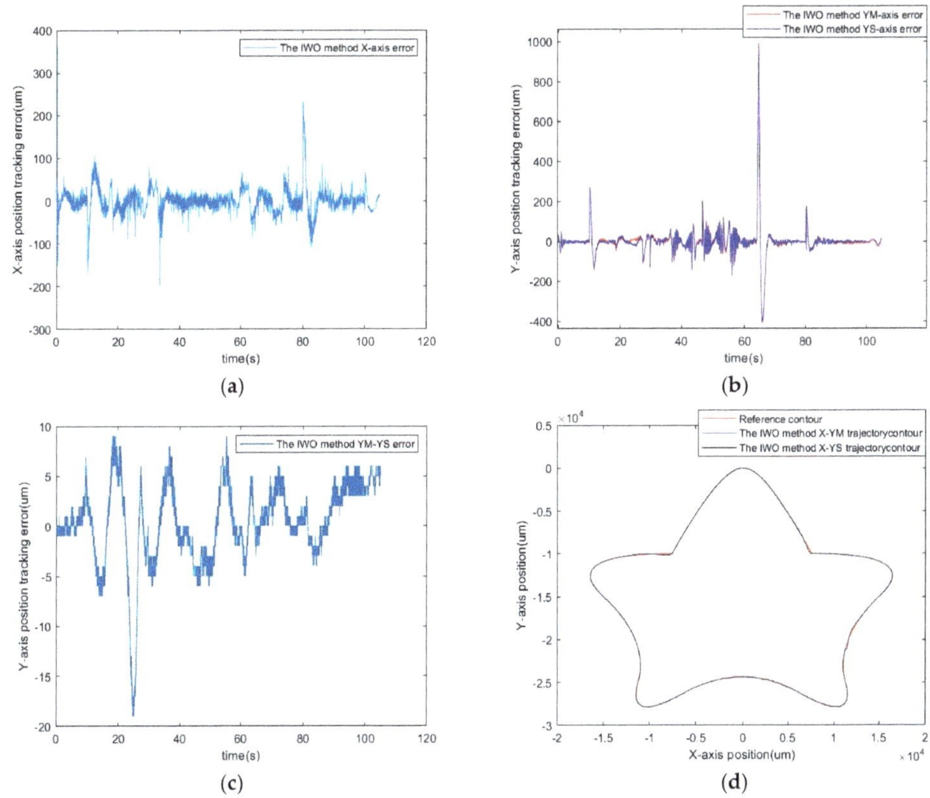

Figure 11. Experimental results of the star contour tracking by using IWO algorithm, (**a**) position tracking error on X−axis, (**b**) position tracking errors on master and slave Y−axes, (**c**) synchronous error, and (**d**) X–Y plane tracking trajectory.

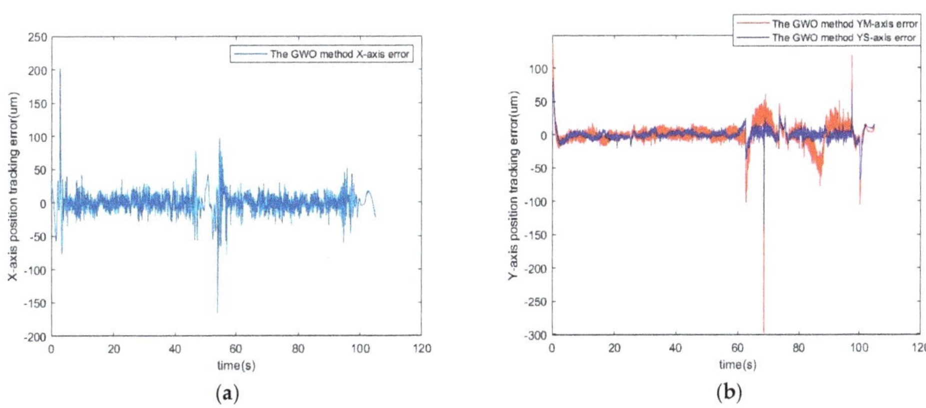

Figure 12. *Cont.*

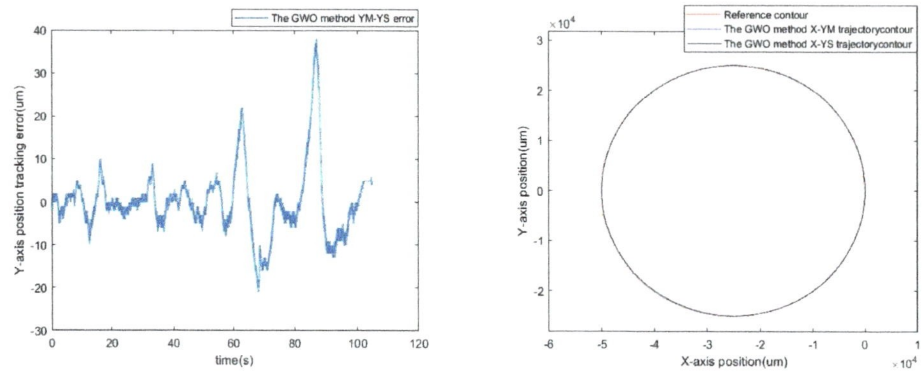

(c) (d)

Figure 12. Experimental results of the circle contour tracking by using GWO algorithm, (**a**) position tracking error on X−axis, (**b**) position tracking errors on master and slave Y−axes, (**c**) synchronous error, and (**d**) X–Y plane tracking trajectory.

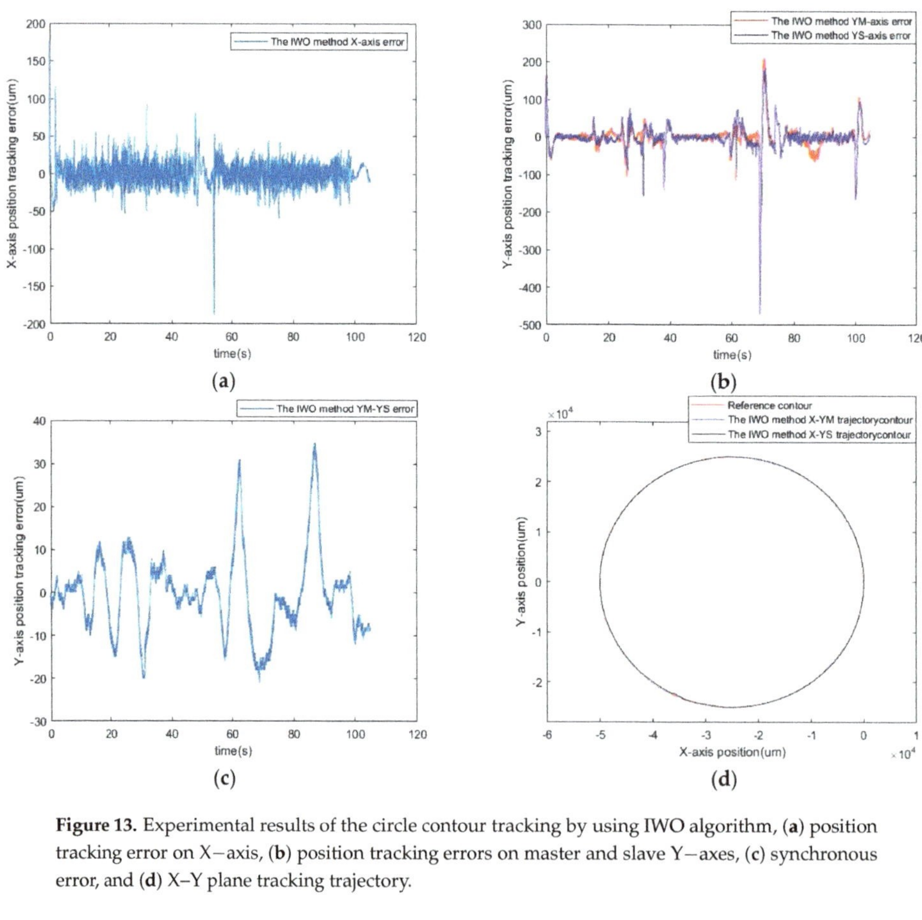

(a) (b) (c) (d)

Figure 13. Experimental results of the circle contour tracking by using IWO algorithm, (**a**) position tracking error on X−axis, (**b**) position tracking errors on master and slave Y−axes, (**c**) synchronous error, and (**d**) X–Y plane tracking trajectory.

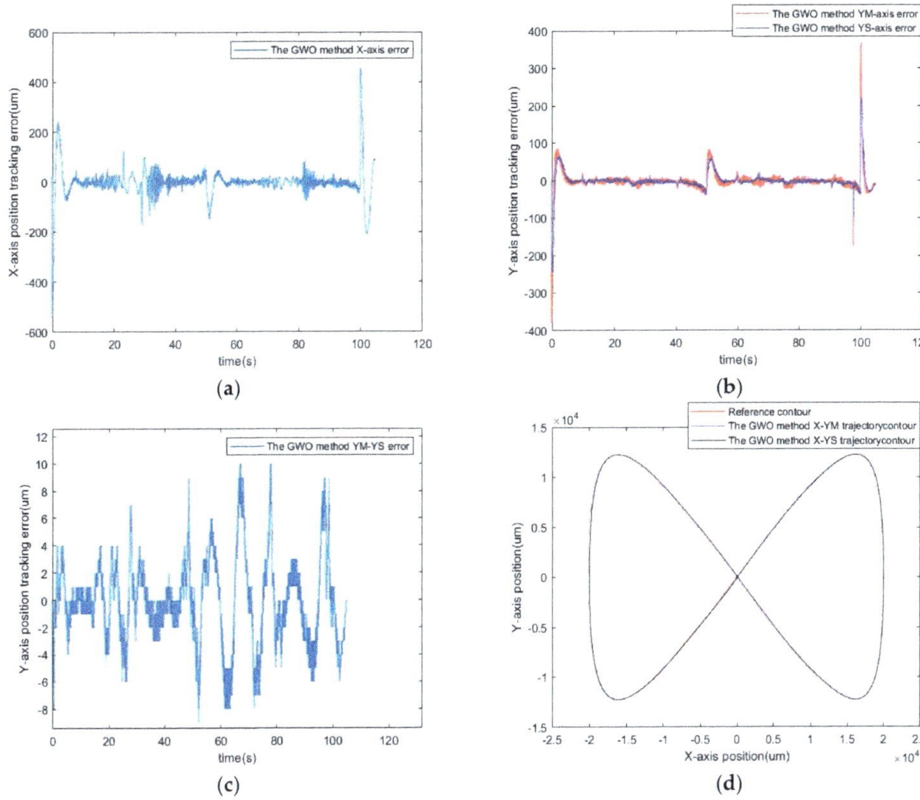

Figure 14. Experimental results of the bow contour tracking by using GWO algorithm, (**a**) position tracking error on X−axis, (**b**) position tracking errors on master and slave Y−axes, (**c**) synchronous error, and (**d**) X–Y plane tracking trajectory.

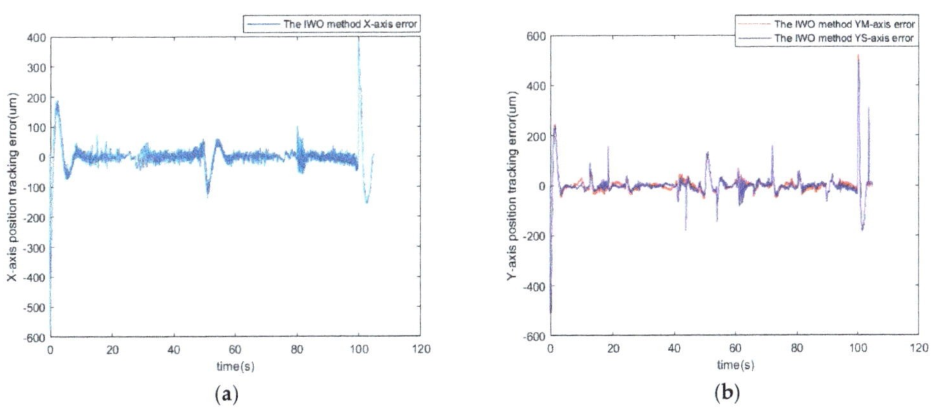

Figure 15. *Cont.*

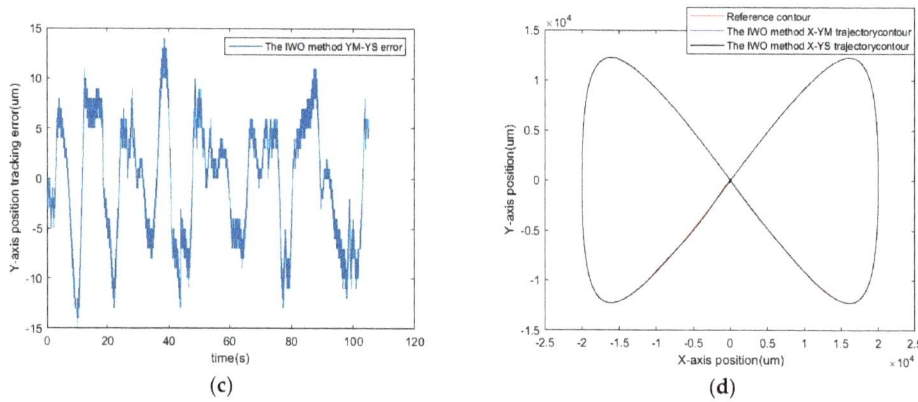

Figure 15. Experimental results of the bow contour tracking by using IWO algorithm, (**a**) position tracking error on X−axis, (**b**) position tracking errors on master and slave Y−axes, (**c**) synchronous error, and (**d**) X–Y plane tracking trajectory.

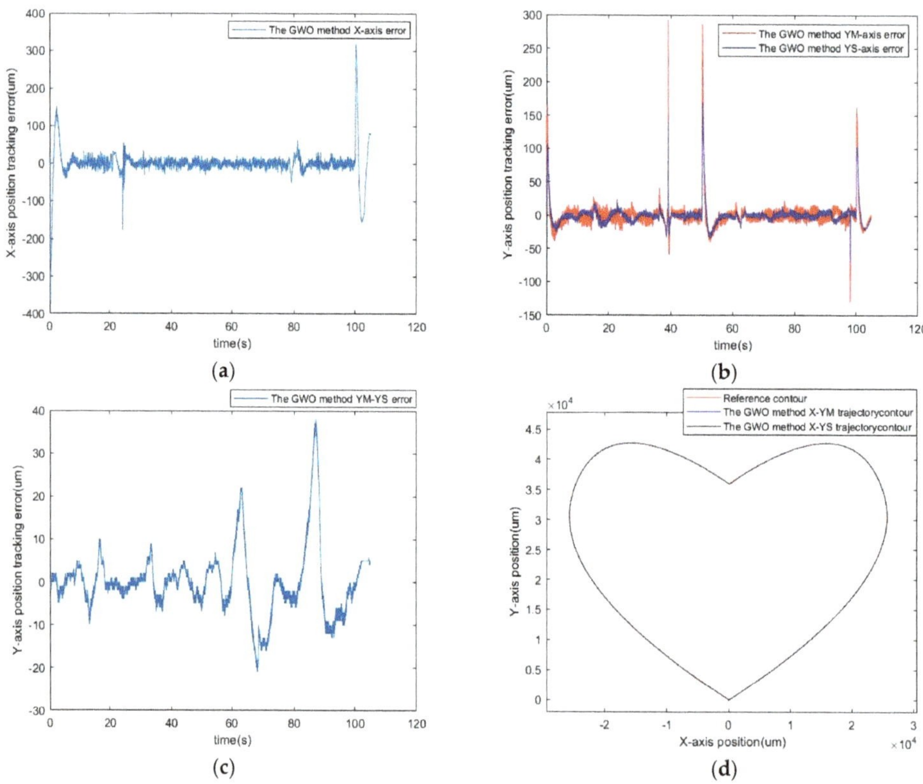

Figure 16. Experimental results of the heart contour tracking by using GWO algorithm, (**a**) position tracking error on X−axis, (**b**) position tracking errors on master and slave Y−axes, (**c**) synchronous error, and (**d**) X–Y plane tracking trajectory.

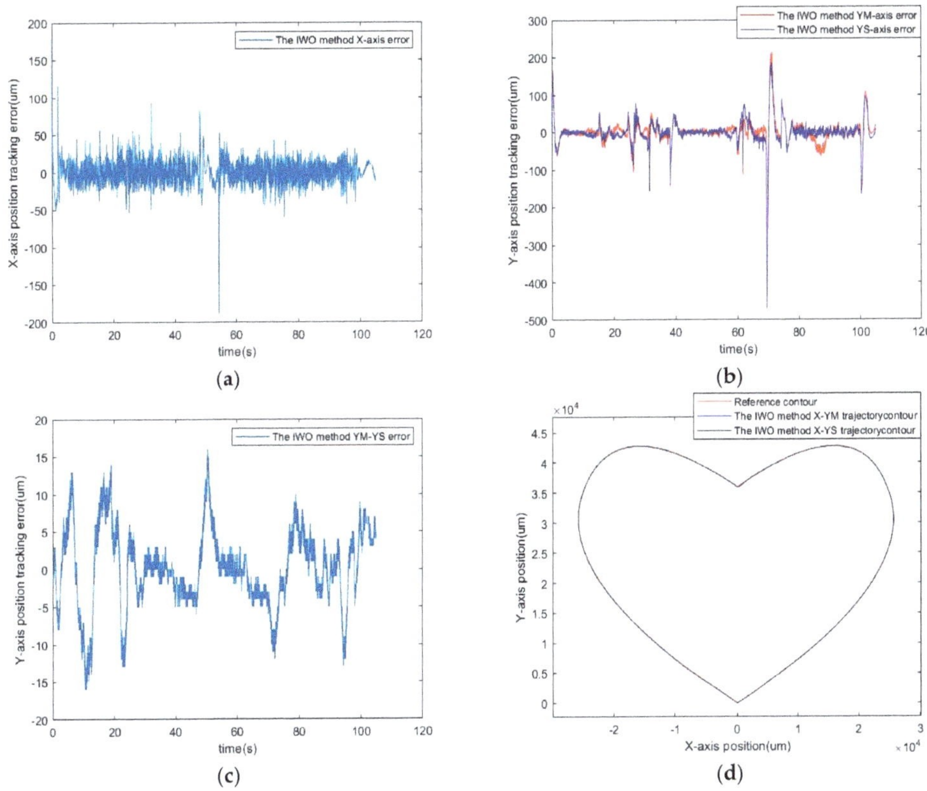

Figure 17. Experimental results of the heart contour tracking by using IWO algorithm, (**a**) position tracking error on X–axis, (**b**) position tracking errors on master and slave Y–axes, (**c**) synchronous error, and (**d**) X–Y plane tracking trajectory.

Table 6. The experimental results of all trajectories.

Method	ATE (μm)	TESD (μm)	ITAE
	Circle		
PSO	12.33468	19.06461	1000.13697
IWO	22.55877	39.85242	1018.96457
BBO	13.65512	15.22419	1009.078
GWO	7.93084	8.69547	998.86251
	Heart		
PSO	17.05340	23.22570	1011.88779
IWO	23.88164	36.07943	1015.39364
BBO	18.09240	27.08182	1008.25875
GWO	9.09414	16.49567	994.75943
	Star		
PSO	19.17965	21.18270	997.62259
IWO	23.93769	29.72738	1007.70703
BBO	21.82199	24.02363	1009.45364
GWO	14.13845	15.14002	993.72111

Table 6. *Cont.*

Method	ATE (μm)	TESD (μm)	ITAE
	Bow contour		
PSO	16.95719	28.80572	1018.65117
IWO	23.79299	42.70955	1018.99118
BBO	23.44690	39.53237	1014.40448
GWO	14.36346	24.53757	976.54349
	Average		
PSO	16.38123	23.06968	1007.07463
IWO	23.54277	37.092195	1015.26410
BBO	19.25410	26.46550	1010.29870
GWO	11.38172	16.21718	990.97163

6. Conclusions

An evolutionary computation-based FOFPID controller is developed in this study to control a two-axis gantry platform. The fractional-order controller benefits from the flexibility of the parameters, and consequently outperforms conventional PID variants. Incorporating the fuzzy logic control structure helps increase design flexibility in the control law. Several evolutionary computation algorithms are tested and compared in simulation and experiment: PSO, IWO, GWO, and BBO. These are used to optimize the FOFPID control parameters while minimizing the tracking error index as measured by the ITAE for four contours, circle, heart, star, and bowtie. The optimization processes are implemented in MATLAB/Simulink simulations and the acquired parameters are then examined in a series of experiments using a practical gantry platform.

The simulation and experimental results verify that the control design could cope with the synchronous control issues and mitigate contour tracking errors. The GWO algorithm outperforms other optimization methods using ATE 11.38172 μm, TESD 16.21718 μm, and ITAE 990.97163 when measured using the average of all contours. Compared to PSO, BBO, and IWO, the GWO algorithm showed a performance advantage of 1.6%, 1.9%, and 2.4% in ITAE, respectively. The demonstrated control scheme effectively compensates for synchronous tracking errors, which subsequently shows no significant peaks in turning, and non-smooth positions of the contours. The contribution of this research is to integrate the evolutionary computation algorithms with the FOFPID, optimize the controller parameters, and compare their performance via simulations and experiments. The control scheme is implemented on a PMLSM-actuated gantry platform to tackle the synchronous error and achieve superior tracking results.

Author Contributions: Conceptualization, W.-L.M.; methodology, W.-L.M. and C.-Y.K.; software, C.-Y.K.; validation, W.-L.M. and C.-Y.K. and S.-H.C.; formal analysis, C.-Y.K.; investigation, C.-Y.K.; resources, W.-L.M.; data curation, C.-Y.K.; writing—original draft preparation, S.-H.C. and C.-Y.K.; writing—review and editing, S.-H.C.; visualization, C.-Y.K.; supervision, W.-L.M. and S.-H.C.; project administration, W.-L.M.; funding acquisition, W.-L.M. All authors have read and agreed to the published version of the manuscript.

Funding: This research was funded by Ministry of Science and Technology, grant number 111-2221-E-224-057-.

Data Availability Statement: No new data were created or analyzed in this study. Data sharing is not applicable to this article.

Conflicts of Interest: The authors declare no conflict of interest.

References

1. Nunez, C.; Alvarez, R.; Cervantes, I. Multi-motor synchronization techniques. *Int. J. Sci. Eng. Technol. Res.* **2014**, *3*, 319–322.
2. Cheng, M.H.; Chen, C.Y.; Bakhoum, E.G. Synchronization controller synthesis of multi-axis motion control. *Int. J. Innov. Comput. I* **2011**, *7*, 4395–4410.
3. Koren, Y. Cross-coupled biaxial compute control for manufacturing system. *J. Dyn. Syst. Meas. Control.* **1980**, *32*, 265–272. [CrossRef]
4. Lorenz, R.D.; Schmidt, P.B. Synchronized motion control for process automation. In Proceedings of the 1989 IEEE Industry Applications Annual Meeting, San Diego, CA, USA, 1–5 October 1989; pp. 1693–1698.
5. Kung, Y.S. Design and implementation of a high-performance PMLSM drives using DSP chip. *IEEE Trans. Ind. Electron.* **2008**, *55*, 1341–1351. [CrossRef]
6. Ting, C.S.; Chang, Y.N.; Shi, B.W.; Lieu, J.F. Adaptive backstepping control for permanent magnet linear synchronous motor servo drive. *IET Electr. Power Appl.* **2015**, *9*, 265–279. [CrossRef]
7. Hsieh, M.F.; Yao, W.S.; Chiang, C.R. Modeling and synchronous control of a single-axis stage driven by dual mechanically-coupled parallel ball screw. *Int. J. Adv. Manuf. Technol.* **2007**, *34*, 933–943. [CrossRef]
8. Chu, B.; Kim, S.; Hong, D.; Park, H.K.; Park, J. Optimal cross-coupled synchronizing control of dual-drive gantry system for a SMD assembly machine. *JSME Int. J. Ser. C Mech. Syst. Mach. Elem. Manuf.* **2004**, *47*, 939–945. [CrossRef]
9. Lin, F.J.; Chou, P.H.; Chen, C.S.; Lin, Y.S. DSP-based cross-coupled synchronous control for dual linear motors via intelligent complementary sliding mode control. *IEEE Trans. Ind. Electron.* **2012**, *59*, 1061–1073. [CrossRef]
10. Dimeas, I.; Petras, I.; Psychalinos, C. New analog implementation technique for fractional-order controller: A DC motor control. *AEU-Int. J. Electron. Commun.* **2017**, *78*, 192–200. [CrossRef]
11. Said, L.A.; Radwan, A.G.; Madian, A.H.; Soliman, A.M. Fractional order oscillators based on operational transresistance amplifiers. *AEU-Int. J. Electron. Commun.* **2015**, *69*, 988–1003. [CrossRef]
12. Saxena, S. Load frequency control strategy via fractional-order controller and reduced-order modeling. *Int. J. Electr. Power Energy* **2019**, *104*, 603–614. [CrossRef]
13. Li, G.; Li, Y.; Chen, H.; Deng, W. Fractional-order controller for course-keeping of underactuated surface vessels based on frequency domain specification and improved particle swarm optimization Algorithm. *Appl. Sci.* **2022**, *12*, 3139. [CrossRef]
14. Li, H.S.; Luo, Y.; Chen, Y.Q. A Fractional Order Proportional and Derivative (FOPD) Motion Controller: Tuning Rule and Experiments. *IEEE Trans. Control Syst. Technol.* **2010**, *18*, 516–520. [CrossRef]
15. Petráš, I.; Vinagre, B. Practical application of digital fractional-order controller to temperature control to temperature control. *Acta Montan. Slovaca* **2002**, *7*, 131–137.
16. Kumar, A.; Pan, S. Design of fractional order PID controller for load frequency control system with communication delay. *ISA Trans.* **2022**, *129 Pt A*, 138–149. [CrossRef]
17. Swethamarai, P.; Lakshmi, P. Adaptive-Fuzzy Fractional Order PID Controller-Based Active Suspension for Vibration Control. *IETE J. Res.* **2022**, *68*, 3487–3502. [CrossRef]
18. Shalaby, R.; El-Hossainy, M.; Abo-Zalam, B.; Mahmoud, T.A. Optimal fractional-order PID controller based on fractional-order actor-critic algorithm. *Neural Comput. Appl.* **2023**, *35*, 2347–2380. [CrossRef]
19. Das, S.; Pan, I.; Das, S.; Gupta, A. A novel fractional order fuzzy PID controller and its optimal time domain tuning based on integral performance indices. *Eng. Appl. Artif. Intell.* **2012**, *25*, 430–442. [CrossRef]
20. Kennedy, J.; Eberhart, R. Particle Swarm Optimization. In Proceedings of the IEEE International Joint Conference on Neural Networks, Perth, Australia, 27 November–1 December 1995; Volume 4, pp. 1942–1948.
21. Mehrabian, A.R.; Lucas, C. A Novel Numerical Optimization Algorithm Inspired from Weed Colonization. *Ecol. Inform.* **2006**, *1*, 355–366. [CrossRef]
22. Mirjalili, S.; Mirjalili, S.M.; Lewis, A. Grey Wolf Optimizer. *Adv. Eng. Softw.* **2014**, *69*, 46–61. [CrossRef]
23. Simon, D. Biogeography-Based Optimization. *IEEE Trans. Evol. Comput.* **2008**, *12*, 702–713. [CrossRef]
24. Cao, J.Y.; Cao, B.G. Design of Fractional Order Controllers Based on Particle Swarm Optimization. In Proceedings of the 2006 IEEE Conference on Industrial Electronics and Applications, Singapore, 24–26 May 2006.
25. Kommula, B.N.; Kota, V.R. Design of MFA-PSO based fractional order PID controller for effective torque controlled BLDC motor. *Sustain. Energy Technol. Assess.* **2022**, *49*, 101644.
26. Obaid, B.A.; Saleh, A.L.; Kadhim, A.K. Resolving of optimal fractional PID controller for DC motor drive based on anti-windup by invasive weed optimization technique. *Indones. J. Electr. Eng. Comput. Sci.* **2019**, *15*, 95–103. [CrossRef]
27. Verma, S.K.; Yadav, S.; Nagar, S.K. Optimization of Fractional Order PID Controller Using Grey Wolf Optimizer. *J. Control. Autom. Electr. Syst.* **2017**, *28*, 314–322. [CrossRef]
28. Yeşil, E.; Güzelkaya, M.; Eksin, İ. Self tuning fuzzy PID type load and frequency controller. *Energy Convers. Manag.* **2004**, *45*, 377–390. [CrossRef]
29. Oustaloup, A.; Levron, F.; Mathieu, B.; Nanot, F. Frequency-band complex noninteger differentiator: Characterization and synthesis. *IEEE Trans. Circuits Syst. I. Fundam. Theory Appl.* **2000**, *47*, 25–39. [CrossRef]
30. Noshadi, A.; Shi, J.; Lee, W.S.; Shi, P.; Kalam, A. Optimal PID-type fuzzy logic controller for a multi-input multi-output active magnetic bearing system. *Neural Comput. Appl.* **2016**, *27*, 2031–2046. [CrossRef]
31. Pieg, L.; Tiller, W. *The NURBS Books*, 2nd ed.; Springer: Berlin/Heidelberg, Germany, 1997.

32. Chen, S.Y.; Lai, Y.H.; Lu, H.T. Contours Planning and Visual Servo Control of XXY Positioning System Using NURBS Interpolation Approach. *Invent. J. Res. Technol. Eng. Manag.* **2016**, *1*, 16–23.
33. Gopi, M.; Manohar, S. A Unified Architecture for the Computation of B-Spline Curves and Surfaces. *IEEE Trans. Parallel Distrib. Syst.* **1997**, *8*, 1275–1287. [CrossRef]

algorithms

MDPI

Article

A Shadowed Type-2 Fuzzy Approach for Crossover Parameter Adaptation in Differential Evolution

Patricia Ochoa [1], Cinthia Peraza [1], Oscar Castillo [1] and Zong Woo Geem [2,*]

[1] Tijuana Institute of Technology, TecNM, Calzada Tecnologico s/n, Fracc. Tomas Aquino, Tijuana 22379, Mexico; martha.ochoa18@tectijuana.edu.mx (P.O.); cinthia.peraza@tectijuana.edu.mx (C.P.); ocastillo@tectijuana.mx (O.C.)

[2] College of IT Convergence, Gachon University, Seongnam 13120, Republic of Korea

* Correspondence: geem@gachon.ac.kr

Abstract: The shadowed type-2 fuzzy systems are used more frequently today as they provide an alternative to classical fuzzy logic. The primary purpose of fuzzy logic is to simulate reasoning in a computer. This work aims to use shadowed type-2 fuzzy systems (ST2-FS) to dynamically adapt the crossing parameter of differential evolution (DE). To test the performance of the dynamic crossing parameter, the motor position control problem was used, which contains an interval type-2 fuzzy system (IT2-FS) for controlling the motor. A comparison is made between the original DE and the algorithm using shadowed type-2 fuzzy systems (DE-ST2-FS), as well as a comparison with the results of other state-of-the-art metaheuristics.

Keywords: shadowed type-2 fuzzy logic; interval type-2 fuzzy controller; differential evolution

1. Introduction

Fuzzy logic is a modern tool, and one of its most important applications is process control. It has shown rapid growth as it can solve problems related to information or knowledge uncertainty, providing a formal method for expressing knowledge in a way that is understandable for humans. It uses linguistic variables for this purpose.

The success of applying fuzzy logic is primarily due to its ability to utilize ambiguous concept models, which helps in reducing the intuitive complexity of a process. This allows for control operations to be carried out, albeit in an approximate or heuristic manner, on nonlinear or time-varying processes [1–5].

Fuzzy logic has achieved significant success in industrial control. While there are various versions of controllers that employ fuzzy logic, the term "fuzzy controller" typically refers to a control system with an internal structure that includes a fuzzy system to govern the controller. One of the frequently mentioned advantages of fuzzy controllers, in comparison to other controller types, is their ability to be designed even in the absence of an exact model of the plant to be controlled, as they are rule-based [6–15].

A new type of fuzzy sets of higher order, known as type-2 fuzzy sets, was proposed by Zadeh in 1975 as an enhancement to fuzzy sets. These sets can handle system uncertainties by considering degrees of membership. The literature demonstrates the development of numerous works that utilize type-2 fuzzy controllers, which exhibit improved results [16–25]. Therefore, in this work, an interval type-2 fuzzy controller is implemented for this reason.

Similarly, this work also presents the utilization of shadowed type-2 fuzzy systems, which represent an alternative branch in fuzzy logic. The concept of shadowed sets was originally introduced to enhance the interpretability of type-1 fuzzy sets and address the issues of excessive precision [26–30]. In this work, ST2-FSs will be employed to dynamically adapt the crossover parameter (CR) of differential evolution, with the primary objective of improving the results.

The aforementioned aims to demonstrate the significance of this development, wherein the CR parameter is dynamically utilized in DE. Few works in the literature showcase the performance of the dynamic CR parameter, hence emphasizing the main reason for its adoption. Furthermore, we have an interval type-2 fuzzy system controller for the motor, which is commonly employed in the state-of-the-art technologies. Moreover, this work presents the integration of these two concepts to validate the potential of their combined application and assess their effectiveness.

The contribution of this article is to utilize a novel approach, shadowed type-2 fuzzy systems (ST2-FS), for dynamically adapting the crossover parameter of differential evolution (DE), in this way obtaining a new variant of DE. This adaptation aims to enhance the performance of the DE algorithm when applied to the optimization of the motor position control problem with interval type-2 fuzzy logic.

This paper provides the following content: Section 2 presents the definition of ST2-FSs, Section 3 introduces the DE theory, Section 4 describes the utilization of the DE algorithm with shadowed fuzzy, Section 5 presents the controller, Section 6 outlines the Results, and Section 7 concludes the paper.

2. Shadowed Type-2 Fuzzy Systems

Fuzzy logic, initiated in 1965 [31,32], is mainly based on the way we perceive the world that cannot always be defined in terms of true or false sentences, that is, it is logically applied to concepts that can take a value and any truth within a set of values.

The evolution of fuzzy logic over time was type-1 fuzzy systems (T1-FS), then intervals type-2 fuzzy systems (IT2-FS), and later generalized type-2 fuzzy systems (GT2-FS); the mathematical equations of each of these systems are presented in Equations (1)–(3) respectively:

$$\tilde{A} = \{(x, \mu_A(x)) | x \in U, [0,1]\} \quad (1)$$

In Equation (2) J_x is referred to the primary membership of x in $\tilde{A}$. For each value of x, denoted as $x = x'$, the two-dimensional (2D) plane formed by the axes u and $\mu_{\tilde{A}}(x', u)$ is known as a vertical slice of $\tilde{A}$.

A secondary membership function corresponds to a vertical slice of $\tilde{A}$, denoted as $\mu_{\tilde{A}}(x', u)$, where $x' \in X$ and $\forall_u \in J_{x'} \subseteq [0,1]$. It can be described as follows:

$$\tilde{A} = \{(x, u), u_{\tilde{A}}(x, u) | \forall x \in X, \forall u \in J_x \subseteq [0,1]\} \quad (2)$$

A generalized type-2 fuzzy set, denoted by $\tilde{A}$, is defined by a type-2 membership function $\mu_{\tilde{A}}(x, u)$, where $x \in X, u \in J_x \subseteq [0,1]$, and $0 \leq \mu_{\tilde{A}}(x, u) \leq 1$. It can be represented by:

$$\tilde{\tilde{A}} = \left\{ \left((x, u), \mu_{\tilde{A}}(x) \right) \middle| \forall x \in X, \forall u \in J_x^u \subseteq [0,1] \right\} \quad (3)$$

Figure 1 depicts the type-1 and interval type-2 fuzzy sets, while Figure 2 illustrates the generalized type-2 fuzzy set, where the orange and yellow colors represent the primary membership function of a trapezoidal, the green color represents the secondary membership function of a Gaussian, and finally the blue color represents the fraction of uncertainty of the kernel and the support of the secondary membership function respectively.

It is widely recognized that the utilization of generalized fuzzy systems entails a significant computational cost for their execution. In order to mitigate this, alternative approaches have been proposed that offer lower computational overhead. These alternatives include Z slices or vertical slices, as well as geometric approximations [33]. Additionally, the literature presents another option known as horizontal sections or α-representation of planes [34–36].

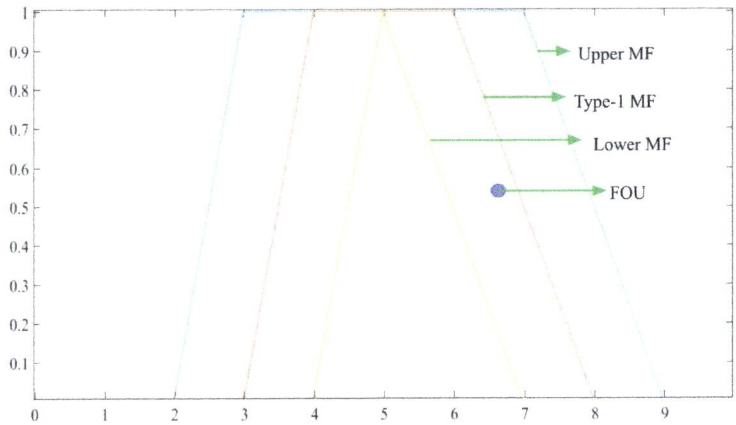

Figure 1. Illustration of the type-1 and interval type-2 fuzzy sets.

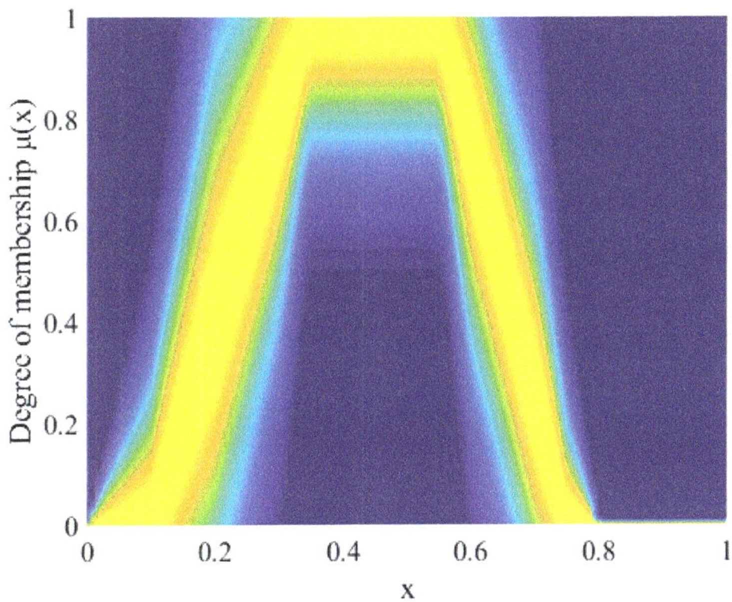

Figure 2. Illustration of the general type-2 fuzzy set.

Taking into account the alternatives discussed in the literature, this paper investigates the utilization of α-planes. Equations (4) and (5) outline the structure of an α-plane and the combination of an IT2-FIS with an α-plane to model a GT2-FS, respectively.

$$\widetilde{A}_\alpha = \{((x,u),\alpha) | \forall x \in X, \forall u \in J_x \subseteq [0,1]\} \tag{4}$$

$$\widetilde{\widetilde{A}} = \bigcup \widetilde{A}_\alpha \tag{5}$$

The elimination of excessive precision is one of the main ones that is sought to be carried out when using a ST2-FS, since this helps to reduce the computational cost. To achieve the elimination of excessive precision, a GT2-FS is modeled using only 2 α-planes; this idea was proposed in Pedrycz concepts, thus creating the theory of shadowed sets [37–40], where the main contribution is the creation of optimal α-planes.

Equation (6) explains the mathematical form of the shadowed sets; this formula is built from 2 α-cuts on a T1-FS, with α and β values, producing three intervals.

$$S_{\mu_A}(x) = \begin{cases} 1, & if\ \mu_A(x) \geq \alpha \\ 0, & if\ \mu_A(x) \leq \beta \\ [0,1], & if\ \alpha \leq \mu_A(x) \geq \beta \end{cases} \tag{6}$$

According to the theory of shadowed sets, optimal values for the variables α and β are proposed, which can be computed using Equation (7). Figure 3 illustrates the process of obtaining the values of α and β, along with the three corresponding areas: the raised area, the reduced area, and the shaded area. Each area is represented by a different color.

$$elevated\ area_{(\alpha,\beta)}(\mu_A) + reduced\ area_{(\alpha,\beta)}(\mu_A) = shadowed\ area_{(\alpha,\beta)}(\mu_A) \tag{7}$$

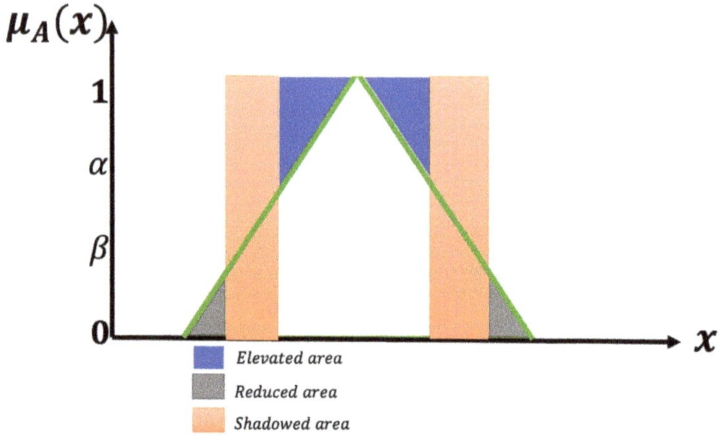

Figure 3. Illustration of the shadowed set.

Moreover, the optimal α and β values are obtained by the optimization of the $V(\alpha, \beta)$ function described in Equation (8).

$$V(\alpha,\beta) = \left| \int_{x \in A_r} \mu_A(x)dx + \int_{x \in A_e} (1 - \mu_A(x))dx - \int_{x \in S} dx \right| \tag{8}$$

3. Differential Evolution

The differential evolution (DE) algorithm is a population-based stochastic search strategy that was proposed in 1995 by Storn and Price. Its main purpose is to solve optimization problems involving real parameters.

In the literature, several works utilizing DE can be discussed as follows: the differential evolution (DE) algorithm is considered to be a practical and effective method for numerical optimization. It is known for its ease of understanding, simplicity of implementation, reliability, and efficiency. This article attempts to comprehensively describe DE, providing illustrations, valuable insights, and empirical advice. It acknowledges that globally optimal solutions are often challenging to obtain, with many problems being intractable [41].

When dealing with functions that have numerous interacting local optima, the application of fuzzy sets in the job-shop scheduling problem (JSP) with fuzzy processing time and completion time (FJSP) allows for a more comprehensive modeling of scheduling. Fuzzy relative entropy provides a method for evaluating the quality of a feasible solution by comparing the actual value with the ideal value, which is the due date. Consequently, the multi-objective FJSP can be transformed into a single-objective optimization problem that can be solved using a hybrid adaptive differential evolution (HADE) algorithm. This algorithm considers the maximum completion time, total delay time, and total energy consumption of jobs as optimization criteria. HADE employs a mutation strategy based on DE/current-to-best and makes its parameters (CR and F) adaptive and normally distributed. The selection of new individuals in HADE is based on the fitness value (FRE) obtained from a population consisting of N parents and N children [42]. Maximizing the traffic capacity of an intersection and reducing the delay rate of vehicles have always been challenges in traffic control research. The coordinated control of urban traffic signals is considered a multi-objective optimization problem. In this study, we examine a mathematical model for urban trunk traffic. We establish models for average delay, average queue length, total delay calculation at intersections, and vehicle exhaust emissions to formulate an optimization model for a new coordinated control system for traffic trunks. To address this, a study that combines fuzzy control theory with the adaptive sequencing mutation multi-objective differential evolution algorithm (FASM-MDEA) was offered in [43].

In our proposed model, we utilize two well-known statistical methods, the Pearson correlation coefficient and one-way analysis of variance, to select cost adjustment factors that have a high correlation with the actual effort. Subsequently, we employ the fuzzy C-means clustering algorithm with three cluster heads to group similar projects in the COCOMO-81 dataset. Furthermore, we utilize an improved self-adaptive differential evolution algorithm to optimize the parameters of the constructive cost model [44].

This paper focuses on the use of differential evolution to improve the approximation properties of function approximation models based on fuzzy partitions. Two cases are considered, fuzzy transform and fuzzy projection, and the design of hybrid evolutionary fuzzy systems is studied. Even though function approximation techniques based on fuzzy partitions have been well studied, few papers consider the problem of centroid selection of the basic functions. Thus, in most cases, uniform fuzzy partitions are considered. By using an evolutionary algorithm, a systematic approach on the selection of the partition is provided. The optimization problem involves the determination of the model parameters, which, in our case, are the fuzzy partition's membership functions' locations [45].

Type-3 fuzzy theory is a recent proposal in the literature. In a recent work, a study by varying an important element of interval type-3 fuzzy sets, known as the LowerScale (λ) parameter, was performed. By manipulating this parameter, different proposed fuzzy systems are utilized to dynamically adjust a parameter of the differential evolution algorithm during its execution, aiming to enhance its convergence [46].

Although DE is considered an algorithm with an exceptionally simple evolutionary strategy, it also proves to be significantly fast and robust. It relies on a small number of parameters, namely:

NP: the number of parent vectors, corresponding to the population size or the number of individuals.

F: the mutation factor or scale factor, typically chosen from the range [0,1].

CR: the recombination factor or crossover rate.

G: the maximum number of generations to be executed.

The performance of the algorithm is highly sensitive to these control values, and each problem may exhibit different responses to different parameter settings.

The mathematical form of DE is expressed by the equations described in the following sections.

3.1. Population Size

DE's implementation, known for its versatility, consists of two vector populations. Each population contains Np D-dimensional vectors with real-valued parameters. The current population denoted as P_x is comprised of vectors $x_{i,g}$ that have been deemed acceptable either as initial points or through comparison with other vectors.

$$P_{x,g} = (x_{i,g}),\ i = 0,1,\ldots,Np-1,\ g = 0,1,\ldots,g_{max}, \tag{9}$$

$$x_{i,g} = (x_{j,i,g}),\ j = 0,1,\ldots,D-1, \tag{10}$$

Indices start with 0 to simplify working with arrays and modular arithmetic. The index, $g = 0, 1, \ldots, g_{max}$, indicates the generation to which a vector belongs. In addition, each vector is assigned a population index, i, which runs from 0 to $Np - 1$. Parameters within vectors are indexed with j, which runs from 0 to $D - 1$. Once initialized, DE mutates randomly chosen vectors to produce an intermediary population, $P_{v,g}$, of Np mutant vectors, $v_{i,g}$:

$$P_{v,g} = (v_{i,g}),\ i = 0,1,\ldots,Np-1,\ g = 0,1,\ldots,g_{max}, \tag{11}$$

$$v_{i,g} = (v_{j,i,g}),\ \ j = 0,1,\ldots,D-1, \tag{12}$$

Each vector in the current population undergoes recombination with a mutant vector, resulting in the creation of a trial population, P_u, comprising Np mutant vectors $u_{i,g}$.

$$P_{u,g} = (u_{i,g}),\ i = 0,1,\ldots,Np-1,\ g = 0,1,\ldots,g_{max}, \tag{13}$$

$$u_{i,g} = (u_{j,i,g}),\ \ j = 0,1,\ldots,D-1 \tag{14}$$

where:

P_x: current population.
i: index of the population.
g_{max}: maximum number of iterations.
j: parameters within the vector.

During recombination, trial vectors replace the mutant population, allowing a single array to hold both populations.

Initialization of the population requires specifying upper and lower bounds for each parameter. These bounds are collected into two D-dimensional initialization vectors, bL and bU, where subscripts L and U indicate the lower and upper bounds, respectively. Using a random number generator, each parameter of every vector is assigned a value within the specified range. For instance, the initial value (at $g = 0$) of the jth parameter of the ith vector is determined as:

$$x_{j,i,0} = rand_j(0,1)\cdot\left(b_{j,U} - b_{j,L}\right) + b_{j,L} \tag{15}$$

The random number generator, *randj*(0,1), returns a uniformly distributed random number from within the range (0,1), i.e., $0 \leq$ *randj*(0,1) < 1. The subscript, j, indicates that a new random value is generated for each parameter. Even if a variable is discrete or integral, it should be initialized with a real value since DE internally treats all variables as floating-point values regardless of their type.

3.2. Mutation

Specifically, the differential mutation utilizes a random sampling equation to combine three randomly chosen vectors and create a mutant vector.

$$v_{i,g} = x_{r_0,g} + \mathrm{F}\cdot\left(x_{r_1,g} - x_{r_2,g}\right) \tag{16}$$

The scale factor, $\mathrm{F} \in (0,1)$ is a positive real number that controls the rate at which the population evolves.

3.3. Crossover

To complement the differential mutation search strategy, DE also uses uniform crossover. Sometimes this is known as discrete recombination. In particular, DE crosses each vector with a mutant vector as indicated by the following expression:

$$u_{i,g} = u_{j,i,g}\begin{cases} v_{j,i,g} \ if \ (rand_j(0,1) \leq Cr \ or \ j = j_{rand}) \\ x_{j,i,g} \ \ otherwise \end{cases} \tag{17}$$

3.4. Selection of the Best Individual

If the test vector $u_{i,g}$ has a value for the objective function equal to or less than its target vector, $x_{i,g}$, then it replaces the target vector in the next generation; otherwise, the target retains its place in the population for at least another generation:

$$x_{i,g+1} = \begin{cases} u_{i,g} \ if \ f(u_{i,g}) \leq f(x_{i,g}) \\ x_{i,g} \ \ otherwise \end{cases} \tag{18}$$

The process of mutation, recombination and selection are repeated until the optimum is found, or a pre-specified terminating criterion is satisfied.

4. Proposed Shadowed Fuzzy using DE Algorithm

The main contribution of this article is the utilization of a novel optimization technique, shadowed type-2 fuzzy systems (ST2-FS), for dynamically adapting the crossover parameter of differential evolution (DE). This adaptation aims to enhance the performance of the DE algorithm when applied to optimize the motor position control problem with interval type-2, specifically by identifying the optimal structure of the membership functions.

Figure 4 displays a flowchart illustrating the procedure employed in this article's general proposal. It demonstrates the utilization of ST2-FS to dynamically adjust the CR parameter, followed by its simulation in the motor controller featuring an IT2-FS.

The equations utilized for constructing the fuzzy parameters of the input and output are presented in Equations (19) and (20), respectively.

$$Generations = \frac{Current\ Generation}{Maximun\ of\ generations} \tag{19}$$

$$\mathrm{CR} = \frac{\sum_{i=1}^{r_{CR}} \mu_i^{CR}(CR_{1i})}{\sum_{i=1}^{r_{CR}} \mu_i^{CR}} \tag{20}$$

The number of rules in the fuzzy system for CR is denoted by r_{CR}; CR_{1i}, represents the output result for rule i of CR, while μ_i^{CR}, represents the membership function (MF) of rule i of CR.

The fuzzy system structure integrated into the DE algorithm consists of the following characteristics. We refer to the combination of ST2-FS with the DE algorithm as DE-ST2-FS. The system comprises an input representing the generations used in the DE algorithm, and the output is the CR parameter that represents the crossover. In the original algorithm, this parameter is defined within the range of [0,1]. Both the input and output are divided into three membership functions (MFs), as depicted in Figure 5.

The rules that form the fuzzy system are presented below. These rules were developed based on experimentation, which demonstrated that decreasing the CR parameter during the algorithm's execution yields favorable results.

1. If generation is low, then CR is low.
2. If generation is medium, then CR is medium.
3. If generation is high, then CR is high.

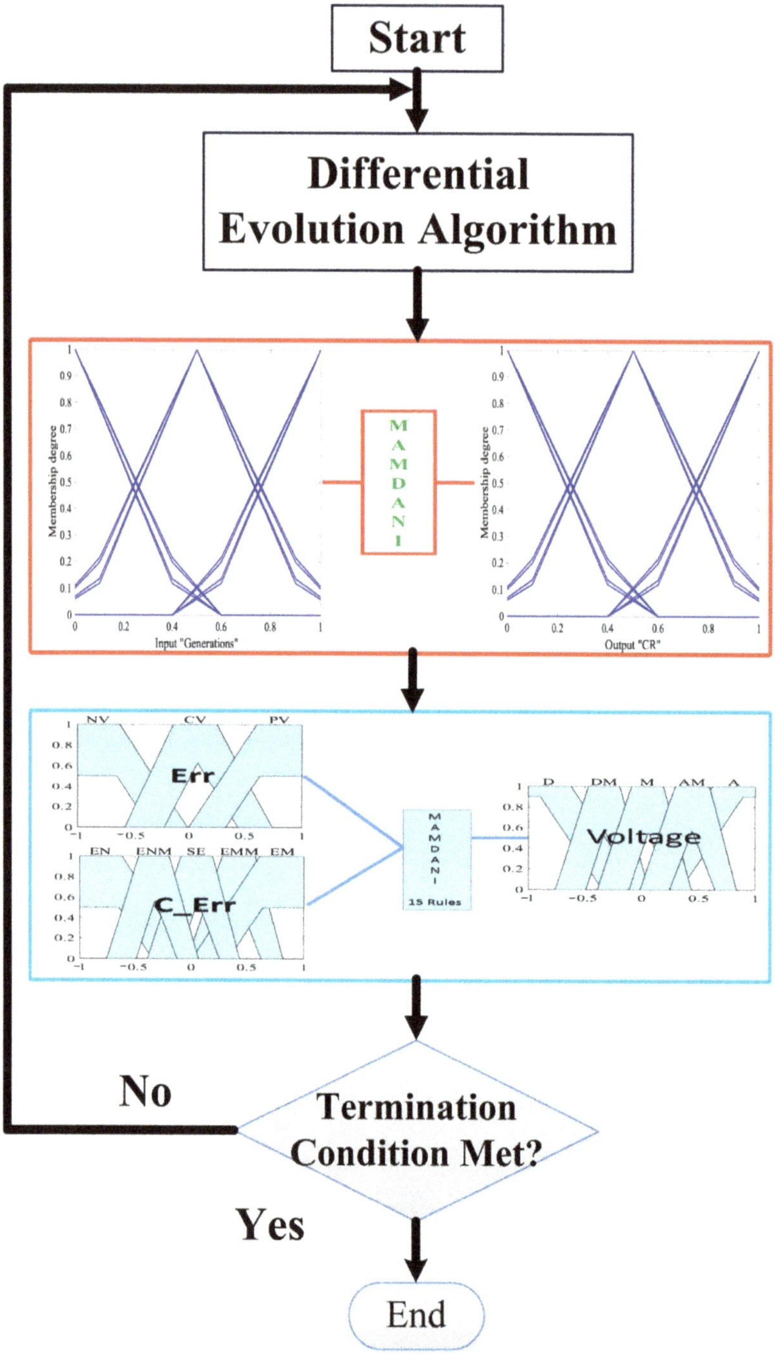

Figure 4. Proposal flowchart.

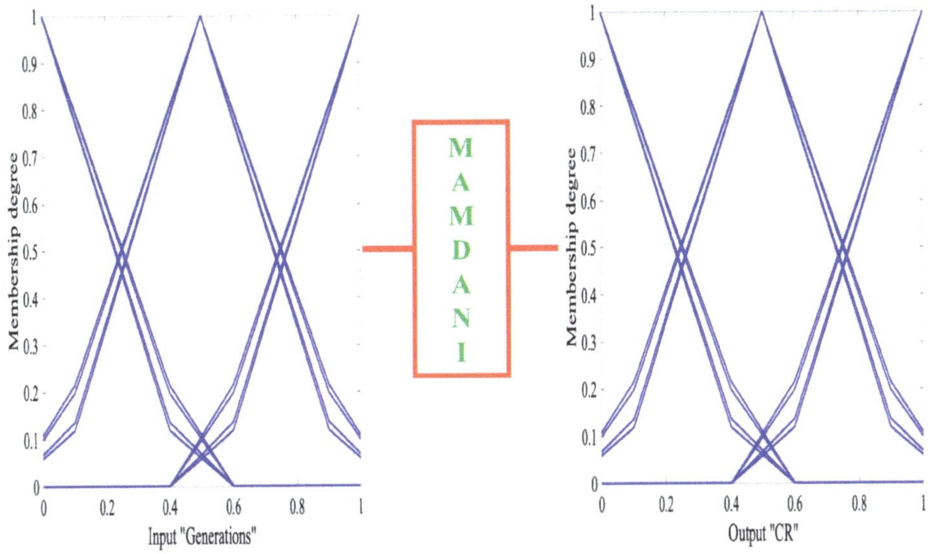

Figure 5. Shadowed fuzzy system integrated with the DE algorithm (DE-ST2-FS).

5. Interval Type-2 Fuzzy Systems Controller

Position control of a direct current (DC) motor is a circuit capable of controlling the position of any DC motor with the simple movement of a potentiometer that acts as a positioner, and it does so through proportional control [47–50]. One of the purposes of this work is the optimization of the interval type-2 fuzzy controller, which we will call (IT2-FLC), which is structured as illustrated in Figure 6.

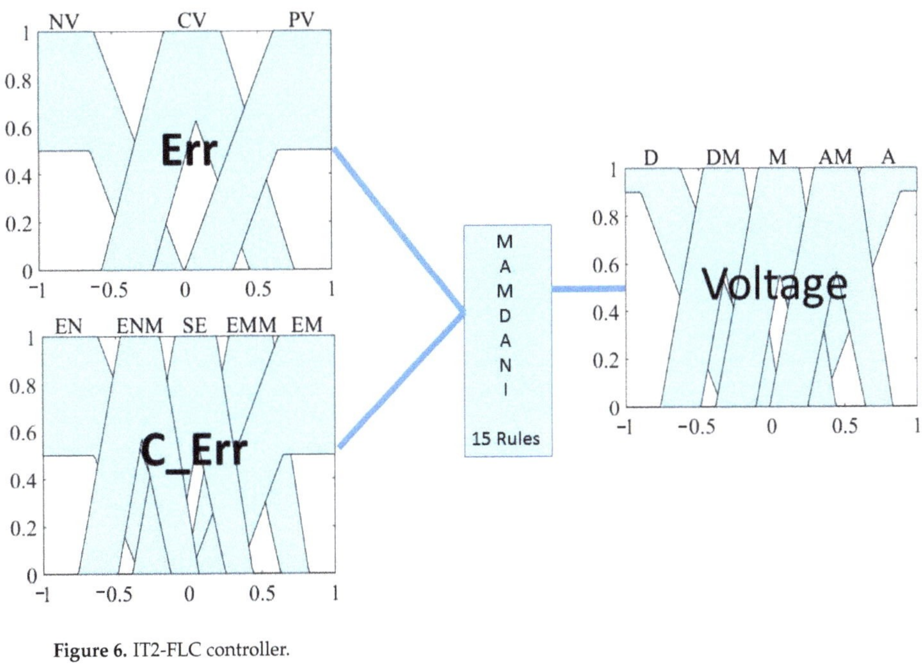

Figure 6. IT2-FLC controller.

The fuzzy system is defined as: the inputs are the error "Err" and the error change "C_Err", the output corresponds to the voltage "Voltage", the "Err" input contains three MFs, the ends are of type *"trapIT2mf"*, and the center is *"triIT2mf"*. The equations that describe the knowledge of each function are shown in Equations (21) and (22).

The second input "C_Err" contains five membership functions, the ends are of type *"trapIT2mf"*, and the three central functions are of type *"triIT2mf"*.

Finally, the output "Voltage" consists of five membership functions, the ends are of type *"trapIT2mf"*, and the three central functions are of type *"triIT2mf"*.

$$trapIT2mf(x, [a_1, b_1, c_1, d_1, a_2, b_2, c_2, d_2, \alpha]) = \begin{cases} a_1 < a_2, b_1 < b_2, c_1 < c_2, d_1 < d_2 \\ \mu_1(x) = \max\left(\min\left(\frac{x-a_1}{b_1-a_1}, 1, \frac{d_1-x}{d_1-c_1}\right), 0\right) \\ \mu_2(x) = \max\left(\min\left(\frac{x-a_2}{b_2-a_2}, 1, \frac{d_2-x}{d_2-c_2}\right), 0\right) \\ \overline{\mu}(x) = \begin{cases} max(\mu_1(x), \mu_2(x)) & \forall x \notin (b1, c2) \\ 1 & \forall x \in (b1, c2) \end{cases} \\ \underline{\mu}(x) = min(\alpha, min(\mu_1(x), \mu_2(x))) \end{cases} \quad (21)$$

$$triIT2mf(x, [a_1, b_1, c_1, a_2, b_2, c_2]) = \begin{cases} a_1 < a_2, b_1 < b_2, c_1 < c_2 \\ \mu_1(x) = \max\left(\min\left(\frac{x-a_1}{b_1-a_1}, \frac{c_1-x}{c_1-b_1}\right), 0\right) \\ \mu_2(x) = \max\left(\min\left(\frac{x-a_2}{b_2-a_2}, \frac{c_2-x}{c_2-b_2}\right), 0\right) \\ \overline{\mu}(x) = \begin{cases} max(\mu_1(x), \mu_2(x)) & \forall x \notin (b1, b2) \\ 1 & \forall x \in (b1, b2) \end{cases} \\ \underline{\mu}(x) = min(\mu_1(x), \mu_2(x)) \end{cases} \quad (22)$$

IT2-FLC rules are outlined in Table 1.

Table 1. IT2-FLC rules.

		C_Err				
		EN	**ENM**	**SE**	**EMM**	**EM**
Err	NV	D	D	D	D	DM
	CV	AM	AM	M	DM	DM
	PV	AM	A	A	A	A

6. Results and Statistical Comparison

In this section, we are presenting the experimentation that were performed, the parameters used, and the objective function used for the experimentation.

The root means square error (RMSE) represents the objective function for our experimentation, where we seek to measure the difference between the desired and the obtained in the controller. The formula that represents the RMSE is described in Equation (23), where x_t is the estimated value of the reference control signal, $\hat{x}_t$ is the observed value control-signal, and N represents the total number of observed samples.

$$\text{RMSE} = \sqrt{\frac{1}{N} \sum_{t=1}^{N} (x_t - \hat{x}_t)^2} \quad (23)$$

The parameters that involve the experimentation of the DE-ST2-FS algorithm are described in Table 2, where we can importantly rescue the parameter CR that is dynamic due to the ST2-FS.

Table 2. Parameter configuration of the DE-ST2-FS.

Parameter Configuration	
NP	20
D	25
GEN	20
F	0.5
CR	Dynamic
Number of experiments	30

The conducted experimentation is summarized in Table 3, which demonstrates the usage of the DE-ST2-FS proposal without applying noise to the controller. Subsequently, the performance of a type-2 controller in handling intervals was evaluated by introducing Gaussian random noise at three different levels: 0.3, 0.5, and 0.9.

Table 3. DE-ST2-FS fuzzy system.

	DE-ST2-FS without Noise	DE-ST2-FS with Noise 0.5	DE-ST2-FS with Noise 0.7	DE-ST2-FS with Noise 0.9
Min.	5.48×10^{-1}	5.28×10^{-1}	9.38×10^{-2}	1.31×10^{-2}
Max.	6.08×10^{-1}	6.01×10^{-1}	9.78×10^{-2}	7.63×10^{-2}
Average	5.99×10^{-1}	5.63×10^{-1}	9.58×10^{-2}	5.92×10^{-2}
Standard D.	1.23×10^{-2}	1.55×10^{-2}	6.22×10^{-4}	2.15×10^{-2}

An analysis of Table 4 shows that the utilization of the controller with a noise level of 0.5 is better in terms of minimum error compared to the proposal without applying noise to the controller.

Table 4. *Z*-test parameters.

Parameter	Value
Level of Confidence	95%
Alpha α	5%
H_a	$\mu_1 < \mu_2$
H_o	$\mu_1 \geq \mu_2$
Critical Value	-1.645

On the other hand, it is also observed that, in comparison to the minimum error, a better result is obtained when a noise level of 0.9 is applied compared to a noise level of 0.7.

Regarding the averages of the experimentation, they all have the same order, but it can be observed how the average decreases when the noise level increases.

Figure 7 shows a comparison of the experimentation with the different noise levels.

The analysis of Figure 7 shows us that with a higher noise level, the DE-ST2-FS proposal shown in this work obtains better results; however, not applying noise to the DE-ST2-FS controller has a similar behavior to DE-ST2-FS with noise 0.5, while DE-ST2-FS with noise 0.7 and DE-ST2-FS with noise 0.9 have very similar behaviors. Overall, a better result is observed with DE-ST2-FS with noise 0.9.

The results of the minimum values obtained in Table 4 are represented in Figures 8–11, showcasing the four different experimental scenarios: DE-ST2-FS without noise, DE-ST2-FS with noise 0.5, DE-ST2-FS with noise 0.7, and DE-ST2-FS with noise 0.9.

Figure 8 shows the minimum RMSE of the simulation of the 30 experiments performed with DEST2-FS without noise, where the value obtained was 5.48×10^{-1}. In Figure 6, when starting the simulation, it exceeds what is desired, but later it stabilizes in the second 0.12 to 0.14 and later it exceeds again from the second 0.14 to 0.2.

Figure 9 illustrates the minimum RMSE of the simulation of the 30 experiments carried out with DE-ST2-FS with noise 0.5, where the value obtained was 5.28×10^{-1}. In the figure, when starting the simulation, it exceeds between seconds 0.06 and 0.1, later a stabilization is observed from second 0.16 to 0.2.

Figure 10 shows the minimum RMSE of the simulation of the 30 experiments carried out with DE-ST2-FS with noise 0.7, where the value obtained was 9.38×10^{-2}. In the figure, the controller has stability from 0.1 s to 0.16 s, while between 0.16 s and 0.2 s the controller output drifts slightly from the desired reference.

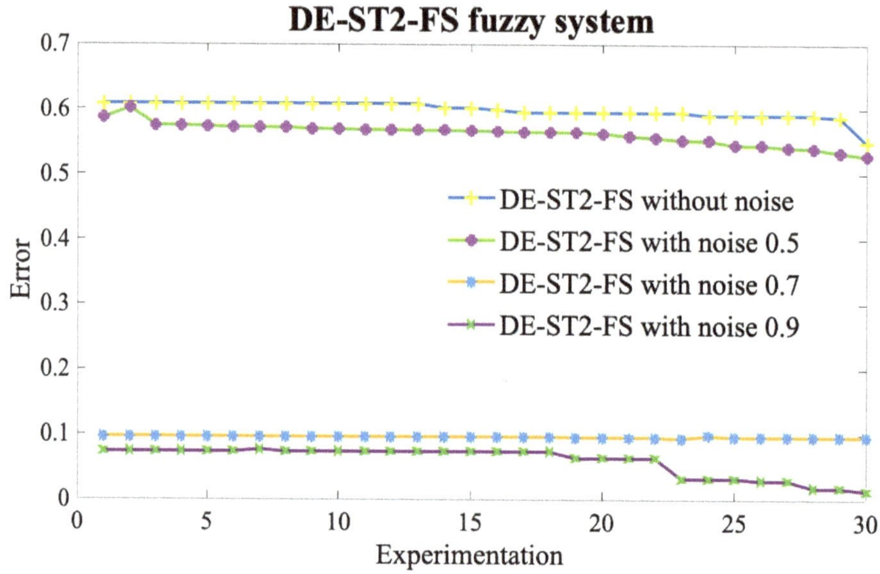

Figure 7. Graphical comparison of experimentation.

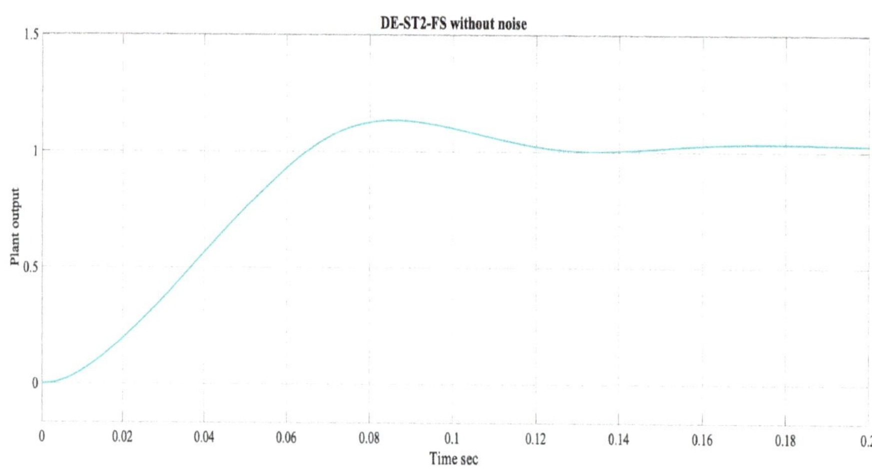

Figure 8. Best result DE-ST2-FS without noise.

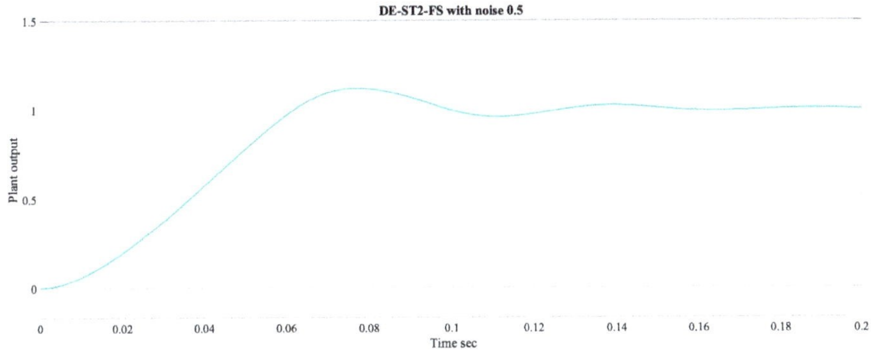

Figure 9. Best result DE-ST2-FS with noise 0.5.

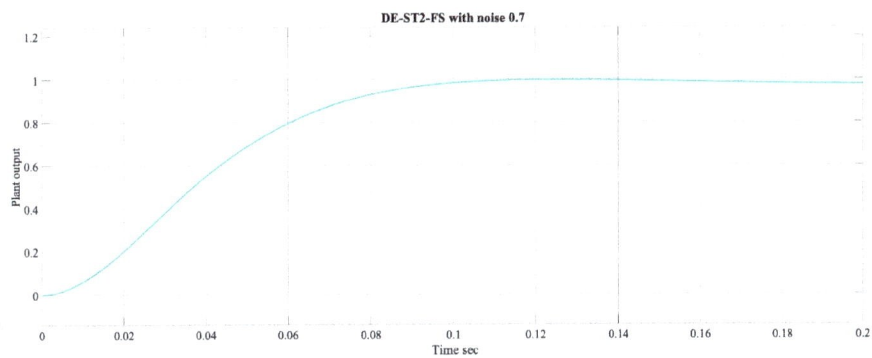

Figure 10. Best result DE-ST2-FS with noise 0.7.

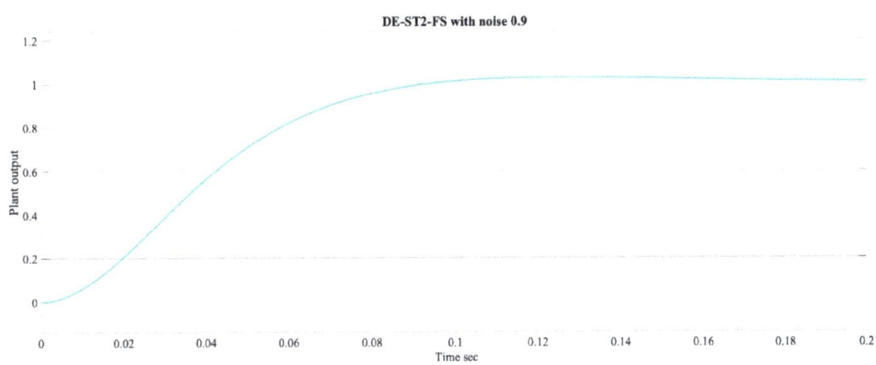

Figure 11. Best result DE-ST2-FS with noise 0.9.

Finally, Figure 11 shows the RMSE of the simulation of the 30 experiments carried out with DE-ST2-FS with noise 0.9, where the value obtained was 1.31×10^{-2}. In the simulation obtained, it is observed that from second 0.1 the output of the plant has stability, but in between seconds 0.16 and 0.2 it is possible to stabilize.

In order to demonstrate that better results are obtained when using DE-ST2-FS with a high noise level, a statistical test was performed. The statistic used in this work is the

Z-test, the parameters used are shown in Table 4, and Equation (24) was used to calculate the Z value.

$$Z = \frac{(\overline{X}_1 - \overline{X}_2) - (\mu_1 - \mu_2)}{\sigma_{\overline{X}_1 - \overline{X}_2}} \tag{24}$$

The objective of the statistical test is to show that DE-ST2-FS with noise 0.9 has a lower average than the other three variants of experimentation carried out: DE-ST2-FS without noise, DE-ST2-FS with noise 0.5, and DE-ST2-FS with noise 0.7.

Three statistical tests were performed, where μ_1 is equal to DE-ST2-FS with noise 0.9 and μ_2 represents each of the statistical tests carried out. The results of the tests are outlined in Table 5.

Table 5. Z-test results.

Case Study	μ_1	μ_2	Z Value	Evidence
Controller	DE-ST2-FS with noise 0.9	DE-ST2-FS without noise	−119.3636	Significant
	DE-ST2-FS with noise 0.9	DE-ST2-FS with noise 0.5	−104.1108	Significant
	DE-ST2-FS with noise 0.9	DE-ST2-FS with noise. 0.7	−9.3201	Significant

The results of the tests show that the greater the uncertainty, the better results are obtained. The three statistical tests carried out show that DE-ST2-FS with noise 0.9 has a lower average than the other three proposals carried out.

Next, a comparison was made with other works found in the literature, in order to be able to validate the proposal to make CR dynamic in the DE and having an interval type-2 controller.

We use as reference "Shadowed Type-2 Fuzzy Systems for Dynamic Parameter Adaptation in Harmony Search and Differential Evolution" [51]. In this previous work, two metaheuristics are used, where one of the parameters is dynamically adapted with a ST2-FS, and the difference with the reference is that the controller used is a T1-FS compared to ours, which is an IT2-FS.

Table 6 exhibits the results from the literature and the results of the best experiments carried out in our work with ST2-FS with noise 0.9, reporting the averages and standard deviations.

Table 6. DE-ST2FS with noise 0.9 comparison.

	ST2FHS-FLC FLC with Noise [51]	ST2FDE-FLC with Noise [51]	DE-ST2-FS with Noise 0.9
Average	4.62×10^{-1}	2.1×10^{-2}	5.92×10^{-2}
Standard D.	2.83×10^{-2}	1.90×10^{-2}	2.15×10^{-2}

Using the data from Table 6, two statistical tests were performed to check if our proposal has a lower average than other methods in the literature. The previously shown Z-test was used, according to Equation (23), and the same parameters used in Table 4 were employed.

For the statistical test, μ_1 is equal to DEST2-FS with noise 0.9 and μ_2 is equal to the two different methods ST2FHS-FLC with Noise and ST2FDE-FLC with Noise [51]. Table 7 reports the Z-test results for the two tests.

The test results indicate that we have sufficient significant evidence to conclude that DE-ST2-FS with noise 0.9 has a lower average than ST2FHS-FLC with Noise. However, for the second statistical test, we do not have enough significant evidence to claim that DE-ST2-FS with noise 0.9 has a lower average than ST2FDE-FLC with Noise.

Table 7. Statistical Z-test results.

Case Study	μ_1	μ_2	Z Value	Evidence
Controller	DE-ST2-FS with noise 0.9	ST2FHS-FLC FLC with Noise [51]	−62.0761	Significant
	DE-ST2-FS with noise 0.9	ST2FDE-FLC with Noise [51]	7.1395	Not Significant

7. Conclusions

For our conclusions, the main contribution is the use of the dynamic CR parameter in differential evolution, as well as the ST2-FS, as this combination is new and there are no current works that utilize our DE-ST2-FS proposal.

This work demonstrates that the use of uncertainty improves the obtained results. In the DE-ST2-FS proposal we used the ST2-FS controller without applying noise and later the noise level was increased in order to demonstrate that at higher noise levels, the IT2-FLC has better stability. The statistical test supports that DE-ST2-FS with noise 0.9 has a lower average than DE-ST2-FS without noise, DE-ST2-FS with noise 0.5, and DE-ST2-FS with noise 0.7.

Figures 8–11 illustrate the improvement achieved by increasing the noise level, as they display the minimum RMSE obtained from each of the different experiments. The comparison with the two methods, namely ST2FHS-FLC with Noise and ST2FDE-FLC with Noise, reveals that our proposal exhibits a lower average than ST2FHS-FLC with Noise. However, we did not obtain significant evidence in favor of our proposal compared to ST2FDE-FLC with Noise. In the latter case, the reference method utilizes a ST2-FS, which makes the F (mutation) parameter of the differential evolution algorithm dynamic. We believe that this is the reason why we lack significant evidence in our proposal. Previous works have statistically confirmed that making the F parameter dynamic yields better results than making the CR parameter dynamic.

Author Contributions: C.P., P.O. and O.C. conducted the state-of-the-art review, literature review, and developed the main idea. O.C. and Z.W.G. provided supervision. All authors have read and agreed to the published version of the manuscript.

Funding: This research received no external funding.

Data Availability Statement: Not applicable.

Acknowledgments: We would like to thank the Tijuana Institute of Technology and TecNM for their support.

Conflicts of Interest: The authors declare no conflict of interest.

References

1. Rossi, F.; Sembiring, J.P.; Jayadi, A.; Putri, N.U.; Nugroho, P. Implementation of Fuzzy Logic in PLC for Three- Story Elevator Control System. In Proceedings of the 2021 International Conference on Computer Science, Information Technology, and Electrical Engineering (ICOMITEE), Banyuwangi, Indonesia, 27–28 October 2021; pp. 179–185. [CrossRef]
2. Krishnan, R.S.; Julie, E.G.; Robinson, Y.H.; Raja, S.; Kumar, R.; Thong, P.H.; Son, L.H. Fuzzy Logic based Smart Irrigation System using Internet of Things. *J. Clean. Prod.* **2019**, *252*, 119902. [CrossRef]
3. Belman-Flores, J.M.; Rodríguez-Valderrama, D.A.; Ledesma, S.; García-Pabón, J.J.; Hernández, D.; Pardo-Cely, D.M. A Review on Applications of Fuzzy Logic Control for Refrigeration Systems. *Appl. Sci.* **2022**, *12*, 1302. [CrossRef]
4. Chen, X.; Hu, Z.; Sun, Y. Fuzzy Logic Based Logical Query Answering on Knowledge Graphs. *Proc. Conf. AAAI Artif. Intell.* **2022**, *36*, 3939–3948. [CrossRef]
5. Almadi, A.I.M.; Al Mamlook, R.E.; Almarhabi, Y.; Ullah, I.; Jamal, A.; Bandara, N. A Fuzzy-Logic Approach Based on Driver Decision-Making Behavior Modeling and Simulation. *Sustainability* **2022**, *14*, 8874. [CrossRef]
6. Zhao, Z.-H. Improved fuzzy logic control-based energy management strategy for hybrid power system of FC/PV/battery/SC on tourist ship. *Int. J. Hydrogen Energy* **2022**, *47*, 9719–9734. [CrossRef]
7. Kenjrawy, H.; Makdisie, C.; Houssamo, I.; Mohammed, N. New Modulation Technique in Smart Grid Interfaced Multilevel UPQC-PV Controlled via Fuzzy Logic Controller. *Electronics* **2022**, *11*, 919. [CrossRef]

8. Atoui, A.; Boucherit, M.S.; Benmansour, K.; Barkat, S.; Djerioui, A.; Houari, A. Unified fuzzy logic controller and power management for an isolated residential hybrid PV/diesel/battery energy system. *Clean Energy* **2022**, *6*, 671–681. [CrossRef]
9. Zhu, Y.; Wang, Z.; Guo, X.; Wei, Z. An improved kinetic energy control strategy for power smoothing of PMSG-WECS based on low pass filter and fuzzy logic controller. *Electr. Power Syst. Res.* **2023**, *214*, 108816. [CrossRef]
10. Afaq, M.; Jebelli, A.; Ahmad, R. An Intelligent Thermal Management Fuzzy Logic Control System Design and Analysis Using ANSYS Fluent for a Mobile Robotic Platform in Extreme Weather Applications. *J. Intell. Robot. Syst.* **2023**, *107*, 11. [CrossRef]
11. Ahmad, I.; M'Zoughi, F.; Aboutalebi, P.; Garrido, I.; Garrido, A.J. Fuzzy logic control of an artificial neural network-based floating offshore wind turbine model integrated with four oscillating water columns. *Ocean Eng.* **2023**, *269*, 113578. [CrossRef]
12. Moutchou, R.; Abbou, A.; Jabri, B.; Rhaili, S.E.; Chigane, K. Adaptive Fuzzy Logic Controller for MPPT Control in PMSG Wind Turbine Generator. In *Artificial Intelligence-Based Smart Power Systems*; IEEE Press: Piscataway, NJ, USA, 2022; pp. 129–140. [CrossRef]
13. Wang, X.; Xu, B.; Guo, Y. Fuzzy Logic System-Based Robust Adaptive Control of AUV with Target Tracking. *Int. J. Fuzzy Syst.* **2022**, *25*, 338–346. [CrossRef]
14. Liu, J.; Wei, T.; Chen, N.; Wu, J.; Xiao, P. Fuzzy Logic PID Controller with Both Coefficient and Error Modifications for Digitally-Controlled DC–DC Switching Converters. *J. Electr. Eng. Technol.* **2023**, 1–12. [CrossRef]
15. Vijayalakshmi, K.; Kn, S. Intelligent Control of Switched Reluctance Motor Using Fuzzy Logic and SMC Controller for EV Applications. *Int. J. Eng. Educ.* **2023**, *4*, 42–57. [CrossRef]
16. Tan, D.W.W.W. A simplified type-2 fuzzy logic controller for real-time control. *ISA Trans.* **2006**, *45*, 503–516. [CrossRef]
17. Castillo, O.; Aguilar, L.; Cázarez, N.; Cárdenas, S. Systematic design of a stable type-2 fuzzy logic controller. *Appl. Soft Comput.* **2008**, *8*, 1274–1279. [CrossRef]
18. Wu, D.; Tan, W. A type-2 fuzzy logic controller for the liquid-level process. In Proceedings of the 2004 IEEE International Conference on Fuzzy Systems (IEEE Cat. No. 04CH37542), Budapest, Hungary, 25–29 July 2005; IEEE Press: Piscataway, NJ, USA, 2005. [CrossRef]
19. Zhang, Q.; Wang, Y.; Cheng, J.; Yan, H.; Shi, K. Improved filtering of interval type-2 fuzzy systems over Gilbert-Elliott channels. *Inf. Sci.* **2023**, *627*, 132–146. [CrossRef]
20. Bernal, E.; Lagunes, M.L.; Castillo, O.; Soria, J.; Valdez, F. Optimization of Type-2 Fuzzy Logic Controller Design Using the GSO and FA Algorithms. *Int. J. Fuzzy Syst.* **2020**, *23*, 42–57. [CrossRef]
21. Sain, D.; Praharaj, M.; Bosukonda, M.M. A simple modelling strategy for integer order and fractional order interval type-2 fuzzy PID controllers with their simulation and real-time implementation. *Expert Syst. Appl.* **2022**, *202*, 117196. [CrossRef]
22. Laib, A.; Talbi, B.; Krama, A.; Gharib, M. Hybrid Interval Type-2 Fuzzy PID+I Controller for a Multi-DOF Oilwell Drill-String System. *IEEE Access* **2022**, *10*, 67262–67275. [CrossRef]
23. Saraswat, R.; Suhag, S. Type-2 fuzzy logic PID control for efficient power balance in an AC microgrid. *Sustain. Energy Technol. Assess.* **2023**, *56*, 103048. [CrossRef]
24. Liu, X.; Zhao, T.; Cao, J.; Li, P. Design of an interval type-2 fuzzy neural network sliding mode robust controller for higher stability of magnetic spacecraft attitude control. *ISA Trans.* 2023; *in press*. [CrossRef]
25. Jovanović, A.; Kukić, K.; Stevanović, A.; Teodorović, D. Restricted crossing U-turn traffic control by interval Type-2 fuzzy logic. *Expert Syst. Appl.* **2023**, *211*, 118613. [CrossRef]
26. Wijayasekara, D.; Linda, O.; Manic, M. Shadowed Type-2 Fuzzy Logic Systems. In Proceedings of the 2013 IEEE Symposium on Advances in Type-2 Fuzzy Logic Systems (T2FUZZ), Singapore, 16–19 April 2013; pp. 15–22. [CrossRef]
27. Castillo, O.; Peraza, C.; Ochoa, P.; Amador-Angulo, L.; Melin, P.; Park, Y.; Geem, Z.W. Shadowed Type-2 Fuzzy Systems for Dynamic Parameter Adaptation in Harmony Search and Differential Evolution for Optimal Design of Fuzzy Controllers. *Mathematics* **2021**, *9*, 2439. [CrossRef]
28. Tahayori, H.; Sadeghian, A. Shadowed fuzzy sets: A framework with more freedom degrees for handling uncertainties than interval type-2 fuzzy sets and lower computational complexity than general type-2 fuzzy sets. In *New Concepts and Applications in Soft Computing*; Springer: Berlin/Heidelberg, Germany, 2013; pp. 97–117. [CrossRef]
29. Zhou, J.; Lai, Z.; Miao, D.; Gao, C.; Yue, X. Multigranulation rough-fuzzy clustering based on shadowed sets. *Inf. Sci.* **2018**, *507*, 553–573. [CrossRef]
30. El-Hawy, M.A.; Wassif, K.T.; Hefny, H.; Hassan, H.A. A proposed shadowed intuitionistic fuzzy numbers. In Proceedings of the 2015 Tenth International Conference on Computer Engineering & Systems (ICCES), Cairo, Egypt, 23–24 December 2015; pp. 153–160. [CrossRef]
31. Zadeh, L.A. Fuzzy sets. *Inf. Control* **1965**, *8*, 338–353. [CrossRef]
32. Wagner, C.; Hagras, H. Toward General Type-2 Fuzzy Logic Systems Based on zSlices. *IEEE Trans. Fuzzy Syst.* **2010**, *18*, 637–660. [CrossRef]
33. Coupland, S.; John, R. Geometric Type-1 and Type-2 Fuzzy Logic Systems. *IEEE Trans. Fuzzy Syst.* **2007**, *15*, 3–15. [CrossRef]
34. Mendel, J.M.; Liu, F.; Zhai, D. α-Plane Representation for Type-2 Fuzzy Sets: Theory and Applications. *IEEE Trans. Fuzzy Syst.* **2009**, *17*, 1189–1207. [CrossRef]
35. Mendel, J.M.; John, R.I.; Liu, F. Interval Type-2 Fuzzy Logic Systems Made Simple. *IEEE Trans. Fuzzy Syst.* **2006**, *14*, 808–821. [CrossRef]

36. Ontiveros, E.; Melin, P.; Castillo, O. High order α-planes integration: A new approach to computational cost reduction of General Type-2 Fuzzy Systems. *Eng. Appl. Artif. Intell.* **2018**, *74*, 186–197. [CrossRef]
37. Dorantes, P.N.M.; Mendez, G.M. Non-iterative Wagner-Hagras General Type-2 Mamdani Singleton Fuzzy Logic System Optimized by Central Composite Design in Quality Assurance by Image Processing. In *Recent Trends on Type-2 Fuzzy Logic Systems: Theory, Methodology and Applications*; Springer International Publishing: Cham, Switzerland, 2023; pp. 201–216. [CrossRef]
38. Pedrycz, W. From fuzzy sets to shadowed sets: Interpretation and computing. *Int. J. Intell. Syst.* **2008**, *24*, 48–61. [CrossRef]
39. Pedrycz, W.; Song, M. Granular fuzzy models: A study in knowledge management in fuzzy modeling. *Int. J. Approx. Reason.* **2012**, *53*, 1061–1079. [CrossRef]
40. Pedrycz, W.; Vukovich, G. Granular computing in the development of fuzzy controllers. *Int. J. Intell. Syst.* **1999**, *14*, 419–447. [CrossRef]
41. Price, K.V.; Storn, R.M.; Lampinen, J.A. The differential evolution algorithm. In *Differential Evolution: A Practical Approach to Global Optimization*; Springer: Berlin/Heidelberg, Germany, 2006; pp. 37–134. [CrossRef]
42. Wang, G.-G.; Gao, D.; Pedrycz, W. Solving Multiobjective Fuzzy Job-Shop Scheduling Problem by a Hybrid Adaptive Differential Evolution Algorithm. *IEEE Trans. Ind. Inform.* **2022**, *18*, 8519–8528. [CrossRef]
43. Lin, H.; Han, Y.; Cai, W.; Jin, B. Traffic Signal Optimization Based on Fuzzy Control and Differential Evolution Algorithm. *IEEE Trans. Intell. Transp. Syst.* 2022, 1–12, *accepted*. [CrossRef]
44. Gouda, S.K.; Mehta, A.K. Software cost estimation model based on fuzzy C-means and improved self adaptive differential evolution algorithm. *Int. J. Inf. Technol.* **2022**, *14*, 2171–2182. [CrossRef]
45. Korkidis, P.; Dounis, A. On training non-uniform fuzzy partitions for function approximation using differential evolution: A study on fuzzy transform and fuzzy projection. *Inf. Sci.* **2023**, *619*, 867–888. [CrossRef]
46. Ochoa, P.; Castillo, O.; Melin, P.; Castro, J.R. Interval Type-3 Fuzzy Differential Evolution for Parameterization of Fuzzy Controllers. *Int. J. Fuzzy Syst.* **2023**, *25*, 1360–1376. [CrossRef]
47. Chairez, I.; Utkin, V. Direct Current Motor Position Control by a Sliding Mode Controlled Dual Three-Phase AC-DC Power Converter. *IFAC-PapersOnLine* **2022**, *55*, 333–338. [CrossRef]
48. Top, A.; Gökbulut, M. A novel period–based method for the measurement direct current motor velocity using low-resolver encoder. *Trans. Inst. Meas. Control* **2022**, *45*, 711–722. [CrossRef]
49. Runjing, Z.; Yu, D.; Weiting, Y. Application of Fuzzy-PI Controller with Feedforward Control in Direct Current Motor Servo System. In Proceedings of the 2005 International Conference on Neural Networks and Brain, Beijing, China, 13–15 October 2005; Volume 2, pp. 1262–1267. [CrossRef]
50. Karabacak, Y.; Uysal, A. Fuzzy logic controlled brushless direct current motor drive design and application for regenerative braking. In Proceedings of the 2017 International Artificial Intelligence and Data Processing Symposium (IDAP), Malatya, Turkey, 16–17 September 2017; pp. 1–7. [CrossRef]
51. Castillo, O.; Melin, P.; Valdez, F.; Soria, J.; Ontiveros-Robles, E.; Peraza, C.; Ochoa, P. Shadowed Type-2 Fuzzy Systems for Dynamic Parameter Adaptation in Harmony Search and Differential Evolution Algorithms. *Algorithms* **2019**, *12*, 17. [CrossRef]

algorithms

MDPI

Article

Real-Time Interval Type-2 Fuzzy Control of an Unmanned Aerial Vehicle with Flexible Cable-Connected Payload

Fethi Candan [1,*], Omer Faruk Dik [2], Tufan Kumbasar [2], Mahdi Mahfouf [1,*] and Lyudmila Mihaylova [1]

[1] Department of Automatic Control and Systems Engineering, University of Sheffield, Sheffield S1 3JD, UK; l.s.mihaylova@sheffield.ac.uk

[2] Control and Automation Department, Istanbul Technical University, 34467 Istanbul, Turkey; diko@itu.edu.tr (O.F.D.); kumbasart@itu.edu.tr (T.K.)

* Correspondence: fcandan1@sheffield.ac.uk (F.C.); m.mahfouf@sheffield.ac.uk (M.M.)

Abstract: This study presents the design and real-time applications of an Interval Type-2 Fuzzy PID (IT2-FPID) control system on an unmanned aerial vehicle (UAV) with a flexible cable-connected payload in comparison to the PID and Type-1 Fuzzy PID (T1-FPID) counterparts. The IT2-FPID control has significant stability, disturbance rejection, and response time advantages. To prove and show these advantages, the DJI Tello, a commercial UAV, is used with a flexible cable-connected payload to test the robustness of PID, T1-FPID, and IT2-FPID controllers. First, the optimal coefficients of the compared controllers are found using the Big Bang–Big Crunch algorithm via the nonlinear UAV model without the payload. Second, once optimised, the controllers are tested using several scenarios, including disturbing the payload and the coverage path planning area to examine their robustness. Third, the controller performance results are evaluated according to reference achievement and point-based tracking under disturbances. Finally, the superiority of the IT2-FPID controller is shown via simulations and real-time experiments with a better overshoot, a faster settling time, and good properties of disturbance rejection compared with the PID and the T1-FPID controllers.

Keywords: fuzzy PID controller; unmanned air vehicles; nano quadcopter; interval type-2 fuzzy controller; autonomy

1. Introduction

Significant and rapid advances in unmanned aerial vehicle (UAV) technology have made them economically viable and easily maintainable. They have been used in research and in civil, military, and commercial applications, such as military UAVs, search and rescue, and agriculture [1–5]. Even though they can complete tasks, they still face many challenging problems because of the sensor accuracy and the coupled highly nonlinear system dynamics. Considering the controller of the UAV, which is one of the challenging problems, encouraged many researchers to take on such challenges and propose several control designs, such as proportional–integral–derivative (PID) [6,7], fuzzy PID control (FPID or T1-FPID) [8–10], linear quadratic regulator (LQR) [11,12], linear quadratic Gaussian and loop transfer recovery (LQG/LTR) [13], model predictive control (MPC) [12,14,15] and H∞ [16,17] control algorithms.

The controller algorithms and the calculation of their parameters are directly related to the physical dynamics of the system. However, the physical dynamics of the UAV represent a challenge for many of the control algorithms implemented on these UAVs, mainly when the control parameters are determined by using limited known dynamic model parameters. Moreover, knowing all parameters of the physical dynamics is almost impossible due to uncertainties or inaccessible parameters. Therefore, the stable controller parameter might cross to the unstable region in the presence of uncertainty or inaccessible parameters. To explain and illustrate the problem, it is scaled and tested using a mini UAV. For indoor experimental research, nano or mini UAVs have proven their efficiency concerning easy access, small sizes and weights [18]. As a result, researchers have used several commercial UAVs, such as Bitcraze Crazyflie 2.0 [8,19–22], Parrot Mambo Minidrone [9,10,12] and DJI Tello [23–25].

In many studies, the connection with the payload represents a further research challenge [23,26–28]; the control problem under uncertain payloads is solved using reinforcement learning. The UAV has a flexible cable, payloads, and magnets. When using the magnets, the payloads can connect to UAV. Hence, the weights cannot be known, adding additional uncertain parameters. Thanks to model-based meta-reinforcement learning, the system's inputs and outputs are trained and created model-based data using a human-based remote controller. After designing a model-based meta-reinforcement learning dynamic model, a model predictive control algorithm is implemented to cope with such effects [23].

UAVs face other challenges not only due to the payload but also due to wind disturbances. In [27], a path following a control algorithm for a UAV with cable-connected payload is designed under wind disturbances. In addition, near hovering and cruising states are included in the control, as well as an employed position-based tracking control algorithm for the outer structure. A whole system model is developed with payload and disturbance effects, meaning that they are not unknown parameters in [27]. Considering unknown parameters, such as the payload mass, an excellent example of associated research work can be attributed to [26] on adaptive UAV control for a cable-suspended unknown payload. The system is tested with a nonlinear and adaptive PD controller. The coefficients/parameters of the UAV controllers are tuned via many different optimisation methods [29], and each of them has its advantages and disadvantages. In [30], a comparative study of different controllers for UAVs is investigated in terms of limitations and strength parts. In this study, we focus on fuzzy-based PID controllers since they have better accuracy than PID controllers and are computationally efficient, which makes them applicable to UAVs in real time [7].

Contributions

This study shows the successful implementation of the Interval Type-2 Fuzzy PID (IT2-FPID) controller under a nonlinear dynamic model and unknown/uncertain parameters of the UAV with a payload in simulation and real-time systems. The implementation comes from model-based tuned parameters to overcome an unknown weighted flexible cable-connected payload. It is aimed to eliminate the oscillating payload effect on DJI Tello UAV and to follow the given references by using these controllers. PID, T1-FPID, and IT2-FPID are tuned using the Big Bang–Big Crunch (BB-BC) optimisation method [31] on the dynamical model of the UAV without a payload. Due to the unmodelled dynamics, such as inaccessible parameters or uncertainties, the controller coefficients are fine-tuned on a real-time UAV without the payload before being tested with the flexible cable-connected payload. After that, it is expected that the UAV will be able to eliminate disturbing payload effects and demonstrate efficient tracking of the designed trajectory. Moreover, the performance of the IT2-FPID is compared with T1-FPID and PID under the same scenarios. The presented results of the study clearly show that the designed IT2-FPID control system is superior in comparison to its T1 and conventional counterparts. The video file provided in the Supplementary Material shows the real-time control performance of the deployed IT2-FPID.

The rest of the study is organised as follows: Section 2 provides the UAV model, including the DJI Tello model and the problem statement and challenges. Section 3 presents implemented controller methods, which are PID, T1-FPID and IT2-FPID, and the simulation results. Then, Section 4 shows the indoor testing area and the designed offline path. Moreover, the process of position localisation of the UAV is explained in this section. The real-time results of the PID, T1-FPID and IT2-FPID controllers are given in Section 5. Finally; Section 6 presents the conclusions and a perspective on future work.

2. UAV Model and the Problem Definition

This section presents the mathematical model for the dynamics of DJI Tello UAV, and the problem statement and challenges. The first part of this section describes the dynamic model of the UAV. This dynamic model is shown without any payload. After that, the problem of the UAV with a flexible connected payload is explained.

2.1. Model Dynamics of DJI Tello UAV

Before outlining the UAV model, we show the main coordinate frames used in this study: $(.)^I$ represents the global Earth-fixed Earth-centred inertial frame, and $(.)^B$ is the body-fixed frame, fixed at the UAV centre of mass (CoM) as given on Figure 1. There are two types of configurations for the UAV, which are × and + configurations [8,20,32]. In this study, the ×-type UAV is modelled and used.

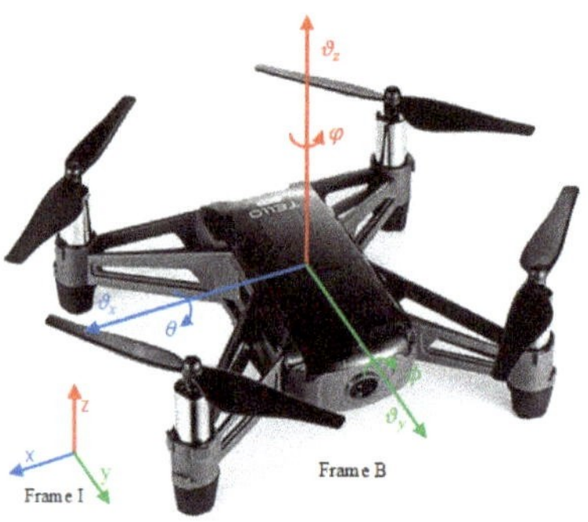

Figure 1. The DJI Tello UAV used in the implementation [33].

The position (p^I) and attitude (η^I) of the UAV with respect to the frame I are defined as follows:

$$\begin{aligned} p^I &= [x\ y\ z]^T, \eta^I = [\phi\ \theta\ \psi]^T, \\ v^I &= \dot{p}^I = Rv^B, \omega^I = \dot{\eta}^I = T\omega^B, \end{aligned} \tag{1}$$

where the vector p^I contains the x, y, and z Cartesian position coordinates of the UAV inertial frame, and v^I and ω^I are the derivative of position and attitude values, respectively. The superscripts $(.)^I$ and $(.)^B$ denote, respectively, the inertial and body frames. The η^I vector contains the angles of roll ϕ, pitch θ, yaw ψ of the UAV body frame, R is a rotational matrix, and T is a translation matrix used in frame conversions. These rotation and transformation matrices are used to calculate the transformation of the inertial frame to the body frame or vice versa. The rotation and transformation matrices are written in Equation (A1) of Appendix A.

The v variable is used to represent the linear velocity, and ω is used to represent the angular velocity. In this study, the heading angle of the UAV, yaw reference (ψ_r) is equal to $\psi_r = 0°$ in order to overlap the inertial and the body coordinate frames of the DJI Tello.

After the defining position and orientation, a nonlinear dynamic equation for the DJI Tello UAV can be written with the Newton–Euler formulation as given below [8,20]:

$$\begin{aligned} m_{\text{uav}}\dot{v}^I &= F^I = F^I_{gravity} + F^I_{thrust}, \\ I^B\dot{w}^B &= -w^B \times \left(I^B w^B\right) + \tau^B_{rotor}. \end{aligned} \tag{2}$$

In Equation (2), m_{uav} is the mass of the UAV to the CoM of the UAV, $F^I_{gravity}$ is the gravity force, F^I_{thrust} is the total thrust force which comes from the propellers, I^B is a moment of inertia, and I^B is referred to as the inertia matrix. The cross product at the right-hand side of the angular velocity dynamics equation comes from the Coriolis force effect. Considering the DJI Tello UAV, this effect can be ignored because of the size of the

UAV. Ref. [8] tested a fixed heading angle and ignored the Coriolis effect on the DJI Tello UAV, which has an almost similar size to the DJI Tello UAV. Therefore, the formula can be written as $I^B \dot{w}^B = \tau^B_{rotor}$, and the UAV torques ($\tau^B_{rotor}$) are expressed by τ_ϕ,τ_θ, and τ_ψ, respectively:

$$\begin{aligned} F^I_{gravity} &= \begin{bmatrix} 0 & 0 & -m_{\text{uav}} g \end{bmatrix}^T, \\ F^I_{thrust} &= R F^B_{thrust}. \end{aligned} \tag{3}$$

To overcome the gravity effect, the force is applied to the CoM of the UAV as $F^I_{gravity}$. The acceleration due to Earth's gravity is denoted as g. The F^I_{thrust} forces are generated by propellers, and the formula is written as Equation (4). The angular velocity of each rotor's propeller is denoted as Ω_i, and the thrust coefficient is referred to as b

$$F^B_{thrust} = \left[0 \;\; 0 \;\; b \textstyle\sum_{i=1}^4 \Omega_i^2 \right]^T, \tag{4}$$

$$\dot{v}^I = \begin{bmatrix} \ddot{x} \\ \ddot{y} \\ \ddot{z} \end{bmatrix} = \frac{b}{m_{\text{uav}}} \textstyle\sum_{i=1}^4 \Omega_i^2 = \begin{bmatrix} s(\phi)s(\psi) + c(\phi)s(\theta)c(\psi) \\ -s(\phi)c(\theta) + c(\phi)s(\theta)s(\psi) \\ c(\phi)c(\theta) \end{bmatrix} - \begin{bmatrix} 0 \\ 0 \\ g \end{bmatrix}. \tag{5}$$

In Equation (5), $s(.)$ and $c(.)$ denote the sine and cosine, respectively. In the equations above, the nonlinear dynamical model for the translational motion of the UAV is represented, and a detailed linear dynamical model of the UAV is written in Equations (A5)–(A7) of Appendix A. The angular velocity dynamics of the UAV also can be found in Equations (A3) and (A4). As aforementioned about the mass of UAV (m_{uav}), it only gives the UAV weight.

In the above equations, mass equals $m_{\text{uav}} = 0.08$ kg, and the length between the CoM and propeller is 0.6 m. The detailed parameters of the DJI Tello UAV are explained in Refs. [24,34].

2.2. Problem Statement and Challenges

In Figure 2, the UAV with the flexible cable-connected payload and its pendulum effects are shown. The figure shows the different perspectives of the UAV with cable-connected payload and the variable payload in detail. A 3D-printed part is created and mounted to provide a UAV connection with a payload cable. The cable length is 35 cm and is chosen as flexible. Taking into account the pendulum effects, forces F_P, F_R and the angles α, ε, β, and λ vary with the acceleration of the UAV due to Newton's second law. The maximum carrying payload is measured with empirical methods, and its maximum value is determined as 75 g for the experiments. This weight (m_{p}) is a significant value when considering the mini UAVs. Then, it is able to rewrite the equations as $m_{\text{total}} = m_{\text{uav}} + m_{\text{p}}$. Instead of rewriting the dynamical equations and calculating the controller parameters using swinging m_{total}, we propose that the compared controllers can eliminate the unknown payload effects and the variable CoM problems without redesigning or the calculation.

Understandably, unknown payloads and disturbances directly relate to the system dynamics. Therefore, the main objective of this work is to overcome these adverse effects. At this point, instead of re-writing the equations of the UAV dynamics and redesigning the controllers by considering the whole mathematical model with the additional dynamics of the swinging payload, the controllers are designed by considering the known dynamics of the UAV itself without taking the payload and disturbance effects into account so that the robustness of the three controllers is compared with each other, then the IT2-FPID controller gives the results in terms of system stability and robustness.

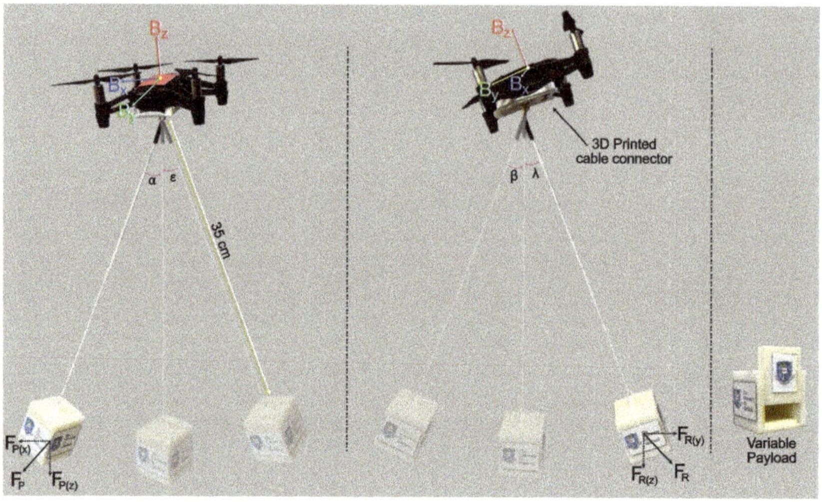

Figure 2. DJI Tello and payload connection.

The most important question is as follows: why do we focus on uncertain parameters, such as unknown payload and flexible cable effects? This system is a simulation of a commercial agricultural UAV problem. Commercial agricultural UAVs may contain liquid or other payloads. However, the problem is that these payloads, such as seeds or pesticides, are unknown loads because of their variable weights and variable centre of masses during the flight.

3. Implemented Controllers

In this study, we design and deploy PID, T1-FPID and IT2-FPID controllers as x-y position controllers that generate the x-y velocity reference signals v_x, v_y (m/s) to be tracked by the on-board velocity controller by DJI Tello UAV. In this context, let us first define the position errors to be minimised by the controllers on the x and y axes e_x, e_y as follows:

$$\begin{aligned} e_x &= x_{ref} - x_{obs} \\ e_y &= y_{ref} - y_{obs} \end{aligned} \tag{6}$$

where (x_{ref}, y_{ref}) and (x_{obs}, y_{obs}) are the references and the feedbacks (actual position of the UAV), respectively. In this study, the reference and feedback units are in meters (m) in the position-based controller. To minimise e_x, e_y, we designed two controllers that generate the velocity signals $u_x = v_x$, $u_y = v_y$. Within the scope of this study, we do not handle the altitude z and yaw ψ control problems of the UAV and use the onboard controller directly. Throughout the study, we set altitude reference $z_{ref} = 90$ cm and heading angle reference of the UAV $\psi_{ref} = 0°$.

In this section, as the x-y position controllers have the same structure, the subscripts (x, y) in e_x, e_y, u_x, u_y are dropped in the rest of the section for a better understanding.

3.1. PID Controller

The PID control law for the UAV is represented as follows:

$$u = K_c\left(e + \frac{1}{T_i}\int e dt + T_d\frac{de}{dt}\right), \tag{7}$$

where u is a reference signal for the inner controller, e is represented as the error, and T_i, T_d, and K_c are the integrator, derivative, and proportional gain, respectively.

3.2. Type-1 Fuzzy PID Controller

In this section, the general structure of the T1-FPID is presented. Before starting T1-FPID, the fuzzy PID control block for T1 and IT2 is shown in Figure 3 [35]. The position error (e), and its rate of change (Δe) are shown as controller inputs [8,9].

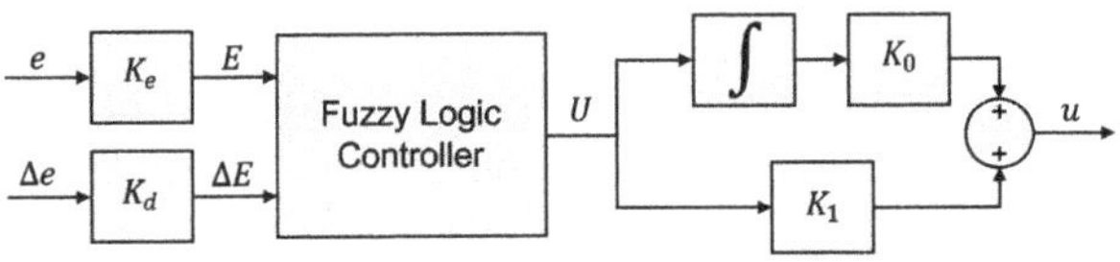

Figure 3. Illustration of the T1- and IT2-FPID controller.

As shown in Figure 3, the input scaling factors (SFs) are denoted as K_e and K_d, while the output scaling factors (SFs) are denoted as K_0 and K_1. The equation is in the form

$$E = K_e e, \quad \Delta E = K_d \Delta e, \tag{8}$$

where E and ΔE denote the FLC inputs. The output of the FLC (U) is transformed to the actual control signal of the T1 or IT2 fuzzy PID controllers (u) as follows:

$$u = K_1 U + K_0 \int U dt. \tag{9}$$

The employed fuzzy logic controller (FLC) is designed with 3 × 3 rules as given in Table 1. The consequent part of the rules is described with crisp singletons. Moreover, they are represented with five linguistic fuzzy terms, which are defined as follows: PB—positive big; PM—positive medium; Z—zero; NM—negative medium; and NB—negative big.

Table 1. The rule table of T1- and IT2-FPID controller.

E/ΔE	P	Z	N
P	PB:1	PM:0.65	Z:0
Z	PM:0.65	Z:0	NM:−0.65
N	Z:0	NM:−0.65	NB:−1

In Figure 4, the membership functions (MFs) of the T1-FPID are presented for the UAV [8,9]. There are three MFs in T1-FPID, N, Z and P abbreviated from "negative", "zero", and "positive", which are the linguistic fuzzy variables. The antecedents are defined with uniformly distributed symmetrical triangular MFs. In this study, triangular MFs are selected instead of Gaussian or other types of MFs. Triangular MFs provide a fast computational time and real-time implementation [7]. Moreover, the MFs values are determined based on empirical evaluations. The resulting control surface is shown in Figure 4. The implemented FLC uses the product implication and operates the centre of sets defuzzification method [36–38]. In this study, the fuzzy weighted average defuzzification method is used, and the equation is written as Equation (10):

$$U = \frac{\sum_{i=1}^{M} y^i f^i}{\sum_{i=1}^{M} f^i} \tag{10}$$

where U is the final output of the Takagi–Sugeno–Kang fuzzy inference system [39], f is the firing function of T1-FPID, y is denoted as consequent MFs, and M is the total number of rules. Table 1 is used for T1-FPID.

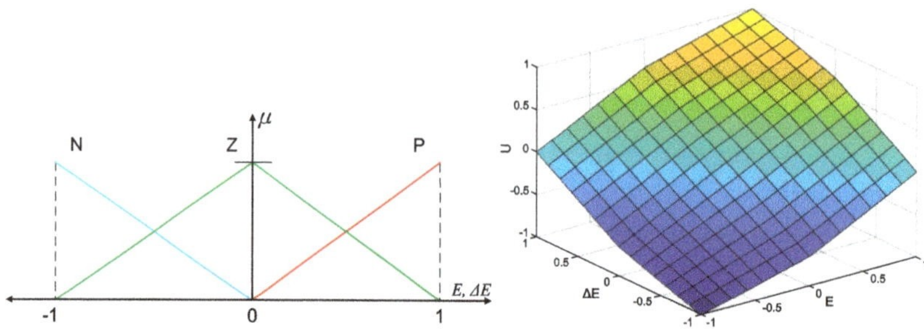

Figure 4. Illustrated T1 fuzzy MFs and control surface.

3.3. *Interval Type-2 Fuzzy PID Controller*

Just like the T1-FPID controller, the IT2-FPID controller is composed of choosing E and ΔE as inputs and the control action of the IT2-FLC U as output as displayed in Figure 3. The IT2-FLC has the same N = 9 rules and is presented in Table 1. The MFs of IT2-FPID are characterised by triangular MFs, and the control surface of the IT2-FPID is given in Figure 5. The linguistic fuzzy variables are N, Z, and P, respectively. Here, m_n is the only parameter that creates the footprint of the uncertainty of the IT2-FPID [40]. We employ the following parameters: $m_2 = \alpha$ and $m_1 = m_3 = 1 - \alpha$ as suggested in [36,40–42]. Therefore, the selection of the parameter (α) is vital because it directly affects U.

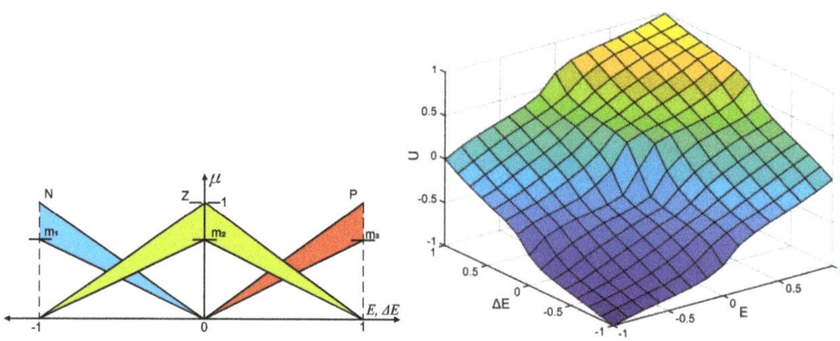

Figure 5. Interval type-2 fuzzy MFs and control surface.

Several methods have been used for the calculation of the controller output (U) [40,43]. In this study, the Biglarbegian–Melek–Mendel method is used [40]. The equation relating to this method is given as follows:

$$\begin{aligned} \bar{y} &= \frac{\sum_{i=1}^{M} f_h^i y^i}{\sum_{i=1}^{M} f_h^i} \\ \underline{y} &= \frac{\sum_{i=1}^{M} f_l^i y^i}{\sum_{i=1}^{M} f_l^i} \\ \mathrm{U} &= \zeta \underline{y} + (1-\zeta)\bar{y}. \end{aligned} \tag{11}$$

where y^i shows consequent MFs, M is the total number of rules (Table 1 is used for IT2), ζ is a weighting parameter for the type reduced set ($[\underline{y}, \bar{y}]$), and U is the output of FLC. Lastly, f_l and f_h are defined as the lower and upper firing functions of IT2-FPID, respectively. In Figure 5, the control surface, which selected $\zeta = 0.25$ and $\alpha = 0.25$ for IT2-FPID, is illustrated.

Parameters of T1-FPID and IT2-FPID are selected aggressively by using rule-based FLCs and MFs. The ζ and α parameters are selected by trial and error so that an aggressive control surface is created for IT2-FPID, then it is defined as $\zeta = 0.5$ and $\alpha = 0.25$ in the study. After that, a comparison of the control surfaces (ΔU) of the T1-FPID (U_{T1}) and IT2-FPID

(U_{IT2}) is presented in Figure 6, taking into account their aggressiveness and smoothness. The differences between them are formulated as $\Delta U = U_{T1} - U_{IT2}$. An aggressive control action is characterised by a relatively higher control action output compared to the others. Specifically, if a line lies above another line in the positive region where $E, \Delta E \geq 0$ (or below in the negative region where $E, \Delta E < 0$), the resulting control action is deemed aggressive. Conversely, if this condition is not met, it is deemed a smooth control action.

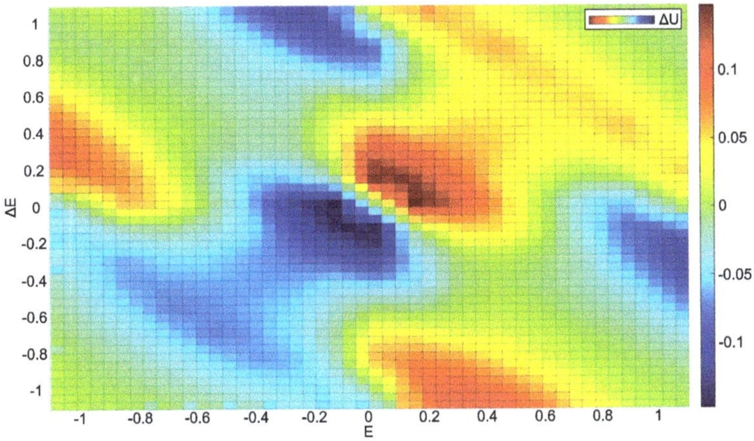

Figure 6. The control surface differences between T1-FPID and IT2-FPID.

3.4. Optimisation Results and Simulation

All implemented controllers are optimised via the BB-BC algorithm, described in Appendix B. The cost function of BB-BC is defined as

$$\text{ISE} = \int (e_x^2 + e_y^2)dt. \tag{12}$$

In the equation above, errors are defined for two axes as e_x, e_y of the UAV. The error values are explained in Equation (6), and integral square error (ISE) is selected for the performance criteria of the optimisation algorithm. In the BB-BC algorithm, the population size is chosen as 50, and the maximum iteration number is selected as 200 for the optimisation process of each controller. The BB-BC optimisation algorithm is used to tune K_c, T_i, and T_d for the PID controller, and the K_e, K_d, K_0, and K_1 parameters for fuzzy-based controllers are tuned using BB-BC, separately. It is noticed that α and ζ are defined empirically. The BB-BC approach evaluation over simulated data is performed within the Matlab environment [44]. The computation times for the controllers are measured between 1 and 4 ms; these values are negligible considering the sampling time in real-time and simulation experiments. The selected controllers and their parameters are in the Python environment [45]. Control signals v_x and v_y are constrained between −12 m/s and 12 m/s during the BB-BC search.

In Table 2, parameters of the controllers and the best performance criteria (ISE) obtained by BB-BC are listed. For tuning to the parameters of each controller, the position reference points are x_{ref} = 1.1 m and y_{ref} = 0.52 m for BB-BC optimisation.

Table 2. Tuned parameters and their performance criteria results.

Controller	Parameters	ISE
PID	$K_c = 0.0472$, $T_i = 0.0052$, $T_d = 0.0445$	82,133.4
T1-FPID	$K_e = 0.019$, $K_d = 0.0019$, $K_0 = 0.0001$, $K_1 = 30$	55,128.2
IT2-FPID	$K_e = 0.019$, $K_d = 0.0019$, $K_0 = 0.0001$, $K_1 = 30$, ($\alpha = 0.25, \zeta = 0.5$) *	36,371.9

*: These parameters have been selected before BB-BC.

The optimised controllers are tested on the simulation model, and the results can be seen in Figure 7. In the simulation, the reference signals are defined as 1.1 m for the x-axis and 0.52 m for the y-axis. They are the same as the references given in the controller parameter optimisation process using BB-BC.

These simulation results show that the IT2-FPID controller leads to the best results, with no overshoot, the slightest steady-state error, and the rise time. In addition, T1-FPID gives a smoother response than the PID controller. Considering the compared controllers, they do not have the same system responses in both axes due to the fact that the feedbacks of the UAV in both axes have different levels of noise. The aim of choosing different levels of noise is that the payload is not connected to the CoM of the UAV, and it will have a directly different effect on the axes. Oscillation and steady-state errors seen in Figure 7 are caused by the Gaussian disturbances added to the simulation model in the testing stage to show the robustness of the compared controllers against external disturbances. Gaussian distribution parameters for the x and y axis are defined as $N(0,5)$ and $N(0,15)$, respectively. After testing the controllers in the simulation, the controllers are implemented in the UAV.

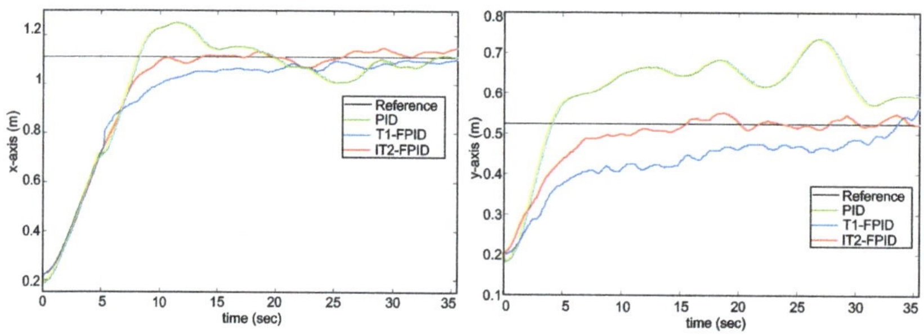

Figure 7. Testing results of the compared controllers in the simulation.

4. Indoor Testing Area

In Figure 8, an overview of the system, including the proposed IT2-FPID-based position controller, is shown. Figure 8 presents the overall structure of the system, including the proposed IT2-FPID-based position controller. Reference signals and controls and position estimates are calculated on the computer controlling the UAV remotely. The computer used in the real-time experiments has Intel i7 CPU, 32 GB RAM and NVidia GTX 1650Ti GPU. The generated outputs of the computer are the reference signals of the UAV. Moreover, the Python 3.10 environment is used in the system [45]. The computer and the UAV communicate via a Wi-Fi communication protocol. The design process of the main system starts with the generation of the reference signals for the desired UAV trajectory. Considering the main system, the process starts with the reference path generation. There are two different reference points in the proposed approach. The first one is about disturbing the payload. It means that when the UAV tracks the reference points using a stick, it is disturbed, and the flex cable-connected payload is a disturbance. Then, the second test is initiated as coverage path planning (CPP). Next, the offline CPP is explained, and the resulting reference points are given [46–48]. The last part is about how to detect the UAV position with a camera and vision-based localisation algorithm. In the following two sections, these are explained intensively.

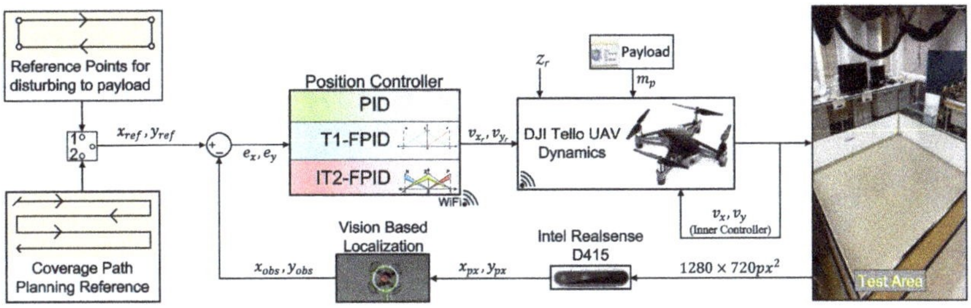

Figure 8. Fuzzy logic-based position control system.

4.1. Intel RealSense Depth Camera and Vision-Based Localisation Method

In this study, an Intel RealSense depth camera is used for the experiments [49], as it is a low-cost localisation system [8,50]. There are several advantages to using this particular depth camera in terms of its size, camera specifications and 3D Cartesian coordinate detection. Moreover, it has a 69° × 42°($\alpha \times \beta$) field of view (FoV) for the RGB sensor, 1280 × 720 px^2 resolution, and a 30 fps RGB frame rate.

To find the localisation of the UAV, RGB colour detection is used to track it. A red-coloured circle piece is put on the region of interest of the area, and the colour parameters are measured as shown in Table 3. These colour parameters are in the hue, saturation, and value colour space (HSV). Moreover, the HSV values have maximum and minimum limits, which are shown in Table 3.

Table 3. Camera HSV parameters.

HSV	Hue	Saturation	Value
Maximum Values	160	60	0
Minimum Values	200	255	255

After detecting the HSV parameters, some trigonometric formulas are used to find the transformed centre points of the UAV. Figure 9 shows the three-axis sizes of the testing area (x, y, z : 200, 150, 250, respectively), camera position, UAV altitude level (z_a : 90 cm), and detected surface on the UAV.

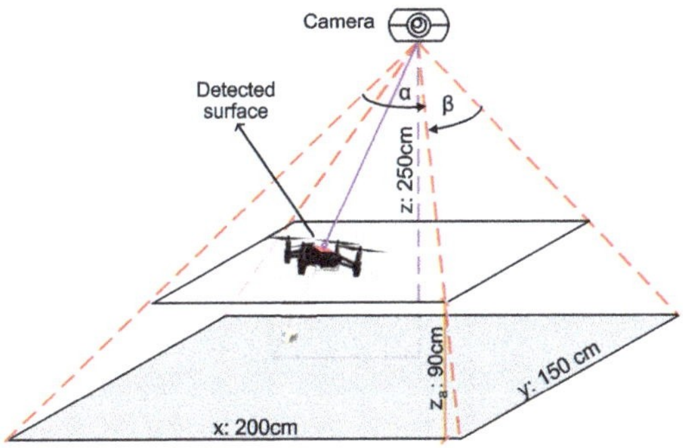

Figure 9. Camera trigonometric formation scheme and the UAV position.

In Equation (13), the raw centre points of the UAV ($\hat{x}_{px}$ and $\hat{y}_{px}$) are defined, which are converged to the transformed centre points. In the matrix, s_x, s_y, sh_x, sh_y and t_x, t_y stand for scale factors, shear factors, and translation factors, respectively. Moreover, these parameters are determined by using "Computer Vision Toolbox for Matlab" [44] and using the following model:

$$\begin{bmatrix} \hat{x}_{px} \\ \hat{y}_{px} \\ 1 \end{bmatrix} = \begin{bmatrix} s_x & sh_y & 0 \\ sh_x & s_y & 0 \\ t_x & t_y & 1 \end{bmatrix} \begin{bmatrix} x_{px} \\ y_{px} \\ 1 \end{bmatrix}. \quad (13)$$

Normally, this calculation is set for the two axes because the z-axis is fixed. For the calculation for the three axes, the trigonometric formula is used via Equation (14). In this equation, M_x and M_y show the total number of pixels for the x-y axes, and also σ_x and σ_y are defined as the relative mounting angles of FoV. Lastly, h (or z-axis) is used for the distance between the camera and the ground or floor. In Figure 9, the x-y-z-axes dimensions are given as 200 cm, 150 cm, and 250 cm, respectively, and by accounting for the following relations:

$$\begin{aligned} x_{obs} &= -\text{ztan}\left(\sigma_x + \beta\left(\hat{y}_{px}/M_x - 1\right)\right), \\ y_{obs} &= -\text{ztan}\left(\sigma_y + \alpha\left(\hat{x}_{px}/M_y - 1\right)\right). \end{aligned} \quad (14)$$

4.2. Coverage Path Planning

This section presents the implemented CPP algorithm. CPP is another challenging problem for UAVs [46–48]. The UAV aims to track the specific points defined by using the CPP method.

In Figure 10, the boundaries, starting point, and the specific reference of the CPP lines are shown and coloured yellow, black, and turquoise, respectively. This is because the UAV has a task: reaching the specific points, which are the endpoints of the path segments. The following relation is used:

$$d = w.(1 - v). \quad (15)$$

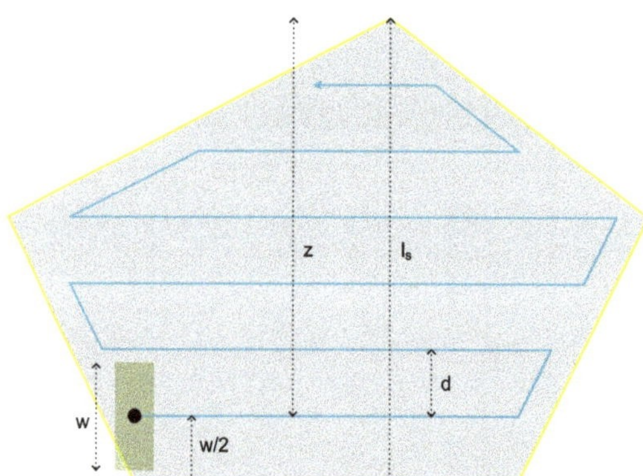

Figure 10. Example of coverage path planning.

The shape, length, and direction of the path constructed by the CPP algorithm depend on d, w, and l_s values, and these correspond to the distance among rows, the half of the camera footprint, and the width of the original polygon, which is swept, respectively, and the percentage of vertical overlap between the width of the camera footprints on consecutive rows are denoted by v and with a total number n of turns equal to

$$n = \begin{cases} 2.\lceil z/d \rceil & \text{if } (z \bmod d) \leq w/2, \\ 2.(\lceil z/d \rceil + 1) & \text{if } (z \bmod d) > w/2. \end{cases} \quad (16)$$

The total number of turns n resulting from the CPP algorithm is given in Equation (16), and this algorithm aims to minimise n to some degree, as it can be seen that this number depends on the z value, which is a function of the polygon width that is $z = l_s - w/2$. Therefore, the direction in which the polygon width is defined determines the value of n.

If the gap between the last row of the created path and the vertex or the edge of the original polygon is greater than half of the camera footprint w, then an extra row is added to the end of the path to reduce the gap as mentioned earlier; therefore, the distance between the last row and the original polygon might be less than $w/2$. In Figure 11, the difference between the distances from the border of the polygon to the initial row and the last row of the CPP path is an example of this case. The optimal line sweep direction and the path are determined by the following algorithm given in Algorithm 1 [46,47].

Algorithm 1 Basic CPP algorithm.

Step 1: (Farthest vertex v from the edge e)
For each edge, find the farthest vertex with respect to Euclidean distance and keep this (e, v) pair and the calculated distance value.
Step 2: (Minimum distance pair (e,v))
Compare the distance values and find the (e, v) pair which gives the minimum distance value.
Step 3: (Orthogonal direction vector)
The optimal line-swept direction is the vector that is orthogonal to the edge from the (e, v) pair found in Step 2, and the rows constructed by the CPP algorithm will be parallel to this edge e.
Step 4: (Path construction)
The path is defined by the way points that are connected by line segments. These way points are placed in such a way that the line segments connecting them are parallel to the edge on which the polygon width is defined and the distance between a way point and the border of the polygon satisfies the camera footprint requirements.

The CPP algorithm is employed in the testing area offline as shown in Figure 11. After reference-point generation by the CPP algorithm, all the controllers implemented in this study are tested over the area.

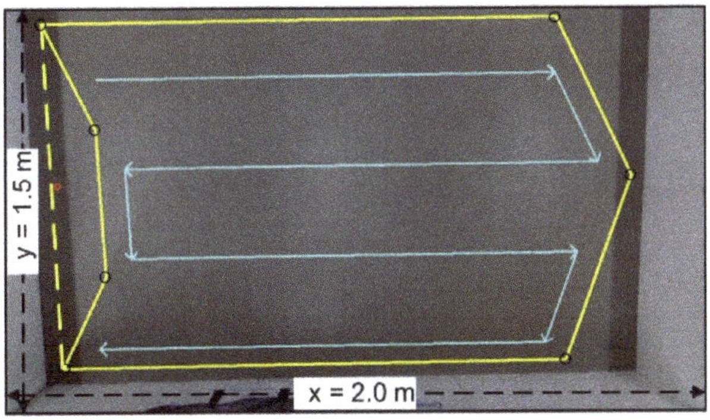

Figure 11. Coverage path planning for the UAV.

In the following section, the training and the testing results of the compared controllers are given, and it is shown that the best performance results are obtained by the IT2-FPID controller.

5. Real-Time Experimental Results

In this section, the performance of the IT2-FPID controller is compared with the PID and the T1-FPID controllers by the data gathered from real-time experiments. All experiments are in two parts: without/with disturbance and payload on the set-point tracking. The tuned parameters without payload using the BB-BC algorithm are employed in the UAV. After that, the set-point tracking shows all the results of the compared controllers under the flexible cable-connected payload and disturbance effects. Comparison results for these controllers are shown as root mean square error (RMSE) values. The sampling time (T_s) is chosen as 055 ms. The selected optimal value of T_s and the UAV IP address are communicated via Wi-Fi from the computer to the UAV. The latencies are taken into consideration, and these have a minimal impact on the real-time algorithm performance. The performance of the proposed approach can be observed via the video file provided as Supplementary Material.

The implemented controllers are tested for three cases. First, the UAV tracks the set point without any disturbance and the payload. Secondly, the controllers try to stabilise the system under disturbance and the payload. Additionally, the square reference points are given to the UAV. The last case is giving the reference path for the UAV by the CPP algorithm. In the CPP scenario, any external disturbance is not applied because when UAV follows the reference trajectory, the flexible cable-connected payload may generate disturbances on both axes due to the fact that the payload is not connected to the CoM of the UAV.

Disturbing the payload aims to investigate the controller responses under disturbance. In the last test, CPP aims to compare the controller performances for minimum time and maximum accuracy. Disturbing the payload and the CPP results show the robustness of the controller in real-time.

5.1. Set-Point Tracking without Disturbance and the Payload

Before testing with the unknown payload, all control methods and their control parameters are tested without a connected payload. The reason for this is that the defined controller parameters may need further fine-tuning.

In Figures 12 and 13, the PID, T1-FPID and IT2-FPID position results can be seen. The reference, PID, T1-FPID, and IT2-FPID are coloured black, green, blue, and red, respectively. The starting point of the UAV is selected as x_0 = 0.2 m, y_0 = 0.2 m, and the reference points are chosen as x_{ref} = 1.1 m, y_{ref} = 0.52 m.

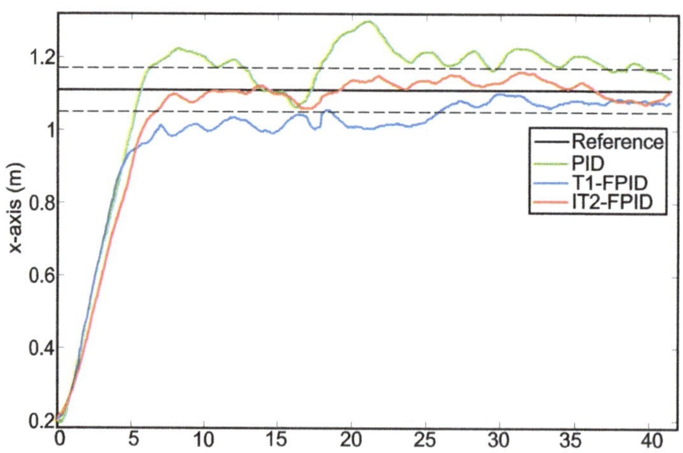

Figure 12. Set-point tracking results on the x-axis.

In Figure 12, the IT2-FPID results show the best performance compared to other controllers regarding settling time, oscillation, steady-state error, and overshoot. PID gives more overshoot and then arrives at coverage of the reference area after 31 s. T1-FPID has a slower response compared with IT2-FPID, but it also reaches the reference faster than PID.

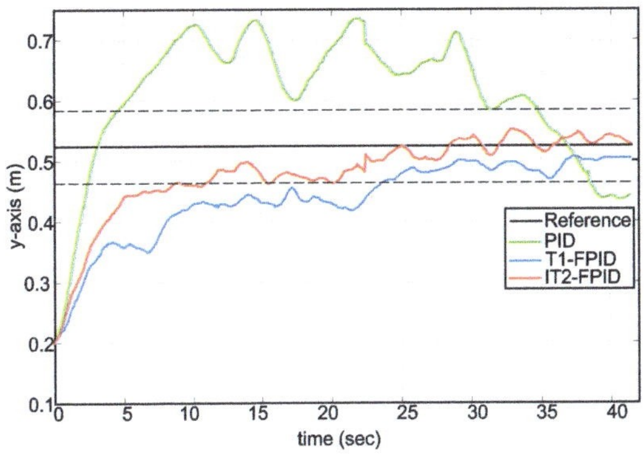

Figure 13. Set-point tracking results on the y-axis.

In Figure 13, unlike the results on the x-axis, all the controllers do not achieve good results on the y-axis. Significantly, the PID controller has an overshoot problem and does not reach the reference or converge to the circle. Moreover, IT2-FPID looks faster than T1-FPID, and the system response is the best.

5.2. Set-Point Tracking with Disturbance and the Payload

The results of set-point tracking with disturbance and the payload consist of two different parts. The first relates to payload disturbing, and the second applies to CPP. In this part, all controller structures are tested under disturbance. The payload is disturbed using a stick to implement the disturbances as external disturbances, directly impacting the system stability. After that, in the CPP scenario, the disturbances are generated by themselves as explained in the aforementioned above section.

In Figure 14, the disturbance effects are seen on the x-axis. PID and T1-FPID give slow responses, and generally, they do not reach the reference points. IT2-FPID is not as affected as the others.

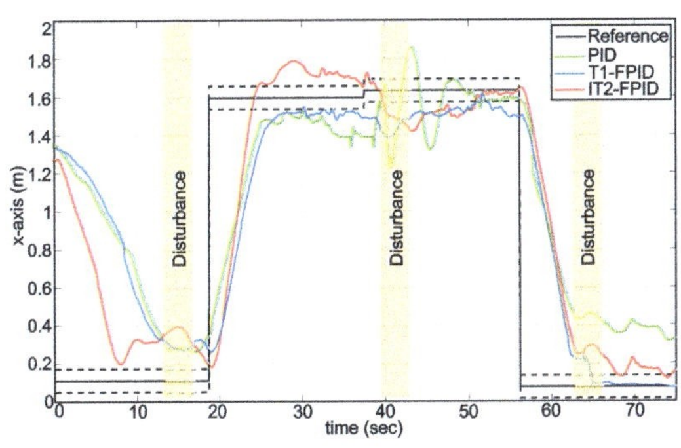

Figure 14. Disturbance results on the x-axis.

In Figure 15, the biggest problem for all controller types is on the y-axis. The PID cannot guarantee stability under disturbance, and T1-FPID and IT2-FPID show a slight overshoot.

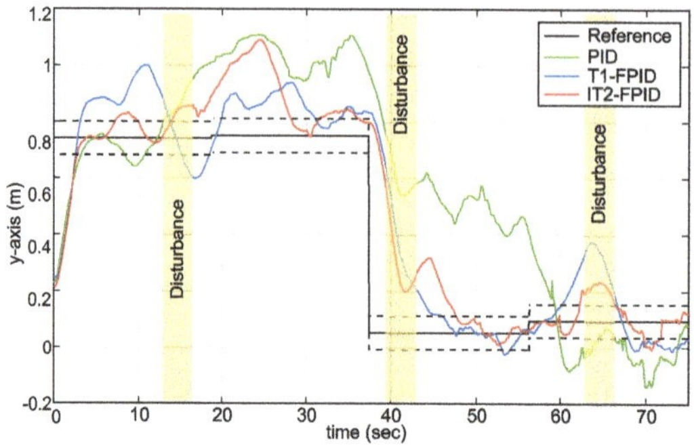

Figure 15. Disturbance results on the y-axis.

After the disturbance-based results, some specific points are given for each controller. The second experiment of the IT2-FPID controller is coverage path planning. Each vertex of the coverage path planning is fixed and determined before the test, and these are given as reference points. The reference point changes to the next vertex when the UAV converges or reaches the current vertex. Considering the task compilation time, IT2-FPID, T1-FPID, and PID complete the task in 74.55 s, 112.35 s, and 120.15 s, respectively. In addition to a faster completion time, IT2-FPID also shows better results in other ways.

The first experiment of the CPP is the PID controller structure for the real-time UAV with a flexible cable-connected payload as shown in Figure 16. PID shows a small steady-state error and slower system response on the x-axis. However, PID has a problem on the y-axis. It does not reach the reference points properly.

In Figure 17, T1-FPID does not show promising results compared with the PID results on the x-axis, but it completes the task time faster than the PID controller; these results are plausible. However, T1-FPID oscillates on the y-axis. This issue can be explained by the fact that the payload is not at the CoM of the UAV but nearer the front side. Therefore, the problem on the y-axis is expected for all of the controller's structures.

The last and the best results achieved with the IT2-FPID are shown in Figure 18. It completes the CPP task in 74.55 s. In addition, it has a better settling time, oscillation, and steady-state error in terms of minor errors and short time. Although the payload position problem on CoM exists for the other controllers, IT2-FPID overcomes the problem steadfastly.

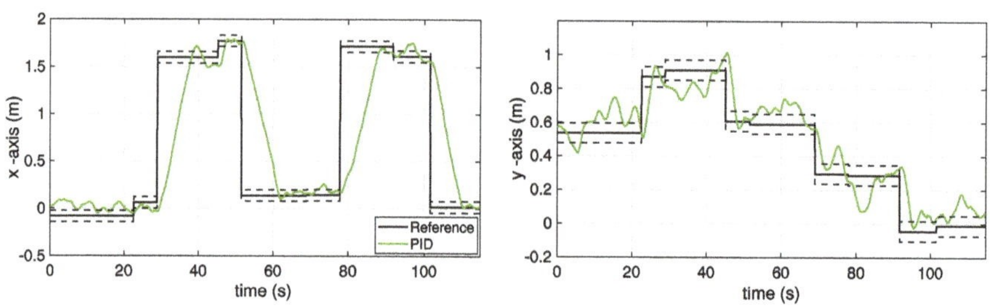

Figure 16. Coverage path planning with PID.

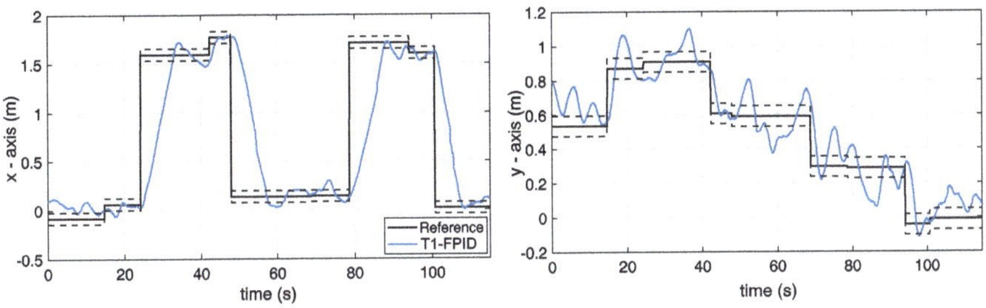

Figure 17. Coverage path planning with T1-FPID.

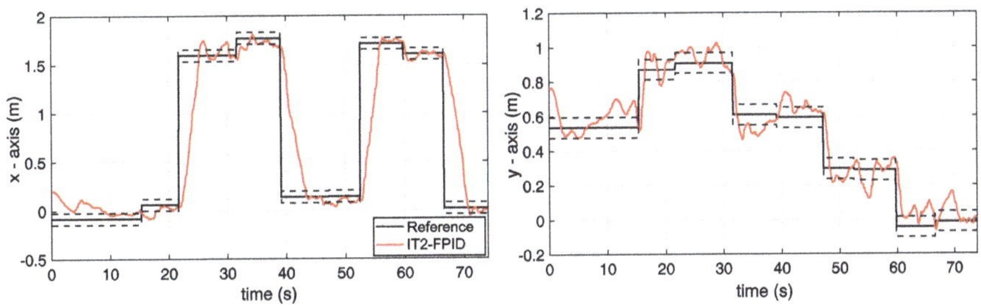

Figure 18. Coverage path planning with IT2-FPID.

The experimental results on each axis are analysed separately. RMSE is chosen as a performance index for the comparison of the controllers. In Table 4, the results of RMSE on the x-axis are shown. The best results of each experiment are IT2-FPID on the x-axis.

Table 4. RMSE values on x-axis.

RMSE Values (m)	PID	T1-FPID	IT2-FPID
Set-Point Tracking	0.2275	0.2255	**0.2218**
Under Disturbance	0.5574	0.5490	**0.4971**
CPP Results	0.5719	0.5597	**0.4540**

As far as the RMSE values obtained in the set-point tracking scenario and in the testing against the disturbance, that is, disturbing the payload with a stick, are considered, IT2-FPID shows almost two times better results when compared to PID and T1-FPID as given in Table 5.

Table 5. RMSE values on y-axis.

RMSE Values (m)	PID	T1-FPID	IT2-FPID
Set-Point Tracking	0.137	0.0964	**0.0805**
Under Disturbance	0.3103	0.1877	**0.1810**
CPP Results	0.1338	0.1298	**0.1068**

In summary, IT2-FPID has the best performance results in all two robustness tests. Considering the aim of the testing for IT2-FPID, the minimum task time, and RMSE values, maximum accuracy is obtained. However, although T1-FPID is not as good as IT2-FPID, it has better results than the compared PID controller. In the simulation, 20 independent tests are conducted, and then 5 independent tests are run in the real-time system.

6. Conclusions and Future Works

In this study, the flexible cable-connected unknown payload, which is a challenging engineering problem, is described. The challenging problems are related to the swinging unknown payloads and point-based reference trajectories. For this challenging engineering problem, a proportional–integral–derivative (PID) controller, type-1 Fuzzy PID controller (T1-FPID), and interval type-2 Fuzzy PID controller (IT2-FPID) are tuned and implemented on a real UAV. The control algorithms are generic and can be applied to different types and sizes of UAVs, although the experiments are performed using a DJI Tello UAV. The performance of the IT2-FPID is also compared against a PID and a T1-FPID controller. After set-point tracking and robustness testing via disturbing the payload with a stick and changing the reference points in coverage path planning (CPP), causing the payload to swing, the experimental results show that the IT2-FPID is better than the controllers. There are different aims for each test, such as minimum task time and RMSE. Disturbing effects of the flexible cable-connected payload on the UAV are shown throughout the experiments. These adverse effects can be eliminated by the three compared controllers to some point, but the results show the superiority of the IT2-FPID. As an example from the experiments, although the PID controller may solve the trajectory-tracking problem, the uncertainties, such as the unknown payload connection via flexible cable and disturbing the payload, lead to highly detrimental results for the PID controller. Thanks to implementing the IT2-FPID controller, these problems are eliminated considerably. Consequently, the system stability is guaranteed without considering the changes in the system dynamics equations and redesigning the controller.

After the controller design, the sensor part of the UAV will be improved to achieve better accuracy. In order to improve the sensor accuracy, the noise distribution will also be investigated, and then the system will be tested both in the simulation environment and in real time. According to the type of distribution, a filter design will be included to eliminate such noise and general disturbances. Lastly, a theoretical analysis of the performance of the proposed approach under internal and external disturbances is a topic of future work.

Supplementary Materials: The following supporting information can be downloaded at: https://www.mdpi.com/article/10.3390/a16060273/s1.

Author Contributions: The authors' contributions are conceptualization, F.C., O.F.D., L.M. and M.M.; methodology, F.C. and O.F.D.; software, F.C.; validation, F.C. and O.F.D.; formal analysis: all authors; investigation: F.C., L.M., T.K., M.M.; resources: F.C., L.M., M.M. and T.K.; data curation: F.C.; writing original draft preparation: F.C.; writing—review and editing: F.C., L.M., T.K. and M.M.; visualization: F.C.; supervision: L.M. and M.M. All authors have read and agreed to the submitted version of the manuscript.

Funding: This research received no external funding.

Data Availability Statement: Not applicable.

Acknowledgments: We acknowledge the Turkish government for funding the doctoral scholarship of Fethi Candan. T. Kumbasar was supported by the BAGEP Award of the Science Academy and the TUBA GEBIP award from the Turkish Academy of Sciences.

Conflicts of Interest: The authors declare no conflict of interest.

Appendix A. UAV Linear Model

The transformation between the body-fixed frame and the inertial frame is achieved with a rotation matrix R for inverse mapping and a transitional matrix T [8,9,32,51] of the form

$$R = \begin{bmatrix} 1 & 0 & -s(\theta) \\ 0 & c(\phi) & c(\theta)s(\phi) \\ 0 & -sin(\phi) & cos(\phi)c(\theta) \end{bmatrix}, \quad T = \begin{bmatrix} 1 & s(\phi)t(\theta) & c(\phi)t(\theta) \\ 0 & c(\phi) & -s(\phi) \\ 0 & s(\phi)/c(\theta) & c(\phi)/c(\theta) \end{bmatrix}. \quad \text{(A1)}$$

In this study, the heading angle of the UAV—yaw (ψ)—is fixed and is equal to $\psi = 0°$. For this reason, the defined rotation matrix form is $R = R_\phi R_\theta$.

Unlike the nonlinear model of the UAV, the definition of the linear model is represented with simpler equations. As a consequence, U shows the control input values of the system of Equation (A2):

$$U = [F^B_{thrust}\ \tau_\phi\ \tau_\theta\ \tau_\psi]. \tag{A2}$$

Equation (A3) is obtained from the equation corresponding to each U input value:

$$U = \begin{bmatrix} F^B_{thrust} \\ \tau_\phi \\ \tau_\theta \\ \tau_\psi \end{bmatrix} = \begin{bmatrix} b & b & b & b \\ -bl & -bl & bl & bl \\ -bl & bl & bl & -bl \\ -d & d & -d & d \end{bmatrix} \begin{bmatrix} \Omega_1^2 \\ \Omega_2^2 \\ \Omega_3^2 \\ \Omega_4^2 \end{bmatrix}. \tag{A3}$$

$$\dot{w}^B = I_B^{-1} \tau^B_{rotor} = \begin{bmatrix} \frac{1}{I_x} bl\tau_\phi/\sqrt{2} \\ \frac{1}{I_y} bl\tau_\theta/\sqrt{2} \\ \frac{1}{I_z} d\tau_\psi \end{bmatrix}. \tag{A4}$$

In the above equations, Ω_i denotes the angular velocity of the UAV propeller, d is the drag coefficient of rotors, and l is the distance between the rotor and CoM. When writing the inertia matrix (I_B) for each torque, they are defined as inertia tensors ($I_x = 0.679 \times 10^{-2}$, $I_y = 0.679 \times 10^{-2}$, $I_z = 1.313 \times 10^{-2}$ [24,34]).

To linearise the equation above by using the Taylor approximation, the following equation is used:

$$U_i = U_i^0 + \frac{dU_i}{d\Omega_i}|_{\Omega_i^0}(\Omega - \Omega_i^0). \tag{A5}$$

In the equation above, the subscript of $(.)^0$ means the hovering mode condition of the UAV. Therefore, the UAV hovering operation point is given by the following equation:

$$U^0 = [mg\ 0\ 0\ 0]^T, \qquad \Omega_i^0 = \sqrt{\frac{mg}{4b}}. \tag{A6}$$

$$\begin{bmatrix} \ddot{x} \\ \ddot{y} \\ \ddot{z} \end{bmatrix} = \begin{bmatrix} g(s(\psi_0)\phi + c(\psi_0)\theta) \\ g(s(\psi_0)\theta + c(\psi_0)\phi) \\ F^B_{thrust} \end{bmatrix}. \tag{A7}$$

Appendix B. Big Bang–Big Crunch Optimisation Method

To find the optimal parameters of the controllers, we use the Big Bang–Big Crunch (BB-BC) optimisation method. The proposed optimisation method has shown a faster response than the global optimisation methods [31]. The BB-BC exists in two primary phases. The "Big Bang phase" involves randomly distributed candidate solutions across the search space, followed by the "Big Crunch phase," which involves calculating the population's centre of mass using a contraction procedure. Like other evolutionary search methods, the initial Big Bang population is produced randomly over the search space. Similarly, all following Big Bang phases are randomly distributed around the centre of mass or the best-fitted individual.

In [31,52], the working concept of this evolutionary approach consists of changing a converging result into a chaotic state, which is a new set of solutions. The algorithm starts by generating a random population of candidates for calculating fitness values. Using Equation (A8), the centre of mass is calculated, and the selection is based on either the best individual (fitness value) or the centre of mass. Similar to evolutionary computing (EC) algorithms, a new set of candidates is generated based on the previously selected individual via adding or subtracting a random number whose value changes adaptively. The whole process is then repeated (without the initialisation) if the stopping criterion has not been met.

During the Big Crunch, a contraction method is used after the Big Bang. The contraction operator computes a centre of mass using the current locations of each candidate, resulting in the population and its associated cost function value. The centre of mass x_c position may be calculated using the following formula:

$$x_c = \frac{\sum_{i=1}^{N} \frac{1}{f^i} x_i}{\sum_{i=1}^{N} \frac{1}{f^i}}. \tag{A8}$$

where x_i is the candidate position, and f^i is the cost function value for each candidate i and population size N. The new value x_i^{new} is

$$x_i^{new} = x_c + \sigma. \tag{A9}$$

where x_i is the new candidate result and σ gives the standard deviation of a standard normal distribution.

For the next iteration Big Bang phase, the new generation is distributed around x_c as follows:

$$\sigma = \frac{r\alpha(x_{max} - x_{min})}{k}, \tag{A10}$$

In Equation (A10), the standard deviation reduces as each repetition progresses. Moreover, r is a random number and α is a parameter bounding the size of the search space and

$$x_i^{new} = x_c + \frac{r\alpha(x_{max} - x_{min})}{k}. \tag{A11}$$

Here, the maximum and minimum limits are given as x_{max} and x_{min}, respectively. Additionally, k is the number of iterations for the optimisation. While, typically, distributed numbers may exceed ± 1, the population must be limited to the search space boundaries. Therefore, the candidate results are constrained inside the search space boundaries due to this narrowing.

References

1. Sun, Z.; Piao, H.; Yang, Z.; Zhao, Y.; Zhan, G.; Zhou, D.; Meng, G.; Chen, H.; Chen, X.; Qu, B.; et al. Multi-agent hierarchical policy gradient for Air Combat Tactics emergence via self-play. *Eng. Appl. Artif. Intell.* **2021**, *98*, 104112. [CrossRef]
2. Bellocchio, E.; Crocetti, F.; Costante, G.; Fravolini, M.L.; Valigi, P. A novel vision-based weakly supervised framework for autonomous yield estimation in agricultural applications. *Eng. Appl. Artif. Intell.* **2022**, *109*, 104615. [CrossRef]
3. Mohamadi, H.E.; Kara, N.; Lagha, M. Heuristic-driven strategy for boosting aerial photography with multi-UAV-aided Internet-of-Things platforms. *Eng. Appl. Artif. Intell.* **2022**, *112*, 104854. [CrossRef]
4. Fu, C.; Ding, F.; Li, Y.; Jin, J.; Feng, C. Learning dynamic regression with automatic distractor repression for real-time UAV tracking. *Eng. Appl. Artif. Intell.* **2021**, *98*, 104116. [CrossRef]
5. Luperto, M.; Amigoni, F. Reconstruction and prediction of the layout of indoor environments from two-dimensional metric maps. *Eng. Appl. Artif. Intell.* **2022**, *113*, 104910. [CrossRef]
6. Argentim, L.M.; Rezende, W.C.; Santos, P.E.; Aguiar, R.A. PID, LQR and LQR-PID on a quadcopter platform. In Proceedings of the International Conference on Informatics, Electronics and Vision (ICIEV), Dhaka, Bangladesh, 17–18 May 2013; IEEE: Piscataway, NJ, USA, 2013; pp. 1–6.
7. Khan, A.A.; Rapal, N. Fuzzy PID controller: Design, tuning and comparison with conventional PID controller. In Proceedings of the 2006 IEEE International Conference on Engineering of Intelligent Systems, Islamabad, Pakistan, 22–23 April 2006; IEEE: Piscataway, NJ, USA, 2006; pp. 1–6.

8. Candan, F.; Beke, A.; Kumbasar, T. Design and Deployment of Fuzzy PID Controllers to the nano quadcopter Crazyflie 2.0. In Proceedings of the Innovations in Intelligent Systems and Applications (INISTA), Thessaloniki, Greece, 3–5 July 2018; IEEE: Piscataway, NJ, USA, 2018; pp. 1–6.
9. Kaplan, M.R.; Eraslan, A.; Beke, A.; Kumbasar, T. Altitude and position control of parrot mambo minidrone with PID and fuzzy PID controllers. In Proceedings of the 11th International Conference on Electrical and Electronics Engineering (ELECO), Bursa, Turkey, 28–30 November 2019; IEEE: Piscataway, NJ, USA, 2019; pp. 785–789.
10. Noordin, A.; Mohd Basri, M.A.; Mohamed, Z. Real-Time Implementation of an Adaptive PID Controller for the Quadrotor MAV Embedded Flight Control System. *Aerospace* **2023**, *10*, 59. [CrossRef]
11. Everett, M.F. LQR with Integral Feedback on a Parrot Minidrone. *Mass. Inst. Technol. Tech. Rep.* **2015**, *1*, 1–6.
12. Okasha, M.; Kralev, J.; Islam, M. Design and Experimental Comparison of PID, LQR and MPC Stabilizing Controllers for Parrot Mambo Mini-Drone. *Aerospace* **2022**, *9*, 298. [CrossRef]
13. Barzanooni, E.; Salahshoor, K.; Khaki-Sedigh, A. Attitude flight control system design of UAV using LQG\LTR multivariable control with noise and disturbance. In Proceedings of the 3rd RSI International Conference on Robotics and Mechatronics (ICROM), Tehran, Iran, 7–9 October 2015; IEEE: Piscataway, NJ, USA, 2015; pp. 188–193.
14. Zhao, W.; Go, T.H. Quadcopter formation flight control combining MPC and robust feedback linearization. *J. Frankl. Inst.* **2014**, *351*, 1335–1355. [CrossRef]
15. Ganga, G.; Dharmana, M.M. MPC controller for trajectory tracking control of quadcopter. In Proceedings of the 2017 International Conference on Circuit, Power and Computing Technologies (ICCPCT), Kollam, India, 20–21 April 2017; IEEE: Piscataway, NJ, USA, 2017; pp. 1–6.
16. Ortiz, J.P.; Minchala, L.I.; Reinoso, M.J. Nonlinear robust H-Infinity PID controller for the multivariable system quadrotor. *IEEE Lat. Am. Trans.* **2016**, *14*, 1176–1183. [CrossRef]
17. Hosseinzadeh, M.; Sadati, N.; Zamani, I. H∞disturbance attenuation of fuzzy large-scale systems. In Proceedings of the 2011 IEEE International Conference on Fuzzy Systems (FUZZ-IEEE 2011), Taipei, Taiwan, 27–30 June 2011; IEEE: Piscataway, NJ, USA, 2011; pp. 2364–2368.
18. Wenzel, K.E.; Masselli, A.; Zell, A. Automatic take off, tracking and landing of a miniature UAV on a moving carrier vehicle. *J. Intell. Robot. Syst.* **2011**, *61*, 221–238. [CrossRef]
19. Palossi, D.; Singh, J.; Magno, M.; Benini, L. Target following on nano-scale unmanned aerial vehicles. In Proceedings of the 7th IEEE International Workshop on Advances in Sensors and Interfaces (IWASI), Vieste, Italy, 15–16 June 2017; IEEE: Piscataway, NJ, USA, 2017; pp. 170–175.
20. Greiff, M. Modelling and Control of the Crazyflie Quadrotor for Aggressive and Autonomous Flight by Optical Flow Driven State Estimation. Master's Thesis, Lund University, Department of Automatic Control, Sweden, Switzerland, 2017.
21. Souza, R.M.J.A.; Lima, G.V.; Morais, A.S.; Oliveira-Lopes, L.C.; Ramos, D.C.; Tofoli, F.L. Modified artificial potential field for the path planning of aircraft swarms in three-dimensional environments. *Sensors* **2022**, *22*, 1558. [CrossRef] [PubMed]
22. Nguyen, N.P.; Lee, B.H.; Xuan-Mung, N.; Ha, L.N.N.T.; Jeong, H.S.; Lee, S.T.; Hong, S.K. Persistent Charging System for Crazyflie Platform. *Drones* **2022**, *6*, 212. [CrossRef]
23. Belkhale, S.; Li, R.; Kahn, G.; McAllister, R.; Calandra, R.; Levine, S. Model-based meta-reinforcement learning for flight with suspended payloads. *IEEE Robot. Autom. Lett.* **2021**, *6*, 1471–1478. [CrossRef]
24. Rao, J.; Li, B.; Zhang, Z.; Chen, D.; Giernacki, W. Position control of quadrotor uav based on cascade fuzzy neural network. *Energies* **2022**, *15*, 1763. [CrossRef]
25. Lee, D.; Park, W.; Nam, W. Autonomous Landing of Micro Unmanned Aerial Vehicles with Landing-Assistive Platform and Robust Spherical Object Detection. *Appl. Sci.* **2021**, *11*, 8555. [CrossRef]
26. Islam, S.; Liu, P.X.; El Saddik, A. Robust control of four-rotor unmanned aerial vehicle with disturbance uncertainty. *IEEE Trans. Ind. Electron.* **2014**, *62*, 1563–1571. [CrossRef]
27. Qian, L.; Liu, H.H. Path-following control of a quadrotor UAV with a cable-suspended payload under wind disturbances. *IEEE Trans. Ind. Electron.* **2019**, *67*, 2021–2029. [CrossRef]
28. Guo, K.; Jia, J.; Yu, X.; Guo, L.; Xie, L. Multiple observers based anti-disturbance control for a quadrotor UAV against payload and wind disturbances. *Control Eng. Pract.* **2020**, *102*, 104560. [CrossRef]
29. Quintero, S.A.; Hespanha, J.P. Vision-based target tracking with a small UAV: Optimization-based control strategies. *Control Eng. Pract.* **2014**, *32*, 28–42. [CrossRef]
30. Shakeel, T.; Arshad, J.; Jaffery, M.H.; Rehman, A.U.; Eldin, E.T.; Ghamry, N.A.; Shafiq, M. A Comparative Study of Control Methods for X3D Quadrotor Feedback Trajectory Control. *Appl. Sci.* **2022**, *12*, 9254. [CrossRef]
31. Erol, O.K.; Eksin, I. A new optimization method: Big bang–big crunch. *Adv. Eng. Softw.* **2006**, *37*, 106–111. [CrossRef]
32. Abdelmoeti, S.; Carloni, R. Robust control of UAVs using the parameter space approach. In Proceedings of the IEEE/RSJ International Conference on Intelligent Robots and Systems (IROS), Daejeon, Republic of Korea, 9–14 October 2016; IEEE: Piscataway, NJ, USA, 2016; pp. 5632–5637.
33. DJI Tello, C. DJI Tello EDU, Ryzerobotics. Available online: https://www.ryzerobotics.com/tello-edu (accessed on 16 June 2022).
34. Giernacki, W.; Rao, J.; Sladic, S.; Bondyra, A.; Retinger, M.; Espinoza-Fraire, T. DJI Tello Quadrotor as a Platform for Research and Education in Mobile Robotics and Control Engineering. In Proceedings of the 2022 International Conference on Unmanned Aircraft Systems (ICUAS), Dubrovnik, Croatia, 21–24 June 2022; IEEE: Piscataway, NJ, USA, 2022; pp. 735–744.

35. Sarabakha, A.; Fu, C.; Kayacan, E.; Kumbasar, T. Type-2 fuzzy logic controllers made even simpler: From design to deployment for UAVs. *IEEE Trans. Ind. Electron.* **2017**, *65*, 5069–5077. [CrossRef]
36. Sakalli, A.; Kumbasar, T.; Mendel, J.M. Towards systematic design of general type-2 fuzzy logic controllers: Analysis, interpretation, and tuning. *IEEE Trans. Fuzzy Syst.* **2020**, *29*, 226–239. [CrossRef]
37. Lee, D.H.; Park, D. An efficient algorithm for fuzzy weighted average. *Fuzzy Sets Syst.* **1997**, *87*, 39–45. [CrossRef]
38. Chang, P.T.; Hung, K.C.; Lin, K.P.; Chang, C.H. A comparison of discrete algorithms for fuzzy weighted average. *IEEE Trans. Fuzzy Syst.* **2006**, *14*, 663–675. [CrossRef]
39. Palma, L.B.; Antunes, R.A.; Gil, P.; Brito, V. Takagi-Sugeno-Kang fuzzy PID control for DC electrical machines. In Proceedings of the 2020 IEEE 14th International Conference on Compatibility, Power Electronics and Power Engineering (CPE-POWERENG), Setubal, Portugal, 8–10 July 2020; IEEE: Piscataway, NJ, USA, 2020; Volume 1, pp. 309–316.
40. Biglarbegian, M.; Melek, W.W.; Mendel, J.M. Design of novel interval type-2 fuzzy controllers for modular and reconfigurable robots: Theory and experiments. *IEEE Trans. Ind. Electron.* **2010**, *58*, 1371–1384. [CrossRef]
41. Kavikumar, R.; Sakthivel, R.; Kwon, O.M.; Selvaraj, P. Robust tracking control design for fractional-order interval type-2 fuzzy systems. *Nonlinear Dyn.* **2022**, *107*, 3611–3628. [CrossRef]
42. Firouzi, B.; Alattas, K.A.; Bakouri, M.; Alanazi, A.K.; Mohammadzadeh, A.; Mobayen, S.; Fekih, A. A Type-2 Fuzzy Controller for Floating Tension-Leg Platforms in Wind Turbines. *Energies* **2022**, *15*, 1705. [CrossRef]
43. Tai, K.; El-Sayed, A.R.; Biglarbegian, M.; Gonzalez, C.I.; Castillo, O.; Mahmud, S. Review of recent type-2 fuzzy controller applications. *Algorithms* **2016**, *9*, 39. [CrossRef]
44. Mathworks, C. Computer Vision Toolbox for Matlab, Matlab. Available online: https://uk.mathworks.com/help/vision/index.html (accessed on 16 June 2022).
45. Python.org. Python3. Available online: https://www.python.org/ (accessed on 14 January 2023).
46. Torres, M.; Pelta, D.A.; Verdegay, J.L.; Torres, J.C. Coverage path planning with unmanned aerial vehicles for 3D terrain reconstruction. *Expert Syst. Appl.* **2016**, *55*, 441–451. [CrossRef]
47. Cabreira, T.M.; Brisolara, L.B.; Ferreira, P.R., Jr. Survey on coverage path planning with unmanned aerial vehicles. *Drones* **2019**, *3*. [CrossRef]
48. Galceran, E.; Carreras, M. A survey on coverage path planning for robotics. *Robot. Auton. Syst.* **2013**, *61*, 1258–1276. [CrossRef]
49. Intel Realsense. Intel Realsense D415. Available online: https://www.intelrealsense.com/depth-camera-d415 (accessed on 16 June 2022).
50. Santos, M.C.; Santana, L.V.; Brandão, A.S.; Sarcinelli-Filho, M.; Carelli, R. Indoor low-cost localization system for controlling aerial robots. *Control Eng. Pract.* **2017**, *61*, 93–111. [CrossRef]
51. Castillo, P.; Lozano, R.; Dzul, A. Stabilization of a mini-rotorcraft having four rotors. In Proceedings of the 2004 IEEE/RSJ International Conference on Intelligent Robots and Systems (IROS) (IEEE Cat. No. 04CH37566), Sendai, Japan, 28 September–2 October 2004; IEEE: Piscataway, NJ, USA, 2004; Volume 3, pp. 2693–2698.
52. Upasane, S.J.; Hagras, H.; Anisi, M.H.; Savill, S.; Taylor, I.; Manousakis, K. A Big Bang-Big Crunch Type-2 Fuzzy Logic System for Explainable Predictive Maintenance. In Proceedings of the 2021 IEEE International Conference on Fuzzy Systems (FUZZ-IEEE), Luxembourg, 11–14 July 2021; IEEE: Piscataway, NJ, USA, 2021; pp. 1–8.

MDPI AG
Grosspeteranlage 5
4052 Basel
Switzerland
Tel.: +41 61 683 77 34

Algorithms Editorial Office
E-mail: algorithms@mdpi.com
www.mdpi.com/journal/algorithms

www.ingramcontent.com/pod-product-compliance
Lightning Source LLC
Chambersburg PA
CBHW061513210926
51850CB00008B/1907
9783725872664